CARMELITE MONASTERY
275 Pleasant Street
Concord, N. H. 03301

MONASTIC SPIRITUALITY

MONASTIC SPIRITUALITY

by Claude J. Peifer, O.S..B

MONK OF ST. BEDE ABBEY

SHEED AND WARD : : NEW YORK

© *Sheed and Ward, Inc., 1966*

Library of Congress Catalog Card Number 66–12267

Nihil obstat:
Adam Raley, S.T.D.
Censor Deputatus

Imprimi potest:
✠ *Lawrence Vohs*
Abbot of St. Bede
August 11, 1965

Imprimatur:
✠ *John B. Franz*
Bishop of Peoria
April 28, 1965

Manufactured in the United States of America

255
P m

Monastic spirituality.
Peiffer, Claude J., O.S.B.

255
P m

MONASTICISM

Peiffer, Claude., O.S.B.
Monastic spirituality.

255
P m

Peiffer, Claude J., O.S.B.
Monastic spirituality. New York, Sheed c1966
555p. 3 indeces, epilogue, bibliography

Note: author monk of St. Bede Abbey.

MONASTICISM
t

255
P m

Peiffer, Claude J., O.S.B.
Monastic Spirituality. New York, Sheed
c.1966.
555p. 3 indeces, epilogue, bibliography

Note: author monk of St. Bede Abbey.

MONASTICISM
t

PATRI FRATRIBUSQUE IN CHRISTO DILECTIS
SUB REGULA SS. P. BENEDICTI
ET PATROCINIO S. BEDAE VENERABILIS
MILITANTIBUS

Foreword

THE CHURCH IN OUR TIME is undergoing a profound experience of self-renewal, in which every aspect of her life is being re-examined, not simply to reject or to destroy, but to rediscover essential values and to bring them into new prominence by clothing them in forms which are meaningful to our times. Monasticism, which has been a vital force in the Church's life for seventeen centuries, can hardly refuse the duty of self-examination; indeed, it must welcome the opportunity to recover its own traditional values. The present volume is offered by way of contribution to this monastic *aggiornamento.*

This book does not pretend, however, to be a study in the adaptation of monastic life to modern times. Its aim is more fundamental: to provide an exposition of the theory of monastic spirituality. It does not treat explicitly of monastic institutions, therefore, except insofar as a discussion of the institutional framework is sometimes helpful in clarifying the underlying principles of spirituality. A prerequisite for making wise judgments about the relevance of institutions is an adequate understanding of the ideology which such institutions are designed to express.

The purpose of the book, therefore, is to explore the essential elements of the traditional spirituality of monastic life, as it has been handed down from ancient times, and to situate this spirituality in the life of the Church. It attempts to explain the nature of religious life and its role in the Church, to distinguish monasticism from other forms of religious life, and to expound the diverse elements which go to make up the total phenomenon of monastic spirituality, discovering their theological significance in the light of their basis in the Scriptures and their expression in the liturgy.

There is, to my knowledge, no other work at present which adequately fulfills this purpose. For many years young monks and nuns in the Benedictine monasteries of this country have used, to a greater or less extent, in their instruction, a small book entitled *Tyrocinium Religiosum.* The present work was originally undertaken in order to replace this book, which for a long time has been recognized as inadequate for its purpose.

The original author of the *Tyrocinium* was Dom Giles Bartscherer, a monk of the abbey of Michelfeld in the diocese of Bamberg, one of the monasteries of the old Bavarian congregation, suppressed in 1803. Born at Neumarkt in 1730, Bartscherer was professed as a monk in 1749 and ordained priest in 1754. He taught theology in the Bavarian congregation's common house of studies at Benediktbeuern and published four books on dogmatic theology between 1761 and 1775. Later he served as novice master for the congregation. In 1783 he was elected abbot of Michelfeld and governed the community until his death in 1799.

In the course of his career as novice master, Dom Bartscherer wrote an instruction on the monastic life for his novices, entitled *Tyrocinium Ordinis S. Benedicti in usum novitiorum Congregationis Benedictino-Bavaricae.* The book was not published, but used in manuscript form in the novitiate. The manuscripts survived the secularization of the Bavarian monasteries and were again used at Metten, where the Bavarian congregation was revived in 1830. From there a copy was apparently brought to the United States by Boniface Wimmer, the founder of St. Vincent Archabbey, from which the American Cassinese congregation stems. At St. Vincent's in the nineteenth century every novice was required to make a handwritten copy of the *Tyrocinium;* some of these carefully written manuscripts still survive in the libraries of the congregation.

Aside from a partial publication in Germany in 1858, the book was never printed until 1894, when it was issued by St. Vincent's Archabbey Press under the title *Tyrocinium Benedictinum seu Synopsis Vitae Monasticae.* Two years later an English translation and revision by Father Vincent Huber was published at St. Vincent's under the title *Tyrocinium Religiosum or School of Religious Perfection.* After his election as first abbot of St. Bede Abbey in 1910, successive printings of the English version continued to be issued by the St. Bede Abbey Press, the eighth and last appearing in 1948. In most monasteries of the congregation and in many other religious houses the novices were regularly introduced to either the Latin or the English version.

It has long been recognized, however, that the book is hopelessly dated. It was already more than a century old before it was published, and essentially reflects the outlook of the eighteenth century rather than, as is generally assumed, the nineteenth; in other words, it is two centuries out of date rather than only one. Abbot Vincent's revision touched only quite minor details, and the successive printings of his translation have remained basically unchanged. It is not surprising, therefore, that demands for a total revision have been heard for a long time.

After several monks to whom this task was assigned were unable to bring the project to completion, it was entrusted to me in 1957. It was immediately evident, however, that Dom Bartscherer's work could scarcely be used even as a basis for an exposition of monastic spirituality which would be meaningful to our times. In the eighteenth century, the monastic order had reached the lowest point in all its long history. During Bartscherer's own lifetime the suppressions had already begun which were to culminate in the general decree of secularization four years after his death. To all appearances monasticism was already a dying institution. In spite of the fact that monasteries in those times still produced some remarkable fruits of sanctity and that attempts at renewal manifested themselves even in the darkest days, the abysmal state of theology, the decadence of monastic institutions and the evils of the social and political situation which conspired to lead the monks into pursuits foreign to their ideals made it impossible to achieve an authentic view of monastic ideology. In short, the *Tyrocinium* is a product of decadence. With all due respect and gratitude for the valiant service it has rendered for nearly two centuries, its retirement is long overdue and it should, without further delay, be accorded an honorable burial.

I have therefore undertaken the task of writing a completely new book, which has no connection whatever with Dom Bartscherer's work, except in the sense that it is intended to fill the same need. The revival of Benedictine monasticism in the nineteenth century, which owed its inspiration to the far-reaching insights of Dom Prosper Gueranger, was fortunately not a restoration of pre-revolutionary monasticism, but an entirely new beginning. While this attempt at a return to sources did not go far enough, it was a start in the right direction, which gave a fresh vitality to the aging monastic order and produced a rapid and vigorous growth. The continuing restoration and foundation of monasteries has been accompanied, especially since the beginning of the twentieth century, by a remarkable revival of monastic studies, which has paved the way for a still more profound return to sources. Proceeding concurrently with the renewal of biblical, theological, liturgical and historical studies in the Church, this revival has brought about a renewed understanding of the original inspiration of monasticism and of its prophetic role in the life of the Church, as well as a number of practical realizations. These developments must be taken into account in an exposition of monastic spirituality today.

While the original reason for writing this book was the need for an introduction to monastic spirituality for the instruction of young monks and nuns in the meaning of their vocation, it is not intended that it be restricted to them. I have deliberately avoided giving it the form of a textbook in the hope that it may appeal to a wider audience.

Monasticism originally was and essentially remains a movement of laymen. The emergence of the laity is one of the most noteworthy phenomena in the present renewal of the Church. A deeper insight into the essence of the Christian vocation and into the different functions which exist in the life of the Church has led to a widespread interest in monasticism. Some notable contributions to the monastic revival have been made by dedicated Christians who are not themselves monks, but who perceive the importance of a vigorous monastic life for the welfare of the Church as a whole.

The vitality of monastic spirituality, therefore, is not a narrowly sectarian or esoteric preoccupation, but a legitimate concern of the Church as a whole, just as is the apostolate, the formation of the clergy, the promotion of the liturgy, the missionary effort, and so forth. "The eye cannot say to the hand, 'I do not need thy help'; nor again the head to the feet, 'I have no need of you' " (1 Cor 12,21). It is important that every Christian perceive not only his own role in the Church, but also that of the other organs of the Body. Monastic spirituality cannot achieve its purpose fully unless its nature and function are understood, not only by monks themselves, but also by other religious, by the laity and by the clergy.

It is the aim of this book to contribute to such an understanding, though it does not pretend to be more than an introduction to the subject. It is a popularization, though I hope not an unscientific one. I have based my work upon the sources, but I do not pretend to any originality. Rather I have attempted to synthesize the assured results of modern scholarship in the fields of biblical, liturgical and monastic studies to describe monastic spirituality according to authentic tradition. I freely acknowledge my dependence upon recent and contemporary scholars whose efforts have provided a solid basis for the renewal of monastic life which is already in progress and shows encouraging signs of future fruitfulness. If this dependence is not explicitly acknowledged in each case, it is because I have thought it best to dispense with footnotes so as not to interrupt the flow of the exposition. I hope that the select bibliography at the end of the book may serve as a partial acknowledgment of my debt to the many writers from whom I have learned what is contained in these pages.

In these times of change, it is impossible to produce a work which is even relatively definitive. New discoveries constantly oblige us to modify our views on this or that point, even though the over-all orientation may be assured. This book has been written over a period of seven years, during which I was frequently interrupted by other duties. I have consequently been obliged to rewrite portions of it several times. One can scarcely wait for the moment which will be suitable for taking a definitive position, for such a moment continues to recede into the future. The text was completed early in 1965, but I have been able to make a few subsequent additions and changes, and to update the bibliography to almost the end of 1965.

Scriptural citations are taken from the CCD version (New Testament 1941; Old Testament 1952, 1955, 1961, St. Anthony Guild Press), with permission of the Confraternity of Christian Doctrine. The *Holy Rule* is ordinarily cited according to the translation of Abbot Justin McCann (*The Rule of St. Benedict in Latin and English*, Westminster, Maryland, 1952), with the authorization of the Newman Press and of Burns and Oates, holders of the American and British copyright, respectively. In a few cases I have modified McCann's version in order to modernize the English. References to the *Rule* are made according to the chapter and verse numbers first proposed by Dom Anselmo Lentini in his edition and commentary (*S. Benedetto: La Regola*, Monte Cassino, 1947). Unfortunately the verse numbers have not yet been used in any English version, though they have been almost universally adopted in other translations and canonized by inclusion in recent critical editions, particularly that of R. Hanslik in the Vienna Corpus. I have used the N.C.W.C. translation of the Second Vatican Council's *Constitution on the Sacred Liturgy*, *Constitution on the Church*, *Decree on Ecumenism*, *Decree on the Apostolate of the Laity*, *Decree on the Church's Missionary Activity*, and of the encyclical *Fulgens radiatur*. All other translations are my own. References to patristic works give only the internal citation, so that the reader who does not have access to critical editions may utilize any edition or translation. The *Regula Magistri* is cited according to the verse numbers of Dom De Vogüé's recent edition.

It remains to express my gratitude to those of my confreres who have generously assisted me in a long and often discouraging task. I am grateful to my abbot, the Rt. Rev. Lawrence Vohs, for giving me a free hand in the work; obviously, his *imprimi potest* does not necessarily imply his agreement with all of the views expressed. Father Marion Balsavich was of invaluable assistance at several stages of the work. Chapter I is based on a draft which he originally prepared before he was prevented from continuing the work. He also contributed valuable solutions to the vexing problem of devising a satisfactory arrangement of the material, read various drafts of the work and made suggestions for improvement on particular points. Father Adam Raley kindly read the entire manuscript and made some felicitous suggestions for changes. I am indebted to Father Owen Fredrickson for contributions which have been incorporated in chapter 5, to Father Charles Speck for checking source material which was unavailable to me, and to all of my confreres for putting up with my bad humor during difficult times.

It is my hope that this book may make some contribution to deepening an understanding and appreciation of the values inherent in monasticism and thereby to furthering the renewal of monastic life, that in all things God may be glorified and men brought to salvation.

December 1, 1965

Contents

PART TWO: THE ELEMENTS OF MONASTIC SPIRITUALITY

PART ONE

The Context of Monastic Life

I What Is Religious Life?

MONASTICISM is one form of religious life. There are many other forms in the Church, which has never ceased to reflect upon the principles of the Gospel and, like the householder who brings forth from his storeroom things new and old, to express the evangelical doctrine in institutions adapted to her present needs. If we wish to situate monasticism in the life of the Church, therefore, we must begin by examining the concept of religious life in general, of which monasticism is a species. All forms of religious life have this in common, that they constitute a means of achieving supernatural perfection through the practice of the evangelical counsels. Once we have seen how this is realized in every form of religious life, we can pass on to an examination of that particular form of it which is called monasticism.

1. CHRISTIAN PERFECTION

God's Glory: Ultimate Purpose of Human Life

Christianity brings a man face to face with the most basic question of human life: Why do I exist? Its answer to this question is that man was created for the glory of God. In the economy of salvation that has been established by the positive will of God, it is man's destiny to give honor and glory to God with and in Jesus Christ, in the unity of the Church, which is the fruit of the Holy Spirit's activity.

Reason can of itself discover the purpose of our existence as creatures. It tells us that all creatures exist to glorify God by sharing in and manifesting his own goodness and perfections. This does not mean, of course, that a creature can add anything to the infinite perfections of the Creator, but only that God wishes to diffuse his perfections by communicating them, in varying degrees, to creatures in the hierarchy of being which his creative activity has established. God's own infinite love and goodness are the all-sufficient first cause and ultimate reason for all things that exist. From this fact every aspect of man's life derives its ultimate meaning; against this fact all of man's actions are judged. Here the human mind discovers a truth of inexhaustible value for the conduct of human life.

In the dimension of faith, however, it finds much more. The divine life and goodness in which man is permitted to share are the life and goodness of the Father, the Son and the Holy Spirit. To glorify God means to share in and to manifest that indescribable exchange of love which is the life of the Blessed Trinity. Furthermore, faith permits us to encounter God himself in Jesus of Nazareth, his incarnate Son, now glorified at the right hand of his Father, where he intercedes for mankind. It is now only through him and with him and in him that man can fulfill the purpose for which he was created: to glorify God in everything.

Glorification of God by Man's Perfection

These truths are basic to the life of any Christian. If one abstracts from them, the meaning of human life becomes insoluble. One must begin with God and with man's absolute dependence upon him. The God of the Christian revelation is both the beginning and the end of the life of every human being. Man has been drawn out of nothingness to glorify God in the image of his incarnate Son. God receives external glory from the perfection of the entire created universe, and it is the destiny of every man to make his own life a harmonious contribution to the symphony of praise which is offered to God by the whole of his creation.

Specifically, how can a man give glory to God through Christ? By achieving supernatural perfection. To say that the purpose of human life is to glorify God is the same thing as saying that it is man's perfection. Man glorifies God to the extent that he shares in God's goodness and manifests God's perfections, therefore to the extent that he himself is perfect. To commit oneself to the pursuit of God's glory in one's whole life is to set out upon the quest for personal perfection. God wills man's sanctification, which is the means by which he is glorified. Man, for his part, need only take care that he does not seek his own perfection as the absolutely ultimate purpose of his existence, but that he constantly refer it to the infinitely greater goodness which is God himself.

Human Perfection: Supernatural Love

A creature is perfect when all its powers are in full possession of the object for which it was created. A man becomes perfect, therefore, when he possesses God, the only object who can satisfy his mind and will. This union with God begins in baptism, when the three divine Persons take up their dwelling within the Christian and communicate to him the divine life of grace. St. Paul addressed his converts as "perfect" and "holy" because they already enjoyed this essential sanctity, even though they did not possess God in the most perfect manner possible.

God does not force this life and friendship of his upon man. The Christian's union with the three divine Persons, which begins in baptism, can be maintained and perfected only if the individual, in turn, moved by the Holy Spirit, loves God with his whole heart and his whole mind and his whole soul. "God is love, and he who abides in love abides in God, and God in him" (1 Jn 4,16). The

Christian's ability to love supernaturally is itself a gift of God: "the charity of God is poured forth in our hearts by the Holy Spirit who has been given to us" (Rom 5,5). Christian perfection essentially consists in that infused love of God whereby man is united to God.

For this reason our Lord declared that charity is not only the greatest of the commandments but the entire fulfillment of the law of God (cf Mt 22,37–40). The new commandment which he gives to men is precisely to live on in the love which he has given them, just as his Father has bestowed his love upon the Son (cf Jn 15,9–11). This love for the Father, like the Father's own love, must overflow to embrace all those who are or can be God's adopted sons. Here again Christ is the model of perfection: "A new commandment I give you . . . that as I have loved you, you also love one another" (Jn 13,34). This union of charity in which men are united to God and to one another is the supreme object of the priestly prayer of Jesus: "That all may be one, even as thou, Father, in me and I in thee" (Jn 17,21). God's glory and man's perfection consist in this sharing of the life and the love of the Blessed Trinity.

Degrees of Perfection

Love for God and union with God can, of course, vary in intensity. Since there are degrees of love, there are also degrees of perfection. The highest degree is that in which God is loved as much as he is lovable. This is realized only in the love which the Father and the Son have for one another in their common Spirit. Only infinite love can love perfectly that which is infinitely lovable; all other love and all other perfection are only relative. The next highest degree of love belongs to the blessed in heaven who enjoy a direct contemplation of God, loving him with a continuous and uninterrupted act which marshals all the power of their being. Next in the scale comes the love of those who possess sanctifying grace in this life. They love God wholeheartedly and habitually, preferring nothing else to him and loving nothing else as much. This is called essentially perfect charity because it possesses all that is essential for an authentic love of God above everything else.

In this charity, however, which is proper to the present life, there is ample room for growth in intensity and hence a wide spectrum of degrees of perfection. The habitual readiness of the soul to love God above all things should be an unfailing source of acts of charity and of other virtues directed by charity, constantly growing more frequent and intense, until the whole of the Christian's life is actually under the control of divine love. This growth in active love tends naturally to the perfection of charity which will be reached in the Beatific Vision. Between essentially perfect charity and the charity of heaven there are innumerable degrees of perfection, measured by the degree to which charity actually influences a man in all the actions of his life.

In willing to share his own life and goodness with men, God desires that every Christian achieve as high a degree of perfection as is possible for him. Growth is the condition of life. Every Christian has the obligation to strive to grow in perfection according to his state in life and the grace which is given to him. The Christian life is neither negative nor static, but is a constant tension toward the perfection of heaven. This is the meaning of the evangelical precept, "You . . . are to be perfect, even as your heavenly Father is perfect" (Mt 5,48). Every Christian is called to perfection.

2. CHRISTIAN PERFECTION IN RELIGIOUS LIFE

The Nature of Religious Life

The purpose of the religious is the same as that of every Christian: to glorify God by union with Christ and his members in as perfect a charity as possible. Religious profession is nothing more than Christian profession made perfect. It is a wholehearted renewal of the promises which all Christians make at baptism. What differentiates religious from other Christians is not their ultimate purpose, for both aim at perfect submission to the Spirit of charity. The principle of distinction is to be found rather in the fact that religious have a special function in the Church, and that they use particular means to achieve the purpose of their Christian existence.

The Gospels reveal that besides the ordinary way of following Christ there is a special and more perfect way. When Christ summoned disciples to live in greater intimacy with him by leaving all things and following him in obedience, he was asking of them something which he did not ask of everyone. He acknowledged that not everyone could make himself a eunuch for the sake of the kingdom of heaven: "let him accept it who can" (cf Mt 19,10–12). To the man who asked what was wanting to him in order to be perfect, our Lord replied, "If thou wilt be perfect, go, sell what thou hast, and give to the poor . . . and come, follow me" (cf Mt 19,16–22). Celibacy and renunciation of material goods are not demanded of everyone. Christ's invitation begins with an "if"; its acceptance is a free act of generosity. The immediate disciples of Christ who accepted his call to a more perfect life were the first "religious" of the Church.

Christ summoned his disciples not only by an external call but also by the internal call of his grace. This interior summons of grace is the authentic source of every religious vocation. Before he invited the rich young man to a life of special fellowship with him, "Jesus, looking upon him, loved him" (Mk 10,21). To his apostles Jesus explained that he had chosen them, shown them a sign of predilection by loving them before they came to love him (cf Jn 15,12–17). In order that a man experience the movement of love which prompts him to the total gift of himself, he must first be looked upon and loved by Jesus. The whole life of a religious must consist in the effort to fathom the depths and gratuitousness of Christ's love. Religious life is a response to a personal call.

Religious Life as Imitation of Christ

Religious life not only begins as a call from Christ but demands an ever more perfect conformity to his life and perfections. It was not only renunciation that Jesus suggested to the rich young man, but also that he "come, follow me" (Mt 19,21). Every Christian must, of course, like a branch on the vine, draw his life from Christ, the source of all grace and union with God; he must strive to make his thoughts, desires, interior dispositions and external actions conformable to those of the supreme Ideal of human perfection. The religious pledges himself to seek in a special way to intensify this dynamic union and moral conformity with Christ. In taking up the cross to follow after Jesus, the religious wills to associate himself more perfectly with Christ in that central mystery to which his whole life tended, his passion, death and resurrection.

Moral imitation of Christ, which should flow from sacramental configuration to him, means seeking to reproduce in oneself the interior dispositions which animated the incarnate Son. From the moment of his incarnation the spirit of religion filled the soul of Christ, supreme high Priest of the human race and sole Mediator between God and man. Religion is that virtue which disposes man to honor God and worship him as the beginning and end of all creation. Throughout Christ's life a constant sacrifice of praise, adoration, thanksgiving and willingness to repair the injury done by sin to God's external glory rose up from his soul to his Father, culminating in his sacrifice upon the cross.

Religious Life as Consecration

The term "religious" for a person who publicly consecrates himself to the observance of the evangelical counsels is not entirely satisfactory. It tends to give the impression that those who do not embrace the counsels are not "religious," that there is something lacking in their practice of the virtue of religion. Yet every Christian, through his baptism, is associated with the worship and sacrifice of Christ. Through his union with him he is consecrated to honor God with interior and exterior acts of worship, and in this sense every Christian is "religious."

The term "religious" also generates another kind of confusion, for it is sometimes used, as we use it in this book, to designate both monks and those who profess a consecrated life in which the work of the exterior apostolate occupies a dominant place, whereas at other times it designates only these latter as distinct from monks. The

Second Vatican Council has retained the term, in the sense in which we use it here, to designate all those who publicly profess the observance of the evangelical counsels. There is need, however, of a new set of terms to correspond to the realities which actually exist in the Church today.

The Council explains the difference between religious and other Christians in terms of the further consecration of the former to divine service. By the fact that he binds himself by vows or their equivalent, "a person is totally dedicated to God, loved beyond all things. In this way, that person is ordained to the honor and service of God under a new and special title" (*Constitution on the Church*, 44). This consecration is merely a further deepening of the consecration of baptism, "that he may be capable of deriving more abundant fruit from this baptismal grace" (*ibid*). By profession of the counsels he is enabled "to free himself from those obstacles, which might draw him away from the fervor of charity and the perfection of divine worship," and is "more intimately consecrated to divine service" (*ibid*).

Religious Life in the Church

In seeking perfection through the following of Christ, the religious always remains a disciple. Now that Christ has ascended to heaven, he has no other way to follow his Lord except under the guidance of those whom Christ has designated to communicate his life, speak in his name and rule with his power. Hence the religious is subject to the Church. There can be no following of Christ nor religious perfection except according to a form of life which has gained the approbation of Christ's Church. From the time of the origins of monasticism, when religious life first emerged as a distinct form of the Christian life, the Church has not ceased to extol it, to recommend it to those who receive the call and to govern it with supernatural wisdom.

The Second Vatican Council has restated this concern of the Church for the religious life and her obligation to regulate it:

> The counsels are a divine gift, which the Church received from its Lord and which it will always observe with the help of his grace. Church authority has the duty, under the inspiration of the Holy Spirit, of interpreting these evangelical counsels, of regulating their practice and finally to build on them stable forms of living. Thus it has come about that, as if on a tree which has grown in the field of the Lord, various forms of solitary and community life, as well as various religious families have branched out in a marvelous and multiple way from this divinely given seed (*Constitution on the Church*, 43).

In order to understand the place which religious life occupies in the Church, we must understand what the Church is. She is the eschatological community of the faithful foretold by the prophets. Composed of the remnant of Israel and a multitude of the Gentiles to whom the doors of salvation were opened, this community has been gathered together by God around Christ, the Messiah. In her the Holy Spirit works, pouring out the abundance of the divine life which issues from the salvific work of Christ. She is, then, the sole and necessary means of salvation, for only through the Church can men enter into contact with the divine life of which Christ is the fullness.

The Church, Divine and Human Reality

The Church is the extension of Christ into the world. We are living in an "in-between" time, between a realized and a future eschatology: salvation has already been achieved in the work of Christ, but it has yet to be consummated in the parousia. The Church is, then, the instrument through which the divine work of Christ is applied to individual men, gathered into the community of God's holy people. Just as Christ is the expression of the divinity in incarnate form, so the Church incarnates and expresses in time the existence and salvific activity of Christ.

The Church continues the incarnation and is thus herself a divine-human reality. She contains the divine life, the first fruits of the

Spirit, the foretaste of the heavenly Jerusalem. But these realities are not yet definitively achieved. Just as Christ unites in his own Person the humanity and the divinity, so the Church is human as well as divine. She is not only reality of grace, but also means of grace. The divine element is both hidden and revealed by the sign of her humanity, her concrete existence in the world. She is a sacramental reality, a sign which not only symbolizes the divine gifts, but also contains and confers them.

The Religious in the Church

As the Body of Christ, the Church is composed of a multitude of organs which have different functions in her structure. St. Paul, who coined this terminology, has pointed out that, while the members have different contributions to make to the well-being of the whole, nevertheless all are necessary to the integrity of the Church and to the fulfillment of her mission (1 Cor 12,12–31).

Insofar as she is the means of grace and sanctification, the Church is composed of clergy and laity; the clergy constitutes the hierarchy of the Church, instituted by Christ and established upon the apostolic college. It is their function in the Church to dispense the means of salvation through the sacramental system and the preaching of the Word. The laity, on the other hand, are the holy people of God, admitted through baptism to the society of the faithful, who are not merely passive, but have an active power to receive the means of grace from the hands of the clergy and to administer some sacraments themselves. The religious life does not pertain to the hierarchical structure of the Church, but it may be adopted by either a layman or a cleric (cf *Constitution on the Church*, 43 and 44).

Insofar as she is reality of grace and sanctification, the Church is composed of seculars and religious. The distinction made between the two does not mean that the latter are consecrated to the service of God and the former are not. All of the faithful are the holy people of God; all are consecrated to his service. Religious life does not constitute a "state" in the same sense in which the priesthood is a state distinct from the lay state. Rather it is a form of life more perfectly adapted to the service of God. The religious is a Christian who, in order to serve God more perfectly, adopts an external form of life structured to correspond to the evangelical counsels. While other Christians remain in the world to work for the spread of Christ's kingdom, the religious leaves the world, at least in some sense, to realize the reality of the Church more perfectly, anticipating the heavenly Jerusalem here on earth. Every religious represents in his own person a certain realization of the reality of grace which the Church contains, to a degree not verified in the case of other members of the Church.

Witness to the Kingdom

Religious, therefore, have a function in the Church which is not adequately fulfilled by any other of her organs and which is of vital importance because it is so closely associated with the most intimate aspect of her being. It is true that through the centuries religious have contributed innumerable works of charity and have enriched mankind with many contributions to human culture. However valuable such things may be, they do not constitute the primary function of religious life in the Mystical Body, but rather are secondary fruits of it. Its primary function is to realize in as pure a manner as possible an essential aspect of the Church's life and thus to bear witness to the world that in the Church the kingdom of God already exists among men, a kingdom of such transcendent value that it demands of men an absolute and uncompromising acceptance.

Through the possession of grace and charity in the unity of the Church, every Christian contains the kingdom of God within himself in a real though imperfect way. The religious life offers a special manifestation of this presence of the kingdom. The community life which is led by most religious is meant to be a mirror of the order and unity of heaven. By that charity which unites the members of a community, and which unites even the hermit to other men, religious manifest to the world the source and model of all unity and peace, the thing which makes heaven to be heaven: the love of the Father, the Son and the Holy Spirit. This charity constitutes the primary apostolic witness of religious.

Further, by a life dedicated to the worship of God in sacrifice and divine praise, by contemplative prayer and the habitual awareness of God's presence, religious anticipate the liturgy of the heavenly Jerusalem and proclaim the fact that all Christians already belong to the heavenly city of the angels and saints. Because of this imitation of the constant prayer and praise of the angels in heaven, religious life, and specifically monastic life, has traditionally been called the "angelic life."

Moreover, religious anticipate the heavenly kingdom by their detachment from material goods and by their virginity, according to our Lord's saying that after the resurrection there will be no more marrying nor giving in marriage, but the redeemed will be like the angels in heaven. By the dedication of their entire being to God in this life religious are already "sons of the resurrection" (cf Lk 20, 34–36). The very fact that fallen human nature can sustain this life of poverty and purity is a striking sign to the world of the presence and power of divine grace. The religious life manifests this aspect of actual possession of the kingdom of God within the Church.

Tension Toward the Kingdom of Heaven

In this life, however, Christians do not yet possess the kingdom of God perfectly and definitively. Here on earth the Church's life is marked necessarily and unmistakably by tension, by a joyous expectation of the final coming of Christ and an eagerness to hasten it. The Church is still engaged in combat, must still finish the course, is still preparing herself to go out and meet the Bridegroom. Every Christian engages in this movement toward the final realization of the kingdom by following Christ's precepts, without which there is no hope of attaining the goal.

For this combat the religious, following the invitation of Christ, strips himself of everything that would hinder him from attaining the goal more surely and more perfectly. He sells all that he has in exchange for the pearl of great price. By his free and wholehearted abandonment of everything that the world values most he bears witness to the good which is measureless. His life proclaims the absolute character of God's claims before a world which loses itself in secondary values. The religious life proclaims the inner need of faith to tend to vision and of grace to tend to glory. In the Church, religious live in its most absolute dimension the tension of Christianity toward the perfect fulfillment of Christ's promises.

Religious Life as a Sign in the Church

The value of religious life as a sign proclaiming the nature of Christ's kingdom has been emphasized by the Fathers of Vatican II:

> The profession of the evangelical counsels . . . appears as a sign which can and ought to attract all the members of the Church to an effective and prompt fulfillment of the duties of their Christian vocation. The People of God have no lasting city here below, but look forward to one that is to come (*Constitution on the Church*, 44).

The *Constitution* goes on to declare that religious life is a sign not only of the presence of the kingdom here below, but also of its consummation in heaven:

> The religious state, whose purpose is to free its members from earthly cares, more fully manifests to all believers the presence of heavenly goods already possessed here below. Furthermore, it not only witnesses to the fact of a new and eternal life acquired by the redemption of Christ, but it foretells the future resurrection and the glory of the heavenly kingdom (*ibid*).

The principle function of religious life in the Church, therefore, is to proclaim the transcendence of the kingdom of God above all purely terrestrial concerns:

The religious state clearly manifests that the kingdom of God and its needs, in a very special way, are raised above all earthly considerations. Finally it clearly shows all men the unsurpassed breadth of the strength of Christ the King and the infinite power of the Holy Spirit marvelously working in the Church. Thus, the state which is constituted by the profession of the evangelical counsels, though it is not of the hierarchical structure of the Church, nevertheless, undeniably belongs to its life and holiness (*ibid*).

Religious Life as Means to the End

Religious life, therefore, with its observance of the counsels, is simply the organization of means to achieve the perfection of charity, means which the experience of the Church has proved to be effective. Religious differ from other Christians, consequently, not in the goal for which they strive, which is the establishment of the kingdom of God as the perfect reign of divine charity, but in the means which they employ to attain that end. The religious embraces as his means of perfection a particular complex of religious and ascetical practices: he makes the law of his life the observance of the evangelical counsels of effective poverty, perfect chastity and voluntary obedience, a religious rule with its approved constitutions, and the laws of the Church which govern religious life and his worship of God.

It is indispensable that the religious see all these things precisely as *means*. Religious perfection consists neither in scrupulous observance of juridical obligations, nor in perfect observance of the common life, nor in assiduous attendance at liturgical functions. It does not consist in frequent reception of the sacraments, or chastisement of the body, or extraordinary states of prayer, or external apostolic works, much less in a purely intellectual appreciation of the religious life. Christ's teaching on perfection is unequivocal: it is interior, and it consists in charity. It was precisely the formalism of the Pharisees which prompted our Lord's thundering condemnation of their religious life. The purpose of all the observances of religious life is to bring men to submit to the rule of divine charity.

To say of means that they are merely means and not ends in themselves does not in any way lessen their value and importance; it merely assigns them their proper function. Determined in their substance by Christ himself, the evangelical counsels have proved throughout the centuries to be suitable and direct means to perfection, though not the only ones, and they retain their value in every age of the Church's life because they formulate an essential aspect of Christianity. The innumerable saints who have attained a high degree of charity in the religious life are eloquent witnesses to the continuing validity of this form of life. By the effective detachment of his profession the religious makes affective detachment from the things of this world and attachment to God alone easier and more secure. The renunciations of religious life are efficacious means to perfection because they free a man from many of the obstacles to actual, wholehearted love of God.

Religious Life an Essential Element?

An efficacious means to perfection, indeed, but is religious life essential to the Church? We can say that our Lord himself is the founder of religious life in the sense that he laid down the ideal and the fundamental principles which are common to every form of religious life in the Church. He made it clear that in addition to the way of perfection which is common to all Christians, there is also a more perfect way of following him. He did not, however, organize these means into a coherent system involving a particular structure of life, but left his followers free to work this out in various ways, according to the needs of the Church in the successive periods of her incarnation in the world. The various religious institutes which have arisen in the Church represent different formulations of the same evangelical principles.

These institutionalized forms of religious life are not essential to the Church. In the first centuries of her existence there were no such organized institutes, and since then many different forms of religious life have appeared and receded according to the needs of the epoch. Religious orders are creations of the Church; they do not pertain to her formal constitutive elements. The Church, which already existed in the apostolic community, is essentially constituted by a bishop surrounded by his flock; nothing more is required for her essence.

However, if we consider religious life, not in the institutionalized forms which it has assumed, but in the intrinsic principles which are common to all of its manifestations, these are essential to the Church because they pertain directly to her end, the sanctification and eventual salvation of all those who are united to the Body of Christ. Religious life is a manifestation of the reality of grace within the Church, of salvation already achieved, and this aspect of the Church's life is of her essence. It is essential to the Church's mission that she bear witness in the world that the kingdom of God is already among us, that this kingdom transcends all earthly realities and that it demands of men a total commitment. The evangelical means to perfection which are common to every form of religious life are essential to the Church because they reveal an essential truth about her nature.

Positive Character of Religious Life

Every religious must have an appreciation for these means which the Church provides for the advancement of God's glory and of his own perfection. Once he has freely engaged himself in the religious life, these means of perfection are no longer optional for him. Hence their importance in his life must be justly estimated. On the one hand, indeed, he must guard against formalism in observance which tends to make the means into ends in themselves. But on the other hand, he must equally guard against a tendency to excuse himself from his religious obligations under the pretext that they are but nonessential means to perfection. Since authentic charity is rooted in humility and obedience, a religious cannot validly excuse himself, under pretext of greater perfection, from any of the obligations which his particular form of life comprises. On the contrary, the most convincing proof of his fidelity to the law of charity will be a sincere observance of his rule without constant calculation of strict obligation.

Religious life, therefore, has an eminently positive orientation. While it is true that renunciation, which aims at the destruction of attachments to the things of this world, plays a large role in every form of religious life, this does not mean that religious life is a completely negative and repressive experience. It is fidelity to the Gospel which dictates that the religious leave all things, as the apostles did; but the same Gospel says that they did so only to follow Christ. The religious life is a living expression of the Gospel paradox that the grain of wheat must die in order to bring forth fruit (cf Jn 12,24). The law of the cross is fundamental to Christianity, but the cross leads to the resurrection. The negative aspects of religious life are endowed with positive content by the fact that they are directed to union with Christ and his members in charity. Moreover, the freeing of oneself from inordinate attachments to creatures demands far more than languid passivity: it requires generous cooperation with God's grace. The effort to arrive at purity of heart ends not in repression but in expansion. The human heart cannot remain empty. As he strives to empty his heart of self, the religious will find that it is more and more filled and moved by the Spirit of Christ.

Religious Life and Christian Freedom

The Spirit of Christ is the Spirit of freedom. St. Paul joyfully announces that the sons of God who through baptism have received the new life of Christ are delivered from slavery to Satan, to sin and to the old law. Since the religious seeks merely to become a perfect Christian, his way of life is especially marked by spiritual liberty. At its very outset it is an act of freedom, for it begins with the free and voluntary decision to leave all things in order to follow Christ. Every authentic religious vocation is a personal call from God to a chosen individual, who must freely elicit a wholehearted response to the divine invitation.

The Council Fathers have insisted that:

> The profession of the evangelical counsels, though entailing the renunciation of certain values which are to be undoubtedly esteemed, does not detract from the genuine development of the human person, but rather by its very nature is most beneficial to that development. Indeed the counsels, voluntarily undertaken according to each one's personal vocation, contribute a great deal to the purification of heart and spiritual liberty. They continually stir up the fervor of charity. But especially they are able to more fully mold the Christian man to that type of virginal and detached life which Christ the Lord chose for himself and which his Mother also embraced (*Constitution on the Church*, 46).

Before man, in his fallen state, can seek God, God must first come in search of him. A religious vocation is a mystery of divine grace and divine choice. The Lord, seeking among his holy people for one to render him special service, casts his glance of special love upon a certain individual. The reason for his choice lies hidden in the infinite mystery of his love. It does not always fall upon those who, to human eyes, may seem best suited or most worthy. The internal grace of vocation may not be accompanied by any sensible inspiration, but only by the ordinary signs of intention and aptitude. Yet it is essentially a call from God, to which the recipient must freely give his answer.

Personal Response to a Personal Invitation

This invitation is a deeply personal one, for what God offers is himself. In the religious life a man seeks his own perfection in charity, seeks to add to the external glory of God. It is correct to say that these things are the purpose of religious life, and yet a man begins to fathom their ultimate meaning only when he perceives that what he is seeking is not something but Someone. It is a Person who invites him and who stands at the end of his journey. This is the all-consuming search of the life of a religious: really to seek

God, in himself and for himself, not simply as men imagine him to be by the light of their own reason, but as he reveals himself in his incarnate Son, in the light of faith. God stands at the end of the religious life as he stands at the beginning, addressing his Word to a man, revealing himself to him. It is in exercising his Christian freedom that the invited one responds, hearkening to the divine Word, accepting the encounter with the living God.

It is not only at the beginning that the religious gives his assent; he must continue to do so throughout his life. His growth in perfection, his progress in the search for God, must likewise be marked by spiritual liberty. Far from considering the obligations which he has undertaken to be no more than external, restraining forces, the religious must grow in his awareness that they are really the guarantees of true freedom. To the extent that he gives generously of himself, his observance will flow less and less from fear or other external, human considerations, and more and more from within, as it were naturally, from the love of what is commanded and from the love of God who draws him onward. It is precisely love which gives religious life its freedom, for charity means liberation from slavery to all that separates from God. When St. Thomas declares that progress in the degrees of charity is the same as progress in the degrees of spiritual liberty (S.T. 2–2, q183, a4, ad 1), he is echoing the ancient monastic tradition which held that the soul expands in charity and freedom once fear has been overcome by the successful conclusion of the ascetical combat.

The Pursuit of Perfection

The search for perfection, then, must continue throughout the life of a religious. In her official pronouncements in the recent past, the Church has often referred to religious life as a *state of perfection.* In this terminology, the use of the word *state* does not imply that religious life is a static condition. Neither does the word *perfection* mean that the person who enters upon religious life must already be perfect, but rather that he takes upon himself a form of life which is structured precisely in view of the pursuit of perfection. Religious life is a state of perfection *to be acquired*, that is, a way of life so organized as to facilitate the search for God. According to the terminology of ancient monastic literature, it is a *school* of perfection. Just as the student entering a school is not expected already to possess the knowledge which the school is meant to impart, so the man who enters religious life is expected only to struggle courageously to achieve the perfection which is the end of religious life.

The term *state of perfection* is not the most felicitous, and is in fact not employed by the *Constitution on the Church* of Vatican II. This document does, however, refer to the *religious state* and says: "The Church not only raises the religious profession to the dignity of a canonical state by her approval, but even manifests that this profession is a state consecrated to God by the liturgical setting of that profession" (45). There need be no objection to the use of the term, so long as it is understood that it is not intended to imply a static condition. Religious life must be a dynamic pursuit of perfection: it is a prophetic vocation.

Those who profess the religious life, therefore, oblige themselves seriously to strive for the perfection of charity. This obligation is implied in the very nature of the life which they profess. Profession is only the beginning; it does not introduce the religious into a static condition in which he can comfortably relax, but into a dynamic forward movement which is impatient to hasten onwards to its goal. He is caught up in the tension toward heaven. He will measure the value of the means provided by religious life in terms of his ardent desire for the final goal. Rather than engaging in vain attempts to measure his own progress and becoming enmeshed in an excessive concern with self, he will be filled with gratitude for the love and mercy God has shown him. The signs which indicate that he is fulfilling his obligation to strive for perfection will be his effort to avoid excessive preoccupation with self, the earnest desire to let his charity expand in works performed with greater generosity and the patient attempt to be faithful in meeting the daily demands of the love and worship of God. His whole life must become an eager response to the Word of God.

3. DIFFERENT FORMS OF RELIGIOUS LIFE

The Principle of Distinction

The fundamental characteristics of religious life which have been outlined in the preceding section are found in every form of religious life which exists in the Church, whether it be of ancient or modern origin. Every religious aims at the ideal of Christian perfection, which is perfect charity. The ultimate purpose of the religious is no different from that of the Christian who remains in the world to work out his salvation in the ordinary circumstances of human life: both aim at the perfection of charity, to be achieved insofar as possible in this life, to be consummated in the vision of the Blessed Trinity in heaven.

Among those Christians who have publicly embraced the observance of the counsels there exist many different forms of religious life. From the time of the first flowering of the ideal of the evangelical counsels in the early Church, there has been a manifold development of religious institutes which have arisen in response to various needs of the Church throughout the ages. We must seek to define the differences among these varied forms of religious life. Here again, it is obvious that the differences cannot reside in the ultimate purpose, which is the same for all religious, as it is for all Christians, but only in the means which are employed to attain it. We may define these differences in means as differences in spirituality.

Definition of Spirituality

What is meant by a spirituality? It may be defined as the organization of a complex of means for the attainment of supernatural perfection. We have seen that human perfection consists in union with God through divine charity. This and this alone is the ultimate purpose of all spiritualities, and consequently there can be no differences among them from the viewpoint of the end. This perfection is supernatural, both in its essence, which is divine grace, a created share in the life of God himself, and in its operation, which consists in the activity of the supernatural virtues, principally charity. Since it is possible to grow continually in grace and in charity, it is the function of a spirituality to organize the means supplied by nature and by the positive will of God into a coherent system which will promote supernatural growth.

However, we must not represent different spiritualities as if they were systems of entirely different means. Not only the end of Christian perfection, but also the basic means for its attainment are determined by the positive will of God and hence cannot vary from one spirituality to another. One cannot define a spirituality by saying, for instance, that it emphasizes prayer, because this is true of every form of spirituality. The most fundamental means of attaining perfection are imposed by revelation itself: every Christian must have contact with the Word of God in the Scriptures, must receive the bread of the Scriptures and the bread of the Eucharist in the liturgy, must be nourished by the other sacraments, must practice mortification, must exercise the theological and moral virtues, must cultivate prayer.

These are essential elements in every Christian's pursuit of perfection, and no orthodox spirituality can dispense with any of them. No form of religious life can claim any kind of exclusive monopoly upon the liturgy, or upon asceticism, or upon the apostolate, much less upon the love of God and neighbor. We cannot seek for the principle of distinction of spiritualities in the use of different means to perfection, at least when it is a question of these basic ones which are common to all religious.

Differences of Spirituality

It is obvious, however, that there are differences among the various spiritualities cultivated by the many religious institutes in the Church. In what do these differences consist? First of all, while the primary elements of every spirituality are the same, the secondary elements may differ. The solitary, for example, will exercise charity for other men by praying for them, the cenobite by caring for the needs of his brethren in the monastery, the active religious by ministering to Christians in the world. Actual physical separation from the world is a secondary element of spirituality which is characteristic of monastic institutes but not of other religious orders, and serves to differentiate the spirituality of the latter from monastic spirituality. These secondary elements are really different modes of implementation of the primary elements which are common to all spiritualities.

What is of greater importance in distinguishing one spirituality from another is the varying proportion which the component elements may assume in the total complex. Every spirituality is made up of many different elements, organized into a harmonious whole in which each part has its specific role to play. While all of the primary elements will be the same in every spirituality, they may be present in different proportions, so that there is room for almost infinite variation in the balance which is struck among them. This proportion is chiefly a question of psychological importance. In one spirituality a particular means may receive a greater psychological emphasis, while in another a different emphasis may be found preferable. Some religious orders center the entire spiritual combat around poverty, others around humility. Both of these virtues must find a place in every system of spirituality, but there is room for great variation in the relative importance which is accorded to them in the total complex.

Differences in Institutions

When it is a question of distinguishing the different forms of religious life, there is, furthermore, another factor which must be considered, that of institutions. In every form of religious life a distinction must be made between the basic ideology, the theory according to which the various means of perfection are harmoniously organized in pursuit of the goal, and the institutions, which are the concrete implementation of this theory in particular structures. The institutions of a religious institute evolve in order to keep pace with changing conditions in the Church and the world around it, while the ideology remains basically the same, although it may be refined and more thoroughly penetrated to bring to light potentialities which previously remained implicit.

The most obvious differences which distinguish one religious institute from another are in the sphere of institutions. They are most obvious because they are on the surface and so do not get to the real heart of the question of differentiation. They are also most subject to change, and can be changed, at least within certain limits, without altering the essential characteristics of the form of life in question. More than one set of institutions can be evolved to give adequate expression to a particular religious ideology. In the sphere of institutions belong such matters as the form of government adopted by an institute, whether centrally organized or admitting of autonomous subdivisions loosely confederated or with no organization at all, the regime of ascetical practices, the liturgical horarium, organization of communal exercises, and so forth.

While there is great flexibility and room for evolution in the matter of institutions, some of these are so intimately related to the fundamental ideology of particular institutes that they could not be abandoned without radically changing the orientation of the spirituality in question. Certain institutions, such as, for example, the common recitation of the divine office or the relative permanence of the office of superior, may be the only possible expression of elements of the spirituality characteristic of a particular institute. In these cases a change in institutional forms would also involve a change in ideology, and would thereby transform the character of the religious institute.

Systems of Spirituality

In the concrete, every individual creates his own spirituality, different to some extent from that of everyone else. Although their outward form of life may be structured in the same way, individual differences are such that it is impossible for any two persons to achieve precisely the same combination of the various means to perfection and always to attribute the same degree of importance, in their own psychological outlook, to the same elements. The vocation of every religious is a personal response to the Spirit, and the Spirit respects individual differences.

It is possible, however, that certain comprehensive patterns developed by great spiritual teachers may be adopted by others who attempt to carry on their own quest for God within the framework of a spirituality which has been proved effective. The complex of means which constitutes a spirituality can be organized on a theoretical basis. Considered from this viewpoint, a spirituality is primarily an ideology, an intellectual system which can be learned even by one who does not practice it. It can, therefore, be assimilated and imitated by others who find it compatible with their own individual characteristics. The great systems of spirituality in the Church, often initiated by founders of religious orders, are broad patterns of organization of the means to perfection, within which men may work out their own individual response to their vocation.

In practice there will be individual variations within each system of spirituality, as many as there are individuals, for each person has to make his own response to the Spirit. Yet it is true to say that all are following the same system of spirituality. The means employed, both primary and secondary, are the same for all, and all achieve approximately the same equilibrium of these elements insofar as their psychological evaluation of them remains relatively constant. Since their striving for perfection proceeds according to the same general pattern, they can be said to follow the same system or school of spirituality.

Freedom and Conformity

A spirituality is not a bed of Procrustes, into which individual inspiration is to be forced even at the cost of its own deformation. The composer who writes a sonata, or the poet who pens a sonnet, does not, if he is a true artist, sacrifice his inspiration to the form. Rather he expresses his own individual genius within the framework of an established pattern. This is what a man does who adopts a particular form of spirituality; he channels his own personal efforts toward perfection within a framework which provides him with a basic ideology and form of life without suppressing the individuality of his own inspiration. Thus both liberty and order are preserved.

Those systems of spirituality which have enjoyed outstanding success and long life in the Church have been precisely those of so broad and profound an inspiration that they continue to exercise an appeal upon men of various times and places. Open-mindedness and breadth of view are essential for the preservation of individual liberty. The system must be an instrument through which the Spirit can work, not an obstacle to his working. The original inspiration of spiritualities which are ancient and traditional must be constantly re-examined, lest nonessential elements be allowed to threaten the equilibrium of the whole and the freedom of the individual within it. This is particularly true of the institutional elements of the spiritualities of religious orders, which require a process of constant updating so that they remain the servants of the ideology and do not become its masters.

Each religious institute has its own spirituality, different to some degree from that of every other. We have seen what is the basis for the distinction. In the description of a particular spirituality, such as we wish to undertake in this book, it is necessary to examine the various elements of which it is composed. Those secondary elements which are proper to it must be isolated, and the others studied in their relation to the total complex to see what role they play in achieving the total equilibrium. Institutional elements, while usually not essential, can shed some light upon the question insofar as they are valid expressions of the ideology. It is this kind of examination which we propose to undertake in regard to monastic spirituality.

2. What Is Monastic Life?

WHILE IT IS TRUE that monasticism is one form of religious life, this manner of stating the question may seem to imply that monasticism is a later development of some earlier and more general form of religious life. Exactly the contrary is true. Historically, monasticism came first and for many centuries was the only form of religious life in the Church. While in the Eastern Church it has remained the only form down to the present day, many other types of religious institutes have grown up in the West since the Middle Ages. Although it has certain features in common with these other institutes, monasticism has always been regarded as a distinct form of life; it is only in recent times that monks have been juridically assimilated to other religious, and this practice has had the disadvantage of obscuring the distinctive features of the monastic order. Because monasticism is such an ancient phenomenon, we must view it against its historical background if we wish to form a clear idea of the characteristics of monastic spirituality and to distinguish it from subsequent forms of religious life.

1. THE ORIGINS OF MONASTICISM

Survival of the Patristic Period

The first thing that strikes the observer of monasticism is its antiquity. In the monastic life we encounter an uninterrupted tradition which goes back to the early centuries of the Church. The basic structures of the monastic life were established during the patristic period and thus put us into contact with the golden age of Christianity. Monasticism is a survival of the religious life as it was conceived during the era of the great Fathers of the Eastern and the Western Church.

While this antiquity may at first sight seem to make the monastic life merely an interesting historical curiosity or an anachronistic museum piece, upon closer examination we find that it is, rather, a testimony to an inspiration so authentically Christian that it has an enduring value. In our time, when the Church has rediscovered the necessity of a return to sources, a survival of the patristic period is not likely to be regarded a priori as anachronistic. The rediscovery of the Fathers has shown us that their spiritual teaching continues to be valuable, not because it is old, but because it is such an authentic expression of the essence of Christianity, in such intimate contact with the sources of revelation.

Likewise the teaching of the monastic Fathers and the form of life in which it found expression enjoy a continuing validity because they incarnate the simplicity and authenticity of the Christianity of the early centuries, which had the genius of offering a synthetic view of the pure teaching of the Gospel, unencumbered by the compartmentalization and casuistry which grew up in later times. Monasticism has found a renewed appeal today precisely because it contains those very values toward which the movement of return to sources has led the Church with unerring instinct. It is not a relic of the past, but a living tradition.

Origins of Monasticism

The origins of monasticism are shrouded in obscurity. We know that already in the primitive Church there were ascetics who adopted a more rigorous form of life than their fellow Christians, following the invitation of the Gospel tradition and St. Paul's warm recommendation of the practice of virginity. Later on, in retrospect, the monks looked back upon the primitive Church of Jerusalem as the first monastic community. During the early centuries, Christians of both sexes, while remaining in the world and taking part in the normal life of the Christian community, practiced continence as a means of following Christ.

This, however, was not yet monasticism as a distinct form of life; it was merely the practice of asceticism within the framework of the community. The essential feature which distinguished the first monks from these ascetics was their physical separation from the Christian community. History does not permit us to identify accurately the first manifestation of flight from the world. We know only that sometime in the latter part of the third century certain ascetics abandoned the Christian community in which they had hitherto lived and retired into solitude. Because our earliest documentation comes from Egypt, it has generally been thought that the movement originated there, but it is possible that it began in Syria. In any case, this phenomenon marks the origin of monasticism.

Hypotheses about Monastic Origins

Many theories have been advanced to explain the origins of monasticism. The hypotheses elaborated in the nineteenth century depended chiefly upon parallels, real or supposed, between the ascetical practices of the early monks and those of ascetics of other religions. Thus it was proposed that monasticism derived from the recluses of the temple of Serapis in Egypt and was Christianized only by St. Basil in the East and St. Jerome in the West (Weingarten). Others found in early monasticism the influence of the Greek cynics, Buddhist monasticism and the Jewish therapeutae mentioned by Philo, currents which began to affect Christianity after it became open to the world due to the peace of Constantine (Zöckler).

The pan-Hellenistic school held that monasticism was a synthesis between the Gospel and the ideals of the Stoic, Neo-Pythagorian and Neo-Platonist philosophers (Reitzenstein). Another theory maintained that it derived its origin from heretical movements in the early Church, such as the Montanists and Encratites, as a reaction against the secularization of the Church in the Constantinian period. Unlike the heretics, however, the monks arrived at an understanding with the hierarchical Church and agreed to a peaceful coexistence (Harnack).

While it is true that certain similarities can be found between the ascetical practices of the early monks and those of non-Christian ascetics, they are for the most part quite superficial and do not touch the real ideology of the monastic life. It is now generally accepted by historians of all persuasions that there is no need to seek for the derivation of monasticism outside of Christianity itself. Aside from a few superficial contacts on nonessential points, the Bible and the Christian tradition of asceticism are quite sufficient to account for the flight of the first monks to the desert. Hypotheses of non-Christian origin are now merely historical curiosities.

The Qumran Sect and Monasticism

There is one possible source of influence, however, which has aroused considerable interest in recent years. This is the community of Jewish sectaries whose monastery and library have been discovered at Qumran, on the northwestern shore of the Dead Sea. It was already known from Pliny that there were Jewish ascetics in the first century A.D. who lived near the Dead Sea and whom he, like Philo and Josephus, calls Essenes. The discovery since 1947 of ancient Hebrew manuscripts in caves near the Dead Sea led to an excavation of the Qumran ruins between 1951 and 1956 which revealed the existence of a monastic complex of buildings inhabited by a community of ascetics. It is now generally admitted that the Qumran sectaries formed a branch of the Essene movement.

Something of their manner of life is known from the excavations and from their sectarian literature, principally the so-called *Manual of Discipline*, which was the rule of the Qumran community, and the *Damascus Document*, which legislated for a related branch of the sect. They lived a common life, though there were also solitaries who inhabited nearby caves. They renounced material possessions and marriage, at least in the stricter branch of the movement, and withdrew into solitude, cutting themselves off from official Judaism, which they regarded as secularized and irremediably corrupt. Through asceticism they sought to achieve domination of the passions. Their time was spent in working, reading their sacred books, attending liturgical assemblies and devoting themselves to contemplation. There was a great concern for ritual purity and a vibrant eschatology. The community was hierarchically organized and there was a detailed procedure for the admission and training of postulants, as well as a penal code which regulated punishments for the infraction of discipline.

It is evident that many parallels can be found between the Qumran community and Christian monasticism. In the present state of our knowledge, however, it is impossible to establish any direct dependence of the latter upon the former. The chronology is an insuperable obstacle to direct dependence, for the Qumran community ceased to exist in 68 A.D. and monasticism did not originate until the second half of the third century. While the Essene movement may have survived for a time in some form, there is no evidence that it continued to exist down through the patristic period. Furthermore, the differences between the two movements are no less significant than the similarities: The whole inspiration of the Qumran ideology is thoroughly Jewish, while that of monasticism is profoundly Christian. At present we cannot postulate more than an indirect dependence, transmitted through the ascetical doctrine and practice of the

Judeo-Christian communities of Syria, which may have been influenced by the Essene movement and in turn produced primitive monasticism.

Biblical Prototypes of the Monastic Life

When the ancient monks sought to elucidate the problem of their origin they, unlike nineteenth-century scholars, never thought of turning to any other source than the Bible and Christian tradition. This was, of course, an interpretation: our documentation is later than the actual origins of the movement and is already stylized and idealized. Nevertheless it is significant that the monks regarded themselves as a purely Christian phenomenon, firmly rooted in the biblical tradition. In the Old Testament they found precursors of monasticism in the prophets Elijah and Elisha, who lived a solitary life, dressed in skins, fasted, carried on a continual dialogue with God and organized groups of disciples into a kind of school of asceticism. The monastic Fathers did not hesitate to refer to them as "monks of the Old Testament" (Jerome, *Epist* 125,7).

A still closer model for monks was John the Baptist. He too wore the prophetic garb which became the habit of the monk, lived in the desert of Judea, adopted an ascetical way of life and was completely absorbed in the imminent coming of the eschatological kingdom. The appeal of the desert and the spirituality of flight from the world find their justification in the Precursor, the man of whom Jesus said: "among those born of women there has not risen a greater than John the Baptist" (Mt 11,11). Modern scholars suspect that John may have had some connection with the Qumran sectaries, whose center was so close to the scene of his labors, whose community was flourishing at that very time and whose religious ideas are in some respects similar to his preaching. The ancients were unaware of this, but they recognized him as a kindred spirit.

Another biblical prototype, to which the cenobites later appealed, was the primitive Jerusalem community, where "the multitude of the believers were of one heart and one soul, and . . . had all things in common" (Acts 4,32). These early Christians "continued steadfastly in the teaching of the apostles and in the communion of the breaking of the bread and in the prayers" (*ibid* 2,42). While Jerome was content to note the similarities between the lives of the early Christians and those of the monks (*De viris illustribus* 8 and 11), Cassian went so far as to declare that this was the actual origin of the cenobitic life. According to him cenobitic monasticism first appeared when certain Christians withdrew from the rest to counter the relaxation which had entered the Church after the Council of Jerusalem (*Conf* 18,5–8). While this myth of monastic origins is of no historical value, it shows the concern of the ancient monks to attach their way of life to the spirituality of the New Testament.

Motives for Withdrawal

Above all, the monks regarded their life as an imitation of Christ. Whatever influences may have been exerted upon monasticism on the level of external practice by the Hellenistic and Jewish milieux in which it grew up, its inspiration is essentially a product of Christianity. When the monks went to the desert, they were conscious of answering the invitation of Jesus in the Gospel, which they regarded as personally addressed to them. Their life did not profess to be anything more than an imitation of their Lord, who himself practiced the supreme degree of renunciation and had invited them to "come, follow me." The monks fled to the desert simply to become better Christians. If they renounced human values and the normal structures of human life in the world, it was only to live more perfectly for God. They had no other intention than to carry out the teaching of the Gospel to its logical conclusions.

But why did they seek solitude to do this? Indeed, the Christian vocation demands a rejection of the world in the sense which the Gospels sometimes attach to this term: that complex of men and attitudes and practices which represent rebellion against God and opposition to his grace. The world in this sense must be abandoned by every follower of Christ, for it is inimical to God and intent upon seducing by its attractions those who belong to him. No Christian can compromise with the kingdom of Satan. But previously it had been possible to renounce worldly ways and carry on an ascetical life while remaining in the Christian community. Why did the first monks interpret the logic of the Gospel as requiring an actual physical separation?

Secularization of the Church

The sources give us no explicit answer to this question, but we can find at least a partial answer in the historical circumstances of the period. In the early centuries of the Church the entire Christian community lived somewhat separate from the world. During the age of the persecutions Christians were despised, looked down upon and discriminated against, when not actually subjected to physical suffering. The very fact of becoming a Christian cut a man off to an appreciable extent from wealth, social position and the mainstream of public life.

But in the third century, as Christians became accepted, and especially after the peace of Constantine, Christianity was no longer regarded as dishonorable. As Christians began to take a more active part in civic and social life, a certain secularization of the Church set in. Instead of being an enemy, the state now lavished honor and material gifts upon the Church. A flood of conversions brought in men of less lofty ideals than the heroic Christians of the age of the martyrs. What was gained in quantity was lost in quality. To be a Christian was no longer a challenge. To men of fervent ideals, it seemed that Christianity had begun to compromise with the world. Therefore one could escape the world only by withdrawing to the margin of the Church. The monks were seeking the radicalism and total self-sacrifice of the age of the martyrs. They could find it only in the desert, where they became the successors of the martyrs, a new generation of giants.

The Solitaries of the Desert

The first monks were the great solitaries of the desert. In the course of the fourth century the bleak deserts of Egypt became peopled with men who had fled from the world in search of solitude. Great numbers of monks also began to appear in secluded regions of Syria, Palestine and Mesopotamia, and, a little later, in Asia Minor. It was not long before the movement spread to the West as well. But it was Egypt, with its vast stretches of forbidding desert, that constituted the real paradise of monks, and it was from there that the earliest monastic literature came. The colonies of monks settled principally in the deserts of Nitria and Skete in the western delta area and in the Thebaid, the great desert which stretches along both sides of the Nile further south.

The monks of this early period were hermits, as they believed that solitude constituted the best climate for the search for God. In practice, however, groups of them often lived in the same locality, coming together for certain common exercises, such as the celebration of the Eucharist. Such a colony was later called a *laura.* Absolute solitude, in which a monk lived totally apart from his fellow men, was generally attempted only by those who had already had long experience in the monastic life. In the early days there was great variety in the manner of life adopted, as each monk was free to create his own style.

The most celebrated of the early solitaries, and the first of whom we have reliable information, was the great Anthony, whom St. Athanasius immortalized in his *Vita Antonii.* It is now generally agreed that this work contains elements of undeniable historical value, though far from being a biography in the modern sense. Its intention is rather to eulogize Anthony as the ideal monk and to propagate the monastic life. It was eminently successful in achieving its purpose and is of inestimable value in informing us of the earliest monastic ideal. Also valuable for this purpose are the *Apophthegmata,* or *Sayings of the Fathers,* pronouncements of the early Coptic monks which reveal their concept of the monastic life. While the collections of these sayings date from a later period, some of the material in them is very ancient.

Entrance into Monastic Life

What was life in the desert like? Apart from the innumerable variations in observance, the principal elements were the same for all. A man who felt a call to the desert disposed of all his property and presented himself to one of the ancients. The reception of the habit constituted his profession. At first the habit was given to anyone who asked for it, but this practice introduced so many misfits that a period of trial was instituted and acceptance of a candidate was subject to the judgment of the fathers. The young monk placed himself under the direction of a spiritual father, a man of long experience, sound doctrine and great wisdom, who taught him how to wage the ascetical combat.

The monastic institute was a charismatic phenomenon. Outside of the mainstream of ecclesiastical life and parallel to the hierarchical structure of the Church without claiming independence from it, the monks were directly subject to the Holy Spirit. There was no rule, no conventual discipline, no structure of authority; the only hierarchy was one of holiness. The *abbas*, or *father*, was one who had reached a lofty degree of perfection and was regarded as a "bearer of the Spirit." He was a "man of God," who acted under direct divine inspiration and often enjoyed extraordinary supernatural gifts. In the light of his own experience and charismatic gifts, he was able to form other monks by sharing his wisdom and transmitting the Spirit. Therefore the teaching of the elders was held in great esteem. It was handed down from one generation to the next, so that a tradition grew up which is incorporated in the *Sayings of the Fathers.*

The Daily Life of the Hermits

Once a monk had renounced everything connected with the world and had withdrawn into solitude, he had to learn the technique of asceticism. He built his own hut near to that of his spiritual father. Then he had to go about the harsh task of the battle to overcome himself. The enemy was twofold: the demons and his passions. The monks often confused the two, for they attributed many things to demonic influence which we would regard as purely natural phenomena. Thus the passions were personified into demons. In the quiet of his cell the hermit prayed, meditated upon the Scriptures, worked, fasted, kept vigils and afflicted his body. He manifested his inmost thoughts to his spiritual father, who was thus able to guide him according to his needs. The monks supported themselves by their labors and gave any superfluities to the poor. They were diligent in performing acts of charity for one another and for travelers who came out to the desert to be edified and counseled. They visited one another from time to time to discuss spiritual subjects. They rose at night to pray for long hours and said numerous prayers during the day, though there was no uniform rule regulating their prayer life.

All of this was very hard work. But it was merely a means to the end. The monk aimed at scaling the heights of perfection, which he would reach only when he enjoyed uninterrupted contemplation of God. The ascetical combat was merely the active phase of his life, which brought him to domination over his lower nature. This state was called *hesychia*, quiet or rest, for in it he was no longer troubled by the rebellion of the flesh. His heart expanded in charity and opened the door to the blessed *theoria*, or contemplation of God. In this state the saint tasted the privileges of perfect tranquillity, spiritual joy, habitual prayer which often became ecstatic, knowledge of the hidden mysteries of the Scriptures, dominion over nature and the wild beasts, and the power of working miracles. Probably those who reached this state of perfection were relatively few, but it was the goal to which every authentic monk aspired.

The first monks in Egypt were unlearned Coptic peasants who devoted themselves to the exercises of monastic life without theorizing about them. Nevertheless their brusque maxims contain some real gems of profound if homely wisdom, and some of these monks attained a high degree of sanctity. In the latter part of the fourth century they were joined by well-educated Greek-speaking monks who developed the theory of monastic perfection into a complete system. The leader of this development was Evagrius of Pontus, who applied the theology of Origen to the monastic life, and whose writings had an incomparable influence upon the later evolution of ascetical and mystical theology.

Pachomius, Founder of Cenobitic Monasticism

While the solitary life afforded real advantages to the monk who sincerely aspired to the search for perfection through renunciation of earthly values and total surrender to God, it had its dangers for the immature and was open to abuse by the insincere. The individualism inherent in this form of life sometimes led to bizarre practices which cast discredit upon the monastic life. The esteem in which extreme feats of asceticism were held led to rivalries which were not always holy. The absence of any kind of regulation of the life opened the doors to many pseudo-monks who soiled the reputation of monasticism by their evil habits. Some became zealous defenders of unorthodox doctrine, and the large bands of warring monks who filled the East during the period of the Christological controversies created a difficult problem for Church authorities.

The grouping of solitaries around an elder whose authority and personal integrity were widely recognized was already a step toward a more communal form of life, but the first organizer of a genuinely cenobitical form of monasticism was St. Pachomius. A soldier and convert from paganism, he embraced the solitary life under the direction of the abbot Palamon for seven years. There he discovered how difficult the eremitical life is for all but the strongest and how many attempts to practice it ended in tragedy. He resolved to organize a form of monastic life in common which would eliminate the arbitrariness so often found in the desert, regulate the exercises of the monks according to a rule, and make a systematic use of obedience as an ascetical practice. In spite of great difficulties, he organized a cenobitic monastery at Tabennisi about 320, which later grew into a whole confederation of monasteries ruled by a superior general.

The monasticism of Pachomius was more individualistic than that of later cenobitic founders, but was a great innovation in comparison to the preceding eremitical life. Pachomius had no intention of rejecting the solitary life, but regarded it as the summit of perfection for which his own institute would serve as a preparation. His form of cenobitism should not be regarded as merely a transitional phase in the development of monasticism; it was already a viable form of the common life, faithful to the best in monastic tradition and endowed with a remarkably profound spirituality. Enough of the Pachomian sources have been preserved to give us a reasonably complete idea of the monastic ideal of this founder who had a notable influence upon the development of monasticism.

The Common Life under St. Basil

The fact that St. Basil is regarded as the patriarch of the monks of the Eastern Church is a curious paradox, since the form of life which he promoted was not monastic in the usual sense and he never uses the word monk in reference to his disciples. His work is not a development of Egyptian monasticism: although he had been in Egypt, he was not attracted to the solitary life and probably had no contact with the Pachomian institute. His ideal is rather in the line of contemporary developments in Asia Minor, where the secularization of the Church in the fourth century had inspired a great enthusiasm for asceticism. Under the leadership of Eustathius of Sebaste, whole families were caught up in a rigorist movement which exalted spiritual realities at the expense of earthly values and urged the practice of the Gospel counsels upon everyone. Basil worked within the context of this enthusiast movement, but attempted to purge it of heresy, sectarianism and instability.

To meet the needs of the ascetical current which he directed he searched the Scriptures to draw out the pure evangelical teaching regarding the perfection of the Christian. It was with the formation of Christians that he was concerned, as they lived together in a local church, not with a special group such as the Pachomian community. For the Christian there could be no other rule than the Scriptures, and Basil's ascetical writings are simply the application of biblical texts to particular cases. The separation from the environment of the normal Christian community which was so essential to Egyptian monasticism is absent from the work of Basil. He aimed at forming a fully Christian community constructed according to the integral teaching of the Gospel. Consequently his principal emphasis was upon the community as Body of Christ and the precept of fraternal charity as the first law of Christianity. His ascetics engaged in works of mercy such as instruction and caring for the sick. They did not live on the margin of the Church, but themselves constituted the local church.

The ideal of Basil has much in common with the monastic ideal which had prevailed hitherto, but added a new emphasis upon works of charity and the bond between the ascetics and the Church. The brotherhoods of Christians which he founded resembled monastic communities so much that they tended to become identified with them. In his writings one can trace an evolution toward a more developed organization of the brotherhoods as new problems arose. Shortly after his death they were being called monasteries and the whole terminology of monasticism was applied to them. But their inspiration was quite different from the cenobitism of Pachomius. Basil had a tremendous influence upon later monasticism, both in the East and in the West.

The Cenobite and the Hermit

Already in the fourth century the two basic forms of monasticism which have persisted down to the present day were constituted in their essential framework: the solitary life and the cenobitic life. There has always been discussion as to which is superior. Throughout the course of monastic history one can trace two attitudes toward the cenobitic life: either it is regarded as having a value in itself superior to eremitism, or it is looked upon as being merely a training ground for the desert. Among the ancient monks of the East, the Cappadocians were the only ones who unhesitatingly adopted the first viewpoint. Basil and his associates quite frankly rejected the solitary life as contrary to man's nature and to the ideal of the Gospel. The hermit has no opportunity to practice love for neighbor, the supreme law of Christianity, no one to correct him, no scope for the exercise of humility and obedience. Only the cenobitic life is fruitful and perfectly fulfills the evangelical ideal. In the West, the great authority of St. Augustine enthusiastically rallied to this opinion.

For the other eastern monks, however, the solitary life remained the supreme ideal. The Egyptians never departed from the epoch-making intuition of Athanasius, who had proclaimed Anthony the exemplar of Christian perfection in its most noble form. For them cenobitism was a safer way which was more practical for the majority of men, but it was only a school of perfection which would normally advance its graduates to the eremitical life. The hermit did not dispense himself from either obedience or charity; he merely exercised them in a different way. Evagrius makes it clear that the solitary's separation from his fellow men does not sever the bonds of charity which unite all the members of the Mystical Body: "a monk is one who is separated from all and yet united to all" (*De oratione* 124). Only the anchorite could hope to scale the heights of contemplation, engage in incessant prayer and achieve the life of the angels here on earth. Jerome and Cassian in the West, while admitting that the cenobium is better for the vast majority, nevertheless followed the Egyptians in their theoretical preference for the eremitical life. We shall see that this was also the position taken by St. Benedict.

2. THE BENEDICTINE TRADITION

Monasticism in the West

Monasticism was not an original development in the Western Church, but entirely derived from the East. We know little about its origins, which go back to the fourth century. The first contact with eastern monasticism seems to have been made when Athanasius came to Rome in 340, accompanied, it is said, by two disciples of Anthony, and there communicated the enthusiasm for the life of the Egyptian monks to which he would later give permanent expression in the *Vita Antonii.* In the succeeding decades there were both cenobites and solitaries in Italy and Spain, though little is known of their life. Jerome gave a great impulse to the movement when he came to Rome in 382, fresh from his eremitical experiment in the desert of Chalcis, and spread his enthusiasm for the monastic life among the wealthy ladies of the Aventine.

In Gaul the most influential though probably not the first monk was St. Martin of Tours. After a long career in the army, he began to live as a hermit, first in Milan and then on the island of Gallinaria. In 361 he accompanied St. Hilary on his return to Poitiers and established himself in a hermitage at Ligugé, just south of the city. In the ten years that he spent there his fame spread through the surrounding region and he attracted numerous disciples. In 371 he became bishop of Tours, where he remained until his death in 397. As bishop he continued to live as a monk, withdrawing from the city to a desolate place which became the monastery of Marmoutier. Many disciples joined him there, living in cells excavated in the mountainside. Martin did not give any organization to his institute, which was reminiscent of the *lauras* of Egypt.

During his lifetime Martin worked untiringly to propagate the monastic ideal. His example was responsible for so many monastic vocations that some two thousand monks paid tribute to him at his funeral. After his death his influence continued to grow, due to the *Vita Martini* published almost immediately after his death by his disciple Sulpicius Severus. This work, which glorified Martin as the model of monks, had an influence in the West comparable to that of the *Vita Antonii* in the East. In the fifth century monastic centers were widely spread in western Europe, notably on the island of Lerins off the southern coast of France, and in Ireland, under the influence of St. Patrick.

The Clerical Monasteries

In the middle of the fourth century a phenomenon began to appear in western monasticism which had been unknown in the East. Eastern monasticism was always essentially a lay movement, although there were a few priests among the solitaries and in the Pachomian *cenobia.* In the West, however, monasteries were established which consisted entirely of clerics. These institutes were the fruit of the enthusiasm which certain saintly bishops conceived for the ascetical life. They organized the common life for their clergy, who submitted to a rule and lived a quasi-monastic form of life, while at the same time carrying out their clerical duties in the cathedral church. The first organizer of such an urban monastery seems to have been Eusebius of Vercelli. He was imitated by Paulinus of Nola and, most important of all, by St. Augustine.

Augustine, who had come into contact with monasticism in Italy, carried the ideal back to his native Africa. When he became bishop of Hippo he established a monastery next to his cathedral, where he lived the common life with his clergy. The universally recognized authority of Augustine assured the spread of this practice throughout Christian Africa. The influence of his monastic writings has extended down to our own time. While Augustine admired the virtues of the eastern solitaries, his own preference was for the common life, in which, he believed, the evangelical ideal of mutual charity in the Body of Christ was perfectly realized. Clerical monasteries of the type which he popularized underwent a vast development in the West. In Rome they were established next to the basilicas, in which the monks assured the daily execution of the liturgy. In the Middle Ages these urban monasteries developed into orders of canons regular.

The Contribution of John Cassian

A contemporary of Augustine who played an important role in the development of western monasticism was John Cassian. Of unknown origin, he entered a monastery in Bethlehem in his youth, after receiving an excellent classical education. After a few years he and his friend Germanus set out for Egypt, with the reluctant permission of their superiors, to be schooled in the ascetical life under the direction of the famous masters of the desert. Cassian was fascinated by what he found there and spent some fifteen years visiting the various monasteries and discoursing with the Egyptian monks, principally in Skete. He probably made the acquaintance of Evagrius at his cell in Cellia, for his later works show that he had absorbed the teaching of that master of ascetical theology. In 399 he left Egypt, due to the Origenist controversy, and went to Constantinople, where St. John Chrysostom ordained him deacon. In 405 Cassian shared the exile of the patriarch and went to Rome to appeal to the Pope on behalf of Chrysostom's supporters.

A few years later we find him in Provence, where he was raised to the priesthood, if his ordination had not already taken place at Rome. At Marseilles he founded two monasteries, one for men and one for women, and worked for the reform of western monasticism, which was then disorganized, undisciplined and often subject to the scorn of the faithful. Cassian saw that an organized cenobitic life had to be developed, which he proposed to establish upon the basis of Egyptian monasticism but in a form adapted to the climate of Gaul and the temperament of the people.

It was to serve the purpose of this interpretation of eastern monasticism that Cassian composed his two famous works: the twelve books of *Institutes*, in which he describes the monastic customs of the East and outlines the combat against the eight principal vices; and the twenty-four *Conferences*, in which, under the form of conversations supposedly held with the Egyptian monks, he treats all the principal questions of the ascetical life according to Egyptian teaching. While he does not mention his sources other than his own personal contacts, he seems to have been well-read in the monastic literature of the East, with a preference for Origen and Evagrius. Thus he became the principal channel through which the monastic teaching of the East became available to western monks. He was the favorite author of St. Benedict.

Western Monasticism in the Sixth Century

By the sixth century a certain degree of order had been introduced into the chaos of western monasticism. In spite of the troubled character of the times, monastic foundations had sprung up everywhere and were no longer regarded with contempt by the populace. There was no uniformity of observance, for each institute followed its own local tradition in the matter of ascetical practices and disciplinary measures.

Many monastic rules were written during this period, a few of which have survived. They were the work of bishops or abbots, usually anonymous, attempting to codify the basic observances of a particular monastery. These rules were dependent upon the eastern tradition as handed down by Cassian. None of them was universally adopted, and some monasteries made use of more than one rule. Monastic rules were written for cenobitic monasteries and so were intended to treat of only the first stage of the spiritual life, the "active" phase, which is alone subject to legislation. They attempted to establish a solid framework for a community life in which the spiritual combat could be wisely waged so as to lead the monk to his goal of contemplation.

In spite of the diversity in observance, there was a basic unanimity in the sixth century as to the nature of monastic life. The frequency of contacts at this period contributed to the formation of a common patrimony, dependent upon the eastern tradition, relative to monastic theory. In this sense, the rules known to us are more striking for what they hold in common than for their divergences. Their substantial agreement on ideology makes it difficult to determine the provenance of a particular rule. When St. Benedict arrived upon the scene, there was already a commonly accepted monastic tradition.

The Dialogues of St. Gregory

For information about St. Benedict we are entirely dependent upon the second book of the *Dialogues* of St. Gregory the Great. This is not a book of biography, and its principal concern is not to provide historical facts. The literary form of the book is that of spiritual teaching expressed through the medium of edifying stories. As in most ancient hagiography, the point of the stories related is a theological one designed to bring out some aspect of the saint's life and works which identify him as an authentic representative of the traditional monasticism.

In the *Dialogues* St. Benedict appears as the man of God, the wonder-worker, the prophet, the apostle—traditional monastic themes which go back to the *Vita Antonii.* Benedict possesses the gifts of all the great men of sacred history and exemplifies their way of life. St. Gregory sums up his purpose, in remarking that Benedict "was filled with the spirit of all the just" or, to be more precise, "he possessed the Spirit of the One who has filled the hearts of all the elect with the grace of the redemption which he has bestowed on them" (*Dial* 2,8). He is, therefore, the Spirit-bearer, the great charismatic. Obviously it is not of decisive importance in this kind of literature whether or not the accounts that serve as vehicle for the theological teaching are historically accurate.

At the same time, there is no reason to doubt the basic historicity of the outline of St. Benedict's career which the *Dialogues* provide. Gregory was writing only half a century after his death, and he explicitly names the men who furnished him with his information about the saint. These were four monks who had been immediate disciples of St. Benedict, who were still living in Gregory's time and whom the great pope knew personally. The reliability of his information about the basic facts of St. Benedict's life cannot therefore be seriously questioned, whatever may be said of the details and the numerous edifying stories which he liberally intersperses in his account. The *Dialogues,* which were extremely popular in the Middle Ages, immortalized St. Benedict, the *vir Dei,* just as Athanasius had done for Anthony and Sulpicius Severus for Martin.

The Life of St. Benedict

St. Benedict was born about the year 480 at Nursia in Italy. As a youth he was sent to Rome for his education, but was so distressed by the low moral tone of the environment there that he determined, like so many great monks before him, to flee from the world. After a short time spent at Affide with sympathetic Christians, he withdrew to a solitary place near Subiaco, where he received the monastic habit from a monk of a nearby monastery and practiced the eremitical life in a cave for three years. Like the hermits of Egypt, he preached the Word of God to people of the countryside who sought him out in his solitude.

Attracted by his fame, some cenobites from a monastery at nearby Vicovaro succeeded in persuading him to become their abbot. They proved, however, to be some of the undisciplined pseudo-monks who so often gave the monastic state a bad name in those days, and Benedict's zeal found no chord of response in them. When finally they tried to poison him, he saw that they were incorrigible, and returned sadly to his beloved solitude. It was not long until he was joined there by numerous disciples, whom he organized into twelve monasteries of twelve monks each, probably according to the Pachomian system. His reputation for sanctity induced certain noble Roman families to entrust their sons to him to be trained in the monastic life.

We do not know how long St. Benedict remained at Subiaco. According to Gregory, he left because of the envy of a neighboring priest who attempted to bring spiritual ruin upon his disciples. With a few monks he set out for Monte Cassino, halfway between Rome and Naples, where he established a single cenobitic monastery. Here, above all, he is portrayed as the great ascetic and charismatic, endowed with discernment of spirits, incessant prayer with the gift of tears, power of miracles and of reading hearts, authority over the demons, confident intercession with God. The exercises of the active life had brought him to the summit of contemplation. He remained at Monte Cassino until his death, which occurred around the middle of the sixth century. Sometime during his stay there he wrote a monastic rule.

St. Benedict and Monastic Tradition

If St. Benedict had been no more than a great ascetic immortalized in hagiographic literature, his influence would have been of the same order as that of Martin of Tours. It is the *Rule* which has made him patriarch of all the monks of the West. Like many abbots of his time, he wished to fix in writing the structure of the life which he prescribed for his monks. There is no evidence that he was commissioned by the Holy See to write the *Rule* as an official code. The only rule known to us to be certainly of Italian provenance, it represents the most mature monastic legislation in all the ancient literature. Universally adopted at a later period as the norm of western cenobitic life, it sums up all that is best in the ancient tradition and constitutes one of the foundation stones upon which western civilization is built.

St. Benedict has often been represented as an innovator and the *Rule* as a highly original work of inventive genius whose success was due to the fact that it boldly broke with previous monastic structures and launched out on new paths. St. Benedict would have opposed the ascetical tradition of eastern monasticism as too extreme and too individualistic. His own experience as an anchorite would have revealed the deficiencies of this form of life, which he later rejected and regarded as less perfect than the common life, in which the individual quest for perfection is overshadowed by the mystique of the community.

This image of the legislator of Monte Cassino is arrived at by reading later developments of Benedictine monasticism into the *Rule*, not by an objective exegesis of the text against the background of St. Benedict's environment. Practically all of the observances of the *Rule* are borrowed from the East. It is a manual of ascetic discipline for the individual monk and regulates the structure of a cenobitic environment in which the active life may be fruitfully pursued. Cenobitism is regarded as safer for the majority, but it is a training school for the more perfect life of the desert, and it is not excluded that some may pass on to the eremitical life. Indeed, its legislation is marked by moderation, but this is merely a realization of the concrete possibilities of the men for whom it was written. Far from being an innovation, it is a highly traditional statement of monastic principles, as are the other western rules known from this period.

The Holy Rule *and the* Regula Magistri

In the past twenty-five years the whole question of the composition of the *Rule* and even of its attribution to St. Benedict has been reopened and subjected to a lively debate. This development has stemmed from a renewal of interest in another monastic rule, of unknown authorship, commonly though incorrectly called the *Regula Magistri.* Although three times as long as the Benedictine rule, it has many passages in common with it, particularly the prologue and the first ten chapters, which closely correspond to the prologue and first seven chapters of St. Benedict. Scholars had long believed that it was a work of the seventh or eighth century which freely borrowed material from St. Benedict. Since 1938, however, when Dom Augustine Genestout first proposed that the *Regula Magistri* is the earlier of the two rules, many scholars have adopted the view that St. Benedict borrowed from it. Others, while agreeing that the *Regula Magistri* dates from the sixth century, think that its author and St. Benedict used a common source.

We cannot here elaborate upon the reasons for postulating the priority of the *Regula Magistri,* nor upon the many ramifications of the discussion upon other aspects of the study of the *Rule.* No definitive solutions have yet been reached, and so far the controversy has raised more problems than it has solved. It suffices for our purpose to observe that the question of composition must now be posed in a different manner than was traditionally done.

The most radical solution denies St. Benedict's authorship of the rule traditionally ascribed to him, holding that it is more likely that the *Regula Magistri* is the rule which he wrote. The "Rule of St. Benedict" would be the work of an anonymous author of the seventh century who added certain passages to an abbreviated edition of the *Regula Magistri.* This extreme view, however, is rejected by the majority of scholars, who advance weighty arguments in favor of St. Benedict's authorship of the rule attributed to him, though most admit that he used the *Regula Magistri* as a source. The authenticity of the *Rule* is still in possession, though the theory of composition has been modified. It is precisely those chapters which contain the principal spiritual teaching of the *Rule* which seem to have been borrowed.

Traditional Character of St. Benedict's Rule

If the dependence of St. Benedict upon the *Regula Magistri* should be established beyond all doubt, however, this will not in any sense lessen the importance of the *Rule* in the evolution of monasticism. The theory that St. Benedict was an original thinker who organized a new form of monasticism has already been recognized as untenable on other grounds. There is a great body of evidence to show that he was dependent upon Cassian, Pachomius, Basil and many other monastic legislators of both East and West. He did not regard himself as a reformer or a founder of a new institute, but as the father of a community, who handed on the traditional monastic teaching of the past, which he had received from others. He was not the first to introduce monasticism into the West, nor the first who attempted to adapt the teaching of the oriental monks to a European situation.

The sixth century was a period in which monastic life was flourishing in Italy and Gaul, in which the ancient tradition was being assiduously studied and new rules being composed. For the authors of these rules, there was no question of producing something new, but of collecting, assimilating and propagating the venerable traditions of the past, of harvesting the fruits of the cenobitic experience of the fourth and fifth centuries. This movement in the West was largely an anonymous one; we do not know the authors of most of the rules which have survived from this period. Monastic teaching was possessed in common; there was little sense of literary ownership. Anyone who found something good in another rule was well advised to make use of it. This is what St. Benedict seems to have done with the *Regula Magistri*, as he did with other products of the tradition. This rule, which has its weaknesses and contains some bizarre regulations, is nevertheless a coherent exposition of monastic theory in which he could find much of value.

Superiority of the Benedictine Rule

This does not mean that the *Rule of St. Benedict* has no special value beyond that of the other rules of the period. Tradition has not erred in assuring that this rule alone would remain down to the present as the living norm for almost all the monks of the West, while the others are now merely relics of the past. For the *Holy Rule* surpasses them all in its intrinsic excellence. It is precisely its superior quality which was responsible for its rapid diffusion from the eighth century onward and its success in displacing all the others by the eleventh century. This rule, better than all the others, knew how to isolate the essentials of monastic tradition and to distinguish them from the accidentals. Instead of entering into innumerable details of observance, which would soon become obsolete, it went straight to the heart of the matter, to the essential religious values of monasticism.

While preserving the central monastic values, the *Rule* leaves sufficient leeway for personal initiative; it knows how to find the right measure. That is why St. Gregory, who seems to have been referring to this rule, praised it for its discretion. This does not mean merely moderation or a kind of benevolent tolerance, but the ability skillfully to adapt the means to the attainment of the end, to find the right measure in everything, "that the strong may still have something to long after, and the weak may not draw back in alarm" (64,19). St. Benedict was not the founder of an order; he was a great teacher, a man who had steeped himself in the monastic tradition of his eastern and western predecessors, who perceived the real values in it and was able to communicate them to others in brief but trenchant form. This is the real genius of the *Rule* and the reason for its longevity. The sources of the *Rule*, proximate or remote, are a secondary question as far as its value is concerned.

Reform Measures of Benedict of Aniane

The early diffusion of the Benedictine rule is rather obscure. In the course of the sixth and seventh centuries it gradually became known in other parts of Italy and in Gaul. It is occasionally quoted by ecclesiastical writers and seems to have been used in some monasteries. It is hazardous, however, to qualify monasteries as Benedictine at this period, for it was the custom in many places to follow more than one rule simultaneously. The *Rule* was certainly used in England in the seventh century, and was carried to the German countries by Anglo-Saxon missionary monks in the eighth century. In Spain it does not seem to have been adopted until the tenth century.

The man most responsible for the exclusive use of the Benedictine rule was St. Benedict of Aniane. A former hermit and abbot of a large community, he was commissioned by Louis the Pious, son and successor of Charlemagne, to reform the monasteries of the Frankish empire. Convinced that the multiplicity of rules and observances was the principal cause of decadence, Benedict imposed the *Rule of St. Benedict* upon all the Frankish monasteries at the Council of Aachen in 817 and insisted upon a uniform observance under his central authority. As a consequence of this prescription, all other monastic rules soon went out of use.

The reform of Benedict of Aniane, however, involved more than simply the literal observance of the *Rule*, for it added a number of elements extraneous to it. These were the result of the gradual influence of urban monasticism upon the regular monasteries. Since those *devoti* who carried out the liturgical services in the basilicas led a quasi-monastic life, a confusion developed between them and the monks, and each group borrowed observances from the other. Thus the monks adopted an increasing emphasis upon the solemnization of the liturgy and extra-liturgical prayers, which grew apace with the fusion between Frankish customs and the Roman Rite in Carolingian times. The Carolingian reformers introduced into Benedictine life the element of ritualism which was to mark it throughout the Middle Ages.

Reform Movements: Cluny and Citeaux

While the reform faltered after the death of Benedict of Aniane in 821, it was taken up again a century later with the foundation of Cluny, an event of unparalleled importance in the subsequent history of western monasticism. Cluny was the most powerful influence upon the reform of the Church in the early Middle Ages, and eventually succeeded in capturing the papacy. It became the center of a vast order of monasteries regulated according to a common observance and under a single authority, the transposition of the feudal system to the monastic sphere. The Cluniacs changed the character of Benedictine life by the abandonment of manual labor, an excessive emphasis upon splendor in liturgical services and ritualism in every phase of daily life, and the progressive clericalization of the monastic order. Nevertheless Cluny provided a disciplined asceticism and an insistence upon the contemplative orientation of monasticism which was eminently faithful to tradition and productive of a remarkably attractive monastic spirituality.

The eleventh and twelfth centuries witnessed a vast flowering of reform movements which attempted to recover the primitive simplicity of the monastic ideal. The variety and spontaneity of these reforms testify to a burning desire to return to sources and freely to adapt institutions so as to regain a vital contact with the primitive tradition. These movements all emphasized poverty and simplicity, austerity of life and the ideal of contemplation. A concern for solitude manifested itself in the semi-eremitical movements of Camaldoli, Fonte Avellana and Chartreuse, and in a great burgeoning of lay movements. In other foundations solitude was reconciled with the cenobitic life, as at Vallombrosa and Citeaux.

Many of these monastic orders still exist, but Citeaux has always been the most influential. The early Cistercians, impelled by a burning thirst for authenticity, wished to interpret the *Rule* in the light of its monastic background and to recover its original simplicity. Their life was marked by a real detachment from the world, a love of solitude and silence, poverty and simplicity, austerity and manual labor, prayer and holy reading, all within a cenobitic framework which laid great stress upon the value of fraternal charity in the common life. There is an attractive genuinity about this reform, which was not merely an archeologizing return to the past, but a recapturing of the primitive monastic ideal and an attempt, largely successful, to express it in structures suitable to the times. The school of spirituality which the white monks produced, dominated by St. Bernard, is no less notable for its charming humanity than for its authentically contemplative orientation.

Decline of the Monastic Order

We cannot follow the details of monastic history down to the present time. For the purpose of describing monastic spirituality, the period from the origins to the twelfth century is of the greatest importance, for it was during this time that the broad lineaments of its ideology were laid down. The subsequent history of monasticism, in spite of the complex developments and the interplay of various influences which can be discerned in it, has contributed nothing essentially new to the ideology. The historical context of monastic spirituality is circumscribed within the period between its origins and first development in the East and the Benedictine centuries in the West.

The diverse tendencies which can be found in the monasticism of the eleventh and twelfth centuries have followed various paths down to the present day. After the energetic outburst of renewal in this period there followed a long era of decline among both black and white monks, and leadership passed to the newly founded mendicant orders. The monasteries were too much involved in worldly concerns, lacked the inner spirit of renewal, and were often reduced to pitiful conditions by the wars and disturbances of the times and by the evils of the *commendam* system. Clericalization of the monastic order became universal and monks undertook the work of the external ministry. Devotional currents which stressed affective and anthropocentric piety exercised so strong an influence upon the monks that their spirituality was sometimes scarcely distinguishable from the other schools of spirituality of the time.

Yet between the thirteenth and eighteenth centuries there were numerous reform movements, some of which flourished for considerable periods of time. While none of them constituted a complete rethinking of the monastic ideal and a thorough return to sources, they nevertheless produced a disciplined monastic life in which the ancient virtues once more shone out. Such were the congregations of Monte Oliveto in the fourteenth century; of Bursfeld, St. Justina of Padua and Valladolid in the fifteenth; and of St. Vannes, St. Maur and the Cistercian reform of La Trappe in the seventeenth. The union of monasteries into congregations was first decreed by the Fourth Council of the Lateran in 1215, but was not actually achieved until the fifteenth century and, on a wider scale, in the post-Tridentine period. The French revolution and similar secularizing movements in other countries put an effective end to most of the monasteries of Europe in the late eighteenth and early nineteenth centuries. Here the monastic order reached the lowest point in its history.

Restoration and Renewal

The nineteenth and twentieth centuries have been a period of restoration, consolidation and renewal for both the white and the black monks. The most important figure in Benedictine life in the nineteenth century was Dom Prosper Gueranger, who in 1833 reestablished monasticism in France with the reopening of Solesmes. What was significant about his work was that it deliberately refused to be a continuation of pre-revolutionary monasticism, but sought its inspiration in an earlier and better age. The high Middle Ages were Gueranger's ideal and, if he was not free from the romanticism which so strongly colored this period, his intuition was nevertheless the indispensable beginning of a return to sources. While Gueranger's effort was a work of restoration of the past more than of a vital renewal, it provided a firm foundation from which those who followed him have penetrated deeper to the original inspiration of monasticism.

The nineteenth century witnessed an encouraging number of monastic realizations. At the end of this century and throughout the twentieth, the return to monastic sources has proceeded apace with the same movement in other areas of the Church's life. The biblical, liturgical and theological renewal has revealed the inner harmony of monastic spirituality with the deepest sources of Christian life and thought. Profound study of the *Holy Rule* has made it possible to understand its teaching against the background of the earlier eastern and western monasticism and to see St. Benedict once more in his real environment, freed from the excrescences which have obscured his thought over the centuries. Thus the original inspiration of primitive monasticism stands revealed in all its strength and simplicity.

Monasticism today, therefore, finds itself in a period of renewal. The challenge which it faces is that of making its spirituality fully relevant to the modern world. This requires the adaptation of monastic institutions so that they may become appropriate expressions of the inner vitality of the authentic monastic ideal. Before the revision of structures can proceed confidently, however, there is need for a thorough assimilation of the ideology of monasticism, purged of extraneous and mutually contradictory elements and reduced to its own compelling logic. There must, therefore, be a sincere attempt to arrive at an authentic understanding of the original form of the monastic ideal and of the legitimate evolution which it has undergone throughout the centuries, against the background of the total monastic tradition. The spirit of renewal will thus enable monastic spirituality to become once again a vital force in the life of the Church, as it was in the days of its origins.

3. MONASTIC SPIRITUALITY IN THE CHURCH

Monasticism in its Theological Context

We have attempted to situate monasticism in its historical context in order to see how this form of spirituality arose in the Church and what evolution it underwent during the period of its expansion and development. It is necessary now to place it in its theological context, i.e., to examine the monastic ideal in its relationship to the nature and life of the Church in order to see what place the monk occupies in the economy of salvation.

We have previously discussed the question of spirituality in general in order to find a basis for distinguishing one religious order from another. It is now necessary to pursue this investigation in regard to monasticism in order to answer the question, "What is a monk?" While it is clear that his adoption of the evangelical counsels distinguishes the monk from the Christian who remains in the ordinary circumstances of human life, since this involves a use of different means to attain their common end, what distinguishes the monk from other religious who also practice the counsels? How can we approach the complex problem of identifying and describing the total complex of means which constitutes monastic spirituality? How is it presented by the ancient literature and how can it be accurately defined? Is a single definition applicable to all the various forms which monasticism has assumed throughout the many centuries of its history?

Finally, what is the role of monasticism in the Church? What is the monk's contribution to the Church? What is the place of a monastery in the Church's structure? All these are questions for which we shall attempt to find an answer in the present section.

The Problem of Diversification

If monastic spirituality is a particular complex of means for the attainment of supernatural perfection, then it can be defined only by pointing out those elements which are peculiar to it and consequently serve to distinguish it from other forms of spirituality. We have already seen that the primary elements are common to all forms of spirituality; it is only in the secondary elements that there is room for diversification. These secondary elements often consist merely of the specific form in which primary elements appear. In addition to this, a principle of distinction can be found in the balance and proportion achieved among the various elements, and the psychological importance which is attributed to some of them in preference to others. Every spirituality is a complex phenomenon, because it brings many different elements into play. Consequently a description of a spirituality is a delicate matter which cannot be adequately summarized in a few words.

There is a further difficulty, too, in the fact that in its practical implementation a spirituality is a vital thing, a thing that is meant to be *lived*. Considered as a doctrine, it is a theoretical system which can be conceptually perceived and expressed in logical concepts. But when it has been reduced to practice, it takes on a vital aspect, employing all of the faculties of man, and thus becomes a phenomenon which it is easier to experience than to explain. In other words, a spirituality is not simply static, but is an existential reality. To explain what monastic spirituality is means to describe an experience, the experience of many men who have, in their own lives, over a period of many centuries, employed a particular complex of means to arrive at union with God. This reality must therefore be approached in a descriptive manner, by characterizing each of the principal elements which go to make up the synthesis and by showing what role each of them plays in constituting the total phenomenon.

The Continuity of Monastic Tradition

But is there such a thing as a *single* monastic spirituality? The brief historical sketch which we have presented above indicates, in its broad outlines, how complex a phenomenon monasticism is in its historical aspect. In view of the many differences among the various branches of the monastic family, and even within the same ones at various periods of time, is it possible to demonstrate that there is such a thing as a single monastic spirituality? Is there a uniform monastic tradition?

It is true that there are many varieties within the monastic tradition. The most fundamental division is that between hermits and cenobites. Within the eremitical life, which is the result of an intensely personal inspiration, there are almost as many variations as there are individuals. The cenobitic life, too, has appeared in many forms, which have sometimes differed considerably. Even within the Benedictine tradition itself there has been great variation. The differences between Cluny and Citeaux, which once generated so much heat, were really quite insignificant by comparison with other cases in monastic history. There has been a penitential monasticism, a liturgical monasticism, a missionary monasticism, etc. The Benedictine tradition is not monolithic. Some of the forms which have appeared have no doubt been deviations from the authentic tradition; yet not every variation is an abuse. The seed planted by St. Benedict was polyvalent, and the various possibilities inherent in it have issued in a multiform growth. It is possible to develop one aspect of tradition more than another without disfiguring the whole.

Many of the differences which have appeared in monastic history are purely institutional differences which do not necessarily affect the substance. When we examine the ideology of monastic tradition, on the other hand, aside from the real deviations we can discover a broad area of agreement that runs like a continuous thread through monastic history. There are broad lines of monastic spirituality which characterize all authentic monks of all ages and serve to distinguish them from other religious. All the many branches of the monastic family, despite the almost infinite variety of differences which separate them, possess these fundamental characteristics in common: the same elements combined in approximately the same proportion to constitute a synthesis. It is here that we touch upon the real consistency of the continuous monastic tradition which enables us to isolate a characteristic monastic spirituality.

Withdrawal from His Fellow Men

What are the specific secondary elements which distinguish the spirituality of monks from that of other religious? The first and most immediately evident is that of physical separation from the world. Every religious must, of course, leave behind worldly ways of thinking and acting; every Christian, in fact, must live as one who is not of this world. But there is an equivocation in this use of the term "world": it is here used to signify the attitudes and policies of those who are still under the dominion of the kingdom of Satan, the "prince of this world." To say that the Christian must abandon the world in this sense is merely to say that he must live the new life of the redemption. When we say that the monk abandons the world, the term is here used in the sense of human society; he withdraws from his fellow men in order to work out his salvation in solitude.

While every Christian must find a measure of solitude in his life in order to commune with God (cf Mt 6,6), a definitive and permanent withdrawal from human society is not an element of every Christian vocation, nor of every religious vocation. On the contrary, most Christians and even most religious have a vocation to remain in society and there to work for the transformation of the world, the construction of the kingdom of God among men through the works of fraternal charity by which love for God is concretely manifested. The monk, on the other hand, withdraws from his fellow men, not because he is unconcerned about their salvation, but because his vocation constitutes another way of contributing to it. The monk and the religious who is active in the world have two different roles to play in the Church. While neither of these roles is totally exclusive of the other, they represent different emphases on essential elements of the Christian life.

There can be no monastic life without solitude, without a distinct separation from the ordinary framework of life in human society. While there can be degrees of separation, as between the cenobitic and solitary life, any spirituality which is not firmly based upon a real withdrawal from the world ceases by that very fact to be monastic. From the day when the first monk left his native village and set his face toward the vast stretches of the inhospitable desert, this has been the most characteristic feature of monasticism. It is, in fact, his solitude which gave the monk his name.

Interpretation of the Term Monachos

The Greek word *monachos*, which has passed almost unchanged into most of our modern languages, came into Christian usage in the second century from its use in the Greek versions of the Bible; in the fourth century it began to be used in Egypt to designate the first monks. The original meaning of the term was "solitary," or "alone"; hence it was appropriate for the early monks who led a secluded life alone in the desert. The earliest monastic literature, like the *Vita Antonii*, always uses the term in this original sense, and St. Jerome insisted upon it: the monk is one who lives alone with God.

Later, however, with the introduction of cenobitism, the word took on a broader meaning. We find it used not only of cenobites in the strict sense, but even of ascetics who continue to live in the world. This is a purely semantic phenomenon: the use of the word began to be extended without regard for its original meaning. Consequent upon the wider use came a new interpretation: the monk is one who is not divided by worldly concerns, but marked by an interior unity in that all his efforts are directed to the search for God. The idea of solitude is replaced by that of single-mindedness. St. Augustine went still further in his interpretation: the word *monachos*, he says, being derived from *monos*, "one," signifies unity among many. The monk is intimately united with others, with whom he shares "one heart and one mind"; the community thus forms a single whole. This explanation, quite consonant with Augustine's emphasis upon fraternal charity in the one body, contains a profound theological observation; but it is a total departure from the original meaning of the term.

Solitude and unity with other men: these are the two poles of the monk's existence. It is a striking realization of the Christian paradox that it is in his separation from men that he becomes truly united to them in the bond of supernatural charity. The many forms of monastic life which have developed through the ages might be characterized by the relative emphasis which they have given to one or the other of these terms. In any case, the idea of solitude represents the original inspiration of monasticism and must be considered essential to it. To say that solitude is a relative term is merely to affirm that one can be more or less a monk, that is, more or less withdrawn from the world, so long as there is a real separation. The solitary is more a monk than the cenobite. But the cenobite, too, is a solitary, that is, a monk, in the sense that he lives separate from the world and maintains an interior solitude in the midst of his brethren.

Place of Prayer in the Monastic Life

Another distinctive secondary element in the monk's spirituality is the orientation of his whole life toward prayer and the contemplation of God. Prayer is obviously an essential element of every Christian's spirituality; it is not prayer alone, but the exclusivism of prayer that sets the monk apart. His spirituality does not include any other essential duty than that of his own sanctification, accomplished in the context of the Church's life, directed to the glory of God, and leading him, together with his brethren, to union with God through contemplation.

To put this in a negative way, we may say that the monk, unlike other religious, does not have any secondary purpose. Subsequent religious founders deliberately modified the exclusivism of the monastic ideal in order to permit their religious to engage in works of mercy among their fellow men. Their principal aim remains the glorification of God by their acquisition of supernatural perfection, but to this they have added, as a secondary purpose, the fulfillment of some particular work for the benefit of the Church. Thus there have arisen successively orders and congregations devoted to preaching the Word of God, furthering the work of Christian education, nursing the sick, caring for the poor and the unfortunate, and even, at one period of history, taking up arms to recover the holy places and redeeming the captives who had fallen into the hands of the enemy.

The monk, who lives outside the ordinary structures of human society by reason of his withdrawal, does not exist for any of these reasons, even though he may engage in such activities when the occasion presents itself. He exists only to serve God through his asceticism and prayer. His love for God is realized directly rather than through service to his fellow man. This means that prayer occupies a dominating position in his spirituality in a way which is not true of other religious. It is the primary activity in his life not only in a qualitative sense but quantitatively as well. Because of this monastic spirituality is eminently disinterested; it is not a means to the accomplishment of anything else in this world, but is directed solely to the kingdom of God.

Component Parts of the Synthesis

Aside from physical separation from the world and the special orientation of the monk's whole life toward disinterested contemplation, there are no other elements in monastic spirituality which are really distinctive. The monk shares all of his other means to perfection with other religious. These means do, of course, take on special nuances in monastic spirituality by reason of their place in the total synthesis. This is also true of monastic institutions: while none of them is exclusively practiced by monks, in their totality they become concrete expressions of the whole ideology which they are designed to implement.

If we wish, therefore, to gain a total view of monastic spirituality we must examine all of the principal elements of which it is composed in order to see what role each one plays in the synthesis and what particular aspect each assumes in view of the distinctive orientation of the whole spirituality. It is only thus that we can gain an insight into the equilibrium which exists among all of the component parts, what emphasis is given to each, what function it performs in the monk's quest for perfection, worked out in solitude and tending toward the goal of contemplative union with God.

In the second part of this book we shall undertake an examination of each of these elements and attempt to assess their contribution to the total effort of the monk. Most of these elements are common to the entire monastic tradition; some are proper to the ideology of cenobitism. We shall be concerned to investigate the place which they occupy in the thought of St. Benedict and in the Benedictine tradition. One cannot in advance, simply by defining the distinctive elements, convey an adequate idea of the character of monastic spirituality; it is only after seeing each of the elements in its proper place in the whole that one can gain a synthetic view of the total reality.

Themes and Analogies of the Monastic Life

This is the manner in which the ancients approached the question of monastic spirituality. They were not concerned with offering a precise definition of monastic life or with distinguishing it from other forms of Christian spirituality. Monasticism was the only form of religious life in the early Church, and the ancients, far from opposing it to the Christian life as lived by the majority of men, were concerned to show that the monk is the true and ideal Christian. While legitimate, the problem of offering precise definitions and distinctions is a preoccupation of more recent origin. The concern of the ancient monastic literature is to make this form of life known, to extol it and to propagate it. In so doing, they approach monastic spirituality descriptively rather than analytically: they attempt to convey some of the richness of the total phenomenon by presenting it under the form of metaphors, analogies and themes.

Through the study of such themes, which invariably have a biblical orientation, we can penetrate into the Fathers' understanding of the monastic life. These themes became traditional in monastic literature and were handed down from one generation to the next. The medieval monks and hagiographers inherited them from primitive monasticism and sometimes developed them elaborately. The principal ones remain constant throughout the tradition, while the spread of cenobitism opens the door to new themes illustrating the common life. Thus the monastery is conceived of as the house of God, the school of divine instruction, the *palaestra,* or training ground of virtue; the community is the family of God, the primitive Jerusalem community, the miniature Church.

The older metaphors, which go back, for the most part, to Egyptian monasticism, represent the monk as the martyr, the crucified who imitates Christ in his sufferings, the athlete in training for the race, the slave in the service of his divine master, the soldier fighting in the army of the heavenly king, the pilgrim on a journey to his heavenly home. He is compared to the prophets and apostles, to Adam in paradise and to the angels who continually praise God before his heavenly throne. His activity consists of flight from the world into blessed solitude, renunciation of all that the world most values in order to gain the greater value of the kingdom of God, the ascetical combat, which is conceived of as an *agon,* a harsh struggle against the twofold enemy of the demons and his passions, and as a liturgy, a complete holocaust of himself offered in praise of God. The ideology of monastic life is thought of as the true philosophy in contrast to the deceptive wisdom of the world. We shall encounter many of these themes in the course of our exposition.

The Monk and the Christian Vocation

Many of these themes, of course, are simply biblical concepts which can be applied with equal relevance to the Christian life in general. The fact is that the ancient monks thought of themselves simply as Christians rather than as a special class in the Church. Today the clericalization of the monastic order has tended, in the popular mind, to associate monks with the clergy. This obscures the fact that monasticism is essentially a lay movement and the monk essentially a lay Christian. The reception or non-reception of sacred orders is quite accidental to his status as a monk. He is simply a Christian who aspires to the perfect fulfillment of the Gospel precepts.

Monastic profession is simply a renewal of the baptismal profession, which already involves a renunciation of the world and of the works of Satan and a solemn commitment to live for Christ. However, it transposes the baptismal promises to another level, deeper, more exacting, more logical, for it commits the monk not only to forego the attitudes and practices of the world, but even its real values: here again the double meaning of the term "world" is decisive. The monk embraces more radically the suffering and death of Christ into which he was plunged in the font in order to follow him more radically and renounce the world more effectively. He is the integral Christian who chooses to live out the mystery of his baptism to its most far-reaching consequences.

The monk's motive for fleeing the world, then, is solely that he may become a better Christian. It is not a question of rejecting or despising his fellow men, of setting himself up against or even alongside the Church. While he recognizes that the world is good in itself, he knows that it is still under the dominion of Satan, groaning in travail as it awaits its final redemption. He wants to escape the obstacles which it presents to the fructification of the baptismal grace, to escape the dissipation which causes forgetfulness of God, to seek an atmosphere where he may stand face to face with the ultimate realities of life, lay bare the depths of his soul and thus embrace the Christian commitment in its most authentic and radical form.

The Monastery and the Church

Does the monk have any particular role in the Church, since he is essentially a lay Christian who applies himself to the struggle for perfection with the methodical use of particular means? A monastic theme which goes back to the origins of cenobitism represents the monastery as an institution which realizes the nature of the Church herself as described in the Scriptures. The ancients did not model the monastery upon or compare it to any profane type of society, such as the Roman family, but saw in it an imitation of the structure of the Church herself. The ecclesiological themes of the Bible, such as the people of God, the temple of God, the vineyard of God, the Body of Christ, are applied to the monastery in the cenobitic literature. The hierarchy of the monastery is compared to that of the Church, its rule to the tradition which governs her life.

There can be no doubt, therefore, that the cenobitic founders intended to produce in their communities a realization of the people of God as described in the Old and New Testaments. Hence the frequent references to the Israelites in the desert under the direction of Moses and the elders, and to the primitive community of Jerusalem as described in the Acts of the Apostles. This does not mean, however, that the cenobitic community constitutes a particular church in the sense of a fully distinct ecclesiastical unit. In this sense it is lacking one of the constitutive elements of a local church, the sacramental priesthood. Abstracting from the present law, which requires that an abbot be a priest and makes him an ordinary, the monastic hierarchy of its nature is not ecclesiastical, but simply a hierarchy of holiness. The abbot is essentially a charismatic, not an ecclesiastical official whose position depends upon apostolic succession or canonical authority.

If the monastery is not a local church, however, it is the type of the ideal Church. It is a Christian community which strives with all its energy to realize the reality of the Church's life: to be the holy people of God, obedient to the Word of God as its law, living the message of salvation in all its fullness. It strives to realize the ideal of sanctity which is of the essence of the Church, to reproduce here on earth a type of the heavenly Church, the new Jerusalem. It is the vanguard of the whole Church, a witness to what the Church most intimately is.

Contribution of the Monk to the Church

Monasticism consequently has a different function in the Church from that of other religious orders. While all religious, due to their renunciation, manifest to some degree the eschatological aspect of the Church's life, this is more pronounced in the monastic orders. The religious who is active in the world is called upon to contribute to the growth and functioning of the Church militant. He operates primarily within the order of efficient causality, contributing to the salvation of his fellow Christians by providing the means of grace. Clerical religious function within the framework of the ecclesiastical hierarchy, assisting the bishops and their clergy in the task of evangelization and sanctification.

The monastery, on the other hand, operates primarily within the order of exemplary and final causality. Outside of the mainstream of ecclesiastical life, it does not exist in order to accomplish any particular goal. It cannot be defined in terms of what it does, but only in terms of what it is. Its role in the Church is to manifest what the Church really is as reality of grace: to reproduce the biblical model of the Church and anticipate the being of the heavenly Jerusalem. The meaning of monastic life in the Church cannot be found in any objective in the line of efficiency; its meaning is contained in its very being. It exists in order to *be* the Church, to bring to realization a society of the elect whose lives are oriented entirely toward God and toward the final consummation of the redemption.

This does not mean that the monk is somehow outside of the Church militant or that his life has no effect upon it. He, too, is subject to the Church, dependent upon her for his sacramental life, committed to contribute toward her apostolate. But his contribution is of a special kind; it is not a goal consciously sought, but one which follows almost imperceptively, in the order of grace, from what he is. In living apart and dedicating himself to the worship of God through asceticism and prayer, he reminds men of an essential aspect of their condition, witnesses to the transient character of this world and to the fact that every Christian is a pilgrim on the way to his heavenly home. It is not by calculated programs of activity that the monastery makes its principal contribution to the Church; it is by being itself, by remaining faithful to its own vocation to realize the ideal image of the Church through an integrally Christian life.

3 The Coordinates of Monastic Spirituality: The Bible and the Liturgy

OF THE VARIOUS ELEMENTS which compose monastic spirituality, there are two whose influence is so all-pervasive as to set them apart from the rest. More than merely particular elements in the complex of means which the monk employs to achieve perfection, they are rather the foundations upon which all the others rest. Everything in the monk's life is a response to the Word of God contained in the Scriptures, which are the living voice of God speaking to him. The Bible, however, would be a dead letter outside of the living context of the Church, which ceaselessly proclaims the Word, the living and enduring message of salvation, through the liturgy. Bible and liturgy are inseparable: it is only in the Bible that the liturgy discovers its message, only in the liturgy that the Bible comes to life. The Bible and the liturgy are the coordinates of monastic spirituality.

To say this is not to imply that other forms of spirituality disregard or underestimate the Bible and the liturgy. No form of Christian spirituality can dispense with them; they are basic to the Christian life in all its manifestations. There can, however, be considerable variation in the concrete manner in which a system of spirituality seeks its inspiration in and makes use of the Scriptures and the liturgy. Monasticism, to the extent that it is faithful to its own traditions, maintains an intimate contact with these vital sources of the Church's life. In this chapter we wish to determine the precise roles of the Bible and the liturgy in the spirituality of the monk.

1. THE BIBLICAL INSPIRATION OF MONASTICISM

The Bible and the Monastic Vocation

In general, two characteristics of the traditional monastic attitude toward the Bible can be singled out. The first is the quantitative predominance of the Bible in the monk's life, both in his vocation to the monastery and in his reading and prayer. The second is its qualitative predominance. Monastic life is not merely based upon the principles of the Gospel, as is every form of the Christian life, but every aspect of it, down to details of observance, has its roots in the inspired Word of God. The entire mentality of the monk is formed by the Bible, so that the proportion of the various elements in his spirituality is the same proportion as is found in revelation itself.

The monastic vocation has traditionally been conceived of as an obedience to the summons of the Scriptures. This is the theme of the first monastic vocation of which we have any details, that of St. Anthony. The orphaned son of a wealthy Christian family, he was in church one day as a young man when he heard these words proclaimed in the Gospel: "If you wish to be perfect, go sell all you have and give it to the poor, and come, follow me, and you shall have treasure in heaven" (cf Mt 19,21). For the first time he heard these words as if spoken to him personally, and in prompt obedience to the Gospel, sold all his property and gave the money to the poor, keeping only a small sum for the support of his sister. But again he heard the Gospel warning him: "Do not be solicitous for the morrow" (Mt 6,34). This time he gave away all the rest, entrusted his sister to the care of some virgins, and devoted himself to asceticism, gradually withdrawing further into solitude. (*Vita Antonii* 2–3).

The theme of a monk receiving his vocation during the reading of the Scriptures thereafter became a commonplace in monastic hagiography. The monk takes his place in the divine economy of the Scriptures by responding to God's call as did the great men of the Old Testament. God's summons is contained as truly in his written word as it was in the theophanies recounted in the Bible. Thus the call of the monk was often compared to that of Abraham, and his reply was equally uncompromising: leaving behind his country, his kinsfolk and his father's house, the monk withdrew into the land which the Lord showed him (Gen 12,1; cf Cassian, *Conf* 3,4).

St. Benedict and Vocation

St. Benedict also thought of the monastic vocation as God's summoning the individual through his Word in the Scriptures. In the Prologue he declares that "the Scripture arouseth us" (Pr 8), and follows this with a mosaic of invitations from the Bible. Then he represents God himself summoning the monk through the words of Psalm 33: "The Lord, seeking his workman among the multitudes to whom he thus crieth, saith again: 'What man is he that desireth life and would see good days?' And if hearing him thou answer, 'I am he,' God saith to thee: 'If thou wilt have true and everlasting life, keep thy tongue from evil and thy lips that they speak no guile. Turn away from evil and do good: seek after peace and pursue it' " (Pr 14–17).

The monk's role, according to this concept, is to respond to the summons of the Scripture. "What can be sweeter to us, dearest brethren, than this voice of our Lord inviting us? Behold in his loving mercy the Lord showeth us the way of life" (Pr 19–20). The voice of God is audible to one who is attentive to the Scriptures.

The Prologue continues with still another quotation to show that a monastic vocation is a summons of the Scriptures. The monk is represented as holding a dialogue with God, the words being provided by Psalm 14. To his question, "Lord, who shall dwell in thy tabernacle, or who shall rest upon thy holy hill?", God answers through the Bible: "He that walketh without blemish and doth that which is right; he that speaketh truth in his heart, who hath used no deceit in his tongue, nor done evil to his neighbor, nor believed ill of his neighbor" (Pr 23–27). Thus it is the Scriptures which not only contain the invitation, but also provide the program for the monk's spiritual life.

The Ancient Monks and Bible Reading

It was not only in the beginning of his vocation, however, that the monk found himself face to face with the Word of God in the Scriptures. They were the principal formative influence upon his entire monastic life. The reformers of the sixteenth century totally rejected monasticism on the grounds that it was unbiblical. This judgment has been entirely reversed by modern scholarship. From beginning to end the ancient monastic literature is filled with biblical texts and allusions, showing that the monks not only devoted an immense amount of time to reading the Bible, but consciously sought in the Scriptures the justification for every detail of their monastic practice.

The Bible was the favorite and sometimes almost the only book which the ancient monks read. In this they were faithful to the general tendency of the patristic period, which regarded all Christian literature as an extension of the Scriptures. The monastic literature of both East and West is filled with recommendations to read and study the Bible and with eulogies of its value. Even the illiterate Copts who first filled the deserts of Egypt did not remain aloof from the Bible because of their lack of human culture. If they could not read themselves, they could listen to the reading of the Scriptures and allow the divine Word to sink in and take root in their hearts. It was read aloud particularly in their liturgical assemblies.

If the ancients read less than we, they nevertheless read more profoundly and developed prodigious memories. They looked upon the Bible as a book not merely to be read or listened to, but to be memorized, so that Scriptural texts could be recited over and over again during periods of work or repose. St. Benedict requires his monks to learn the Psalter by heart (8,3); St. Basil the Gospels (*Shorter Rules* 235–236); St. Pachomius the Psalter and the New Testament (*Praecepta* 140). Palladius tells with evident admiration of certain great heroes of the desert who memorized the entire Bible (*Lausiac History* 32). "Meditation" consisted of pronouncing the words of the sacred text over and over again so as to fix them in the memory and engrave the divine precepts upon the heart, where they would take root and grow up to bear spiritual fruit. Cassian prescribes that "the entire series of the Sacred Scriptures should be carefully committed to memory and constantly repeated" (*Conf* 14,10).

The Bible as Monastic Rule

The purpose of this assiduous study of the Bible was to learn how to live according to the will of God, which he makes known through his Word in the Scriptures. The monks were convinced that the Scriptures are of themselves an adequate rule of life. St. Athanasius begins the great discourse of Anthony to the Egyptian monks with the words, "The Scriptures are truly sufficient for our instruction" (*Vita Antonii* 16). The rules which were written for cenobites were not intended to replace the Bible as the supreme rule of life, but rather to collect the biblical precepts which are applicable to the monastic life and to interpret them for practical use. The frequency of scriptural texts in all the ancient rules is sufficient evidence of the concern of their authors to prescribe nothing which does not have a biblical justification.

This is most evident in the case of St. Basil, for whom the Bible alone was the exclusive rule. He had no intention of writing a separate rule. Instead he searched the Scriptures for a solution to every problem that arose in his brotherhoods. His *Morals* consist simply of a series of statements, each one supported by a series of New Testament citations. His later work, now called the *Longer and Shorter Rules*, was not entitled *Rule* by Basil himself, and is merely a series of counsels and answers to questions, consisting largely of quotations from Scripture. Basil explains clearly that the Scriptures are his rule of life when he discusses the question whether a person may ever do or say what he thinks right without the support of the Bible (*Shorter Rules* 1).

Thus the Bible is the criterion for judging the legitimacy of every monastic observance. If the monk lived apart from the world, it was because the Lord said, "A prophet receives no honor in his own country" (Jn 4,44), and the psalmist, "Turn your ear, forget your people and your father's house" (Ps 44,11). If he practiced self-denial, it was because the Gospel says, "If anyone wishes to come after me, let him deny himself, and take up his cross, and follow me" (Mt 16,24). If he worked, it was because St. Paul said, "If any man will not work, neither let him eat" (2 Thes 3,10). Poverty, continence, incessant prayer, obedience, fraternal charity, are all supported by reference to the Bible. Even such details as the number of hours in the divine office and the exact times of prayer depend upon biblical prescriptions (cf *Rule* 16,1–5; Cassian, *Inst* 3,3; Basil, *Longer Rules* 37).

The Bible in the Holy Rule

In this as in so many other respects, St. Benedict is entirely in the line of the earlier tradition. It is not only the treatment of the monastic vocation in the Prologue which depends upon the Bible, but the entire rule. Most of its precepts are based upon biblical texts which give them authority or are at least phrased in terms reminiscent of Scripture. Like St. Basil, St. Benedict thought of his rule as an interpretation of the Bible and an application of Scriptural precepts to particular cases. For him a monk is a Christian who hearkens to the Scriptures and obeys them literally.

It is not surprising, then, that his rule is little more than a mosaic of biblical quotations and allusions. In the short compass of the *Holy*

Rule, scholars have discovered some 130 biblical quotations, including 118 distinct biblical passages. Of these 72 are from the Old Testament, 46 from the New. The book which appears most frequently is that of the Psalms, which is quoted 53 times; it had long been the book of predilection of the ancient monks, and St. Benedict prescribed its daily use in the divine office. Proverbs and the other sapiential books hold second place. In the New Testament it is the Gospels to which most frequent reference is made, especially that of St. Matthew, so highly esteemed in the ancient Church, and then the Pauline epistles.

More comprehensive than the direct citations from the Bible are the frequent allusions to Scriptural passages. By a word, an image, a simple allusion, the holy patriarch shows that he is thinking in terms of the sacred history of the Bible. Thus in speaking of the abbot he often alludes to the Good Shepherd (2 *passim;* 27,8–9). This procedure shows an unusual familiarity with the Bible, and the ability to think in the categories of revelation itself.

Biblical Mentality

This means that for St. Benedict the Bible was much more than merely a collection of instructions in writing. He believed that the Holy Spirit is present in the Scriptures, speaking through them directly to the individual and communicating to him a vital and efficacious message. The frequent allusion to Scripture is not merely a façade used to ornament his own thought constructions, previously worked out in other categories. Rather, the substance of the *Rule* and its very language were derived directly from the Word of God and breathe its spirit.

It is this that is distinctive about the biblical inspiration of monasticism. The use of Scripture is not a studied thing, but springs forth spontaneously from a mind which is so steeped in the sacred history of the biblical account that it expresses itself naturally in its language. The things which he has to say to his monks cannot be expressed except in the words of Scripture, for it was in that mold that they were formed. This formulation does not merely convey to the reader a precept coldly stated, but evokes in him the echoes and overtones of the great themes which resound throughout the Bible. It conveys an atmosphere.

Exegesis of St. Benedict

The Bible contains words of life. The individual has only to hearken to them, to open his mind and his heart and to gain an intimate familiarity with the divine Word. Every part of Sacred Scripture is equally suitable for the profit of the monk. In his use of the Bible, St. Benedict makes no distinction between the Old and the New Testament. The two together form a whole, which is God's message to the human race, the revelation of God in the economy of sacred history. The ancients had a profound sense of the unity of the two testaments. It is the same Holy Spirit who speaks to us in every inspired word of Scripture, hence a verse from the Psalms or from Proverbs contains a divine precept equally as valid for the monk as the words of Jesus in the Gospels.

St. Benedict's faith in the divine presence in the Scriptures and their efficacy for the needs of the individual is evident from the manner in which he cites it. He calls it "the divine voice" (Pr 9), "the voice of the Lord" (Pr 19; 7,32) and "the divine word" (31,16). Citations are introduced by such phrases as "let us hear the Lord answering" (Pr 24), "the Lord says" (Pr 33.38; 5,5.11.13; 39, 9), and "may he hear from the Lord" (64,21). His faith in the power of the Scriptures was so strong that he believed them capable of healing the spiritual sickness of a monk who refused to amend his life; in this case he refers to them as *medicamina scripturarum divinarum* (28,3).

The exegesis of St. Benedict is consequently marked with a great liberty of spirit. He may quote only part of a text, or quote from memory, or combine a text from the Old Testament with another from the New. He indulges in moralizing allegory, in the tradition of Origen, which so strongly marked the exegesis of the period. The ladder of Jacob represents the degrees of humility (7,6–9); the

Babylonian infants dashed against the rock are evil thoughts, which must be shattered against the Rock which, according to the saying of the Apostle, is Christ (Pr 28; 4,50). Yet he penetrates profoundly into the moral teaching of the Bible. What may seem arbitrary to us is often not intended as a studied exegesis but is merely the expression of concepts in a biblical language which has become so familiar as to be used almost unconsciously.

Predominance of the Bible

Thus formed himself in the mentality of the Bible, St. Benedict strives to communicate the same formation to his monks. The Holy Scriptures are to be the principal food of their souls. They are to hold first place in the monks' library, "for what page or what utterance of the divinely-inspired books of the Old and the New Testament is not a most unerring rule of human life?" (73,3). The other books which St. Benedict recommends to his monks, the works of the Fathers and of the preceding monastic writers, are conceived of as nothing more than commentaries upon Sacred Scripture.

The Scriptures form the principal part of the divine office as it is outlined by the *Rule*, the whole Psalter being recited every week and the greater part of the other books occurring annually in the cycle of the lessons. The Bible most probably provided the substance of the public reading also, in the refectory and at the reading every night before Compline. We are certain that the Bible was read in the latter case, for here the *Rule* explicitly excludes the Heptateuch and the Books of Kings, which are not to be read then, but at other times (42,4).

In addition to this, the *Rule* provides for about four hours a day of *lectio divina* in private, of which more will be said in a later chapter. This was devoted either to the Scriptures themselves or to other works which served as commentaries upon them. The Lenten reading seems to have been devoted exclusively to the Bible: the term *bibliotheca* (48,15) probably does not mean *library*, as it is usually translated, but the collection of nine codices into which the Bible was then divided. This frequent reading of the Scriptures and "meditation" upon them is in evident continuity with the earlier monastic tradition.

Contact with the Scriptures

More important than the purely quantitative predominance of the Scriptures in the monk's spirituality is the mentality which they imprinted upon him. Authentic Benedictine tradition has always attempted to maintain this vital contact with the sources of revelation. In general, all the medieval monastic literature is conceived of as a commentary upon the sacred books, and everything in the monastic life preserved an intimate relationship with the divine economy of biblical history.

In this mentality, the monastic experience becomes a continuation of sacred history. The Christian, and pre-eminently the monk, is a fulfillment of the types to be found in the Old Testament. Living in the final phase of the kingdom whose history is traced throughout the pages of the Old and New Testaments, he is able to perceive the profound unity of the entire economy and the *divina dispensatio* which infallibly guides it. He takes his place in this economy, the heir and fulfillment of those who went before, and the preceding phases of the sacred history become the guide for the itinerary of his own soul toward God, who is the end as well as the beginning of the entire economy. God does not change: the history of his dealings with his people will be reproduced in the soul of the monk. The Bible is like a mirror in which the monk can see the story of his own salvation reflected.

The holy monk, the saint, fully realizes in himself all the stages of the divine economy of the Bible. The life of each individual must repeat the framework of the biblical history: rejected from Paradise because of sin, he must return to God through Christ. This profoundly biblical background is the basis of monastic hagiography, which almost invariably refers the various stages of the life of a saint to the successive phases of the kingdom of God traced in the Bible.

Medieval Exegesis

This mentality presupposes an attitude toward the Scriptures which modern times have largely lost. The patristic period knew a method of exegesis which began with Origen and reached its climax in St. Gregory, from whom it passed to the entire Middle Ages and became known as the fourfold sense of Scripture. The historical sense, the basis of all the others, sought to trace the development of sacred history as it is set forth in the Bible. From this the exegete passed to the allegorical sense, the doctrinal sense of Scripture, in which he discovered the mysteries of the faith, and to the moral sense, which dealt with the supernatural perfection of the Christian. The anagogical sense looked forward to the future consummation of the kingdom in the heavenly Jerusalem.

For these men the Bible, as interpreted by tradition, was the sole source of revelation. The Scriptures were not isolated from other aspects of the Christian life, but the Word of God as a living reality, read and heard in the Church, was the source from which the Christian sought his daily sustenance. Consequently the entire science of theology was considered to consist in the interpretation of Sacred Scripture. It appealed not only to the intellect, but to the whole man, through a vital, existential relationship. The monk not only read the Bible, he lived it, day in and day out, in the monastic liturgy which was for him the sacramental actualization of sacred history, and in his own personal life. Monasticism itself was the continuation and fulfillment of the divine economy.

Developing an Outlook

This vital contact with the Sacred Scriptures and the assimilation of them into the monk's daily life have always remained aspects of monastic spirituality, but the changed mentality introduced especially since the Renaissance had adulterated the purity of this concept. The tremendous effort which is being expended upon the Bible by modern scholars is directed chiefly toward the recovery of the literal sense. There is increasing recognition among modern exegetes, however, of the values inherent in patristic and medieval exegesis, and a growing attempt to recover the vital contact with the sources of revelation which was experienced in those times.

There can be no question of returning to outmoded methods of exegesis which have been left behind by modern progress in biblical studies. But what was of value in the ancient approach to the Scriptures must be recovered. This is precisely the biblical mentality which regarded the Christian life, and particularly the monastic life which was its most perfect expression, as a continuation of sacred history. Thus every aspect of the monk's life was looked upon in relation to the revealed divine economy.

Monks in our day will penetrate to the heart of their monastic vocation only if they cultivate such a mentality. The monk who has come to the monastery from the world and is accustomed to thinking in different categories and according to a more or less secularized set of values must give himself wholeheartedly to the world of the supernatural, which is the world of the Bible. Only daily reflection upon the truths of Scriptures can produce the habit of seeing all things in the unity and continuity of the divine economy. Normally, his introduction to the world of the Bible will be accomplished through his living in the world of the liturgy.

The Bible and the Monk

The monk must approach the Scriptures with a profound reverence for the Word of God. The ancients regarded it as the daily spiritual food of the Christian, in close relationship to the Eucharist. Just as Christ is the Word of God, who is the perfect manifestation of his Father to the world, so the Scriptures are also that Word of God which manifests the divine mysteries to us. The Bible participates in the Incarnation; it is a sacrament in the broad sense of the term, at once signifying and revealing the sacred mysteries which are contained therein.

Underneath the letter of the historical sense, the Scriptures contain Christ, and it is their Christological sense that the monk must try to perceive. For in the unity of the two testaments and the living continuity of the entire economy, the whole of revelation speaks of Christ. A truly spiritual approach to the Bible can never be satisfied with arriving at the literal sense alone. The Bible is adapted to the needs of all, and everyone can profit from it. But to read with profit requires both good dispositions and divine grace, and also a persevering effort to acquire a biblical mentality.

The monk, then, must give himself up joyfully to the study of the Scriptures. In his study of theology it should be his primary concern to learn sacred doctrine as it is exposed in the categories of revelation itself. He will neglect none of the means which modern biblical studies have put at our disposal for a more fruitful understanding of the Bible. He will not stop, however, at a purely scientific approach to the Scriptures, but will continue to read and meditate upon the Bible within the context of the Church and the liturgy, and will make it the norm of his spiritual life and the daily nourishment of his soul.

2. THE LITURGICAL INSPIRATION OF MONASTICISM

Monasticism and Liturgy

In modern times, due to the role which monks have played in the contemporary liturgical movement, particularly in Europe, the popular mentality automatically associates the liturgy with Benedictine monasteries. Monks themselves, while rejecting the suggestion that the liturgy is in any sense their private property, as has sometimes been implied, will readily concede that it does occupy an important place in their spirituality. Monastic spirituality is not identical with liturgical spirituality but, in the Benedictine tradition, it is one form of it. In fact, monasteries seem to flourish and to attain a high degree of supernatural vitality and influence within the Church to the extent that they cultivate the liturgy.

Has this always been the case? Have monasteries always been

centers of liturgical worship? Actually, the modern emphasis upon the place of the liturgy in monastic spirituality goes back only as far as the nineteenth-century restoration under Dom Gueranger. In his mind, the revival of monastic life was inextricably joined to the revival of the liturgy. This concept of Dom Gueranger, however, was not an innovation without precedent in monastic tradition, but rather the rediscovery of a value which the monks of the high Middle Ages held in peaceful possession. While the ritualism of Cluny was excessive, a sane and sober emphasis upon the communal liturgy was a part of the authentic tradition in all its branches during the Benedictine centuries. Its roots go back to St. Benedict himself.

Early Monks and Liturgy

The important role assigned to the liturgy, however, is a feature of the Benedictine tradition which does not go back to the origins of monasticism. Liturgical spirituality is communal by its very nature, for its purpose is to effect the sharing of many in the one sanctity and worship of Christ. It is not to be expected, therefore, that the liturgy would play a predominant role in the spirituality of the first monks, who were solitaries and whose approach to supernatural perfection was on an individual level. The liturgy is, of course, an element which cannot be dispensed with in any orthodox form of spirituality, but there can be vast differences in the degree to which it is cultivated and in the importance which the individual Christian attributes to it in his search for perfection.

Within these limits it can be affirmed that the spirituality of the early monks did not accord a prominent place to the liturgy. The anchorites emphasized continuous prayer, but their prayer was not of a liturgical character: it consisted chiefly of the private recitation of psalms. Their principal emphasis was upon a radical personal asceticism. Although they assisted at the Eucharistic celebration and received the sacraments, this was simply taken for granted as the normal Christian practice of the time. From a quantitative viewpoint the liturgy received relatively little emphasis in their spirituality and there is nothing like a theology of liturgical worship in the early monastic literature. However, their basic outlook was not really foreign to the liturgy, for it was derived from the Bible, upon which the liturgy depends and with which it is in perfect harmony. Moreover, the monks conceived of their asceticism as a liturgy in itself, for it was offered to God as a holocaust and effected their sanctification.

When the solitaries began to live together in groups, separated from each other by relatively short distances, they ordinarily gathered together at a common church or oratory on Sunday for common prayer and the celebration of the Eucharist. But it was only with the growth of strictly cenobitical forms of monasticism that a community liturgy began to be developed. In the Pachomian system a good deal of freedom was still left to individual initiative in matters of worship as well as asceticism. In the West the performance of the liturgy was associated with the urban monasteries from the beginning. Since the ascetics who inhabited these monasteries were clerics, their principal activity was the carrying out of the liturgy in the cathedral or parish church.

St. Benedict and Liturgical Worship

It is with St. Benedict that the liturgy begins to occupy a truly important place in the spirituality of monks. While he generally followed the Egyptian monastic tradition, in this respect he seems to have been influenced by the urban monasteries of the West and by the liturgical practices of the Roman basilicas. Together with work and the *lectio divina,* the common performance of the divine office becomes one of the monk's principal activities, and from a qualitative viewpoint assumes an important role in determining his spirituality. The divine office, of course, is not simply to be equated with the liturgy, though it is one of its major parts. We are not very well informed about the sacramental practices of St. Benedict's monastery. The Eucharist was celebrated only on Sundays and feast days, and the sacramental life of the Church certainly played a less important role than it does in monasteries today. This, however, was consonant with the common practice of the universal Church at that time.

Accordingly we cannot make St. Benedict out to be a theorist of the theology of liturgical worship or of liturgical spirituality. His thinking was predominantly in the line of the oriental tradition which stressed the relationship of the individual monk to God, although there is a greater concern for the common life in the *Rule* than in many earlier works of monastic legislation. His prescriptions regarding the divine office derive more from his concept of the communal nature of cenobitic life than from theological considerations. But he sowed the seed of a development which has grown logically enough from his theory of monastic life in community. In the course of monastic history the liturgical practices of monasteries have sometimes been exaggerated to the point of obscuring the simplicity which is certainly more in the logic of St. Benedict's thought. Nevertheless a sober emphasis upon the value of the liturgy in the development of the monk's spirituality is in accord with authentic Benedictine tradition.

What Is Meant by the Liturgy

It is important that the monk have a clear idea of precisely what the sacred liturgy is. It has too often been misunderstood and consequently caricatured. Even today, in spite of the efforts of the modern liturgical movement which have culminated in the eloquent declarations of the Second Vatican Council, it is sometimes still regarded as the visible, ceremonial aspect of Christian worship, the complex of rites and ceremonies which are officially organized and regulated by the Church. Such a view leaves out the most important element of the liturgy: the divine element. It caricatures it as a collection of minutiae which may offer abundant material for the esthete and the perfectionist but can only be a waste of time for the practical Christian intent upon a vigorous spirituality.

The liturgy is the worship which the Church, the Mystical Body of Christ, offers to God together with her Head, and his response to that worship in the form of the sanctification of the Church. This worship and sanctification are accomplished under the form of a complex of sacred signs, perceptible by the senses. Some of these signs were instituted by Christ himself, others by the Church. They not only symbolize the interior reality of worship and sanctification, but also contain it, though in different ways. The whole is accomplished through the mediatorship of Christ, the High Priest of the New Covenant, in the abiding presence of the Holy Spirit. The liturgy is therefore a dialogue between God and man, the place where the human and divine meet. It is the supreme manner in which the Church accomplishes its mission on earth, continuing the action of Christ himself.

While the Second Vatican Council has offered no formal definition of the liturgy, it has described what is essential to it in the following terms: "Rightly, then, the liturgy is considered as an exercise of the priestly office of Jesus Christ. In the liturgy the sanctification of man is signified by signs perceptible to the sense, and is effected in a way which corresponds with each of these signs; in the liturgy the whole public worship is performed by the Mystical Body of Jesus Christ, that is, by the head and his members" (*Constitution*, 7). The Council concludes from this that "every liturgical celebration . . . is a sacred action surpassing all others; no other action of the Church can equal its efficacy by the same title and to the same degree" (*ibid*). Although "the sacred liturgy does not exhaust the entire activity of the Church" (9), it is "the summit towards which the activity of the Church is directed; at the same time it is the fount from which all her power flows" (10).

Christ in the Liturgy

The liturgy, therefore, is an exercise of Christ's priesthood, "an action of Christ the priest and of his Body which is the Church" (7). The Christ who acts in the liturgy is the glorious Christ. During his earthly life his divine glory was hidden under the veil of the human nature which he had assumed. During his public life, the initial phase of his mission, "he went about doing good and healing all who were in the power of the devil; for God was with him" (Acts 10,38). But his mission was consummated only with his own glorification. St. John uses this term to refer to the mystery of his passion, death and resurrection, which put the seal of God's approval upon his work and exalted him in glory to the right hand of his Father. "This Jesus God has raised up . . . therefore, exalted by the right hand of God, and receiving from the Father the promise of the Holy Spirit, he has poured forth this Spirit which you see and hear" (Acts 2,32–33). It is the triumphant and glorious Christ who accomplishes the definitive act of salvation.

This work of Christ was a priestly work. The epistle to the Hebrews represents him as the great High Priest, who accomplishes the salvation of men by entering into the heavenly sanctuary and there presenting redeemed humanity to his Father. His priesthood is the only true priesthood in the new dispensation; he is sole mediator between God and man. Nor is his priestly activity a thing of the past. He continues to exercise it in the heavenly sanctuary before the throne of the Father, and on earth through the ministry of men who share in his priesthood. In the liturgy he is present once again to his followers; his Word is addressed to them; above all, the ritual action which is performed in the liturgy is the activity of the glorious Christ himself. His priestly activity, the salvific work which he performed on earth and consummated by his glorification, is continued in the liturgy on earth as it is in his heavenly intercession.

Mystical Body and Liturgy

Christ is no longer present to us in the same manner as he was during his earthly life, but he is present in a new way through the Church. He promised that he would be with his disciples until the end of time. This extension of Christ into time and space is accomplished through the Church which he established. The Church is the society of believers, gathered together about the now glorious

Christ as members in relationship to him as their Head. He lives among them still by his mystical presence.

The Church is therefore the continuation of the Incarnation and of the salvific work of Christ. His Holy Spirit dwells in her in such a fashion that the Spirit can truly be called the soul of the Mystical Body of Christ. It is he who vivifies the Church and works within her, dispensing the divine life which is the fruit of Christ's salvific work. The individual members of the Body can achieve contact with the divine life only through their membership in the Body and their participation in its supernatural activity. There is no way to Christ except through the Church, as there is no way to the Father except through Christ.

The liturgy, consequently, is not an activity of isolated individuals, but the activity of the entire Church, and it is this which gives it priority over individual forms of worship and makes them subordinate to and dependent upon it. The liturgy is essentially communal because its purpose is to bring about the communion of many in the one sanctity and worship of Christ, who, as the Second Vatican Council declares, "always associates the Church with himself in the great work wherein God is perfectly glorified and men are sanctified" (*Constitution* 7). Christian sanctity and worship are essentially social, since they are a shared sanctity and worship derived from a common source, the priesthood of Christ. Consequently the liturgy "is the outstanding means whereby the faithful may express in their lives, and manifest to others, the mystery of Christ and the real nature of the true Church" (*ibid* 2).

Liturgy and Sacred Signs

Just as the divine activity of Christ was hidden and at the same time manifested by his human nature, so the continuation of his activity takes place under the veil of symbols. The liturgy, which includes the sacrifice of Christ, the sacraments, the sacramentals, the formulae of prayer and the other rites which surround these things, is a great complex of sacred signs. The supernatural realities, the interior worship which the Church offers to God in Christ and the sanctification which it receives from him, are hidden under signs perceptible by the human senses.

The ancient world, in which the Christian liturgy had its origin, gave greater attention to the value of signs than is customary in our modern mentality. In the elaboration of the signs which play such an important role in our liturgy, there was a certain influence of the neo-Platonic mentality of many of the Fathers, according to which the material creation is a symbol of the realities of the supra-terrestrial world. But the essential value of the concept of sign is not dependent upon human philosophy, for it is found in revelation itself.

It was the intention of God himself, in inspiring the human authors of Sacred Scripture, that the persons, places and events of the Old Testament should be types of the reality of salvation which he would bring about in the fullness of time. This biblical typology is the basis of the symbolism which the liturgy exploits. The dispensing of the realities of salvation won for us by Christ and the expression of our interior worship under the form of sacred signs are, therefore, according to the positive will of God himself.

Significance of Liturgical Signs

The signs used in the liturgy include words, songs, gestures, objects and persons. This sacramentalism of the liturgy is simply a continuation of the Incarnation itself. The human nature of Christ is the supreme sign. The signs of the liturgy have a religious significance, determined by the positive will of God or the intention of the Church, depending upon whether they are of divine or ecclesiastical institution. Accurate historical study of the individual rites is necessary to define precisely the significance of each particular sign.

Every liturgical sign signifies that in which the liturgy essentially consists: the worship which the Church renders to God through Christ and in the Holy Spirit, and the sanctification of the Church by God through Christ in the Holy Spirit. Both of these aspects are present in some manner in the meaning of every sign, but there is infinite variety in the manner in which they are expressed. A sign may stress one aspect more than another.

The liturgical sign signifies the salvific action of Christ, accomplished in his passion, death and resurrection, as well as its previous foreshadowings in sacred history. At the same time it signifies the supernatural realities which are present here and now in the liturgical act: the interior worship which the Church offers to God through Christ the Mediator and the reality of grace which is communicated to the Church in the encounter with God in Christ. Connected with this is the moral disposition of the subject and his obligation to make his own life conformable to what is signified in the liturgical action, according to the adage *imitamini quod tractatis*. Finally, the liturgical sign is also eschatological, for it signifies, too, the consummation of that salvation whose first fruits we receive in the liturgy: eternal glory and the heavenly liturgy.

Efficacy of the Liturgical Sign

The liturgical signs not only signify but also effect the worship of God and the sanctification of the Church; but they do not all do so in the same manner. The rites which are of divine institution produce their effect principally *ex opere operato*, that is, by the very fact that the sacred action is performed, provided that all the conditions for validity are observed and the subject places no obstacle. Those rites which are of ecclesiastical institution, on the other hand, produce their effect principally *ex opere operantis Ecclesiae;* that is, the cause of the effect is not the action itself, but the merits and intercession of the Church, to which God proportions the grace which he confers.

The sacrifice of the Mass and the sacraments, therefore, produce their effect by the very fact that the action is validly performed: the minister must have the requisite power, the recipient must oppose no obstacle and the act itself must be freely and validly placed.

This does not mean that the dispositions of the subject are of no importance; it merely means that they do not constitute the cause of the effect, but only the condition.

The other liturgical rites derive their efficacy principally from the action of the Church. God regards the moral dignity of the subject who places the action. But in the case of the liturgy this subject is the Church herself, the Spouse of Christ, his Mystical Body. Consequently the impetratory power of the liturgical rites is greater than that of any individual, even though he be a member of the Church, for in them it is the Church herself, with her indefectible mark of holiness, who is the subject.

It is for this reason that liturgical worship is more efficacious than any individual worship, no matter how worthy that may be in itself. For it is the worship of God by Christ himself, joined to his Body, the Church, and is therefore the official worship which is intended by God to be the place of meeting where he encounters his holy people. Consequently individual prayer and worship also gain in dignity and efficacy to the extent that they are an overflow and continuation of the liturgical action.

The Liturgy and Sacred History

Viewed under the aspect which we have attempted to sketch here, the liturgy is nothing other than the re-presentation and continuation of the sacred history which is delineated in the pages of the Bible. It is a particular phase of that history, the period in which the salvation which Christ has won for us is applied to the individual members of his Body, gathered together in the Holy Spirit, through the means which have been determined by him and further elaborated by his Church.

In the liturgy the whole of the divine economy which was manifested in history is presented to us, and is presented precisely in that form in which revelation has made it known. We see the plan of God, conceived from all eternity, realized in the creation and elevation of man, then frustrated by man's rebellion and sin. Then comes the long period of preparation for the repair of the damage, in which man is pitted against the forces of evil, but lives on in faith and in hope of the redemption to come. We see this redemption realized in Christ, definitively accomplished by his death, resurrection and entry into glory at the right hand of his Father, and dispensed to those who become members of his holy redeemed people and enjoy contact with the realities of salvation through the means which he has established, looking forward with hope to the final phase of that kingdom when he will return in glory to consummate his kingdom and present it to his Father.

It is here precisely that we have the point of insertion of the liturgy into monastic spirituality, for we have already seen that the monastic life was traditionally conceived of as a continuation of sacred history. The monk realizes in his own life the divine economy described in the biblical history. But it is precisely in the liturgy that he realizes it to the fullest degree. The sacramentalism which marks every aspect of the monastic life finds its fullest expression in the liturgy, where the saving economy of God is actualized in the context of the Church under the guidance of the Holy Spirit.

Liturgical Spirituality

If a spirituality is a complex of means through which men can achieve supernatural perfection, then the Church herself provides us with such a spirituality in the liturgy. The liturgy not only presents to us the great truths of revelation manifested in the course of the history of salvation, but also deduces from them the moral implications which are the consequences of these truths and urges us to reduce them to practice.

We have seen that spiritualities differ in the relative balance which they achieve among the various elements which are common to every orthodox form of spirituality. Now liturgical spirituality is distinguished by the fact that this balance is determined by the liturgy itself. The hierarchy of order among the various truths of revelation is that which is found in the liturgy. And this is the order found in revelation itself, for the presentation of the liturgy is in turn determined by the biblical history. Liturgical spirituality, therefore, unifies all of the individual's efforts toward supernatural perfection by forming them according to and incorporating them into the liturgical action of the Church.

This means that the liturgy itself becomes a complete form of the spiritual life for one who adequately penetrates into its spirit. It does not mean that there can or need be no other spiritual activity in his life, but only that extraliturgical activity is subordinated to the liturgy and becomes either a preparation for or a continuation of the liturgical action. The equilibrium which is established in the psychological attitude of the subject is derived from the liturgy itself, according to the axiom *sentire cum Ecclesia.*

Convergence with Monastic Outlook

It has often been said that liturgical spirituality is objective, theocentric and communal. But since these characteristics must to some degree be the marks of every orthodox spirituality, they do not sufficiently distinguish it from others. It must be added that liturgical spirituality possesses these characteristics in a particular way: the outlook of the subject is formed by the liturgy, which gives predominance to the objective events of sacred history over the subjective state of consciousness which reflection upon them creates in the believer; to the role of God in salvation over human activity; to the community of God's redeemed people over the individual considered in isolation. Here again the liturgy is simply following the viewpoint of revelation itself, and the believer in conforming his own mentality to this view is adopting the outlook of the Church herself and taking his place in the present phase of sacred history, which extends from the ascension to the parousia.

Thus the liturgy actualizes and the participant experiences in his own life the great themes which the Bible traces throughout the successive stages of sacred history. Among these themes several may be singled out as having particular significance for the monk: it is here that we observe the coincidence between liturgical and monastic spirituality. The continual struggle between the city of God and the city of Satan is a theme of frequent recurrence in the liturgy and coincides remarkably with the combat against the devil which led the early monks into the desert to do battle with him in his own stronghold. The struggle against Satan has become a constant theme of monastic tradition. The theme of the return to paradise likewise strikes a sympathetic chord in monastic tradition, as we shall see more fully later on. The liturgy's emphasis upon the social dimension of Christianity coincides with the cenobitic theme of the monastery as house of God and church of God, in which the bond of fraternal charity produces "one heart and one soul." In view of these points of coincidence, the evolution of monastic spirituality over the centuries toward a more liturgical orientation seems to be quite in harmony with the intrinsic character of cenobitic life.

The Monk and the Liturgy

Together with the Bible, then, the liturgy provides the monk with the primary orientation of his spirituality. Through it he turns daily to God to offer him the worship of one who recognizes his own impotence and the vast gulf which separates the creature from the Creator, and to receive from him the supernatural sustenance which permits him to advance continually in the search for God.

To say that the Bible and the liturgy are the primary sources of the monk's spirituality is not to say that they are in any sense his exclusive property. The Church presents them to all her children as the foundation stones of their supernatural life. Biblical and liturgical spirituality are capable of almost infinite variation to suit the needs of all the faithful. The monk will be more absolute, more logical, perhaps, in the use of the Bible and the liturgy than other Christians; above all they will assume in his life a quantitative predominance which cannot be as fully realized in the spirituality of other groups among the faithful. But monastic spirituality is only one species of biblico-liturgical spirituality.

The attitude of the monk toward the liturgy will be determined by the interior character of his vocation and his relationship to God and a consequent concern for authenticity. If he is to be the integral Christian, then he must seek the authentic and essential values in the life of the Church rather than the peripheral and accidental. He must try to develop a profound sense of the sacramentalism of the liturgy which will overflow into every area of his life. But his attitude toward the signs which constitute the liturgy must be a deeply spiritual one: he must not remain upon the level of the sensible signs, still less of the esthetic experience he may derive from them, but must seek the authentic and essential supernatural values toward which they point. The signs will be for him a means of penetrating more profoundly into the world of the supernatural, and there discovering God and himself in the unceasing dialogue of the liturgy.

3. THE EUCHARIST IN ANCIENT MONASTICISM

The Eucharist in the Church

Just as the liturgy is the "summit towards which the activity of the Church is directed" and at the same time "the fount from which all her power flows" (*Constitution* 10), so the Eucharist is the summit and the fount of the whole liturgy. The Eucharist is the very center of the Church's life, for it is this sacrament which continually builds up the Church and is "the outstanding means whereby the faithful may express in their lives, and manifest to others, the mystery of Christ and the real nature of the true Church" (*ibid* 2). Through the paschal mystery which is renewed in the Eucharist men are brought to a share in the life of the Blessed Trinity through union with Christ. Therefore the Church is never more herself than when she offers the Eucharistic sacrifice.

In the Eucharist Christ, who promised that he would never abandon his Church, perpetuates his presence among his followers. He offers them a memorial of his redemptive act, gives himself to them as nourishment, and draws them into the unity of his Mystical Body. The Eucharist is the supreme sign of Christ's love for the

Church, the node about which all the other sacraments revolve and to which they are directed. It is "a sacrament of love, a sign of unity, a bond of charity, a paschal banquet in which Christ is eaten, the mind is filled with grace, and a pledge of future glory is given to us" (*ibid* 47).

If the monk is to be an integral Christian, therefore, his life must be centered upon the Eucharist. His ascetical efforts, his prayer, his life in community and his apostolate will have supernatural value to the extent that they are directed to and flow from the Eucharist. The monastic community's celebration of the Eucharist is its principal bond of unity with the universal Church and its most noble contribution to the Church's life. When he offers the Eucharistic sacrifice, and is nourished with the paschal banquet, the monk enters into contact with the life of glory in the heavenly Jerusalem, of which the Eucharist is a pledge. In this section we wish to examine the place of the Eucharist in monastic spirituality.

Individualism of Anchorites

At first sight it would seem that the Eucharist played scarcely any role in the spirituality of the earliest monks. In its origins the monastic movement was a flight from the world, and seemingly even from the Church herself. The great solitaries separated themselves unequivocally from their fellow Christians and hid themselves in the forbidding wastes of the desert. We hear of monks who spent many years in a place of seclusion without laying eyes upon another human being.

We have already observed that these early monks attributed relatively little importance to the liturgy. Their spirituality was of an individual character, dominated by private prayer and a harsh asceticism. Using these means, they worked out their salvation alone in the wilderness. Such a spirituality naturally lays little stress upon common liturgical prayer, upon the unity of the entire Christian community in worship and upon a common sacramental life. In retiring to the desert, they would seem to have deliberately cut themselves off from the sacramental life of the Church.

Devotion to the Holy Eucharist

Upon closer examination, however, we find that the monks' seclusion from the sacramental life of the Church was far less radical than this portrait suggests. They never had any intention of setting themselves up as a kind of charismatic church in competition with the hierarchic community of the faithful. On the contrary, they remained united to the Church by their subjection to the hierarchy, their apostolate and their contact with the sacramental system.

It is true that the monks did not cultivate a liturgical spirituality to any appreciable degree before the rise of cenobitic forms of monasticism. Even the sacraments did not occupy a position of quantitative importance in their religious outlook. But this does not mean that they cut themselves off from the sacramental life of the Church, a position that could not be adopted by any authentically Christian movement. On the contrary, we find them intensely devoted to the Eucharist.

The opinion that the monastic movement was a rebellion by ascetic laymen against the hierarchical Church has been vastly exaggerated and is not supported by the testimony of the sources. The monastic literature does mention some monks who refused to take part in the sacramental life of the Church, but it is clear that they belonged to the unorthodox lunatic fringe which always plagued the authentic monastic movement. Cassian tells of a monk who refused to leave his solitude to go to church with the other monks, but he denounces him for this and other indiscretions which eventually led to his unhappy downfall (*Conf* 2,5). Later on he speaks of other monks who received the Eucharist only once a year, but makes it clear that he does not approve of such a practice (*Conf* 23,21).

Eucharistic Practice among Ancient Monks

We have seen that the solitaries of Egypt and Syria ordinarily lived in groups at a reasonably short distance from a common center.

Here there was a church, at which they assembled on Saturdays and Sundays for the common celebration of the divine office and the Eucharistic liturgy and to receive Holy Communion. Usually one of the monks was a priest. Cassian found this arrangement fully developed during his sojourn in Egypt at the end of the fourth century.

Some solitaries, however, withdrew into more remote places where it was impossible for them to assist at the Eucharistic sacrifice for long periods of time. St. Anthony is said to have spent twenty years on the outer mountain of the Thebaid without seeing anyone, though many came in hopes of visiting him and to bring him a supply of bread (*Vita Antonii* 12). From other sources we are informed, however, that these solitaries carried the sacrament with them into their seclusion so that they could partake of the Body and Blood of the Lord from time to time. In some places it seems to have been the practice of those who went to church on Sunday to take the sacred Bread home with them so that they could communicate on weekdays when no liturgy was celebrated (cf Basil, *Epist* 93).

There is an abundance of testimonies from the ancient monastic literature to indicate that the early monks held the Eucharist in the highest esteem and accorded it a place of honor in the development of their own spirituality. There is considerable evidence of the practice of daily communion in certain localities, as in the monasteries of St. Augustine (cf also *Regula Magistri* 21;22;80). In some places weekly or twice-weekly communion seems to have been the rule. However, it is true that the monastic spirituality of the period laid less emphasis than might be expected upon the importance of the Eucharist for spiritual growth. The custom of individual reception tended to shift the emphasis almost entirely to the aspect of divine nourishment and to neglect the other aspects of the Holy Eucharist.

St. Benedict at Subiaco

St. Gregory pictures the youthful St. Benedict in his cave at Subiaco as completely cut off from the society of men for three years. His only contact was with the monk Romanus, who could not reach his cave, but lowered food to him upon a rope (*Dial* 2,1). Nothing is said of his receiving the Eucharist during this time; on one occasion, in fact, he was not even aware of the occurrence of the feast of Easter (*ibid*).

It is, however, extremely unlikely that St. Benedict went without the reception of the Eucharist for three years. To do so would have been contrary to the entire monastic tradition, if we except the deviations which were justly condemned by the orthodox representatives of the movement. It would even have been contrary to the general mind of the Church of the period. (A contemporary provincial synod, held at Agde in Gaul under the presidency of St. Caesarius of Arles, required the faithful to communicate at least on the three greatest feasts of the year.) The monks never considered themselves exempt from the general practice of the Church.

It seems much more likely that St. Benedict attended the celebration of the Eucharistic synaxis from time to time in the church of the nearby monastery to which the monk Romanus belonged, or at least received the Eucharist alone in his cave. The fact that the *Dialogues* make no mention of this need not surprise us if we take into consideration the literary genre of St. Gregory's account. He had no intention of offering us a detailed biography of the saint in the modern sense, nor did he have the materials for such an undertaking. In evoking St. Benedict's sojourn in the cave, he no doubt wished to portray him as the ideal monk who had left the world behind to commune with God alone in the solitude of the desert. It was not the place to comment upon his Eucharistic devotion.

The Eucharist in the Rule

The *Holy Rule* takes it for granted that the Eucharist will be celebrated on Sundays and feast days; the order of the day does not make provision for a daily synaxis. Here St. Benedict is simply adopting the custom of his monastic predecessors. Daily communion was in favor in some monastic circles: St. Basil defended it (*Epist* 93), and St. Augustine discussed the respective merits of daily or weekly reception (*Sermo* 57,7). A weekly Eucharist, however, seems to have been the custom in Cassian's monastery: there are some texts where he seems to make reference to daily communion, but the weight of the evidence rather favors a weekly reception.

St. Benedict prescribes that the monks shall receive communion in their regular order (63,4), and that the reader should drink a little wine mixed with water before beginning to read to prevent any irreverence to the sacred species (38,10). There is a clear reference to the weekly reception of the sacrament in 38,2, where it is prescribed that the reader should receive the blessing on Sunday after communion. The term *officium altaris* refers to the Eucharistic sacrifice in 62,6, where the *Rule* prescribes that a priest or deacon may exercise the "service of the altar" if the abbot permits him to do so. There are no other certain references to the sacrifice of the Mass in the *Holy Rule*.

Difference of Mentality

It is significant that St. Benedict nowhere offers any precise legislation regarding the celebration of the Eucharistic sacrifice or the reception of Holy Communion. The Eucharistic practice which was common among monks of his time is simply taken for granted. The *Rule* deals with specifically monastic practices, and there seemed no necessity for treating of matters which were held in peaceful possession by all Christians.

It must be recognized that the mentality of the *Rule* is quite different from our own. While it implies no lack of esteem for the Eucharist, nor any underestimation of the value of the sacrament in the lives of Christians, it nevertheless lacks a positive emphasis upon the central place of the Eucharist in the development of the supernatural life. In this respect our theological outlook has evolved together with the evolution of Eucharistic practice. In our day a monastic rule which fails to emphasize the centrality of the Eucharist in the lives of monks seems to be lacking something, and in fact the *Holy Rule* has on this point been completed by the constitutions of the various monastic congregations, which justly lay emphasis upon the daily conventual Mass as the supreme act of corporate worship in the monastic day.

We are here in the presence of a legitimate development. In their attitude toward the Eucharist, monks of our time cannot overlook the changes in theological outlook and piety which have taken place over the centuries. We must make explicit what was left implicit in the teaching of St. Benedict. Not the least of the fruits of the modern liturgical movement has been to restore the Eucharist to its place of honor at the very center of the Christian life and practice and to re-establish a balanced appreciation of its many-sided riches which had been obscured by controversy and theological decline. It is incumbent upon the monk, therefore, to acquire a profound understanding of the place which this supreme sacrament occupies in the life of the Church and in his own spirituality.

4. THE EUCHARIST IN THE CHURCH

The Eucharist in the Early Church

If we wish to examine the significance of the Holy Eucharist in the life of the Church, the best place to begin is with the Eucharistic celebrations of the early Christian community. There we find the original significance of the rite explained by the inspired writers of the New Testament. From them we learn that both in the primitive community of Jerusalem and in the Pauline communities, such as that of Corinth, the rite called the "breaking of bread" was celebrated.

It was characteristic of this rite that it took place in the course of a meal and in an atmosphere of intense joy. The "breaking of bread," an expression which soon became a technical term for the celebration of the Eucharist, was the principal religious rite of the early Christians. The meal was simply a continuation of those meals which the disciples had taken in common together with the Master during his earthly life, when they had accompanied him on his journeys throughout Galilee and Judea. The last of these meals had a particularly solemn character, celebrated as it was in the atmosphere of the Jewish paschal feast and with overtones of the tremendous events which were to befall Jesus immediately afterward.

The breaking of the bread was a continuation also of the meals which they had eaten together with Jesus during the time he spent with them after his resurrection. During those forty days he had on numerous occasions appeared in their midst and partaken of food and drink with them. These were occasions of intense spiritual joy, for the Master was with them once more, alive and conversing with them about things which they had not been able to understand before. It was in this breaking of the bread that they recognized him and acknowledged that he was truly risen and had entered into his glorious state: it was an encounter of faith. When he departed once more, they continued to hold these joyous repasts, confident, now with the certitude of faith, that he was still present among them.

Jesus at the Last Supper

Of all the meals which they shared with him, however, there was one that stood out with particular vividness in their memory. This had taken place on the last night before his arrest and subsequent passion and death. It was a meal to which he had looked forward with intense anticipation: "I have greatly desired to eat this passover with you before I suffer; for I say to you that I will eat of it no more, until it has been fulfilled in the kingdom of God" (Lk 22,15–16). After washing the feet of the disciples, Jesus reclined at table with them in an atmosphere of mutual love and profound religious devotion.

The meal took place in the setting of the Jewish paschal feast. It was the week of the Passover, when the Jews flocked into Jerusalem to celebrate the memory of the deliverance from Egypt, the greatest act of God's sovereign power on behalf of his people. While problems of chronology have created some difficulties in regard to the paschal character of the Supper, the indications of the evangelists are sufficient to show that Jesus intended to institute his new rite within the context of the Jewish Passover. The events of the Supper can be situated without difficulty in the framework of the traditional Jewish Passover ritual.

In the course of this ritual meal, Jesus took bread, blessed and broke it, and gave it to them, saying, "Take; this is my body." Later he took a cup of wine, gave thanks over it, and gave it to them to drink with the words, "This is my blood of the new covenant, which is being shed for many" (cf Mk 14,22–24). In this brief account we have the essence of the rite which Jesus there instituted. What significance did he wish to attach to it?

Jesus Offers His Life in Sacrifice

First of all, the Lord indicated his intention of sacrificing his life for mankind. He made it clear that this was to be the last of the meals which he would share with them during the period of his ministry, because on the morrow he would go forward to his death. The apostles had been unable to understand the previous announcements which he had made to them of his impending passion, intent as they were upon the terrestrial aspects of Jewish messianism. The threefold prediction of his sufferings upon which Mark lays so much emphasis had gone unheeded. Now, on the eve of the passion, he enforced his prediction with a symbolic action.

The bread and wine which he distributed to them are themselves symbols of his death. The bread is broken, as his body would be by the torments of his persecutors. The wine, whose very color is suggestive of blood, is the vital fluid of the living grape, as blood is of the living body. The bread and wine are given separately, in reference to the separation of body and blood which constitutes death.

The formulae which Jesus pronounced explain the symbolism. His blood is shed for many, an expression which in the Semitic idiom means for all men. The Pauline tradition has preserved a similar pronouncement over the bread. The sense of the statement is clear: Jesus intends to sacrifice his life, his body and blood, for mankind.

He will offer it to his heavenly Father as a sacrifice, a holocaust of atonement which will effect the reconciliation of sinful mankind with the Creator.

Fulfillment of Prophecy

In assuming this role, Jesus was consciously fulfilling the prophecies of the suffering servant of Yahweh from the second part of the book of Isaiah. This mysterious figure was to be a man "spurned and avoided by men, a man of suffering, accustomed to infirmity, one of those from whom men hide their faces, spurned, and we held him in no esteem" (Is 53,3). He would accept suffering and death with heroic patience: "Though he was harshly treated, he submitted and opened not his mouth; like a lamb led to the slaughter or a sheep before the shearers, he was silent and opened not his mouth" (Is 53,7).

This suffering was to be endured on behalf of others, for whom it would have a vicarious value: "It was our infirmities that he bore, our sufferings that he endured . . . he was pierced for our offenses, crushed for our sins; upon him was the chastisement that makes us whole, by his stripes we were healed . . . the Lord laid upon him the guilt of us all" (53,4–6). His sufferings would satisfy for the sins of others and gain pardon for them: "Through his suffering, my servant shall justify many, and their guilt he shall bear . . . he shall take away the sins of many, and win pardon for their offenses" (53,11–12).

During his ministry Jesus had already presented himself as the fulfillment of the servant prophecies. A saying preserved by Mark is evidence that he was consciously assuming the role of the vicarious sufferer: "The Son of Man also has not come to be served but to serve, and to give his life as a ransom for many" (Mk 10,45). In another passage he explicitly quotes Is 53,12 and applies it to himself: "I say to you that this which is written must yet be fulfilled in me, 'And he was reckoned among the wicked' " (Lk 22,37). There are other allusions to Isaiah in the accounts of his baptism, transfiguration and the predictions of his passion which show that he wished to present himself as the fulfillment of the prophecies.

Now, at the Supper, we reach the climax of the identification. His words repeat the very terms of the prophetic texts: his life will be *given* for *many*. He will suffer, and the fruits of his passion will be extended to all men in a universality of salvation which goes beyond the horizons of the prophet. His life will be given as a ransom.

The Old Covenant Sealed in Blood

In the Isaian prophecies Yahweh says to the servant: "I formed you, and set you as a covenant of the people, a light for the nations" (Is 42,6). Here there is a contact between the Isaian theme of the servant and another common Old Testament theme, that of the covenant. On Mt. Sinai God had formed a covenant with his people, an event which ties together all the successive phases of the history of God's people.

The covenant was sealed in blood. In the account of its ratification, the book of Exodus tells how Moses sacrificed young bulls and spilled half the blood of the sacrifice upon the altar. Then he announced the terms of the covenant to the people, who agreed to abide by them. Next he sprinkled the rest of the blood upon the people, with the words: "This is the blood of the covenant which the Lord has made with you in accordance with all these words of his" (cf Ex 24,3–8). The paschal feast was the yearly commemoration of this covenant of Sinai first entered into when Yahweh delivered his people from the bondage of Egypt.

Institution of A New Covenant

Unfortunately the chosen people had not kept the covenant: the rest of their history is a long tale of constant infidelity. While the prophets thundered threats of punishment against them for their faithlessness, they yet held out hope for the future with the announcement that God would give them a new covenant, one to which they would be faithful, and which would last forever. Jeremiah is the prophet of the new covenant: "The days are coming, says the Lord, when I will make a new covenant with the house of Israel and the house of Juda . . . I will place my law within them, and write it upon their hearts; I will be their God, and they shall be my people. . . . All, from least to greatest, shall know me, says the Lord, for I will forgive their evildoing and remember their sin no more" (Jer 31,31–34).

Jesus was mindful of all this when he announced at the Supper: "This is my blood of the new covenant" (Mk 14,24). He is instituting the new covenant foretold by the prophet, and extending it to the "many" for whom he offers his life. He accepts the traditional Jewish principle that a covenant must be sealed in blood. But for the sacrifices of the old law he substitutes a new one, the sacrifice of himself, and it is his own blood that ratifies the covenant. The author of the epistle to the Hebrews would comment later:

> If the blood of goats and bulls and the sprinkled ashes of a heifer sanctify the unclean unto the cleansing of the flesh, how much more will the blood of Christ, who through the Holy Spirit offered himself unblemished unto God, cleanse your conscience from dead works to serve the living God? (Heb 9,13–14).

Jesus Gives Himself as Food and Drink

In recalling the covenant of Sinai at the annual celebration of the Passover, the Jews did not content themselves with retelling the story. They went further than that and relived it. The family gathered together to eat the same meal of which their forefathers had partaken on their last night in Egypt: unleavened bread, bitter herbs, a lamb of which no bone was broken. The commentary during the supper explained the significance of the rite. But it was by actual participation in the meal that they associated themselves with the experience of their ancestors.

At the paschal supper which he augmented with a new rite, Jesus acted in a similar manner. He did not merely explain to the disciples that he was about to offer his life for them, that he was the suffering servant, that he was inaugurating a new covenant. He reinforced the instruction with a realistic action that would make them sharers in his sacrifice: he gave them the bread and wine that contained his redemptive death and instructed them to eat and drink it.

Human nature possesses no more intimate means of communication than through eating and drinking, by which food is assimilated into the very substance of the person. Jesus chose this means. The bread and wine were symbolic of his suffering and death, but his action goes far beyond this symbolism. He wished not only to offer his life for men, but to give it to them under the form of food and drink. They would become sharers in the gift of his life, of his own substance.

The Eucharist as a Memorial

Jesus did not merely perform this rite, rich in symbolism, at the Last Supper, he also instructed the disciples that they should repeat it after him. The Pauline tradition explicitly recalls his command, and the practice of the infant Church, which began to celebrate the Eucharist immediately after Pentecost, can only be explained by the will of Christ himself that the rite should be renewed. For the early Christians it constituted a memorial of the Lord: a solemn commemoration of his salvific activity and of his Person through the repetition of the sacred rite which actualized his sacrifice.

The Eucharist is a memorial. Primarily it commemorates the cross, the salvific act of Christ which is the greatest testimony of divine love. But it does not restrict its retrospective vision to the cross alone, extending it to the entire salvific activity of Jesus. This includes, first of all, the resurrection and ascension, which are not only exemplary causes of the redemption but participate in its efficient causality as well. It then includes all of the events of sacred history, both those which led up to the redemption and which God had designed to prepare for the work of Christ, and those which resulted from the redemption and extend the vision of the Christian forward to the final glorious consummation of the kingdom.

The principal expression of the Eucharist as a memorial occurs in the prayer called *anamnesis*, "the remembrance," which in the Roman liturgy begins with the words *Unde et memores* and follows immediately upon the consecration. Christ had commanded that the rite be repeated "in remembrance of me" (1 Cor 11,25; Lk 22,19): the liturgy fulfills this precept immediately after the repetition of his words of institution. The Roman *anamnesis* recalls by name the passion, resurrection and ascension, the principal mysteries of salvation; other liturgies also include other phases of sacred history.

The Church and Sacred History

It is of the nature of Christianity, which exists in an "in-between" time, to look both back upon the past and forward to the future. Unlike other religions, its horizons are not restricted to the world of nature. Christianity is essentially an historical religion, based upon the historical fact of the redemption. God has intervened in human affairs, and thus has left an ineffaceable mark upon human history.

The decisive element of Christianity is its historical character. The Church cannot abstract from its heritage, it cannot live without reference to its sacred history. The Christian is necessarily conscious of the position which he occupies with reference both to the past and to the future. His life is not merely a natural existence reinforced by certain supernatural aids. It is radically supernatural, because its source is the free decision of God to intervene in human affairs.

Nor does this historical character consist merely in the psychological consciousness of the Christian. The memorial is efficacious. In the Eucharist, which is the great sign of Christ's continuing presence and continuing salvific activity, sacred history is re-presented with a dynamic actuality which places the individual participant in a personal relationship with the Author of that history.

The Memorial in the Liturgy of the Word

The *anamnesis* occupies a privileged position in the Eucharistic liturgy because the Eucharist is essentially a sacramental remembrance. In this the Church is faithful to the wishes of the one who instituted the rite. At the Supper Jesus was conscious of fulfilling the Old Testament by assuming the role of the suffering servant and by replacing the Old Covenant with the new one which had been foretold by the prophets. The *anamnesis*, in extending the object of the memorial to the whole of sacred history, is simply developing a feature which was inherent in the Supper itself and was evolved by the earliest liturgies.

But the *anamnesis* is not the only feature of the Eucharistic liturgy which develops the theme of the memorial. There is an inseparable connection between the synaxis itself and the biblical readings which precede it in the liturgy of the Word. Like the Jews from whom they borrowed this usage, the Christians wished to recall the powerful works of God on their behalf which had marked all the stages of his successive interventions, as well as the religious teaching which accompanied them. Thus the Supper takes its place in the whole sweep of the history of salvation, coming as the climax of the preparatory stages which led up to the definitive act of Christ which is renewed in the Eucharist.

But the Scriptural readings do not merely recall the past; they find their realization here and now in the present, in the sacramental action itself. The historical work of salvation is made present to the mind and heart of the believer, who hears the Word of God proclaimed and receives it with faith. Thus is created an atmosphere of faith which is necessary for the reception of the mystery; faith leads the believer to participation in the Eucharistic action, which is a mystery of faith. There the work of salvation is made present not only psychologically, but sacramentally. The entire Eucharistic liturgy is a liturgy of the divine Word: first of the spoken word which appeals to faith, then of the Incarnate Word, truly present in the re-presentation of his redemptive sacrifice.

The Eucharist as Thanksgiving

The remembrance of the past which the Church makes in the Eucharistic liturgy is expressed in terms of thanksgiving for the wonderful works of God on our behalf in the course of sacred history. Here we come into contact with another essential element of the Eucharist: the thanksgiving service. It is this element which has given its name to the entire rite, for the Greek word *eucharistia* means thanksgiving. It gradually came to be adopted as a technical term to replace the earlier expression, "the breaking of bread."

The element of thanksgiving likewise goes back to Jesus's own action at the Last Supper. The synoptics and St. Paul agree that Jesus gave thanks before he distributed the bread and wine to the disciples. The early Christians were developing a concept inherent in his own intentions when they considered the Eucharist as a great act of thanksgiving for all of God's benefits. The bread and wine themselves, which symbolize God's creation, are the starting point for the thanksgiving. They introduce the participants into the thanksgiving theme, which from the elements of the sacrifice proceeds to all the benefits of creation and redemption. This is closely related to the memorial, for the recollection of God's past interventions gives rise to the sentiments of gratitude which are expressed in the thanksgiving.

The Thanksgiving in the Anaphora

After the biblical readings of the liturgy of the Word have stirred up the faith of the participants, the great Eucharistic prayer engages them in an expression of gratitude to God. The celebrant exhorts them to "lift up their hearts" and to "give thanks to the Lord our God." This constitutes the introduction to the great thanksgiving of the Mass which is contained in the anaphora, or consecratory prayer, principally in the part which precedes the words of consecration.

The theme of this prayer is thanksgiving for the entire work of creation and redemption. The anaphoras which have come down to us from ancient times and those which are still used in the eastern liturgies are very rich in content, tracing the entire history of salvation through its various phases. The mystery of the Blessed Trinity is evoked, then the progressive interventions of God in human history: the creation of man and his subsequent fall, the promise of redemption, the long preparation for the redeemer in the Old Testament, the realization in the historical work of Christ, his incarnation, life, death, resurrection and ascension, with reference to the second coming.

In the Roman liturgy, which is more sober, the thanksgiving theme is contained principally in the Preface, which really belongs to the anaphora, despite its apparent separation. Instead of including all the phases of sacred history in a single anaphora, it distributes them according to the feast or cycle of the liturgical year which is being celebrated. Thus in the course of the liturgical year all of the wonderful works of God successively appear as objects of our gratitude. While the number and variety of Prefaces is greatly reduced in the present liturgy from what it was in ancient times, nevertheless the thanksgiving theme is clearly present. It will probably be brought into clearer focus in the revision of the Roman missal which is now in progress.

The Eucharist as a Sacrifice

The thanksgiving expresses the gratitude of the Church in words, but this is not yet the whole of the rite. These same sentiments receive their further and more emphatic expression in the presentation of an offering. The Eucharist is not only a remembrance and a thanksgiving; it is furthermore, and even primarily, a sacrifice. Among these essential elements there is no contradiction; on the contrary, the sacrifice itself is the principal reason for both the memorial and the thanksgiving. The Eucharist is an *oblatio rationabilis*, a spiritual offering.

At the Last Supper Jesus offered himself in sacrifice and incorporated his sacrifice in the elements of bread and wine: as often as the rite would be repeated, the sacrifice would be renewed. From the earliest times the Christians regarded the Eucharist as a sacrifice, the renewal of Christ's offering of himself to the Father on behalf of mankind. If the concept of sacrifice has in recent centuries been overemphasized by the theological preoccupations of the period to the point of obscuring the other constitutive elements of the Eucharist, it is nonetheless essential. The priest who offers the Mass is acting in the person of Christ: it is his sacrifice which he renews. The liturgy insists upon this.

At the same time, however, the Eucharist is also our sacrifice, the sacrifice of the entire Church. This concept is also clearly expressed in the liturgy. The whole of the Christian life has a sacrificial character, for it is entirely a life of divine charity, in which the whole Church and each of her members perform a continual self-oblation to the Father. This sacrifice of the members of Christ finds its supreme realization in the sacrifice of the Mass, in which their offering of themselves is united to the sacrifice of Christ and thus presented to the Father.

The Offering of the Whole Church

The Mass, consequently, is both the sacrifice of Christ and the sacrifice of the Church. It is the offering of the whole Christ, both Head and members. It is the Head who has provided the matter of the sacrifice by offering himself upon the cross and continuing to renew his offering through the Eucharist; he places it, as it were, in the hands of the Church, who presents it to the Father with Him. Christ did not wish to offer his sacrifice alone; he wished to include in it all those who become incorporated in him through baptism. The new covenant, like the old, is ratified by all those to whom it is extended. They are the *plebs sancta,* the elect, the priestly race, able "to offer spiritual sacrifices acceptable to God through Jesus Christ" (1 Pt 2,5).

To the offering of Christ the faithful add their own offering, which is absorbed in the Eucharistic action and rendered worthy because of it. It is not a question simply of passively receiving the benefits of Christ's sacrifice, but of actively offering it, so that it becomes the expression of our own love for and obedience to the Father, modeled upon that of his Son. Sacrifice is meaningless unless it expresses the adoration of those who offer; and hence those who share in the sacrifice of Christ must likewise share in the sentiments with which he offered it. The liturgy expresses this in the prayers *Supra quae* and *Supplices te rogamus* immediately after the *anamnesis*, in which we beg God to accept our sacrifice as he did those of the patriarchs and to receive it into his divine presence. The request concerns not the offering of Christ, which is already definitively accepted, but that which we join to it, and which demands an interior attitude like that of Christ.

The sacrifice of the Church receives expression also in the rite of the offertory. The bread and wine are symbols of the offering of ourselves. This is not the offering of Christ's sacrifice, but it is a necessary introduction: we begin by making our own offering, the declaration of our love and obedience, which in the consecration will be transformed into the offering of Christ, to be thus presented to the Father. The offertory gifts are symbolic of the whole material creation: it is our whole lives and ourselves that we offer in union with Christ's sacrifice.

The Sacrament of Christ's Presence

Christ and all of his members are therefore united in the celebration of the Eucharist. Christ is present among them, for the Eucharist is the sacrament of his presence. It is, indeed, both a memorial of the past and a pledge of the future, but past and future come together in the enduring present of the Eucharist, for the great act of salvation which Christ accomplished once for all is extended into a present which already shares in the character of the eschatological times.

A new world has come into existence since the glorification of Christ. Through his resurrection and ascension he has entered into the new state of belonging totally to the Father. He alone pertains fully to this new world, for only he, by the power of his resurrection, has been completely freed from the old world of subservience to sin and death. We belong to it only insofar as we are incorporated into the risen and glorified Christ, who is "the first fruits of those who have fallen asleep" (1 Cor 15,20), the "house not made by human hands, eternal in the heavens" (2 Cor 5,2). Through contact with the risen Christ, we also enter into the glorious state in which he lives: "As in Adam all die, so in Christ all will be made to live. But each in his own turn, Christ as first fruits, then they who are Christ's, who have believed, at his coming" (1 Cor 15,22–23).

This incorporation into Christ will not be completed until the final day of our own resurrection, when we will be definitively snatched from the world of sin and death and ushered into the new world of conclusive belonging to the Father. But the eschatological times have already begun; our glorification is already in progress, for the last times are already incipiently realized. Our incorporation in Christ is already a reality. We contact the risen Lord through faith and through the sacraments: in the present life this contact attains its fullest realization in the Eucharist.

Christ's Presence Real and Physical

Christ wanted to remain present to his members. He promised never to abandon them: "Behold, I am with you all days, even unto the consummation of the world" (Mt 28,20). This could have been accomplished merely through the contact of faith in his Word and through the possession of his Spirit. But God is accustomed to take man as he is and to deal with him according to his nature. Man does not consist of soul alone, but of body as well, and it was the intention of Christ, in giving the symbol of bread and wine, to make himself, as it were, present to the senses.

The sacrament is symbolic of the presence of Christ, but it is a symbol which produces what it signifies. Christ is *really* present in the Eucharist, not only symbolically. The whole process of our salvation in Christ is a concrete and realistic thing. If we are to be re-created in Christ, then our bodies as well as our souls must be incorporated in him. He gives us his real body and blood, and gives them as food, so that the whole man, body and soul, may be united to his risen and glorified humanity and thus brought into the realm of his new and glorious life.

The glorified body of Christ is a "spiritual body," but nonetheless a real one. Consequently his presence is real, though it transcends the realm of flesh and blood. "My flesh is food indeed, and my blood is drink indeed. He who eats my flesh, and drinks my blood, abides in me and I in him" (Jn 6,56–57). How this can be is indeed a mystery: the Roman liturgy calls it *mysterium fidei.* A mystery of faith, precisely, because it addresses itself to the faith which the Holy Spirit stirs up in the hearts of those who believe. Without faith in Christ's Word man cannot penetrate beyond the species to the real presence within.

The Unity of Christ's Body

The real presence of Christ in the Eucharist, symbolized by and contained in the bread and wine, is itself symbolic of a further reality: the incorporation of all Christ's members into his Body. Christ contains within himself, as it were, the whole of humanity, of which he is the Head. The human race, united unto destruction under the headship of Adam, has been re-created unto the new life of grace under the headship of Christ, the new Adam. There is no salvation except in Christ. In order to enter into the new world of salvation, every man must be incorporated into Christ through faith and the sacraments. By putting us into physical contact with the Body of Christ, the Eucharist unites us to him, making us members of his Body, and to all the other members who belong to him.

"The bread that we break, is it not the partaking of the body of the Lord? Because the bread is one, we though many, are one body, all of us who partake of the one bread" (1 Cor 10,16–17).

The expression "Mystical Body of Christ" was applied first to the Eucharist and only later came to be used of the Church. The union of Christians in Christ, the society of the elect, is itself the result of the Eucharist, for it is only by continued participation in the one body which he has given us in this sacrament that we become more and more closely united to the Body of the Church. Sharing in the Eucharist is an encounter not only with Christ the Head, but with all the members of his Body. The building up of the Church is, therefore, a direct effect of the Eucharist. The Eucharist is pre-eminently the sacrament of charity.

Significance of Communion

This means that an essential feature of the Eucharist is the communion. The meaning of the term communion is not restricted to the modern understanding of reception of the Eucharist by an individual: communion is not the private business of the one who receives. The term, a Latin version of the Greek *koinonia*, means *union with;* however, this does not signify merely the encounter of an individual with Christ, but *union among* many brethren. One does not enter into communion with Christ alone, but with the whole community of the redeemed, the *plebs sancta.*

Sharing in the same gift is the outward symbol of the union of charity among all God's people. The *communio sanctorum* which is a participation in sacred things is the symbol and the cause of the *communio sanctorum* which is unity among the saints. All those who are united by bonds of charity in the body of Christ are invited to demonstrate their unity by their sharing in the banquet which is the completion of his sacrifice.

Because it is essentially a *communio,* the Eucharist must be a common meal, in which all the participants come together to enjoy a common share in the fruits of Christ's sacrifice. It is through sharing in the same gifts that we receive the grace to live together in mutual charity. The Roman liturgy sums up the whole point of the communion in the remarkable postcommunion prayer of the Friday after Ash Wednesday: "Pour forth in us, O Lord, the Spirit of your love: so as to make us one in charity, after having filled us with the one heavenly bread."

Eucharist and Eschatology

The Eucharist extends Christ's salvific action into the present to draw men into his Mystical Body, but it also opens their horizons to the future. St. Paul said of the Eucharist: "As often as you shall eat this bread and drink the cup, you proclaim the death of the Lord, until he comes" (1 Cor 11,26). This is an indication of the eschatological significance of the Eucharist: it is the pledge of future glory. The sacrament testifies that the reality of salvation, now conferred in an incipient manner, will one day be consummated in glory.

Possession and expectation, these are the two poles about which the Eucharist revolves. It is the banquet in which the whole Church shares in the goods won for us by Christ's victory, but it is not yet the definitive banquet: it points ahead to the final Messianic banquet when the risen Savior will appear again upon the clouds of heaven. It sums up the whole past in the memorial, the thanksgiving and the sacrifice, and offers reconciliation with God and their fellow men to all those who share a common faith and common sacraments. But, at the same time, it directs the gaze of the whole city of the redeemed to the future glory of the kingdom, when all things shall be subject to the Son, and he with his whole kingdom subject to the Father, that God may be all in all (cf 1 Cor 15,28).

Thus the Eucharist is the node of sacred history, the center of the whole life of the Church and of the individual Christian. Everything in the Church is centered upon the Eucharist, not only the entire liturgy, including the other sacraments, but the Church's activity of government and apostolate as well. Man cannot be sanctified nor render worship to God unless he is in contact with the salvific activity of the glorious Christ. The Eucharist is, in the whole period from Pentecost to the parousia, the place of encounter with Christ, the whole Christ, Head and members, and the springboard to the consummation of the new life in Christ in the kingdom that is still to come.

5. THE EUCHARIST AND THE MONK

Centrality of the Eucharist

The preceding section has attempted to point out the place which the Eucharist occupies in the life of the Church and consequently in the spirituality of the individual Christian. Its position at the very center of the Church's life and activity is of such importance that no form of orthodox spirituality can prescind from the Eucharist. We have seen previously that ancient monastic teaching and practice likewise held the Eucharist in high regard, though their emphasis upon the role played by the sacrament in the development of the monk's spirituality was generally implicit rather than explicitly formulated.

The Eucharist must be central in the monk's spiritual life, as it is central in the life of every authentic Christian. A monk cannot claim any special kind of relationship to the sacrament of our Lord's body and blood: the Eucharist is important for him because he is a Christian, not because he is specifically a monk. The reason for devoting a section of this book to the Eucharist is not that monastic spirituality has any kind of monopoly upon it, but simply that no orthodox spirituality is complete without according it a central position.

The centrality of the Eucharist must be for the monk not merely an objective reality but also an actual condition of his subjective attitude. He must penetrate thoroughly into its meaning *for him*, and accord to it in the development of his own spirituality the place which it occupies by right in the objective order of redemption. Accordingly it will not be superfluous to point out, in the present section, how the themes of the Eucharist join the themes of monastic spirituality in an encounter of mutual harmony.

The Monk and the Memorial

We have seen that the monk's spirituality is nourished by an intimate contact with the Bible and the liturgy. The themes which dominate it, conversion, penance, compunction, humility, are attitudes assumed by a man who has reflected upon the meaning of God's interventions in human history. The virtues which the monk practices are those which these attitudes command, and the activities in which he engages, prayer, work and *lectio divina,* are designed to bring to full realization his basic relationship to the God of history. The monk stands in the stream of sacred history, looking backwards upon the *mirabilia Dei* of which his vocation is the continuance, and forward to the consummation in glory of what he now possesses only in the form of first fruits.

In view of this, the themes of memorial and thanksgiving in the Eucharistic celebration strike a sympathetic chord in his spirituality. The Eucharistic liturgy recalls all of God's wonderful works on behalf of his people, culminating in the salvific activity of Christ's passion, death, resurrection and ascension, and offers thanks to God for all the phases of sacred history. The monk, whose psychological perception has been attuned to the historical character of Christianity by long reflection, can join wholeheartedly in the memorial and the thanksgiving of the Eucharist and through it unite his own sentiments to those of the whole Church.

In this connection, the readings of the liturgy of the Word play the same role for the monk as the *lectio divina* and the readings of the divine office. They are a meditation upon the themes of sacred history, the various salvific acts of God which foreshadowed and, in the complex development of the historical process, prepared for the ultimate deliverance effected upon Calvary. But the readings of the liturgy of the Word give way to the Eucharistic anaphora, in which the entire Church solemnly recalls and gives thanks for all these events, and this in turn leads into the ritual memorial in which the act of salvation is renewed upon the altar. Here then, the memorial is not merely psychological, but real and objective, and in it the monk realizes and lives to the fullest degree his participation in the drama of sacred history.

The Monk and the Offertory

In a similar way, the rite of the offertory will strike a note of sympathy in the heart of the monk. In the offertory, we have said, the Church offers herself to God. It is not yet the oblation of Christ's sacrifice, but the addition to it of the personal sacrifice of the participants. Taking the elements of bread and wine as their point of departure, they offer the entire material creation to God, from whom it has come, including their own sentiments of love and obedience. It is a question of Christ's members adopting the same attitude of humble submission to God's will which the Lord himself demonstrated in the hour of his passion.

The monk should be able to feel the significance of the offertory rite with even greater intensity than his fellow Christians. Like them, he will express his gratitude to God for all the gifts of his creation and will be inspired to offer them in return to God as an expression of his love. Like them, he will approach the sacrifice with sentiments of loving submission to the Creator and the desire to unite his own offering to that of Christ. But the monk's offering of himself should be more radical, more total, than that of the Christian in the world. He has already renounced the values of this world in an effort to give himself unreservedly to God. The offertory of every Mass should be for the monk an intense rededication of himself to his vocation, a renewal of the monastic profession which he has made once for all but must repeat and intensify every day.

The offertory should be on the part of the monk an effort to fulfill St. Paul's admonition: "Have this mind in you which was also in Christ Jesus" (Phil 2,5). He must attempt to reproduce in himself the sentiments of complete abandonment of self to God which animated Christ throughout his life, but particularly at the moment of his impending suffering. The whole life of the monk, according to the ancient monastic theorists, is nothing more than an imitation of Jesus. The offertory is the ritual expression of this basic exigency of his spirituality.

The Ultimate End of the Eucharist

The offering of oneself, however, is not yet the ultimate reality of the Eucharist. Its final purpose consists in its effect upon the Mystical Body: the unity of charity among the members of Christ. This is the last of three stages which theologians distinguish in the Eucharistic action. The first of these is the *sign:* the ritual celebration, including all the words and gestures which go to make up the rite and the bread and wine which are the material of the sacrifice. This sign symbolizes and effects a reality, the second stage in the Eucharistic action, which is the real presence of Christ and the re-presentation of his sacrifice on Calvary. This is called the *symbolic reality* because, while it is a reality in reference to the sign, it is itself symbolic of a further reality.

This further reality, which we encounter in the third phase of the action, is called the *ultimate reality*. It is the final purpose of the sacrament, the effect which it is intended to produce among the faithful. It consists in the unity of the Mystical Body, the sanctification of all of Christ's members through their union of charity with their Head and among themselves. The Eucharist was not instituted merely to re-present the sacrifice of Christ and to insure his continuing presence among us. The liturgy is not its own end; its ultimate purpose is not attained unless there is an effect of sanctification upon those who celebrate it and upon the entire Church.

This purpose, however, is not achieved automatically. The third phase of the action, the production of the ultimate reality, will take place only if no obstacle is placed by the recipients. The unity of the

Mystical Body is not automatically effected merely by celebrating Mass. The sacraments are not machines. The sanctification of the recipients will not follow without their cooperation.

Incorporation into the Body of Christ

When the ultimate reality of the Eucharist is attained, the Body of Christ is built up. By the positive will of God the mystery of redemption which is made present in the Eucharist has a communal character: the law of salvation in common is basic to the entire divine economy. Like the economy of the Old Testament, the redemptive economy of the New Testament is a covenant between God and his people, not primarily a relationship with individuals. No one can be saved except by belonging to the *plebs sancta*, the holy community of the redeemed, which is the one Body of Christ.

St. Paul develops the theme of the Body of Christ with remarkable realism. It is not a mere metaphor intended to explain symbolically the collectivity of the faithful gathered into an organization. The Christ of St. Paul is not a mystical Person, but the real Christ who became incarnate, rose from the dead, and has now been glorified at the right hand of the Father. The Body of Christ, which we call the Mystical Body, is not a supra-personal collectivity, but is the real Person of the glorified Christ. This concept of Christ corresponds to what is known in Hebrew thought patterns as a corporate personality: a person who sums up and contains in himself the whole multitude of those who are united to him. This is the foundation for the vicarious efficacy of his salvific acts.

There is no salvation outside of the real Body of the risen and glorified Christ. The Christian must surrender himself, body and soul, to the risen Savior to become one body with him. He must become identified with the Person of Christ by an incorporation into his Body, an existential contact with him who has become a "life-giving Spirit" (1 Cor 15,45). The new life of the real Body of Christ then courses through the members who have been grafted on to him. They are united to one another because they are joined to him in a realistic union. It is the dynamic presence of Christ himself which constitutes the bond of unity among Christians.

The Sacrament of Fraternal Charity

In the Eucharist this real, glorified Body of Christ is truly and dynamically present, and is assimilated as food by the participants. The contact with Christ is real and physical. Thus the Body of Christ grows and develops through the Eucharist, for it is in this sacrament that the bodies of his members are grafted on to his Body to share in his risen life, in a union of charity not yet visible except to the eyes of faith, but nevertheless real and meaningful.

The Eucharist is essentially the sacrament of our unity in Christ and hence of fraternal charity. The rites which accompany it stress this point again and again. Even the types of the Eucharist, such as the paschal meal, the manna in the desert and the multiplication of the loaves, emphasize the aspect of common unity in a ritual act. At the institution of the sacrament Christ washed the feet of the disciples to teach them a lesson in fraternal love before proceeding to the supper. The banquet itself, in which the bread is broken and distributed and the common cup shared by all present, is symbolic of the unity of the participants. The composition of the bread and wine indicates that many have become one. The discourse after the supper is a catechesis on charity. The assembly of the faithful, the common voice and gesture with which they worship, the form of the prayers and ritual acts, are all designed to give expression to the union of Christ's members in charity.

All of these, however, are only indications. They belong to the sign, which does not directly symbolize the unity of the Mystical Body. The real symbol of this unity is the one Body of Christ really present, the symbolic reality. It is "because the bread is one" that "we, though many, are one body, all of us who partake of the one bread" (1 Cor 10,17). The one Body is Christ's risen and glorified Person: by partaking of it we are assimilated into him, without losing our own identity. This union of charity reaches its climax at the moment of communion, which is not so much a question of Christ's coming to us as of our being incorporated into him. It was of this that St. Augustine was thinking when he exclaimed, "Oh sign of unity, Oh bond of charity!" (*Tract in Joh* 26,13).

Eucharist and Monastic Unity

It is evident that the Eucharist, considered as the sacrament of our unity in Christ, possesses a vital significance for the monk, especially for the cenobite. In his whole existence he is surrounded by those who are his brothers in Christ. The community is the vital organism about which the whole of monastic life revolves: the *cenobium* is a segment of the Mystical Body of Christ, an image in miniature and a model of the union of many brethren drawn into one by fraternal charity.

It is in the celebration of the Eucharist that this unity achieves its maximum reality. Christ really present in his Body draws the monks into union with himself and with one another. Here the community becomes a real community in fact through the sharing of a supernatural reality. It is no longer merely an organization of individual monks under one head, who holds the place of Christ: it is the real incorporation of all the members of the group into the real Head of the community, who becomes all in all in each one and welds them into the union of charity.

The conventual Mass is the maximum actualization of the unity of the monastic community. The whole monastic body, from the abbot down to the most recently arrived postulant, comes to the altar to worship together and to be sanctified together. The whole of the monastic observance and the ascetical striving of the individual monk reaches its climax in the Eucharist, the dynamic encounter with the risen Christ. It is the supreme moment of the monk's conversion, the fulfillment of his penance, the response to his prayer. With his brethren he is assumed into Christ and anticipates the union of heaven to which his whole monastic life has tended.

Celebration of Conventual Mass

The conventual Mass is the supreme act of worship in the monastic day because it draws the entire community together in the unity of Christ's Body. The monk should therefore esteem the conventual Mass as the most important function of each day in his life. If it is to achieve its purpose of strengthening his love for Christ and his brethren, he must assist in the common sacrifice in a spirit of faith and devotion, with his heart open to the gift of divine love.

The ritual form of celebration adopted for the conventual Mass should correspond to its function in the spiritual growth of the community. All of the monks should participate to the maximum degree in the words, song and gesture of the rite, and approach the Eucharistic banquet as a symbol of their union in charity. A monk who needlessly absents himself from the common celebration of the Eucharist, or who participates only halfheartedly or even uses this time to catch up on his breviary, is withholding his contribution from the common effort of the community to grow up in Christ. Whatever other contributions he may make to the community's welfare, they will be of little value unless informed by the supernatural faith and charity which are proclaimed in the common celebration.

For the monk who is also a priest, there has been for a long time a certain tension between the conventual Mass and the celebration of individual Masses. The priest has been obliged to adopt a form of celebration in which the communal element is reduced to the barest minimum; and at the same time his participation in the conventual Mass has been limited because he could not take part in the common banquet. Psychologically this situation has involved a choice between the exercise of his priesthood and full participation in the common worship of his brethren. This dilemma has now been resolved by the extension of the faculty of concelebration to the daily conventual Mass of religious communities. In those communities which have adopted the practice of daily concelebration, it has again become possible to manifest the unity of the entire monastic body in its supreme liturgical action.

Commitment to Christ in Faith

Ritual participation alone, however, would be meaningless without a profound and fervent faith. We cannot afford to neglect the importance of the personal engagement which is required of every believer participating in the Eucharist. The sacraments are protestations of faith on the part of the recipients. The sole purpose of the sign is to lead on to the reality which it signifies and which it will produce if the subject offers his cooperation. This reality cannot be perceived except by faith: participation is a solemn and public declaration of faith in the reality which the sign signifies. Without faith the ultimate reality of the sacrament cannot be attained.

Faith in the biblical understanding of the term is not merely an intellectual conviction. A living faith, vivified by the ardor of charity, involves the commitment of the entire person. It is an active attitude of the soul, irrevocably pledging itself to Christ. The reception of a sacrament is a solemn and public declaration of this attitude, a consecration of one's whole being to Christ. The sacraments appeal to our faith and our generosity.

The Eucharist is the greatest of the sacraments, because it gives not only the dynamic power of Christ, but his very Person. St. Thomas calls the Eucharist "the consummation of the spiritual life, and the end of all the sacraments" (S.T. 3,73,3 c), and insists that it is necessary for salvation, at least *in voto*, from the viewpoint of the ultimate reality. Consequently the commitment which the Eucharist demands is a summing up of the whole Christian life. The mystery of Christianity is a mystery of love; and the criterion of whether or not we belong to Christ is whether or not we are united to him in mutual love. The Eucharist brings about this union.

The "Amen" which the faithful proclaim at the end of the canon means that they agree to what is being done in their presence. They agree to give themselves to Christ, to commit themselves to a life of charity. All of the moral obligations of the Christian life result from this engagement of charity. Active participation in the Eucharistic liturgy, which is meant to be a symbol of the interior union of charity, is meaningless unless it is the expression of a truly common love in Christ. Faith and self-surrender are required at every step of the Eucharistic action.

Living the Mass: Living in Charity

The celebration of the conventual Mass by the monastic community must be, therefore, an exercise of charity. No matter how perfect the external performance of the liturgy may be, the reality of the Eucharist will not be attained unless the monks really live the Mass. To live the Mass means to live in charity. The conventual Mass is the daily rededication of the whole community to Christ. Through the Eucharist the monks become more deeply grafted into Christ's Body, and obligate themselves to live the life of Christ, which is a life of mutual charity.

The conventual Mass is the center of the monastic day because it activates that charity which is the soul of conventual life. All of the other activities of the day are directed to it as to their end: the monk's work, his prayer, his reading, all find their ultimate fulfillment in the union of his sacrifice with that of Christ. The hours of the divine office are the setting which surrounds the jewel of the Mass. The monk's progress in perfection is the working out in practice of the reality of the Eucharist.

Participation in the Eucharistic liturgy, then, is far more than fidelity to rubrical observances. The perfection of the ceremonies and the chant is important, for it is the symbol of interior unity. But it is only a symbol: faith and generosity are required to lead from symbol to reality. The monk who celebrates, ministers or assists at Mass must give himself entirely to the details of the ritual observance, but he must do so in an interior spirit of self-surrender. He will not be drawn into the unity of the Body of Christ unless he wants to be.

Prayer Before and After Communion

Wholehearted participation in the Eucharist demands an adequate preparation. Rather than the recitation of any particular formulae, although those which have been sanctioned by long usage in the Church may prove helpful, the monk's preparation should consist in the deepening of his prayer life to dispose him for the gift of Christ's love. If he makes an effort to pray the hours of the divine office with attention and devotion, he will be properly disposed for the conventual Mass, for which the office provides the setting. This public liturgical prayer should overflow into private prayer in which the soul of the monk will become attuned to the voice of the Spirit within and readied for the outpouring of charity which is the ultimate reality of the Eucharist. The liturgical texts for each day's Mass can be especially helpful in stimulating prayer and deepening one's understanding of and appreciation for the Eucharist.

After Mass and communion a reasonable length of time should be devoted to thanksgiving. The direct encounter with Christ at the banquet table of the Eucharist should stimulate sentiments of love and gratitude which the monk will long to pour out in silent dialogue afterward. These are precious moments: one could scarcely conceive of a more powerful stimulus to prayer than this personal confrontation with the risen Christ. The monk will want to express his gratitude in his own words, or perhaps without words, simply by an outpouring of the love which floods his heart. The missal contains many excellent prayers of thanksgiving which may be of use, depending upon one's need to stimulate his own prayer. But the most valuable prayer of thanksgiving will be the one that comes from the heart and issues in a growth in charity which extends to every area of one's being. Such prayer is the bridge which unites participation in the Eucharist to living out its implications in one's daily life.

The Eucharist and Total Conversion

Living the Mass, indeed, is a question of allowing it to penetrate into one's entire life. If the Eucharist is the consummation of the spiritual life, then its power must inform every aspect of the monk's life and bring about in him a total conversion. Every action of the day must either be directed toward the Eucharist as a preparation or else flow from it as a result. The Eucharist is the sacrament of charity, and the intensity of the monk's participation in it will be measured by the increase of charity in his life.

The Eucharist looks toward the past, the present and the future. As the office of Corpus Christi expresses it: "The remembrance of his passion is brought to mind, the soul is filled with grace, and a pledge of future glory is given to us." The monk cannot fail to experience a connaturality with this pregnant sense of history. His entire life is in a sense turned toward the past, for he feels a vivid continuity with the whole of sacred history, which has come to realization in the present of his own life. But he is even more turned toward the future, for his vocation is of its nature eschatological: he is a living witness to the reality of the Church's life in God, which will be fully realized only in the kingdom yet to come. But in the Eucharist the eschatological reality is already present as first fruits: it is the Messianic banquet of the last times and a pledge of the consummation in glory, when God will be all in all.

PART TWO

The Elements of Monastic Spirituality

4 The Entrance to Monastic Life

A MAN'S DECISION to embrace the monastic life demands a shift in his values and a change in the direction of his life. He turns his back upon his former way of life and sets his face toward something new. The bridge which leads into the new way of life is his monastic profession. When he crosses this bridge, the monk experiences a process which is one of the constant themes of the Bible and the liturgy: the process of conversion, which is at the very root of the monastic vocation. From the moment of his profession, the monk's life becomes a continual process of turning away from sin and turning toward God.

St. Benedict expresses this in terms of obedience to God. The monk is one who has strayed from God through the "sloth of disobedience." It is, then, only by the "labor of obedience" that he can return to him. He is encouraged to "take up the strong and glorious weapons of obedience to fight for the true King, Christ" (Pr 2–3). The vocation of every Christian demands such a conversion: no one can be a follower of Christ unless he wills to turn from a life of sin to a life of love and service of God. The monk strives to realize this aspect of the Christian vocation in the most radical and absolute manner. His entire life, even in the external form which it assumes, will be a testimony to man's need for conversion. In this chapter we wish to see what is involved in the process of entering upon a new life by crossing the bridge of monastic profession.

1. THE BIBLICAL DOCTRINE OF CONVERSION

Consciousness of Need for Penance

The entire Old Testament is the story of God's repeated attempts to convert his people to himself. At the very beginning, when man had sinned in the garden of paradise, God called to him to return, but Adam fled and hid his face from him. The choice of the patriarchs was a further stage in God's effort to summon mankind back to him. Again in the covenant he offered his people the opportunity to return. But the covenant often went unheeded, despite the frequent admonitions which God addressed to his people through the prophets.

Nevertheless there was always in Israel a consciousness of the need for penance and conversion. From the earliest times both public and private rites of penance were performed to turn aside the wrath of God. Fasting was the principal element in such rites, together with the wearing of sackcloth and ashes, and other penitential practices. There are references in the Old Testament to public liturgies of penance which were performed on the occasion of national calamities, to confess the sin of the people and ask God's pardon and deliverance. In later times the anniversaries of such calamities were observed as days of penance.

Often the prophets severely criticized such penitential practices, but not because they objected to them in principle. What they condemned was rather the attitude of the people in performing them. Without being sincerely repentant, they presumptuously believed that they could placate God merely by performing outward ceremonies. Without the interior conversion of the heart, such rites became a kind of magical ceremony, little better than the pagan rites of their Chanaanite neighbors. The prophets unceasingly demanded inner sincerity.

Theology of the Prophets

It is, accordingly, in the writings of the great prophets of the eighth and seventh centuries that we find an Old Testament theology of sin and repentance. Sin is an infidelity to God, a turning away from him. Its gravity is measured not only by the shocking character of the object which Israel has preferred to God, but also by the benefits which his people had received from him. It is an ingratitude, for Israel was chosen from all other nations to enter into a special covenant relationship with God and received innumerable favors from him. It is a disobedience to God, a refusal to heed the requirements of the covenant. The entire relationship between God and his people is subverted by sin.

Man is incapable of rescuing himself from the abysmal depths into which sin has lowered him. The sinner has walked in the wrong direction, has turned away from God, and he is unable of himself to reverse his direction and return to the right path. The more he sins, the more he closes himself to the true knowledge of God. He becomes hardened and does not even realize the gravity of his condition. Once he has voluntarily rejected and abandoned God, there is nothing he can do to right the wrong.

The Old Testament concept of sin, therefore, does not depend upon natural morality, but upon the personal relationship of Israel to God. It is an offense against God, in the sense that it deprives him of his people whom he has gratuitously loved and chosen for himself. It is a violation of the covenant through which he has united himself to Israel in an enduring bond of love which the prophets compare to the marriage union. It is an evil for man himself, since it deprives him of his most precious possession, the friendship of God, and reduces him to a state from which he is impotent to deliver himself.

Conversion as a Grace

Conversion, then, is not the ideal of any purely natural goodness, but a return to a personal and loving God. It is a restoration of that correct relationship between God and his people which had been destroyed by sin. The sinner begins once more to follow God with his whole heart, to take him and the covenant relationship seriously, to walk again in the right direction. It is a return to obedience to God according to the terms of the covenant. The sinner must abandon all the purely human devices in which he had placed his confidence and rely upon God alone. He must undergo a change of heart.

But sin has so corrupted him that he is unable of himself to work this change. Unless God intervenes to turn him back, he becomes more and more hardened in his sin. Only God can make him aware of the tragic character of his own state. He, in his loving mercy, reveals to the sinner the state in which he has placed himself and the magnitude of his offense against infinite goodness. Through this revelation God makes it possible for him to admit his guilt, to acknowledge that he has departed from God. The very admission of guilt restores the sinner to an attitude of humility and dependence upon God, and opens him to the reception of his gifts. It is itself a return to the conditions of the covenant relation.

This means that conversion is a grace. Man himself can do nothing to accomplish it; God must take the initiative. Unless he makes the sinner aware of his offense and of his need, he will be powerless to save himself from it. But God in his mercy ceaselessly summons his people to conversion. They have only to accept this grace with humility and open themselves to his salvific love. Only God can change the heart.

The Message of John the Baptist

Despite the discouragement of Israel's continued infidelity and refusal to repent even in the face of catastrophe, the prophets looked forward to a time when God would intervene decisively to work the conversion of his people. Jeremiah foretold a new covenant, when God would give his people a new heart, no longer of stone, but of flesh, so that they would know and love their God, and turn to him in repentance and faith. No longer would they seek the old idols, but respond generously to his grace, and accept conversion to him with a sincere heart.

The repeated failures through the subsequent centuries of Israel's history left this magnificent prophecy unfulfilled until the day when John the Baptist appeared in the desert of Judea preaching repentance and announcing that the time of fulfillment had arrived. Conversion was the basic theme of his preaching. The kingdom foretold by the prophets was at hand and judgment would not be long delayed. In the face of the imminent breakthrough of the kingdom only one attitude was possible for man: conversion. What was demanded was a radical break with the sins of the past and a sincere turning to God, who was about to give himself to man in a manner hitherto unsuspected.

The message of John was in the line of that of the prophets, but it had an urgency and a categorical imperative that was new, for it was spoken on the very threshold of the eschatological time. There was no longer any choice but to be converted or to perish in the coming judgment; only an interior change of heart would suffice, with all the necessary ramifications in one's moral life. John's baptism was the symbol of this radical conversion, through which God would create for himself a community of men to accept the kingdom. Conversion was both a grace of God and an obligation for man.

Call of Jesus to Conversion

The call to conversion is the great imperative of Jesus's preaching also. His first recorded words in Mark's account are: "The time is fulfilled, and the kingdom of God is at hand. Repent and believe in the Gospel" (Mk 1,15). With Jesus it is not merely the announcement of an impending reality, as with John; the kingdom is really here, in his very person. The purpose of his coming is to issue the summons to repentance: "It is not the healthy who need a physician, but they who are sick. I have not come to call the just, but sinners to repentance" (Lk 5,31–32). His miracles are likewise a summons to conversion.

Jesus offers men the grace of conversion which was foretold by the prophets. His entire preaching is an invitation to them to accept it. It is a final offer, for the course of sacred history is entering its last phase. If they wish to be saved, they must respond with an absolute and radical conversion, which will involve the whole man. The Holy Spirit, who is Jesus's gift, will confer upon them the new heart of flesh promised by Jeremiah. Christ does not only call upon man to repent, he also gives him the ability to do so. The Holy Spirit will make of him a new creature, no longer attached to sin and wandering from the path of salvation, but making a total gift of himself to God. This kind of conversion is not merely a moral reform, an avoidance of evil: it is the encounter with Christ himself, and the acceptance in the heart of his life-giving Word. The positive aspect of conversion is faith.

Requirements for Conversion

Conversion is not, therefore, a thing which can be accomplished by human effort. One must become another man, and only God can work this profound change in the human heart. Jesus came into conflict with the Pharisees because in their pride they refused to accept the uncompromising requirements for entry into his kingdom. Christ did not despise the Pharisees because they kept the law, nor did he cherish sinners because they did not. The Pharisees were rejected because they relied upon their own efforts at observance, the sinners welcomed because they acknowledged their own impotence and relied upon God.

The condition for receiving the grace of conversion, then, is simply the willingness to accept it. This means abandoning all human supports, not only evil, but anything that can prevent the total surrender of self to God: riches, human traditions, self-satisfaction. One must become like a child, who is without guile and depends entirely upon another. One must be open, recognizing his need for help and being ready and grateful to accept it from God, who can do for man what man cannot do for himself. Man cannot repent until he has acknowledged that he is a sinner.

Humility and faith, therefore, are the basic attitudes required of the man who would be converted and enter into the kingdom. Faith is not only belief in the teaching of Jesus, it is the total gift of self to him, bringing into play the entire man with all his faculties. Where Jesus finds these attitudes, he exercises his mission as Savior: the healing which he works upon sick bodies is symbolic of what he does for the inner man. He forgives the sins of the past; he will send his Holy Spirit as the principle of a new life in God. The baptism of Jesus, which admits the sincere convert into his kingdom, is not merely a symbol of repentance like that of John; it actually brings about his conversion and infuses the new life of the Spirit. The baptism of John was in water alone; but that of Jesus is in the fire which purges and purifies and in the Spirit who creates the new man.

Conversion as an Enduring Process

Given the weakness of human nature, however, man can be unfaithful to his original conversion and fall back again into the evil which he had renounced. Consequently, conversion is not merely an event that takes place once and for all, but must be an abiding attitude of the heart and a dynamic challenge affecting the daily life of the believer. He must continue to live by faith in the newness of life which the Spirit stirs up in his heart. The theologians of the New Testament, St. Paul and St. John, treat of conversion in the context of the new life of faith which the convert pursues under the guidance of the Holy Spirit.

This means that one must continue to follow Jesus along a path that utterly transcends human ways of thinking and acting. The

Christian must take up his cross if he is to bear witness to the Gospel and to the salvation which Christ has offered him. It is the Gospel of St. Matthew which seeks to develop the enduring obligation of the commitment to Christ which the believer has once made. He must produce the fruits which conversion demands by the daily practice of that new justice which is the perfection of the justice of the old law. Having once become a child in the spiritual sense, he must remain such, continually open to the gifts of the Spirit, totally dependent upon God's grace, conscious of his own failures and of his inability to accomplish anything by himself.

It is in this context that our Lord inserted his institution of the sacrament of penance. His own power to forgive sin, to stir up repentance in the heart and to turn men back to God is confided to the authorized ministers of his Church. The Christian is conscious of his continuing need for repentance in view of his repeated infidelities to grace. The gifts of repentance and forgiveness which Christ brought as the basic requirement of entry into his kingdom and of perseverance therein are extended into space and time in the continuation of his Incarnation which is the Church. Through the sacrament of penance Christ continues to hold out his offer of conversion to all men and to confer upon them the very ability to repent. The exigencies of conversion are ever the same for those who are his members.

2. CONVERSION IN THE CHURCH

Preaching of the Apostles

Christ commanded his disciples to go forth and preach the Gospel to every nation and thus bring to realization the universality which is essential to his message. The invitation to conversion had to break through the bonds of Jewish particularism and be addressed to all men. As soon as they had received the Holy Spirit on Pentecost, the apostles addressed themselves to this task.

The call to penance is dominant in their preaching. To the question of the crowd on Pentecost, "What shall we do?", Peter answered, "Repent and be baptized every one of you in the name of Jesus Christ for the forgiveness of your sins; and you will receive the gift of the Holy Spirit. For to you is the promise and to your children and to all who are far off, even to all whom the Lord our God calls to himself. . . . Save yourselves from this perverse generation" (Acts 2,38–40).

Here we see all the essentials of the New Testament doctrine of conversion. It is God who takes the initiative: he calls to man, inviting him. Man needs only to show good will, unlike those Jews who hardened their hearts and refused to accept the invitation of Jesus. In the new covenant conversion is linked with baptism, the sacramental means of repentance which Christ has provided. Through it one receives the Holy Spirit, who effectively brings about the conversion in the heart and reorients the sinner toward a new life in God. The invitation is extended to all, to the Gentiles who are far off as well as to the Jews who are near. And it is given with a sense of urgency, for the eschatological times have arrived, and those who are overtaken unawares will be swallowed up in the judgment.

Penitential Character Essential to the Church

The apostolic Church was therefore oriented toward conversion. The same themes appear again and again in the preaching of the apostles recorded for us in Acts. The great effort of the disciples was directed toward the conversion of all men in the sense which Christ had clarified during his public ministry. Without conversion no one could be united to the group of believers which constituted the early Church. The Church was that body of converts who had responded generously to the summons which God had issued through his Son and continued to issue now through the ministers appointed to bear witness to him.

This means that the Church is essentially a penitential institution. It is the Body of Christ, formed of those members who, in obedience to his call, disavow their previous life of sin. Cleansed of their sins in the saving waters of baptism, they give themselves entirely to God in the new life of faith stirred up in their hearts by the Holy Spirit. Confident that they shall be saved through faith in Christ, they look forward with hope to the end-time when his kingdom shall be consummated in glory.

Meanwhile, however, they live in the intervening period when one must walk by faith and not by vision, when the full glory of the kingdom has not yet been achieved in them. Hence they still experience the misery of the human condition, and are still subject to relapse into sin. So the Church must also be an institution of continuing penance, ever conscious of man's needs and of his total dependence upon God, of his obligation to purify himself and continually to renew his commitment to Christ. Hence the theme of penance recurs constantly in the rhythm of the Church's life: in the Eucharistic liturgy, in the recurring cycles of the liturgical year, in the sacrament of penance and in the sacramentals.

The Mystery of Man Relived

The liturgy is the life of the Church. Through it she relives the whole of sacred history. That history is the story of man's fall from grace, of his miserable state of servitude to sin, of the slow and painful process of his redemption. It is not only the mystery of Christ which the Church relives in the liturgy, but the mystery of man as well. She sees him as a sinful creature, sunk in the depths of the misery which he has brought upon himself, but rescued from it by God to the extent that he is willing to allow himself to be freed from his state of evil by responding to the summons of God.

First of all, then, in her liturgy the Church is supremely conscious of sin. At the beginning of every Mass the faithful beg God's pardon in the *Kyrie eleison.* In the preparatory prayers the priest confesses his sins and asks to be made worthy to approach the sacred mysteries. The *Confiteor* occurs again in the divine office, in the distribution of Holy Communion outside of Mass and in other rites.

In this respect the liturgy is extremely realistic. In the authentic liturgical tradition there is no morbid emphasis upon evil, but there is a consciousness of man's condition as creature, and as sinful creature, which the worshiper is never allowed to forget. The liturgy accepts this fact and continually calls our attention to the needs of sinful humanity. It recognizes sin for what it is, man's ungrateful rejection of God, and continually evokes the stages of sacred history through which God vainly attempted to recall his people to the path of salvation.

The Struggle against Satan

It is primarily the communal aspect which the liturgy emphasizes in sketching a picture of sin. It is all men who have gone astray and are called to return. The sin of Adam is evoked as the fall of the entire race from grace. All men are in the same condition, and no one can escape from it except in Christ.

This solidarity in sin is the background against which the liturgy draws a vivid picture of the continual struggle between the city of God and the city of Satan. Man is not engaged in a struggle against abstract evil or merely against his own passions, but against the fallen angels, powers of evil who seek to attract him into their kingdom. This struggle is not an individual one, but forms part of a drama in which Satan and his followers are pitted against God and his followers, and one which will endure until Christ hands the kingdom over to his Father. It was the kingdom of Satan which Jesus came to war against: the Gospels frequently refer to his work in this way, particularly on the occasion of his miraculous healings.

The individual, then, is not alone in his struggle. Nor is sin merely a matter between himself and God. Every sin is an injury to the entire human race, for it helps to deliver us all into the hands of Satan, to make the work of redemption more difficult. Sin is the cause of all suffering and death in the world. Furthermore, it injures the Mystical Body by placing an obstacle in the way of its salvific function. The liturgy of penance becomes incomprehensible if this communal aspect is not taken into account.

Lent and Penance

It is primarily in the liturgy of the Lenten season that the significance of sin and penance is revealed. By the very fact that it sets aside this recurring season in the ecclesiastical year for particular emphasis upon man's need of conversion, the Church shows that conversion is a continuing necessity. Lent is the time of salvation par excellence, a period which God, in his mercy, grants to the Church for her conversion to him. Just as John the Baptist announced that the crucial moment had come in which men must make their decision, so the Church annually presents us with an opportunity to turn back to God in sincerity of heart through the practice of penance.

The liturgy of Lent repeats again and again the great themes of salvation: the fall of man, his state of misery, the call to repentance and conversion. During Septuagesima, the immediate prelude to the Lenten season, we read the story of the fall of Adam, in whose history the Church sees the life of every man. The succeeding stages of salvation are envisaged as so many summonses of God to sinful man to return to him through repentance. The struggle with Satan is unceasingly evoked. And the invitation is again extended to all: "Now is the acceptable time, now is the day of salvation!" (2 Cor 6,2).

It is in this context that the Christian is invited to do penance. The mortifications of Lent are a means of repairing the excesses which man has committed through original sin and through the personal sins of each individual. They are a share in the sufferings of Christ, which were the supreme means determined by divine Providence for the healing of man's wounded nature. Fasting, prayer and almsgiving strengthen the Christian to make him a valiant soldier of Christ in the battle against the forces of Satan.

Sacrament of Penance

But the most important of all the Church's penitential rites is the sacrament of penance itself. Herein the Church possesses a sacramental means, given to her by Christ himself, of reconciling to herself and thus to God those of her members who have fallen back into sin after their baptism. It is principally through this sacrament that the individual Christian assimilates into his own life the rhythm of the Church's life of penance.

In the early Church penance was a public rite and consequently the role which the Church played in it was more immediately evident. Those who were guilty of grave faults had cut themselves off from the Church; their sin had made them dead members. They had to appeal to the community for reconciliation, and this was not easily granted. After presenting themselves to the bishop or priest, they were given a public penance to perform by way of satisfaction, which often lasted for a considerable time. A grave fault which harmed the community was thought to demand a rigorous satisfaction. When the penance had been performed, the penitent was readmitted to the Church in a public ceremony, usually held on Holy Thursday, the rite of which is still contained in the *Roman Pontifical.*

The public character of this rite brought clearly into view the place of the Church in the reconciliation of penitents. No one can be reconciled to God without first being reconciled to the Church. Later on, when the administration of penance became private and even secret, this aspect of the sacrament was obscured. Today it is brought out in the rite itself only by the gesture of readmission which the priest makes while conferring absolution. Nevertheless its significance is still there and should not be forgotten. The Church shows in this way that she is a penitential organization, not only for those who come to baptism to seek the haven of salvation in her bosom, but also for her wayward members who wander from the path of salvation and must constantly be recalled.

Penance in the Church's Life

Thus the sacramental liturgy, as well as the cycles of the liturgical year, is oriented toward the conversion of the Christian. We have seen that the Mass liturgy requires an admission of sin and request for pardon before one enters into the celebration of the divine mysteries. The various sacramentals often emphasize the same basic truths. Through them the Church sanctifies persons, places and objects, removing them from the sphere of the influence of evil by the exorcism of Satan, into whose power all creation passed through original sin, and consecrating them to the service of God.

Thus the Church continually teaches the fundamental truth that all creation is under the empire of Satan and that mankind through its own disobedience has an inherent inclination to sin. It teaches man's inability to free himself from this domination and the unceasing concern of God's mercy that he be delivered. Hence the invitations to return throughout the course of biblical history, the intervention of God himself in the person of his Son to conquer Satan in his own stronghold, and the gift of the Holy Spirit who stirs up sentiments of repentance in the heart which enable the believer to adhere to God once more through faith.

The Church not only teaches these truths, but relives them day by day in the liturgy. She evokes the events of the past to introduce the faithful into the divine economy of salvation which is still operative on their behalf. Through the sacramental power confided to her she receives into her bosom those who are sincerely repentant and who turn back to God in humility. She looks forward to the future when the kingdom shall be complete and her converts, purified of their sins, will assist at the eternal liturgy of the heavenly Jerusalem.

3. CONVERSION AND THE MONK

Conversion and Spirituality

If the Church is essentially a penitential institution and the aspect of conversion is inseparable from the life which she lives in the liturgy, then it follows that the vocation of every Christian is a conversion. It is not only the initial conversion by which he becomes a member of the Mystical Body of Christ, but a continual process of repairing the evil which sin has wrought in his nature and a continual turning to God in the new life of faith. From all that we have said above, it is evident that penance is not merely a negative thing, a regret for sin and avoidance of it, but the positive dedication of the entire person to God in a profound recognition of one's need of him.

Since this is essential to the Christian vocation, it is clear that it must play a role in every orthodox form of spirituality. But here again it can be realized in an infinite variety of different manners. Conversion is only one aspect of the rich complexity of the Christian life. There are others, and it is precisely the varying emphasis given to the individual elements that make up the total experience which determines the nature of a form of spirituality.

In monastic spirituality the aspect of conversion plays a dominant part. Monasticism by its nature represents that aspect of the Church's life which is expressed in the New Testament teaching on conversion and in the liturgy's presentation of it. The monk is a man who takes Christianity seriously, who carries out to their logical conclusions the requirements expressed in Christ's summonses. Since his spirituality is structured primarily according to the religious values contained in the Scriptures and in the liturgy, it is not surprising that his vocation should be expressed in terms of a conversion.

Monastic Life as Conversion

Conversion is a complete revision of the meaning which a man attaches to life. Whereas previously he had believed that the gods of this world were sufficient to fulfill the desire for happiness which is deeply rooted in every human being, he now understands the Word of the Gospel which proclaims that this world is passing away. Any human life which has no meaning beyond the terms of this present age will pass away with it. A whole shift in a man's outlook is required to lead him to the explicit choice of the kingdom of God over the attractions of the world. He must free himself from the enticements which would make his life meaningful only in terms of the present age.

This is what is involved in a conversion to the monastic life. It is only a more complete and more logical form of the conversion which the New Testament demands of every Christian. Strictly speaking, a Christian is required to renounce only what is sinful and what proximately leads to sin. But the divine summonses can lead a man much further in the logic of conversion, even to the renunciation of things which are in themselves fully legitimate. The monk listens to the call of the Spirit speaking within his heart, and, once he has beheld an interior vision of the pearl of great price to which no other value can be compared, he loses his interest in all other goods and is impelled by love to give himself completely to the search for it.

It is this total dedication to the pursuit of the greater good which causes the monk to abandon the lesser, to withdraw into the desert. His renunciation frees him from the many cares of the present life which threaten to divert his attention from that pearl of great price and to stifle the voice of the Spirit inviting him to the embrace of divine love. He will be tempted by the allurements of created goods and will have to sustain a fierce combat with Satan in his own stronghold, where he will relive the biblical theme of the people of God in the wilderness, and by his renunciation will proclaim the transcendence of the kingdom of God and the invincible power of the love of Christ.

St. Benedict, in conformity with monastic tradition, speaks of the monk's entry into the monastery as his conversion. In the Prologue he invites the prospective monk to embrace the monastic vocation by quoting the words of Ezechiel, "I will not the death of a sinner, but that he should be converted and live" (Ez 33,11; Pr 38). On other occasions he refers to the time of a monk's entry into the monastery simply as the time when he was converted (2,18; 63,7). While he never uses the term *conversio*, it is possible, according to the view of some scholars, that *conversatio* is a synonym for it (cf especially 63,1).

Totality of Conversion

The element of conversion occupies a position of predominance in monastic spirituality which sets it apart from other forms of religious life. While every religious, and indeed every Christian, must be converted to God from a life of sin, others do not erect this into a principle of spiritual progress to the same degree as the monk. For his conversion colors every aspect of his life. It is not only a thing which must be realized interiorly, but it also determines to a large extent the outward form of his life.

In the complete logic of his conversion, the monk abandons not only the evil in his life, but also many aspects of his former life in the world which were good in themselves. He leaves behind his relatives and friends, indeed, to a certain extent the society of all other men, and withdraws into solitude. He even changes his external garb as a symbol of the change of heart that has taken place within him. He abandons such legitimate pleasures as material possessions, marriage and the right to have a family of his own, and the assertion of his own preferences and binds himself to the observance of poverty, celibacy and obedience. He subjects his body and his higher faculties to various forms of mortification. Instead of engaging in the activities which are normative for other men, he devotes himself principally to prayer and reading.

All of these changes in his life are aspects of his conversion. He is not content with those essential aspects of conversion which are required of every follower of Christ: abandonment of sin and dedication of self to the new life of faith. He wishes to become so completely converted that the interior conversion will affect even his exterior form of life, to change completely all of his former habits and make of him a new man. In this sense the monk is a radical, an extremist. He cannot be satisfied with halfway measures.

The Correct Motivation

While being aware of the radical nature of monasticism, the monk must be sure that he understands the motive for it, which is all important. The purpose of the monk's conversion is to turn his heart away from sin and from all that is mundane and ephemeral in a world that is under the domination of Satan, in order to surrender himself completely to God. The exterior aspects of conversion are of little importance unless they really reflect a sincere interior conversion. They are not ends in themselves, but only means. They must be regarded precisely as means if they are to perform their proper function in the monk's life. Once they become promoted to ends, there is an inversion in the person's whole outlook which will be difficult to rectify.

The systematized Manicheism which the Fathers combated is no longer a living issue in the Church. But the dualistic view of creation which was at the root of it has continued to crop up again and again in the course of the Church's history and shows no signs of an early disappearance. There are indications that some of the ancient monks were at times infected by it, and the modern Christian is by no means exempt from the same mentality. The basic error of dualism is a denial of the intrinsic goodness of creation. To be saved one must renounce all created things because there is something evil about them.

The extreme form of this doctrine is obviously incompatible with Christianity. But it is not in its extreme form that it is likely to influence the monk; it is rather a question of his general outlook on the world. Very often it is not an intellectual conviction at all, but rather an emotional attitude, in conflict with what a person knows to be true. For one who is dedicated to a life of renunciation, there is always the danger that he may begin to think of the things which he has renounced as being somehow evil. And then he begins to make of renunciation an end in itself, and in so doing inverts the proper hierarchy of values in his conversion.

Monasticism and Eschatology

If the monk is fully conscious that his vocation is a continuation and fulfillment of the sacred history recounted in the Scriptures, he will not fall into this error. For there is no such dualism in the Scriptures. There is a dualism between the kingdom of God and the kingdom of Satan, between the children of light and the children of darkness, but there is no dualism between nature and grace. We do not become saints by destroying our nature, but by perfecting it. What must be destroyed in us is the influence of Satan, so that we may belong fully to the kingdom of God.

We will not belong fully to the kingdom of God until the eschatological times have arrived. At the resurrection on the last day, this corruptible body will put on incorruption, this mortal body will put on immortality (1 Cor 15,53). Not until then will the whole man's search for God be ended, or his conversion complete. When death is swallowed up in victory, then nature will be seized by glory, not destroyed but perfected and transfigured.

But eschatology is already in the process of realization. The monk is in a hurry to have it realized. In his haste to leave the kingdom of Satan behind him and belong completely to God, he abandons even the good things of his natural life, things which will be of no use to him in the angelic life toward which he aspires and which can be a hindrance on his journey. The monastic life is essentially eschatological, and one who forgets this can never hope to understand it. That is why it is a continual conversion, for Christ has made conversion the *sine qua non* requirement for entry into his eschatological kingdom.

Themes of Paradox

In adopting this manner of life, the monk is simply reliving the great themes of biblical history. He is the prolongation in the Church of the great paradox that runs through the pages of the Scriptures. In renouncing all that he has he loses nothing and finds everything. It is the sort of life that makes no sense whatever according to any kind of human computation. But it is the life that God demanded of the great men of the Old Testament who prepared for the advent of the kingdom, and that Christ required of his followers. The monk repeats the experience of these his forerunners.

The theme of the desert marks the monk's life. Man's rejection from the fertile garden of paradise into the desert was a consequence of sin. But it is precisely in the savage desolation of the wilderness that he finds the way back to God. When Israel was comfortably installed in the promised land she was constantly unfaithful to her covenant with God. In these circumstances, the prophets looked back upon the time of her wandering in the desert as the ideal period when she was close to Yahweh and obedient to him. It was her honeymoon experience. The monk seeks the solitude of the desert for the same reason. There, unencumbered by man-made comforts and distractions, he can encounter God directly.

Further Paradoxes

The theme of sterility is another paradox. Sterility, too, is a result of sin, and the people of Israel regarded it as a curse from God. But it is the sterile whom God chooses to produce the great men whom he sends to his people. Isaac, Samson, Samuel, John the Baptist, are the sons of women who were deserted by nature but remembered by God. Sion herself will become the fruitful mother of children only in the desolation of exile (cf Is 54,1). The voluntary virginity of Mary issues in the divine maternity. The monk has an analogous experience: his life becomes fruitful only when he has renounced all human means and placed his trust in God alone.

There is also the theme of poverty and weakness. It is not the rich, the powerful, or the great men of the world who carry out the designs of God, but the poor, the weak, the despised, the humble. The Jews stand awe-struck and incredulous before the choices made by God. Gideon with his small band of followers shatters the power of Midian; David the humble shepherd boy strikes down the oppressor Goliath and becomes the anointed of Yahweh, whose throne shall endure forever. The prophets are ignored and sometimes persecuted, but they prevail in the end; the poor of the psalms are oppressed by the mighty, but their cry reaches the ear of God.

The Logic of Paradox

There is a divine logic in all this, a logic distressing to human reasoning, for it is the logic of paradox. Such are the mysterious ways of God. Our Lord embraced it fully when he declared that the humble will be exalted, that he who loses his life will find it while he who seeks to save his life will lose it. It is the logic of faith, not of reason, and it is the law of the eschatological kingdom. For on the last day all human standards will be reversed: the mighty will be thrust from their thrones and the lowly exalted; the hungry filled with good things and the rich sent away empty. It is the logic of the Beatitudes. Blessed are the poor, the meek, the mourners, the hungry, the persecuted: of such as these is the kingdom of heaven.

St. Paul understood the logic of paradox. He saw in the mysterious dealings of God a divine principle at work. Human power is of no avail; every accomplishment is God's. Therefore the man who will be successful with God is he who empties himself completely of every human device and renounces every human support. "Strength is made perfect in weakness . . . when I am weak, then I am strong" (2 Cor 12,9–10). "The foolish things of the world has God chosen to put to shame the 'wise,' and the weak things of the world has God chosen to put to shame the strong . . . lest any flesh should pride itself before him" (1 Cor 1,27–29).

The monk, too, enthusiastically accepts the logic of paradox. His entire life is a rejection of the temporal values which the world most prizes, an acceptance of the eschatological values which it most disdains. It is this principle which determines the penitential aspect of monastic life. In the next chapter we shall speak of the various forms of detachment which monastic life has adopted as an application of this principle. But first we wish to see how the monk's conversion is brought to realization within the context of the Church's sacramental system.

4. THE MONK AND THE SACRAMENT OF PENANCE

The Regime of Penance

Of all the means which the monk has at his disposal to bring about his continuing conversion, the most important and the most efficacious is that of the sacrament of penance. We have seen that in the new covenant the return to God of a sinner properly disposed is effected by the Church through the power granted to her by her Founder. This takes place first of all in the sacrament of baptism, when the neophyte is wrested from the kingdom of Satan, cleansed of his sin, engrafted upon the Mystical Body of Christ, and, through membership in the society of the faithful, introduced into a state of friendship with God.

Thus baptism is the gate of entry which gives access to the community of the redeemed and opens the channel of salvific grace flowing from the passion and resurrection of Christ. But our Lord, in condescension for human weakness, also instituted another sacrament for the forgiveness of sins committed after baptism. Because conversion is a continuing process, never complete in this life, man must not only once but repeatedly turn away from sin and back to the merciful love and friendship of God. Pardon and the invitation to return are continually held out to the sinner, and the entire ascetical effort takes place under the regime of the sacrament.

Thus the entire ascetical life of the monk is associated with the sacrament of penance: his basic attitudes of compunction and humility and his practice of mortification must be conceived of either as a preparation for or as a consequence of his reception of the sacrament. Penance dispensed by the Church through her ordained ministers is the normal channel, in the present dispensation, of forgiveness and conversion.

Confession in the Holy Rule

St. Benedict makes no mention in the *Rule* of the sacrament of penance. In his time the practice of private penance had not yet come into general use. The sacrament was still administered publicly and only for very grave sins, which required a long period of public satisfaction before a reconciliation with the Church could take place. It was presumed that crimes such as these would not be committed by monks, or that they would be expelled from the monastery in consequence of them, and hence he did not find it necessary to speak of the administration of penance in the *Rule*.

The *Rule* treats at length, however, of faults committed by monks and of the manner in which satisfaction must be made for them. Two whole groups of chapters, called the penal code, are devoted to this question: 23–30 and 43–46. Admission of guilt is demanded and penances are imposed for public faults. But for secret faults, St. Benedict prescribes a non-sacramental form of confession: "Should the matter be a secret sin of the soul, let him tell such a thing to the abbot alone, or to a spiritual father; for they know how to cure both their own wounds and the wounds of others without disclosing and publishing them" (46,5–6; cf 4,50).

Confession of Devotion

Secret confession thus originated in monasteries, and it was largely the influence of monastic practice which led to the general adoption of private penance as we know it today. Even though not sacramental, and often made to non-priests, such confession has a definite penitential value: the value of reparation for faults and the incentive which it gives to sentiments of humility and compunction. If this be true of non-sacramental confession, it is so a fortiori of the frequent confession of venial sins in our day, when to this intrinsic value is added the actual reconciliation with the Church and thus with God through the sacramental power of the minister.

Accordingly, Pope Pius XII vigorously defended the practice of such confession of devotion against those who had asserted that it was of little value.

> There are many ways, worthy of the highest commendation . . . in which these faults can be expiated; but for a swifter daily progress in the path of virtue, we wish that the devout practice of frequent confession, introduced into the Church under the inspiration of the Holy Spirit, should be especially advocated. Through its use correct self-knowledge is increased, Christian humility grows, evil habits

are rooted out, resistance is offered to spiritual negligence and tepidity, the conscience is purified, the will is strengthened, fruitful direction of souls is ensured, and grace is increased by the power of the sacrament itself. (Encyclical *Mystici Corporis*, June 29, 1943: AAS 35 (1943) 235)

Manifestation of Conscience

It will be noted that some of the effects here listed by the Holy Father are to be found also in non-sacramental confession of faults. This is what we now call manifestation of conscience, and what was for St. Benedict nothing more than the practice of the fifth degree of humility. The fact that modern canon law forbids superiors to extract such a manifestation (*CJC* 530,1) does not mean that the Church wishes to discourage it. On the contrary, the same canon recommends that religious spontaneously open their consciences to their superiors for their own spiritual good, with the proviso that the latter be priests, who alone are now regarded as having the competence to give effective guidance (*CJC* 530,2).

A monk can scarcely hope to make progress in the spiritual life if he depends entirely upon his own judgment, which is never more fallible than in his own case. A superior or prudent spiritual director will ordinarily have the advantage not only of experience but also of an objective point of view. This does not mean, of course, that a monk should be constantly running to a spiritual director to have all his decisions made for him. Spiritual direction should not become an excuse either for abdicating personal responsibility or for manufacturing problems which do not exist. But in the ordinary course of events there will be difficulties enough, and even when there are no special problems, every monk needs reliable guidance on the path to perfection. To set out alone for the spiritual combat, fraught with difficulties as it is, is to lay oneself open to the delusions of self-deception. The monk must begin the struggle by finding a spiritual father who can help him to understand himself and the warring movements which are in conflict for the mastery of his soul.

Function of the Spiritual Father

In ancient times, a prospective monk who wished to strive for perfection first sought out a spiritual father. It was recognized that one did not become a monk merely by following a certain rule of life and practicing certain observances. The monk was rather one who had learned to listen to the promptings of the Spirit within him, to follow the call of grace. The task of renouncing his self-will and learning to discern the movements within his own heart was one which required training at the hands of a master of the art.

Such a master was one who had himself had experience in the art of seeking God. He had himself waged the spiritual combat for many years, was filled with the Holy Spirit and the gift of discernment of spirits, wherefore his sanctity and vast experience enabled him to offer sure guidance and healing to others. He was a spiritual father, a spiritual physician, a man of God, a charismatic, whose own attainment of perfection enabled him to beget spiritual sons by transmitting the Spirit to them by his discernment and counsel. Origen referred to Christ as the "spiritual father" and "spiritual physician," who came to heal the spiritual sicknesses of men. The monks believed that these qualities of Christ were inherited by the ancients whom they called "Abba," who took the place of Christ for their disciples.

The disciple obtained guidance by laying bare his soul to his spiritual father. The ancients did not speak of manifestation of conscience, but of manifestation of thoughts. They were not interested in the past, but in the present state of the soul. What was of concern was what was going on in a man's heart at present, and this was revealed in his thoughts, which the Greeks called *logismoi.* The "thoughts" are the interior movements which attract the soul either to evil or to good. It is not easy for an inexperienced monk to determine the source and the real nature of these interior impulses, for sometimes by trickery Satan makes his own suggestions appear to emanate from an angel of light. Hence the principal charism of the spiritual father is that of discernment of spirits.

Eight Principal Sources of Evil

The purification of the heart is constantly threatened by evil thoughts, which are enticements to seek satisfaction in self rather than in God's will. This is the real battlefield upon which the spiritual combat must be waged; it is in solitude, in the depths of the monk's own heart, that he meets the adversary face to face. He must be prepared to recognize the enemy and ceaselessly to struggle against him. St. Benedict tells us how we must deal with these evil thoughts: "Immediately to dash the evil thoughts which come into one's heart against Christ, and to make them known to the spiritual father" (4,50). It is only the power of the risen Christ which can triumph over Satan in this new battlefield of the monk's soul, just as he once did in the desert of Judea.

These evil suggestions present themselves in manifold form and only experience can teach the monk to discern them. Evagrius and Cassian, the great systematizers of monastic theory, drew up a list of the eight principal vices, the evil thoughts which offer the most powerful enticement. They impel the monk to seek for satisfaction in the goods of the present life or to lapse into an unhealthy state of soul because he cannot attain them. This catalogue became a commonplace in the subsequent monastic tradition; while St. Benedict does not list the eight vices, he is thinking of the same reality when he speaks of the "desires of the flesh" which the monk must not fulfill (4,59).

These eight sources of evil are: gluttony, the temptation to satisfy the body's craving for food and drink; fornication, the urge to satisfy the sexual appetite; love for money, the suggestion that one must insure his security in this world by holding human resources; anger, the desire to follow the dictates of one's lower nature in reacting to unpleasant situations; melancholy, the tendency to feel sorry for oneself and enjoy one's unhappiness at the deprivation of material goods; *acedia*, a dissatisfaction with the monotony of the spiritual combat which manifests itself in instability and distaste for spiritual things; vainglory, the temptation to court the approval of men; and pride, the attributing to oneself of whatever good the Holy Spirit has accomplished in the soul (*Inst* 5–12).

Defense against Evil Suggestions

The monk who has already attained purity of heart will be able to distinguish good thoughts from evil ones by a kind of connaturality: virtue will have become such a second nature to him that he will spontaneously recognize anything that is opposed to it. But one who still possesses attachments that hold him prisoner to the flesh will not be able to make such a judgment without the assistance of a spiritual father. When an impulse has been recognized as evil, it must be resisted from the very outset, before it can grow roots in the soul.

Here the monk must rely upon the strength of Christ operating in him through his Spirit. For this reason a childlike and confident prayer to Christ has been the traditional weapon of the monk: ejaculatory prayer, the invocation of the Holy Name. The oriental monks repeated again and again what is called simply the "Jesus prayer," "Lord Jesus, Son of God, have mercy upon me, a sinner," or quoted texts from Scripture which, following the practice of Jesus in the desert, was regarded as an arsenal against the onslaughts of Satan. An entire work of Evagrius, the *Antirrheticus*, consists of a catalogue of biblical texts arranged for use against various kinds of temptation.

Abbot's Role as Spiritual Father

For St. Benedict the spiritual father who guides his disciples in the combat against evil thoughts is the abbot of the monastery. Faith reveals that he holds the place of Christ, and his name is derived from the saying of St. Paul which manifests his charismatic function: "You have received the spirit of the adoption of sons, whereby we cry, 'Abba, father' " (Rom 8,15; *Rule* 2,2–3). The abbot is looked upon both as a spiritual father (49,9; cf 2,24) and as a wise physician (27,1–2; 28,2). While St. Benedict's abbot has also become the father of the monastic family and the administrator of all the details of its daily life, he is primarily the perfect monk about whom have assembled disciples whom he begets spiritually as his sons and to whom he communicates the Spirit.

The abbot is essentially a teacher, in the line of the *doctores* of the Old and New Testaments, whose authority is charismatic rather than hierarchical, derived from the designation of the Holy Spirit rather than from sacramental ordination. Cenobitic life is simply an institutionalized form of a group of disciples gathered together around their spiritual father. The fact that canon law now requires that he be a priest and invests him with the abbatial blessing to signify his role in the sacramental hierarchy of the Church in no way changes his essential function as teacher and man of the Spirit. The abbot remains the spiritual father of his monks, and even his administrative function is directed toward the growth in perfection of his sons and toward maintaining an atmosphere favorable to their spiritual progress.

While the abbot always remains the principal spiritual teacher of his community and holds the responsibility for the welfare of all of his sons, the administrative burdens of his office do not always permit him to direct each one individually. Hence St. Benedict extends this function also to the elders of the community who have the requisite discretion to cure the spiritual wounds of the monks who seek their advice and will know how to maintain a strict confidence in regard to the secrets of their consciences (46,5–6; cf 4,50). The function of these elders, however, is only an extension of the abbot's and must be exercised in dependence upon him.

The Acts of the Penitent

The penitential practice of the Church has evolved considerably since the time of St. Benedict and now revolves about the frequent reception of the sacrament of penance. The modern monk, therefore, must learn to situate the ancient practice of manifestation of thoughts within the regime of the sacrament. Accordingly it is fitting to consider how the monk should approach the sacrament of penance for a fruitful reception of it and what place it should occupy in his spiritual life.

The Council of Trent has defined that the form of the sacrament consists in the words of absolution pronounced by the priest, which confer reconciliation upon the sinner (Sess 14, ch 3; *Denz* 896). The matter of the sacrament consists of the three acts of the penitent: contrition, confession and satisfaction. Since these acts of the penitent are of vital importance from the viewpoint of the contribution which the recipient must make, some attention will be devoted to them here.

Before we undertake to discuss these acts, however, something must first be said about the exercise of examination of conscience. We must see ourselves with clarity, as we really are, if we are to lay open our conscience in confession. Consequently a careful examination of conscience must precede the reception of the sacrament. In the life of a monk, indeed, self-knowledge should be habitual; a constant awareness of the evil in one's life is nothing other than the attitude of compunction.

This attitude is best kept alive, however, by a periodic examination of conscience which brings into sharper relief those areas which have not yet been illumined by the splendor of Christ's redemption. Accordingly it is customary in most monasteries to set aside a time each day for such examination. Generally two periods are provided: one for a general examination at the end of the day, the other for what is known as the particular examen. The practice of examination of conscience is found already in the ancient monastic literature (cf *Vita Antonii* 55; Basil, *Sermo ascet* 1,5).

The General Examination

The general examination of conscience is one which covers the acts of a particular day. It is accordingly to be performed in the evening before retiring, preferably just before the *Confiteor* of the office of Compline. The spirit of this last hour of the day, more individual and introspective than the hours of Lauds and Vespers, which are principally devoted to praise of God, is one of recollection and compunction. It begins with a confession of sin, and its psalms are designed to stir up in the heart of the monk sentiments of sorrow for sin and gratitude for the divine protection which will accompany him during the night.

It is a time, then, suitable for laying bare one's conscience before God and ending the day in a spirit of contrition and humility. The examination of conscience should help to arouse such sentiments and should enable the monk to see himself clearly in the light of faith. Its purpose is not merely to move him to contrition for his sins, but also to make an accurate inventory and to determine measures which may be taken for amendment and improvement.

The monk should begin the examination by placing himself in the presence of God in a spirit of faith. He may then undertake the examination proper by reviewing in an orderly manner the actions of the day, his fundamental dispositions, temptations, the basic problems with which he has been faced. The examination should concentrate not only on the evil, but also upon his virtuous qualities and actions, so that he may have a complete picture of the day. Next he should determine what needs to be done further to develop what is good and to eliminate the defects. The examination should end with a prayer, first of thanksgiving to God for the graces he has received throughout the day, then of contrition for the faults he has committed, finally of supplication for the divine assistance to enable him to fulfill his purpose of amendment.

Particular Examination

Many monasteries also have a time set aside each day for the particular examen; and even if there is no specified period, it is an exercise which can be fruitful. The particular examen is an examination of one's conscience on some particular point. This may be a particular fault which should be eradicated, or a particular virtue which needs to be developed, or some religious exercise which should be performed more perfectly. It can be of great utility for the monk thus to concentrate upon some particular point in his life which the daily general examination has shown to require special attention.

In its present form the practice of the particular examen is rather recent, but the basic idea behind it is much older and of monastic origin. The ancient monks, in their concern to heal the spiritual sickness of the soul, attempted to analyze the dominant vice which was the source of the disorder and the principal obstacle to spiritual progress. Cassian treats of the combat which must be waged against the dominant vice in his fifth *Conference*. Essentially the particular examen is the same kind of analysis.

The subject matter chosen for the particular examen should be some particular manifestation of weakness in the monk's spiritual life. If a fault is chosen for examination, then it should be the dominant fault, the one which is the source of other difficulties or which vitiates actions that would otherwise be virtuous. Such things as particular manifestations of pride, sensuality or lack of fraternal charity can thus be profitably examined. If a virtue is chosen, it should likewise be something of which he has particular need, such as, for example, discretion or temperance. In regard to observance, he may profitably examine himself on such things as prayer and spiritual exercises, or the practice of mortification. He should strive to see clearly his negligence in particular instances, and especially examine the motives for which he acts, in order that he may adopt measures suitable for eliminating his defects.

The Examination before Confession

The examination of conscience which should precede the weekly confession is in some ways similar to the foregoing, in other ways different. It will be more extensive, for it must cover the entire period of time which has elapsed since the last confession. But the field of investigation is somewhat narrower, for the examination before confession does not require an inventory of virtuous qualities nor of habitual dispositions. Its purpose is only to make the monk aware of the sinful acts which have been performed since the last confession. Evil dispositions are not matter for the sacrament unless they have actually resulted in sin.

If the daily examination of conscience and the particular examen are made well, the examination before confession need be only a summing up of what is already known. Even more important, a monk who lives habitually in a spirit of conpunction will not have to begin anew at the time set aside for examination. A monk's life should not be divided into airtight compartments, so that examination of conscience is restricted to those periods which are especially provided for it. If the attitude of compunction is habitual, such periods can be valuable as concentrated efforts to sum up what he is already conscious of. If he does this regularly, his examination of conscience before confession will consist principally in giving an accurate formulation to his self-knowledge so that his reception of the sacrament will be as fruitful as possible.

First Act: Contrition

Examination of conscience is not one of the acts of the penitent enumerated by the Council of Trent, but is rather a prelude to them. The first of these is contrition. It is also the most important, for the contrition of the penitent is essential to the validity of the sacrament. While absolution may be validly conferred upon one who is unable to confess and to make satisfaction, provided he has the will to do so, it may not be conferred upon one who is not contrite. It follows from the nature of sin itself that a person cannot be reconciled unless he wants to be reconciled.

Why this is so is evident from what we have said of the process of conversion. God is not a tyrant who inflicts arbitrary penalties upon those who disobey more or less arbitrary laws. He is a loving Father who wishes to draw all men into the sphere of his love. Through sin they voluntarily reject his love and turn aside from him. He offers them the means of return: absolution is God's power, made available in the Church through Christ's passion and resurrection, obliterating sin from a contrite heart. But God does not force free will; man must want to accept his offer. And accepting the offer means being sorry, for man cannot be reconciled unless he reciprocates God's love.

Contrition is not a matter of sentiment, but of the will. When sincere and intense, it is likely to overflow into the emotions, but this is not of its essence. One who feels no emotion at all about his sins can nevertheless be truly sorry for them. Interiorly he judges himself guilty, regrets his errors and wills to return to God's love. In this judgment he submits himself to the Church too, realizing that his sin has been harmful to the entire Mystical Body. His contrition must include a confidence in God, a filial trust that God in his mercy will efface his sin, restore him to his place in the economy of salvation and offer him again the chance to respond with gratitude and love to the divine generosity.

Contrition must also include a purpose of amendment. In turning his back upon sin, the penitent must reject it once and for all and determine never again to prefer self-love to the love of God. A man who intended to sin again would not be truly contrite. But this does not mean that the penitent will have any certainty about the future; indeed, in view of the weakness he has shown in the past, he may well foresee the possibility of future infidelities. But such a realization is a matter of the intellect; sorrow is in the will. It is impossible to be *sure* that one will not fall again; all that God requires is the firm *intention* not to do so.

Motive for Contrition

What is the motive that inspires such sorrow for sin? It is clear that the whole question of forgiveness revolves about *love*. It is God's merciful love that grants forgiveness; it is our faith in his love which enables us to approach him. It is only natural to expect that our faith will produce reciprocal love in us. Hence a real love for God is a necessary condition for receiving God's forgiveness.

Contrition is often presented as if there were two separate ways of obtaining pardon: imperfect contrition with the sacrament of penance and perfect contrition without it. This is a false way to pose the problem. It is true that one may regret his sin for imperfect motives, such as disgust for the shamefulness of sin, fear of death and punishment, the desire to lead a humanly upright life and to find happiness. These motives are based upon the love of self, and cannot qualify as that authentic contrition which is based on the love of God. Consequently they cannot of themselves merit the forgiveness of sin. What they can do is dispose the penitent to proceed further until he arrives at that filial fear which is inspired by supernatural charity. At this point the other motives may remain, but they are no longer predominant.

Sin cannot be forgiven unless the heart is contrite. The heart is not contrite unless there is a real love for God. This love is not incompatible with a concern for oneself, which is always involved in the love of another person for his own sake, though in a secondary place. If the penitent has not yet arrived at this love when he approaches the sacrament, then it is infused together with the grace of absolution. But his sins cannnot be forgiven without it.

It should not be imagined that perfect contrition is extremely difficult to attain. Any penitent who is sincerely sorry for having offended God and wishes to return to his love is truly contrite. If some less unselfish motives remain in the background, this is of little consequence. Obviously, there are degrees of perfect contrition; like charity itself, it is open to indefinite growth. The practical conclusion from this is that the monk must constantly strive to perfect his contrition. Consequently his preparation for the sacrament of penance should concentrate much more upon his contrition than upon probing into his conscience to make sure that his confession will be absolutely complete. If he habitually strives to deepen his compunction, then the contrition which is required for the sacrament will be already available and need only be concentrated in a fervent act of sorrow.

Choice of Confessor

In the present economy of salvation, reconciliation with God takes place through reconciliation with the Church. It is necessary, therefore, that this be an exterior act, which is accomplished through the confession of one's sins to an authorized priest. It is the mind of the Church that all religious should confess their sins weekly (*CJC* 595,1,3). What we have already said about the nature of the sacramental economy of penance indicates that the monk's entire life of conversion should be centered about his sacramental participation in Christ's passion and death in the sacrifice of the Mass and in his weekly reception of the sacrament of penance.

If the monk is permitted a choice of confessors, then he should select that priest who seems to correspond best to his needs, and go to him regularly. Frequent changing of confessors according to one's changing whims can only be harmful to oneself. It must be remembered that the essential feature of the sacrament is the absolution, and that any priest can confer this. But secondarily the confessor is also an adviser, and in this respect some priests are more skilled than others.

A confessor should be chosen primarily for his wisdom, for in this matter correct knowledge is more important than personal holiness. He should also be exacting, not content to let his penitents become complacently hardened in their faults. And he should be a person to whom the monk feels that he can open his soul with perfect confidence and freedom. The monk should remember that he is free to go to confession whenever he wishes and is never required to ask permission of superiors for this. He is even permitted, by way of exception, to go to any confessor who has the faculties of the monastery or of the diocese to obtain quiet of conscience (*CJC* 519).

Precision in Confession

The next question is how to go about confessing one's sins. Like anything frequently repeated, regular confession can become tedious, a merely routine procedure that is of little profit because of the lack of proper disposition on the part of the penitent. This can be avoided if one's sins are confessed accurately. A precise and humble confession requires a good proximate preparation and, even more so, an habitual compunction which produces that delicacy of conscience which permits a monk to perceive the true malice of his sins.

It would be impossible to confess all of one's sins, and there is no point in trying to make one's confession absolutely complete. There is a strict obligation to confess all mortal sins, but Pope Pius XII insisted on the value of confessing venial sins and faults also, particularly for those who confess frequently. But instead of trying to confess all his venial sins, the penitent must make a choice. He should confess those faults which will reveal to his confessor the particular needs and problems of his spiritual life. This means that he should choose those venial sins which he commits most frequently, or which are most deliberate and malicious, and therefore constitute a danger and a real problem in his life.

These sins should be confessed precisely, with their particular circumstances, so that they will reveal the state of the soul. Confession should be an accusation of particular sinful acts, with the nuances that render them meaningful, not merely of evil tendencies or of generalizations. One can fail in charity in many different ways: it is one thing to think momentarily about the faults of a confrere, quite another to refuse to speak to him for a week. Being attached to a book and keeping a sum of money without permission are both offenses against poverty, but they are of a different kind and gravity. Laziness can express itself in doing one's work carelessly, or in deliberately sleeping during the divine office.

Confession of Former Sins

It is also recommended that the penitent confess a sin from his past life which has already been absolved. The advantage of this practice is not only that it is an expression of humility and continued sorrow, but also that it applies the grace of the sacrament anew to a weakness which may not yet be entirely healed. Accordingly the sin chosen should be one which has offered special difficulties in the past and may still constitute a weak point.

On occasion it may also be advisable to make a general confession, in which one repeats all the sins of his life or of a determined period of time. This practice can be helpful, especially at times of special decision, to reveal accurately the state of the soul, lay oneself bare before God in humility and contrition, and submit one's entire life to the power of Christ's redemptive Blood. Thus it may be recommended before entering the novitiate, before monastic profession and reception of holy orders, and at other intervals in a person's life. But it should be done only in answer to a real need in the monk's life, not merely out of routine or because it happens to be customary.

Thus the material of confession should always be chosen carefully, so as to enable the confessor to form an accurate judgment of the penitent's needs and to contribute the maximum possible to his spiritual advancement. But the monk's own intention is the all-important thing: confession should be a sincere acknowledgement of the evil he sees in himself and a determined repudiation of it, coupled with the firm intention to avoid all sin in the future.

The Value of Satisfaction

The final act of the penitent is that of satisfaction. The actual performance of satisfaction, like the actual confession, may be impossible in some cases; what is essential is that the penitent have the *intention* of making satisfaction. We may ask what is really meant by satisfaction. It is sometimes presented as a demand of divine justice, as if God required an adequate reparation for the evil of sin. This is clearly a false view of God's justice. In the first place, it is impossible for man to make an adequate reparation for sin; nothing that he might do could ever really atone for the damage he has done. And, in any case, God forgives generously; he is not an exacting tyrant who demands complete compensation for the wrong done to him.

God does not place any conditions upon his forgiveness; he is the merciful and loving Father who magnanimously welcomes the repentant sinner back to his embrace. If reparation is required, it is a consequence of his love, not of a divine justice conceived of as the exaction of a *quid pro quo*. Satisfaction can in no way benefit God, much less satiate a supposed divine appetite for vengeance; it can only be for the benefit of the penitent himself and of his fellow Christians. Sin always produces disorder both within the sinner and in society around him. These effects of sin are not automatically healed when the sin has been forgiven. Within the person there may remain bad habits and the general disorientation produced by his having turned his life in a false direction. In society there may remain the scandal caused by the sin and the injury which it has inflicted upon the health of the Mystical Body.

These effects of sin must still be corrected after the sin itself has been absolved. It is for this that satisfaction is intended. The repentant sinner who truly loves God will wish to destroy these remnants of his sin, to remove the obstacles which his own evil actions have placed in the way of his personal search for perfection and in that of others. Not in servile fulfillment of the arbitrary decrees of a tyrannical master, but in a spirit of generosity prompted by love, he will willingly undertake to undo the consequences of his own selfishness by assuming the duty of satisfaction.

Satisfaction and the Monk

It must not be supposed that the sacramental penance imposed by the priest is of itself sufficient to remove all the evil effects of the sins absolved in confession. In our time these penances have become a very light burden by comparison with the severe penances that were imposed in the early Church. But the sacramental penance is itself a symbol of the constant call to satisfaction addressed to the repentant and forgiven sinner, imposed in order to remind him of the duty of satisfaction which is incumbent upon him because of his own sins and those of others. All of the good works performed by the members of the Mystical Body have a satisfactory value, and the sacramental penance must be seen in the context of the satisfactory effort of the whole Church. The penance is only a symbol of the individual's participation in this general effort.

The monk plays a special role in the satisfactory work of the

Church, for, as we have seen, his life is penitential to a degree not realized by the ordinary Christian in the world. But his satisfaction should be conceived of primarily as an effort to repair the consequences of sin in order to give him a greater freedom to follow Christ. This was the purpose of all asceticism for the ancient monks. A medieval current of spirituality interpreted the individual's satisfactory role as one of compassion, that he might suffer together with Christ. Still later it was thought of as making reparation for the sufferings inflicted upon our Lord, and even as substituting for other sinners who did not do penance themselves.

There is a certain value in each of these viewpoints, but in putting them into practice an exuberant sentimentality has often predominated and thus obscured the authentic value which they contain, which is the basic truth of the solidarity of every Christian with Christ and all of his members in the Mystical Body. It is upon this background that the monk, the integral Christian, must contribute his personal satisfactory effort to that of his monastery and of the whole Church. Consequently he must learn to see his own sacramental penance in the context of his whole ascetical effort and that of the entire Mystical Body. This is another point of contact which should help him to integrate his ascetical life into the regime of sacramental penance.

The Unity of Monastic Life

This integration must be realized if the monk is to make a conscious contribution to the life of the Church. It is essential that he perceive clearly the nature and the value of his life of conversion. We have attempted to show here how conversion is the basic response that man must make to the call of God, that it is the response which Christ demanded of his followers and which the Church realizes in her daily life through the liturgy. Its realization requires of the individual the fundamental attitudes of compunction and humility, based upon a profound consciousness of the reality of sin and of one's personal involvement therein, and it makes use of the means provided by the Church's sacramental system, to which the effort of the individual to purify himself of sin through the practice of asceticism must be joined.

Now this entire process must be seen as a unity. The monk's life must not be divided up and fragmented into isolated acts, withdrawn from the context of the entire movement of conversion which he lives in and with the whole Church. His monastic observance, the virtues which he strives to cultivate, the ascetical practices which he undertakes, must all be seen as so many means designed to bring him to that perfect charity which is the condition for union with God, both here and hereafter. The unifying principle in the entire process is the liturgy. God not only summons us, he also gives us the means to respond. Those means are primarily the sacraments and all the rest of the liturgy which revolves around them. All individual efforts must either be a preparation for or a consequence of the monk's participation in God's own plan for sanctifying him. Thus his life will gain a dynamic purpose and direction which will enable him, as an authentic Christian, to advance continually toward the God who has called him and never ceases to draw him to himself.

5. MONASTIC PROFESSION

Profession as Gateway to the Monastic Life

The gateway to monastic life is the act of profession, by which the prospective monk publicly proclaims his intention to turn his back upon the world and his former way of life and to devote himself to the quest for God in solitude. The solemn public ceremony which now enshrines the profession of a monk is intended to symbolize the monk's gift of himself and God's acceptance of his gift. It is now recognized by the Church as one of the major sacramentals. Profession itself is, of course, only a beginning of that conversion which must continue throughout the monk's life. But it sums up the entire meaning of the monastic life, speaking eloquently of the themes of conversion and penance whose sources we have found in the Bible, the liturgy and the nature of the Church herself.

Monastic profession has assumed a legal aspect, for it is the means by which the Church juridically binds the monk to fidelity to the manner of life which he has freely chosen under the inspiration of divine grace. The juridical character of profession is recognized already in St. Benedict's regulations for the rite. But this is not the whole of the reality. Primarily it is a religious act, involving not only the rendering of worship to God by the monk's gift of himself, but also the reciprocal action of God sanctifying and consecrating the monk to his service. In this section we wish to see how the rite of profession originated and developed in monastic tradition and what meaning was attached to it. The principal themes which occur in the tradition which surrounds the profession rite are those which regard the monastic life as baptism, as martyrdom, as imitation of Christ's passion, as military service, as a consecration. We shall see how profession understood in this sense constitutes the gateway to monastic life.

Adoption of the Monastic Habit

The oldest form of profession rite, which goes back to the earliest days of monasticism, consisted simply in a change of clothing. The prospective monk laid aside his worldly clothes and put on the rough, poor vesture which was commonly worn by monks. The first monks simply assumed the habit themselves. Later it was the custom for them to receive the monastic habit from the spiritual father to whose direction they submitted during their period of training. At the beginning of his eremitical experience at Subiaco, St. Benedict received the habit–*sanctae conversationis habitum*–in this way from the monk Romanus (*Dial* 2,1). In cenobitic monasteries the abbot conferred the monastic habit upon new recruits. St. Pachomius would do this only after the candidate had demonstrated his sincerity during a period of probation (*Reg Pach* 49).

The first monks, like the ascetics who preceded them, did not wear any distinctive kind of garb. They were recognizable, however, from the wretched quality of their clothing: it was an axiom among the desert Fathers that a monk's garment should be so poor that no one would think of stealing it if he should leave it lying about in the open. Soon, however, a distinctive type of garment was adopted, which recalled the vesture of Elijah the prophet and of John the Baptist: the simple garment called *melota*, made of the skin of an animal and held in place with a leather cincture (cf 4 Kgs 1,8; Mt 3,4; Heb 11,37). At the time of his death St. Anthony had two such sheepskins, which he bequeathed to St. Athanasius and Bishop Serapion (*Vita Antonii* 91). St. Benedict wore the same kind of garment at Subiaco: St. Gregory describes him as *vestitus pellibus* (*Dial* 2,1) and speaks of his wearing the *melota* (*ibid* 2,7).

Later on other articles of monastic dress came into use. The tunic replaced the sheepskin or *melota* in the Pachomian monasteries and is prescribed by the *Holy Rule* (55,4.10). The pallium was a mantle worn by philosophers and adopted by some monks in accord with the idea that the monastic life was the true *philosophia*. The scapular probably was a kind of strap worn over the shoulders to protect the tunic during work; it is prescribed by the *Rule* (55,6). The cuculla was originally a hood covering the head and shoulders which was gradually extended until it became a full-length garment (cf *Rule* 55,4.10). In the Middle Ages this garment was so characteristic of monks that they were referred to as the *gens cucullata*.

The Symbolic Value of Monastic Vesture

A symbolic value was widely attributed to these garments. The *melota* brings to mind the prophetic character of monastic life, which belongs to the charismatic order and not to the ecclesiastical hierarchy. It also reminds the monk of the sin of the first parents, the cause of man's need for clothing, and the consequent necessity of conversion: it is a penitential garment. Its poor character is symbolic of poverty, renunciation and asceticism. The tunic is the garment of the soldier of Christ; the scapular symbolizes the asceticism of work and the constant bearing of the cross; the cincture chastity and mortification. However, the monastic habit was also regarded as symbolic of the new life of grace and thus compared to the baptismal robe: this symbolism is generally applied to the cuculla in later tradition. The Byzantine monks today still speak of the great habit worn by the *pneumatikoi* as the "angelic garment."

The habit itself, therefore, spoke eloquently of what is involved in the monastic vocation. For this reason the assumption of the habit was regarded as a sufficient indication of a man's intention of conversion of life, without an oral profession or any liturgical rite whatever. Stripping himself of his secular clothing meant laying aside his whole previous manner of life and fleeing the sinful world with all its attractions. Hence St. Benedict prescribes that a monk unfaithful to his vocation shall be stripped of his habit and clothed once more in his secular garb before returning to the world (58,27–28). Cassian explains that the stripping away of a monk's secular clothing signifies not only the loss "of all his former possessions, but also that he has abandoned all worldly pride, and become subject to the destitution and poverty of Christ" (*Inst* 4,5).

The assumption of the habit which followed signified the putting on of "the new man, which has been created according to God in justice and holiness of truth" (Eph 4,24). The monk thus proclaims his intention to live for God alone, to devote himself exclusively to the service of God and to prayer. At the same time, however, the taking of the monastic habit testifies that this new life, in the present economy, will be one of harsh combat against the flesh and the demons before the monk can scale the heights of contemplation.

Development of Profession Rite

St. Basil seems to have been the first to require an explicit oral promise. We do not know the formula that was used, but he mentions the "profession of virginity" and specifies that it should be pronounced in the presence of an authorized witness representing the

Church (*Longer Rules* 15). So far as we know, this was the first effort to integrate monasticism into the ecclesiastical hierarchy, and is quite consistent with the general tendencies of the Cappadocian movement. As far as the content of profession was concerned, Basil's demands were the same as those of other monastic legislators: renunciation of family and friends, of worldly manner of life, material possessions, the lusts of the flesh, above all of oneself (cf *Longer Rules* 8).

We do not have the profession formula of St. Benedict either, but the *Holy Rule* outlines a more developed ritual of profession than previous monastic legislation (58,17–29). First of all the candidate made his *promissio*, an oral promise to observe all the obligations of the life which he wished to embrace. Unlike his predecessors, however, St. Benedict required that this promise be put in writing, a document which he calls the *petitio*. The novice was to write it himself, or at least sign it, and place it upon the altar; afterward it was to be kept in the monastery as testimony of his profession, and if he ever was unfaithful to his promise, would serve as a witness against him. In this provision we can discern a certain juridical concern which is undoubtedly a product of the western mentality.

Yet the legal aspect is entirely overshadowed by the religious character of the rite. After placing the *petitio* upon the altar, the novice sings the *Suscipe me Domine* (Ps 118,116) and the community repeats it three times, adding *Gloria Patri;* then the novice lies prostrate at the feet of each of his brethren, asking them to pray for him. Finally the rite concludes with that traditional act which was always regarded as essential to monastic profession: the clothing in the habit.

The role of the abbot in this rite is to receive the *petitio* written in his name. There is no indication that he performed any hierarchical function such as imposing of hands or pronouncing a consecratory prayer, and it is gratuitous to suppose that St. Benedict simply takes this for granted, though such a consecration of monks later appears in all the rituals of profession. St. Benedict's mention of the altar seems to place the profession rite in relation to the Eucharistic sacrifice, and in fact the early medieval rituals prescribe that the abbot shall celebrate a Mass of profession and pronounce a benediction over the monk.

Profession and Religious Vows

As far as the content of profession is concerned, St. Benedict had the same understanding as did his predecessors of what is involved in the profession of monastic life. It is a complete conversion: a renunciation of the world and total consecration of one's person to God. The *Rule* specifies that the *promissio* shall concern stability, *conversatio morum* and obedience. This statement has often been taken to mean that the three elements mentioned were to be explicitly vowed as constituting the essential content of monastic profession: the monk's *promissio* would have consisted of three distinct promises, which are frequently referred to as the "Benedictine vows." However, it is an anachronism to attribute to St. Benedict a concept of vows which did not arise until a later period.

The practice of reducing the content of religious life to a determined number of vows, usually three, is a product of the concern of the scholastics for accurate analysis and definition. The vows are an attempt to systematize the totality of religious life under a few briefly stated but comprehensive obligations. Different forms of such systematization are conceivable, but none is entirely adequate, for no classification according to logical and juridical concepts is capable of expressing the complete experiential reality of the renunciation and consecration to God which are entailed in religious profession. The classical division is that of poverty, chastity and obedience. St. Thomas justifies it by explaining that each of these vows corresponds to one of three categories of created goods: exterior goods, goods of the body and goods of the soul (*S.T.* 2–2, q186, a7 c). These are what St. John calls "the lust of the flesh, and the lust of the eyes, and the pride of life" (1 Jn 2,16). These are therefore the *essential* renunciations of religious life.

Each of these renunciations is then conceived of as forming the object of a specific promise by the religious. Here there enters a concept of legal binding force which is a product of the western juridical mind. At its worst it has led to the abuses of unnecessary subtlety, casuistry and legalism. The speculative analysis of religious life, however, and the accompanying classification of the vows are in themselves both legitimate and useful. But it does not represent the mind of St. Benedict nor of ancient monasticism in general.

Ancient Concept of Monastic Profession

We have seen that the ancient monks made no attempt to analyze monastic life speculatively or to define it by identifying substance and accidents. They looked upon it as an existential whole and spoke of its content in metaphors and themes which related it to the biblical prototypes. When a man entered the monastic life he knew what would be required of him and simply undertook to fulfill all that was entailed in that form of life, without inquiring what was essential or what could be disregarded without serious sin. When the custom of oral profession was introduced, the monk explicitly mentioned some of the principal obligations which he was assuming, but there was no attempt to classify them as distinct promises accompanied by legal obligations. We do not know precisely what was mentioned, as none of the ancient profession formulas has survived. It was understood that profession seriously bound the monk for life, and abandonment of his monastic vocation was universally held to be equivalent to sacrilege (cf Basil, *Longer Rules* 14).

St. Benedict's brief statement that the novice must make a promise in regard to his stability, *conversatio morum* and obedience is not a profession formula. These three elements of monastic life, of which the second is of uncertain meaning, are not intended as an enumeration of distinct vows which the candidate must make. They are not presumed to exhaust the content of monastic life, nor even to constitute its essential elements. They are merely a rubrical indication of some of the elements which are included in the content of the *promissio*. They are not the only things the monk must promise, but are partial indications of the content of profession. What the monk promises is to embrace the monastic life in its entirety, as it was traditionally understood. St. Benedict is entitled to suppose that the novice, who has already had the *Rule* read to him three times (cf 58,9–13), understands the absolute character of the renunciation which he must make.

Profession as Consecration

Renunciation, however, is only the negative element in monastic profession, which was regarded positively as a consecration of the person to the exclusive service of God. His intention to embrace the monastic life involved a complete holocaust of himself, body and soul. We have seen that the monk's life was thought of as a liturgy to such an extent that his prayer and asceticism sometimes substituted for participation in liturgical action. The monk's whole life was a continuous prayer, a sacrifice of praise to God. The desert was the temple in which this liturgical offering was made, or the monk himself was regarded as a temple. The monk realized in his person the elements of every religious consecration: he was set apart from all that is profane, and devoted exclusively to divine service.

This holiness, however, was of a purely spiritual and charismatic character; it was not sacramental like the consecration involved in sacred orders. For this reason the assumption of the habit was a sufficient indication of the monk's consecration. Originally there was no liturgical rite for the consecration of a monk, no official acceptance by the Church of his offering nor liturgical intervention to sanctify his person. Such a rite developed, however, at an early period, in consequence of the tendency to integrate monasticism into the ecclesiastical hierarchy. It evolved as a correlative of the consecration of virgins, which is attested as early as the third century.

The first known reference to a consecration of monks occurs in a letter of St. Nilus in the early fifth century. Since he asks a wandering monk which abbot imposed "the hand of consecration" upon him, it appears that the rite then consisted of an imposition of hands accompanied by a consecratory prayer. The first description of such a rite is found in the *Ecclesiastical Hierarchy* of the Pseudo-Dionysius, who wrote in Syria at the beginning of the sixth century (ch 6). He classifies it as a secondary consecration, at which a priest rather than a bishop officiates. The rite includes four elements: an *epiclesis* or consecratory prayer, pronounced over the monk as he stands before the priest; an oral profession by which the monk formally promises to renounce the world and is marked with the sign of the cross; the tonsure; and the vesting in the monastic habit, followed by the kiss of peace. Other ancient rituals from the East contain similar rites, sometimes including also an imposition of hands.

Evolution of the Consecration Rite

In the Eastern Church the consecration of the monk has been developed into an elaborate ceremony in which the dominant theme is the analogy with baptism. The rite gives great prominence to the monastic habit, especially in the case of the consecration of "monks of the great habit," who receive the "angelic garment." In the West it was adopted more slowly. Neither Cassian nor St. Augustine mentions a consecration of monks in the fifth century. At the time of St. Benedict it seems to be unknown to the *Regula Magistri* and to Caesarius of Arles. We have seen that the *Holy Rule* makes no mention of it: while developing the ceremony of monastic profession and introducing a written *petitio,* St. Benedict says nothing of a consecratory prayer or of any intervention by a priest.

In later centuries the rite was widely introduced into Benedictine monasteries and was generally calculated upon the analogy with baptism. The *Penitential* of Theodore of Canterbury in the late seventh century, which seems to be of oriental inspiration, prescribes that the abbot celebrate the Mass and pronounce three prayers over the monk. More than a century later the commentary of the Pseudo Paul the Deacon has a similar provision for an *oratio* over the monk. The present ritual of profession which, though subject to variations, generally contains a Preface with orations *ad faciendum monachum,* is largely based upon a *Roman Pontifical* of the tenth or eleventh century. Thus in the end the consecration ceremony has been added to the simple rite of monastic profession that prevailed among the earliest monks and was reproduced with some elaboration by St. Benedict.

The rite of consecration is a legitimate development and there need be no objection to its introduction. However a sense of balance should be maintained. The primary element is the profession itself, the act of the monk outwardly expressing his will to undertake a conversion of his life, to leave behind the world and all its attractions and to embrace the new life of total self-dedication to God. This, which was considered sufficient by the ancients, should always remain the predominant element of the profession rite. The consecration, by which the Church, acting through the priest, signifies her acceptance of the monk's offering and confers a solemn blessing upon him, is a secondary element and should not be so elaborate as to overshadow the profession itself.

Monastic Life as Military Service

It is the meaning of monastic profession, however, rather than the form which it assumed, with which we are principally concerned. As the gateway to monastic life, profession implied a radical break with the past and conversion to a new life. The ancient monastic literature explores the significance of this conversion in the elaboration of various themes and analogies, some of which we may briefly examine here. The first of these presents profession as induction into military service for a spiritual warfare.

The metaphor of the Christian life as military service is a New Testament theme which was particularly dear to St. Paul. He calls the Christian a "soldier of Christ Jesus" (2 Tim 2,3) and describes the "armor of God" with which he must wage the spiritual warfare: the breastplate of justice, the shield of faith, the helmet of salvation, the sword of the spirit (cf Eph 6,11–17; also 1 Thess 5,8; Rom 13,12; 2 Cor 6,7; 10,4–6). The idea of the *militia christiana* was early applied to the monks, so that the monastic state was frequently referred to as *militia spiritualis* (e.g. Cassian, *Conf* 1,1) and the monk was called the "soldier of Christ" (e.g. Id., *Inst* 1,1), a term which already appears in the Latin translation of the *Vita Antonii.* The monk was one who had enlisted in the army of Christ, lived in a spiritual encampment and armed himself with the weapons of prayer, fasting and vigils (cf Cassian, *Conf* 7,5). Application of this military terminology to the monastic life seemed particularly appropriate because the monk's asceticism was conceived of as a combat against the demons and vices, the spiritual warfare of which St. Paul speaks (cf *Vita Antonii* 21).

The theme of monastic life as military service was widespread in the West in the sixth century and St. Benedict frequently alludes to it. The *Rule* is addressed to those who wish to "fight for the true King, Christ," with "the strong and glorious weapons of obedience" (Pr 3; cf Pr 40). The cenobite is one who "serves (*militans*) under a rule and an abbot" (1,2). There is to be no distinction of persons in the monastery because we all "serve alike in the army of the same Lord" (2,20; cf 61,10). The *Rule* is the "law under which you wish to serve (*militare*)" (58,10). In the *Rule,* however, this military terminology has largely lost the connotation of an armed struggle, and is used rather in the sense of *service.* The enemy is one's self-will, and service of Christ consists precisely in obedience to the rule and the abbot, the foundation for the cenobite's manner of life. The themes of *miles Christi, servus Dei* and *discipulus* began to lose their original meaning at this period and tended to converge.

Monastic Profession: Taking up the Cross

The monastic life was also regarded as an imitation of Christ in his suffering and death. The ascetical program of the monk was a crucifixion and mortification of his passions. Hence he was especially consecrated to the passion of Christ; to put on the monastic habit was to clothe oneself in the passion and agree to follow Jesus upon the way of the cross. As a reminder of this the Pachomian monks wore a red cross on their cuculla. The monastic literature often refers to the Gospel invitation to follow Christ in his sufferings: "If anyone wishes to come after me, let him deny himself, and take up his cross daily, and follow me" (Lk 9,23; cf 14,27). St. Basil comments that to take up one's cross means to be willing to die for Christ, to mortify one's body, to stand firm against every danger and to be indifferent toward this life (cf *Longer Rules* 6). The monk is one who takes up the cross of suffering in this life to follow his Savior: *nudam crucem nudus sequens*, in the lapidary phrase of St. Jerome (*Epist* 58,2).

Cassian comments at some length upon the crucifixion of the monk. He must fulfill the precept of the Apostle, who forbids us to glory in anything but the cross of Christ, "through whom the world is crucified to me, and I to the world" (Gal 6,14). Hence the monk must be dead to the world: the cross is the *sacramentum* under which his life is placed, for he no longer lives, but Christ who was crucified for him lives in him (cf Gal 2,19–20). The monk must carry the cross continually and observe the command of the Psalmist to pierce his flesh with the fear of the Lord (Ps 118,120). The fear of the Lord is his cross, for just as the cross prevents a crucified man from turning aside, so the fear of the Lord constrains the monk not to turn back to the attractions of the world to which he is dead (cf *Inst* 4,34–35).

While this theme is not developed at length in the *Holy Rule*, it is brought out with remarkable clarity at the end of the Prologue: "Persevering in his teaching in the monastery until death, we shall share by patience in the sufferings of Christ, that we may deserve to be partakers also of his kingdom" (Pr 50). Patience for St. Benedict means suffering, sharing in the passion of Christ: "to bear patiently wrongs done to one-self" (4,30); "meeting in this obedience with difficulties and contradictions and even injustice, he should with a quiet mind hold fast to patience" (7,35); "in adversities and injuries they patiently fulfill the Lord's commands" (7,42). Monastic profession is to embrace the cross of Christ.

Monastic Life and Martyrdom

The theme of suffering together with Christ is closely connected with the analogy drawn in ancient times between the monk and the martyr. Although the theme of monastic life as martyrdom does not occur explicitly in the *Holy Rule* (but cf 7,38), it was popular among the oriental predecessors of St. Benedict, as well as among his contemporaries in the West (e.g. *Regula Magistri* 7,59). We have seen how the monks' flight to the desert came at the end of the era of persecutions and may have been partially encouraged by dissatisfaction with the situation of a Church which no longer demanded martyrdom of its members. During the time of the persecutions the martyrs who shed their blood for Christ were the great heroes of the Christian people: they bore witness to their faith with their very lives. When the Church came to be at peace with the state, she needed new heroes, and the monks then stepped in to succeed the martyrs.

It is in this context that the comparison of the monk to the martyr first presents itself in the *Vita Antonii.* St. Athanasius tells us that when the persecution of Maximinus broke out in Egypt in 305 and Christians were being tried and executed in Alexandria, Anthony had such a great desire to suffer martyrdom that he left his solitude and went into the city. He cared for the confessors in the mines and prisons, and at the tribunal he encouraged them to proclaim their faith boldly. Anthony made every effort to achieve martyrdom, even remaining in the city and continuing to frequent the court after the prefect had banished monks from Alexandria, but to no avail. When the persecution ended in 311, "He left and again went back to his cell, and there he was daily a martyr to his conscience, fighting battles for the faith" (cf *Vita Antonii* 46–47). Anthony's battles were the struggles of the ascetical combat, through which he gave expression to the same ardent love for Christ that had inspired the martyrs in their torments. It was thus that the monks took over the martyrs' function in the Church.

Suffering in the Life of the Monk

The comparison of the monastic life to martyrdom caught on quickly. Jerome proclaims: "Bloodshed is not the only thing that counts as confession of the faith, but the service rendered by a devoted heart is a daily martyrdom" (*Epist* 108,32) and "the practice of virginity involves a martyrdom of its own" (*ibid* 130,5). Cassian connects the monk's crucifixion with the idea of martyrdom when he says: "Patience and the strict observance by which they so devoutly continue in the profession which they have undertaken that they never fulfill their own will make them daily crucified to this world and living martyrs" (*Conf* 18,7).

In the West, where St. Martin of Tours was the exemplar of monastic life comparable to Anthony in the East, his biographer proclaimed him a martyr:

> Although the character of the times could not allow him martyrdom, yet he will not be without the glory of a martyr, because by his desire and his virtue he was both able and willing to be a martyr. . . . Although he did not suffer these tortures, nevertheless he achieved martyrdom without bloodshed. For what agonies of human suffering did he not endure out of hope of eternal life: hunger, vigils, nakedness, fasting, the reproaches of the envious, the harassments of the wicked, care for the sick, anxiety for those in danger? (Sulpicius Severus, *Epist* 2).

The analogy with martyrdom rests upon the monk's bearing witness to Christ. The martyr did this by shedding his blood; the monk does it by daily bearing the death of Christ about in his body. Both imitate the sufferings of Christ, the king of martyrs, who bore witness to his Father both by his daily life and by his death. The monk's love for Christ would not shrink, indeed, from the supreme testimony of laying down his life, but it is his vocation rather to bear witness by the daily martyrdom of asceticism. This is a hidden martyrdom, which attracts no honor, may, indeed, arouse resentment and reproaches: it is thus that the monk shares in the passion of Christ. When he makes his profession, he is beginning a martyrdom of love.

The Baptismal Renunciation

Of all the analogies employed to bring out the meaning of monastic profession, perhaps the most common is that which relates it to baptism. The comparison with baptism has had a great influence upon the development of the rite of profession. The importance of baptism in the Christian life was more clearly realized in the early Church than it is today. The renunciation of the world and of Satan which the neophyte made at baptism brought about a noticeable difference in his life, especially in the era of the persecutions. It meant that he had to forego many aspects of the secular society of his time and solemnly promise fidelity to Christ, a promise which might well lead him to martyrdom. The baptismal renunciation was a reality which was acutely felt.

It was only natural, then, that the decision to embrace monastic life should be compared to baptism, for it too was a conversion involving the same elements: renunciation of the world and of Satan, and a solemn pledge to follow Christ. This is already clear in the vocation of Anthony, who renounced his property, his family and all the attractions of the world, and devoted himself to learning the practice of virtue from the ascetics whom he visited (cf *Vita Antonii* 2–4). After the cessation of the persecutions, when the ordinary profession of Christianity had ceased to involve serious risks, monastic profession stood out as the most heroic way of making an effective renunciation and following Christ to the limits of one's possibilities, as only the martyr had done before. As martyrdom had been the most complete working out of the baptismal renunciation and dedication of self to Christ, so now monastic profession became the perfect fulfillment of baptism.

Martyrdom as a Second Baptism

While the parallel between baptism and monastic profession was implicit from the beginning, the first to treat explicitly of profession as a solemn ratification of the baptismal renunciation seems to have been St. Jerome. To Demetrias he wrote: "For you have abandoned the world and for a second time, following your baptism, you have come to an encounter with the adversary, saying to him, 'I renounce you, O devil!'" (*Epist* 130,7). And to Paula, to comfort her after the death of her daughter Blaesilla: "Inasmuch as through the mercy of Christ she was purified four months ago by the second baptism, so to speak, of profession, and thus entered upon a new life, trampling upon the world and thinking only of monastic life, do you not fear that the Savior may say to you: 'Are you angry, Paula, because your daughter has become mine?' " (*Epist* 39,3).

For Jerome, the idea that profession is a second baptism is dependent upon its being a martyrdom. Martyrdom was a baptism by blood, for it was the perfect fulfillment of the renunciation of baptism. From the time of Ignatius of Antioch martyrdom was regarded as the most perfect way to follow Christ, and to it were attributed the remission of sin and the conferral of heavenly glory, just as in the case of baptism. We have seen how the monastic life came to be looked upon as a martyrdom in which the monk is crucified daily by his austerities. If it was a martyrdom, then it was also a baptism. The term *second baptism,* then, really refers to martyrdom, either the actual laying down of one's life or, in the wider extension which the concept of martyrdom received after the age of persecutions, a life of penance.

Monastic Profession: Analogy with Baptism

In the East the comparison between profession and baptism was enthusiastically adopted. The baptismal motif is predominant in the rite of monastic consecration found in the Pseudo-Dionysius and other subsequent oriental rituals. The renunciation of the world, in the form of interrogations, is modeled upon the baptismal rite, as is the formal promise to follow Christ perfectly. Above all, the monastic habit, which is surrounded with such honor in the East, is looked upon as a new baptismal garment indicative of the transformation of the person's life. The Pseudo-Dionysius comments that this rite is comparable to baptism, in which the change of vesture indicates that the catechumen has left the purgative way and entered upon the way of illumination and vision (cf *Ecclesiastical Hierarchy* 6). Other profession rites adopted still more baptismal features: conducting the renunciation in the vestibule; stripping off the monk's old garments before the profession of faith; the *sphragis;* wearing the habit for eight days afterward; referring to profession as "illumination."

In the West, however, the analogy with baptism was not ordinarily drawn in ancient times. The only notable exception to this silence is the *Regula Magistri*, which develops the baptismal theme at some length in the Prologue. The author speaks of candidates for the monastery as those regenerated by baptism who renounce their earthly parents to acknowledge the Church as their mother and the Lord as their father, and also instructs them in the Lord's Prayer, as was done in the baptismal catechesis (Thema Pater 1-11). St. Benedict makes no reference to baptism when treating of monastic profession, unless the novitiate training which he prescribes is modeled upon the catechumenate, with the three readings of the *Rule* corresponding to the *scrutinia.*

The later Benedictine tradition, however, hastened to introduce the baptismal symbolism into the rite of profession. In the early ninth century the Pseudo Paul the Deacon prescribes that the novice's head be covered with the *melota* at profession and uncovered only on the eighth day afterward. He also directs the novice to prostrate after the *Suscipe* while the *Miserere,* the *De Profundis* and other psalms are recited, a rite which brings out the idea that the monk is buried with Christ in order to rise with him, as at baptism (cf Rom 6,3–5). Later in the Middle Ages this idea of mystical death was further accentuated by the use of a funeral pall and candles. These additions to the rite, which are calculated upon the baptismal analogy and are still in use in some monasteries, displace the emphasis from the primary element of the profession, destroy the primitive simplicity of the rite and tend to be theatrical.

Effects of Profession

Another aspect of the baptismal analogy is the belief that monastic profession confers the remission of sins. This idea goes back to the earliest days of monasticism. St. Athanasius tells how Anthony once had a vision in which he was led by certain spirits. They were challenged by evil spirits who demanded an accounting of all of

Anthony's sins from his birth. His guides refused to allow him to give such an accounting because, they said, God had forgiven him all his sins from his birth until the time when he became a monk. Only for the faults he had committed since his monastic profession could they hold him accountable (*Vita Antonii* 65).

Later writers of the eastern tradition as widely separated in time as John Damascene, Theodore Studite and Simeon of Thessalonica clearly affirm the efficacy of monastic profession to forgive sin. In the West this teaching appears in the Middle Ages in the works of such theologians as St. Peter Damian, the school of Bec and St. Bernard. A practical consequence of it was that entry into religion, without any other absolution, was sometimes imposed, instead of the usual public penance, upon those guilty of serious sins.

In the scholastic period, when the distinction between the seven sacraments and the sacramentals had become clear, this teaching created a problem. St. Thomas was concerned both to preserve the traditional doctrine and to avoid making religious profession a sacrament. He teaches that profession is a sacramental, a sign of the monk's devotion to God, which sanctifies him, not *ex opere operato*, but by virtue of the sentiments of faith and charity which inspire his self-devotion. In this sense it is a further perfection of baptism, for it insures the full effects of the sacrament of regeneration (cf *S.T.* 2–2, q88, a7 c; q189, a3, ad3; q65, a l, ad 6).

This problem of an *ex opere operato* efficacy of profession never occured to the ancients, who did not make these distinctions. For them profession was a second baptism because it was a martyrdom. They drew the analogy only on the level of the *opus operantis*, the effort of the individual: profession is like baptism because it is a more absolute renunciation which builds upon the baptismal renunciation and constitutes its fulfillment; and, like baptism, it opens the door to a new life of self-dedication to divine service. Profession in this sense is not merely a transitory ritual act, but the entire life of the monk, a lasting conversion. In this sense the analogy helps to clarify the significance of profession, as the gateway to an existence in which a man turns his back completely upon the world of sin and lives only for God.

5 The Active Life:
I. The Spiritual Combat

ONCE HE HAS ENTERED upon the monastic life through the gateway of profession, the monk must begin the struggle for perfection. The classical theory of monastic perfection was elaborated by Evagrius of Pontus and transmitted to the West by Cassian, who expounds it in his first *Conference*. According to this system there are two phases in the spiritual ascent: the active life (*vita activa*) and the contemplative life (*vita theoretica*). The division is made on the basis of a distinction between the ultimate end (*finis*) of monastic life and its proximate goal (*destinatio vel scopos*). While the end is eternal life, the goal is purity of heart. The active life, or first phase, is the continuous ascent to the goal by means of the ascetical combat. Once attained, purity of heart opens the door to the contemplative life, or second phase, which leads to the final end, eternal life, a reality which can be tasted already in this life through contemplation.

Obviously this systematization is more rigorous than actual experience: in practice, the two phases in the spiritual ascent will often be parallel or alternative rather than strictly successive. Nevertheless it has its value as a classification of the elements of monastic spirituality, and it will be convenient to follow it in our exposition. To distinguish the two phases is not to imply that they will be separate in practice. The active life, with which the ascent begins, is the struggle for purity of heart by the use of the traditional monastic exercises of asceticism. It is the concrete working out of the renunciation to which the monk pledges himself at profession. It represents, therefore, the negative aspect of the spiritual ascent, though it is understood that asceticism is directed to a positive goal and exercised under the inspiration of charity. We shall speak first of the spiritual climate in which the ascetical combat is waged, a climate determined by solitude, discretion, compunction and humility; then of the individual elements of monastic renunciation: asceticism, poverty, virginity, obedience, stability, *conversatio morum* and work.

1. BEATA SOLITUDO

Flight from the World

We have seen that monasticism began with flight from the world. Since the very word *monk* means one who lives in solitude, it was the universal conviction of the ancients that separation from the world constituted the climate that was essential to the pursuit of monastic life. St. Athanasius represented the spiritual ascent of Anthony as an increasingly radical separation from the world, in which four consecutive degrees of flight from human society are traced. First Anthony withdrew to a place just outside his native village (*Vita Antonii* 3); then he took up his dwelling in a tomb some distance away (*ibid* 8); next he withdrew into the desert, settling upon the "outer mountain" in the solitude of Pispir on the east bank of the Nile (*ibid* 12); finally he penetrated into the remotest recesses of the desert between the Nile and the Red Sea and ended his days on the "inner mountain," far from any human habitation (*ibid* 49–50). It is clearly Athanasius's intention to suggest that growth in virtue is correlative with the degree of separation from the world.

The necessity of fleeing the world is emphasized by all the monastic writers of all periods, in both East and West. St. Jerome's vigorous apostrophe to Paulinus of Nola is well known: "If you want to justify your name of *monk*, that is *solitary*, what are you doing in cities, which are not the dwellings of solitaries, but of crowds?" (*Epist* 58,5). St. Benedict stood firmly in the line of a constant monastic tradition when he fled from the corrupt world that he had known at Rome and "withdrew the foot which he had placed on the threshold of the world, so to speak, for fear that if he came to absorb something of the knowledge of it, he too might afterward fall headlong over the fatal precipice" (*Dial* 2, Pr).

Solidarity despite Physical Separation

We have already noted that the term "world" is used in two senses in the Scriptures, particularly by St. John. On the one hand, it designates creation insofar as it has fallen from its original integrity and been reduced to servitude in the kingdom of Satan. From this world every Christian must make his escape, for there is implacable warfare between it and the kingdom of God: "If the world hates you, know that it has hated me before you. If you were of the world, the world would love what is its own. But because you are not of the world, but I have chosen you out of the world, therefore the world hates you" (Jn 15,18–19). In order to escape from this fallen world more effectively, the monk separates himself physically from the world in quite another sense, insofar as the same term designates the society of men whom God loves and seeks to save. In this sense of the term St. John says: "God so loved the world that he gave his only-begotten Son, that those who believe in him may not perish, but may have life everlasting" (Jn 3,16). In isolating himself from human society, the monk obviously does not and cannot rupture the bond of solidarity which indissolubly unites his destiny to that of all his human brothers. Rather his physical separation unites him even more closely to his brethren in another sense.

Whatever may have been the motives that prompted the flight of the early monks–substitution for martyrdom, escape from laxity, desire to seek out the devil in his stronghold, or to find the lost paradise—they did not withdraw from an egotistical desire to find tranquillity in the abandonment of concern for their fellow men. It was not the world of their brethren in Christ that they fled, but the world subject to the dominion of Satan. Authentic monks of all ages, no matter how radical their isolation, have not ceased to be concerned about the world's salvation. Both those who flee the world to find God in the encounter of silence and those who remain in it to find him in their fellow men are realizing an integral aspect of the Christian vocation, in obedience to the Gospel and to the Spirit who summons them.

Spirituality of the Desert

The monk who takes refuge in the desert does so in order to find God. For it is the experience of the whole of sacred history that it is there that God is to be found. The chosen people found him during their forty years' wandering in the wilderness of Sinai: amid the privileges and the trials of this harsh existence they came to understand that he cannot be found amid the wealth and pleasures of Egypt, but only in the stern asceticism of desert life. Later, when their hearts had been seduced by the riches of the Promised Land, and they had gone a-whoring after the fertility gods of their pagan neighbors, the prophets proclaimed that only a return to the desert could bring Israel back to the happy idyll of her espousal to Yahweh that had been consummated in the Exodus.

Elijah, too, and the sons of the prophets, took refuge in the desert, and after them came John the Baptist. The early monks were conscious that their life was a continuation of that of the prophets. Their very garb, their mortified life, their expectation of the coming of the Lord, all reproduced the experience of the prophets. Above all, it was an imitation of Christ himself, who "was led into the desert by the Spirit, to be tempted by the devil" (Mt 4,1). The desert was the dwelling place of demons, whom the monk must engage in combat in the remotest recesses of their own stronghold. He must be put to this test, in which the divine strength is pitted against the power of the enemy, and must win a decisive victory over him as Christ himself had done.

If dwelling in an actual desert is more a symbolic requirement of monasticism than a real one, nevertheless there must be a real separation from the world. The real physical separation is one of the most distinctive traits of monastic spirituality, and, in the exterior form which it assumes, serves to distinguish it from other forms of spirituality. The Gospel demands that every Christian renounce the evil world; it likewise demands that everyone concern himself with the salvation of the world. But it does not require that everyone fulfill these two imperatives in the same way. The monk fulfills them by fleeing into solitude, there to conquer the prince of this world so that he may be free to give himself for the salvation of others.

Necessity of Solitude

Every monk, then, must live in solitude. He must be a pilgrim, seeking the way to the "Jerusalem which is above" (Gal 4,26) through the desert of the present life. He has here "no permanent city, but seeks for the city that is to come" (cf Heb 13,14). Even the cenobite, whose separation from other men is less radical than that of the anchorite, must be in some sense a solitary. The world of his monastery is not the world which is under the empire of Satan, but is already an anticipation of the heavenly Jerusalem. His separation from the world of sin must be as absolute as that of his forerunners in the desert.

St. Benedict insists that the monastery's isolation be preserved at all costs. It is within the enclosure that monks are to exercise the tools of good works (4,78). They are not to go out into the world except in cases of necessity, for this "is not at all expedient for their souls" (66,7), and in these exceptional cases they must be protected by prayer before, during and after their absence (67,1–4). It is severely forbidden to go out without permission (67,7) or to tell others about the affairs of the world outside the monastery (67,5–6).

Equally stringent measures are taken to keep the world out of the monastery: while guests are welcomed, various precautions are taken to see that their visits do not disturb the regular life or the solitude of the monks (53 *passim*). Letters, gifts and any other communication from the outside world must pass through the abbot's censorship before the monk may receive them (54,1–2).

Recollection and Silence

None of these measures in itself, however, will be effective in preserving the monk's spirit of solitude unless he really wants to preserve it. Actual physical separation can only banish distractions and hence is a negative precaution; but the real value of solitude is a positive thing, a continual absorption in God. The monk's whole attention must not only be withdrawn from useless or harmful objects; it must be positively concentrated upon God and the necessities of salvation. This means that he must cultivate the habit of recollection.

It is here that we come to the importance of silence in monastic life. Recollection and prayer are impossible if talking is permitted without limit. Many of the sayings of the desert Fathers were devoted to the value of silence, and Cassian insisted upon its necessity. On this point St. Benedict is entirely in the tradition of the ancient eastern monks. At certain times and places he requires an absolute silence: in the refectory (38,5), in the oratory (52,2), in the dormitory (42,8; 48,5), and everywhere in the monastery at night after Compline (42,8).

At other times and places there is no absolute ban upon speaking; there is only care to restrict and regulate speech so that the atmosphere of recollection may be preserved. Rather than the ascetical value of renouncing speech as a form of mortification, it is the positive value of preserving a spirit of prayer that St. Benedict is aiming at with his legislation. Even his terminology suggests this: when he speaks of absolute quiet, he says *summum silentium* (38,5; 52,2) or *omne silentium* (48,5); but when he means the spirit of silence, moderation in speaking, he usually says *taciturnitas* (6,2–3; 7,56).

Four Types of Speech

In chapter 6, which treats *ex professo* of *taciturnitas,* St. Benedict distinguishes four different kinds of speech. First of all, there are evil conversations, which are obviously excluded by an elementary sense of morality (6,2). These include the various sins of the tongue, whether against justice, truth, charity or temperance. Obvious as this prohibition may be, it is not superfluous to insist upon it, as sins of the tongue are among the most frequent and insidious failings of all men, and monks must be particularly on their guard against them. They are perhaps even more exposed to certain faults of this kind than the Christian in the world, for living close together is bound to produce friction, which may find expression in detraction and uncharitable speech if a monk has not learned to keep a close watch over his tongue.

Undesirable also is speech which is not in itself sinful, but is scurrilous, useless, and leads to laughter and buffoonery. This is talking simply for the sake of talking, without having anything worthwhile to say. St. Benedict forbids this absolutely: "We condemn such things everywhere with a perpetual ban, and forbid the disciple to open his mouth for such conversation" (6,8). The reason is that such idle speech is diametrically opposed to the atmosphere of recollection without which a monastery cannot be a place of prayer, and it destroys in the monk the attitude of seriousness and calm reflection which is essential to his spiritual progress.

The third type of speech consists in necessary communication with others, especially with superiors. Provided that it be restricted to what is truly necessary, this does no violence to the taciturnity of the monastery and is permitted (6,7). Finally, there is the question of edifying conversations. In principle these are for the monk's advantage, but they too must be regulated, and St. Benedict prefers that they be the exception rather than the rule (6,3–5). He gives two reasons: the monk's love of silence, which should urge him to prefer silence even to good speech, and the persistent danger that even edifying conversations may degenerate into a waste of time or even into sins of the tongue.

The Ideal of Taciturnity

The *Rule* makes no provision for recreation periods, nor do the earliest commentaries know of this custom, though it became widespread in later Carolingian times. But certainly St. Benedict did not intend a silence so absolute that his monks were always required to use signs rather than speech; this is prescribed only for the refectory, so that the reading will not be disturbed (38,7). He forbids talking at "unseasonable hours" (48,21), a prescription which supposes that there were times when it was permitted. One of the things that the monk is encouraged to give up for Lent is talking (49,7), which also supposes that it was legitimate at times.

These and other passages of the *Rule* indicate that St. Benedict's ideal was not simply the abolition of all speech, but the habit of temperance in speaking. *Taciturnitas* is the opposite of *loquacitas*, which means unregulated talking with all the evils that accompany it. Silence in itself is of no value; it is the discreet control of the faculty of speech which is a virtue. The man who never speaks is not necessarily a good man, nor is talking the only form of escape from the habit of taciturnity. In the modern world, men sometimes talk too little, for the very atmosphere is too noisy for talking. Fear makes some men enamored of noise, which enables them to forget the serious problems and values of life. The modern attraction toward constant activity is merely a translation of noise from sound to motion. Discord and confusion can be expressed through various media equally opposed to a genuine spirit of recollection and peace.

A right esteem for speech is the sign of a virtuous man. He values the power of speech and the tool of language as gifts of God. While respecting their use, he seeks to avoid and correct their abuse. Language is a sacred sign, through which human and divine knowledge and love can find expression. Speech is neither to be despised nor overindulged. At times silence can be the most eloquent tribute to the presence of God, for often it is impossible to say what one knows and loves. A genuine sense of the sacred inspires wonder, the source of a confident silence.

Listening to God's Voice

The value of silence is that it enables us to listen. St. Benedict insists that "it becometh the master to speak and to teach; but it befits the disciple to be silent and to listen" (6,6). Here again he is in the spirit of ancient monasticism, which placed so much emphasis upon the oral instruction of the novice by the spiritual father. There can be only one authentic teacher in the community, for if everyone offers his infallible opinions, the result can only be confusion and discord. Monks must be ready to accept the sacred teaching from the lips of the abbot, and to speak themselves only with meekness and humility.

The abbot's teaching is not his own, but is the Word of God. The spiritual father is one who possesses the Holy Spirit and is therefore able to communicate it to others. When we are silent, it is in order that we may hear the voice of God speaking to us. This prepares us in turn to engage in the dialogue with God which is prayer, in which it is not we ourselves who speak to God, but the Holy Spirit who speaks in us: we "have received a spirit of adoption as sons, by virtue of which we cry, 'Abba! Father!' " (Rom 8,15). The silence of the monastery should not create a cold, depressing atmosphere, but should be a living, breathing reality, vibrant with the voice of God, who makes himself heard neither in the wind, nor in the earthquake, nor in the fire, but in the whisper of a gentle breeze (cf 3 Kgs 19,11–12).

Preserving Recollection

The spirit of recollection grows out of an authentic compunction and fear of the Lord; it is itself an expression of humility. The proud man wishes to display his knowledge in incessant talking. The humble man is the one who knows how to say the right thing at the right time. Taciturnity is a question of being in harmony with the Spirit of God who dwells in us, of placing oneself in the habitual attitude of contemplation.

Scurrility can only banish the Spirit and introduce dissipation and distraction. In the modern world, which thrives upon noise, a real effort must be made to preserve the spirit of recollection in the monastery by keeping the noise of the world outside. The introduction of radio, television and movies into monasteries is the surest way to destroy the spirit of recollection and peace. Once this is gone, the monastic ideal is in grave jeopardy. Equally dangerous is the unrestricted reading of secular newspapers and magazines.

Recreation is quite another matter, but recreation in the monastery must be different from what the world calls recreation. Its purpose is not to dissipate, but to relax and renew. Fruitful communication with his brethren can help to restore the monk's spiritual strength and enable him to return to the pursuit of his ideal with renewed energy. Recreation is not a time for letting down all the bars; on the contrary, to participate in it in the right way demands an effort. It should not be an interlude in which the monk takes a brief holiday from striving for perfection, but rather a means to further his striving.

Recreation in the monastery should be a fully human activity, and at the same time a supernatural one. It is not a form of entertainment, but a living contact between persons united in the pursuit of a common ideal. This demands the intelligent participation of men who have realized their human potentialities, unlike the half-people who too often animate the television and movie screens. One of the advantages of cenobitic life is that it affords the individual the help of many brethren. Recreation is one of the activities where this advantage can be best realized, for it offers the opportunity of a meeting of minds. The supernatural vitality of a community is at a low ebb if its members are not able to communicate intelligently with one another, or refuse to do so because they prefer to be entertained. Recreation should be a matter of using the God-given gift of speech to draw the whole community closer to God.

2. DISCRETION

Discretione Praecipua

In his solitude the monk must learn to use the weapons of the spiritual combat, or, to use the metaphor of St. Benedict, "the tools of the spiritual craft" which are employed in "the enclosure of the monastery and stability in the community" (4,75–78). The virtue which guides his use of these tools is discretion. Of all the eminent qualities of the *Holy Rule*, it is its discretion which has generally been singled out as most worthy of praise. St. Gregory referred to the *Rule* as *discretione praecipua* (*Dial* 2,36). St. Benedict not only possessed this important virtue himself, but he also insisted upon its necessity for his monks. It is due to this quality that the *Rule of St. Benedict* has enjoyed such a lasting influence in the Church, whereas other monastic rules of greater severity but less breadth of view are now only relics of the past.

"Let all things be done in moderation" (48,9) is a basic principle of the *Rule*, and to the abbot it gives the pregnant advice, "*ne quid nimis*" (64,12). Similar expressions occur throughout the *Rule*. The monks for whom it was envisaged are beginners (73,8), and St. Benedict is cautious not to impose anything "harsh or burdensome," lest the weak "be dismayed and run away from the way of salvation" (Pr 46–48). He is constantly concerned about the weak and the pusillanimous. While insisting upon essentials, he does not hesitate to depart from the customs of his forerunners in regard to the means to be employed, although he revered and admired the oriental monks and held them up as ideals for his monks to imitate. The supreme law is that "souls may be saved and that the brethren may do their work without justifiable murmuring" (41,5).

All of the concrete provisions of the *Rule* are drawn up in function of this outlook. In the matter of corporal asceticism, nothing extraordinary is imposed: sufficient food and drink, clothing and sleep are provided for. The hours of prayer are not excessive. Special provisions are made for the weak, the young and the old. In the matter of punishments for faults the *Rule* is lenient and seeks medicinal rather than vindictive measures. Offenders are given several chances to make good.

Meaning of Discretion

All of this may give the impression that discretion is entirely a question of moderation. It would be a grave error simply to identify the two. Much less is it a kind of diplomacy, an ability to compromise and conciliate opposing interests so as to satisfy everyone. Discretion is concerned not with finding an acceptable compromise but with choosing the means which in particular circumstances are best calculated to achieve the end.

Discretio is the Latin translation of the Greek word *diakrisis*, which appears already in the New Testament and was adopted by the monastic Fathers to denote a virtue which they regarded as of supreme importance. In Hebrews 5,14 the term means the ability to distinguish between good and evil; in 1 Corinthians 12,10 the ability to distinguish authentic charisms from those of diabolical origin. St. Athanasius presents Anthony as the model of *diakrisis:* he had the gift of distinguishing the works of the devil from those of God, that is, of selecting from a number of possibilities that one which would best further his purpose here and now (*Vita Antonii* 22; 35; 44; 88). True discernment is required for this, because the devil sometimes "disguises himself as an angel of light" (2 Cor 11, 14), so that the approach which seems best on the surface, to the carnal man, is actually a diabolical trap. St. Benedict applies this principle of discernment to the acceptance of candidates for the monastery, quoting the advice of St. John (1 Jn 4,1; *Rule* 58,2).

Discretion: Gift of Discerning Spirits

This ability to distinguish the good from the evil, as well as the better from the good, is what is meant by discretion in all the ancient monastic literature. The classic treatise on the subject is Cassian's second *Conference*, which begins by explaining that discretion is a charism conferred by the Holy Spirit: "This is no ordinary virtue, nor one which can be acquired by human effort, but can only be conferred by the gift of divine grace" (*Conf* 2,1). Once when the ancients gathered together for a lengthy discussion to determine what virtue or observance was most necessary for a monk to reach the heights of perfection, various participants expressed different opinions. Finally the great Anthony offered his view, pointing out that while all the things mentioned are of great value, no virtue is more important than discretion, for without it the others are in danger of being frustrated. "Discretion is the source, the guardian and the ruler of all virtues" (*Conf* 2,4). Cassian then goes on to offer numerous examples both of the value of discretion and of the tragedy of indiscretion in the lives of monks. He insists that to possess it one must be truly humble.

Discretion is a corollary of the gift of discernment of spirits. It is a question of taking practical measures in accord with a man's interior impulses. Each individual must hearken to the dictates of the Spirit within his own heart and act in accordance with his directives. The same measure cannot be blindly imposed upon all, because the spiritual condition of each monk is different from that of his fellows. Discretion involves a right proportioning of the exercises which a monk undertakes to the interior dispositions which he possesses here and now.

St. Benedict and Discretion

It is against this background that we must understand St. Benedict's concept of discretion. Echoing Cassian, he calls it "the mother of the virtues" and declares that it enables its possessor to "so temper all things that the strong may still have something to long after, and the weak may not draw back in alarm" (64,19). The word *discretio* appears only three times in the *Rule*, but the reality which it represents is present from one end of the legislation to the other.

For St. Benedict discretion is the ability to strike in all circumstances the balance between excess and defect. Where human actions are concerned, this balance is subject to contingencies imposed by circumstances and by free will, and so cannot be determined a priori. Discretion is the virtue through which a man can find this balance in each set of particular circumstances and thereby determine what is the best thing to do here and now. The *Rule* can only create the framework of monastic life and lay down general rules of conduct. It cannot foresee and solve particular cases, which depend upon contingencies and upon the disposition of each man's heart. Consequently St. Benedict insists that in the concrete it is the abbot who must determine what is best for the community, and the individual monk or his spiritual father who must often decide what is best in his own case.

When the matter is regarded from this viewpoint, it becomes evident that the choice of the best means to attain the end under a given set of circumstances will not always mean the choice of the easiest way. For this reason it is false to equate discretion with moderation. Discretion does, indeed, find a middle way between rigorism and laxism, but the golden mean is not necessarily the easiest way. The discreet thing to do, that is, the thing which out of all possible choices of action is the one best calculated to attain the end, may sometimes be the most difficult of all the possibilities. The perfection of the theological virtues does not consist in a mean, but in the greatest possible measure. Likewise St. Benedict adopts no measure in the renunciation of such things as self-will (3,8; 4,60; 5,7; 7,19.31), private property (33,1) or murmuring (34,6). In these matters, and in the growth of charity (4,21; 72 *passim*), there is no room for moderation. One must learn to recognize the invitation of the Spirit within his own heart and generously follow it.

Discretion for Abbot and Monk

It is the task of the abbot to find the means most suitable for attaining the end of the whole community. For that reason it is in chapter 64, on the appointment of the abbot, that St. Benedict especially develops his teaching on discretion. The abbot must know how to apply the *Rule* to particular cases which arise—a matter in which the *Rule* itself grants him extensive authority—and regulate the life of each individual monk so that the greatest good may be achieved. He cannot be merely a robot who mechanically invokes regulations in a spirit of legalism that can only stifle the spiritual liberty of his monks, but must be a loving father who finds the true mean for each individual by wisely interpreting general principles and applying them to particular cases in such a way that each may find the surest path to his ultimate goal.

But the over-all control of the abbot does not dispense the monk from possessing the virtue of discretion. Obedience should not be the blind annihilation of one's own will, but the voluntary submission of it to a higher norm of action. It cannot dispense the monk from thinking for himself nor from making his own decisions. Whatever good he does will be valueless unless he *wills* to do it; hence the monk himself must be so formed as to have the ability to make right choices. Even when one lives under a rule and an abbot, there are still innumerable cases in day to day living where the individual has to use his own discretion to choose the best of several possible courses of action. One who makes it a policy to do everything that is not strictly forbidden will miss the whole point of his monastic life.

Discretion and True Liberty

St. Paul insisted that Christianity is a religion of freedom that delivers men from the yoke of a "letter that kills" to give them the true freedom of the "Spirit that gives life" (2 Cor 3,6). "Where the Spirit of the Lord is, there is freedom" (2 Cor 3,17). "We are not children of a slave-girl, but of the free woman—in virtue of the freedom wherewith Christ has made us free" (Gal 4,31). The *Rule* is not meant to restrict freedom, but to make true freedom possible. Freedom establishes a law peculiar to itself, which is an interior law written upon the heart. The function of the *Rule* and the abbot is to awaken this law in the heart of each individual by properly forming his mind and his will. Discretion, utilizing the surrender of humility, provides the foundation for a life of freedom lived in the service of God.

Moderation too easily degenerates into mediocrity. Discretion does not, for it has no intention of restricting the generosity of the individual, but rather of guaranteeing it the freedom of infinite expansion. Many Benedictine saints have gone beyond the moderate provisions of the *Rule*. It was St. Benedict's intention that they should do so, for what he required is only "a little Rule for beginners" (73,8), and he ceaselessly holds out to his followers an ideal that has no limitations, for it is a question of divine love. No one has ever gone to excess in the attainment of the ideal, for in this there can be no question of moderation. It is discretion which finds the right path to the ideal.

Discretion, Breadth of View and Wisdom

The monk must be willing to allow the same measure of freedom to others which he himself enjoys under the *Rule* and the abbot. Nothing is more contrary to true Christian freedom than that false equality which seeks to impose a rigid uniformity that would draw everyone down to the same level. The monk does not retire to a monastery to shut himself up in a spirit of isolation and provincialism, nor in that narrow-minded legalism which would seek to impose the same measure upon all. Discretion is broadminded; it recognizes the marvelous diversity in God's creation; it allows each individual to develop his own potentialities as the Spirit of God leads him. Grace builds upon nature, and will build differently upon different natures; it must be left the freedom to do so. The monk who is a man of one idea, or of one book, and refuses to withdraw from the narrowness of his own limitations, shuts out the Spirit and prevents him from accomplishing his work. Discretion is not authentic unless it is accompanied by good zeal.

An equally subtle danger which can be countered by discretion is that of anti-intellectualism. It is a consequence of the preceding, for the false leveling of society leads to a disdain for wisdom. Man can conform his will to God's will only when he knows something about God and about other creatures. Knowledge affords the elements for judgment about what must be done and what must be avoided. Truth in judgment cannot be a matter of chance or of "good intentions"; it must be guided by discretion, which habitually forms the intellect according to reality. The will cannot choose correct means for the attainment of its end unless it is guided by an intellect rightly formed. The man who is discreet sees things as they are and makes his choices accordingly.

Discretion and Prudence

The scholastic theologians absorbed the teaching of the monastic Fathers on discretion into their treatment of prudence. Prudence is a virtue which resides in the practical intellect. Drawing its principles from knowledge and faith, and from the ends pursued by the other virtues, it chooses means which are suitable for the attainment of these ends. It is, then, an intellectual virtue, without which the other faculties cannot function properly; accordingly it is called "the queen of the virtues." It preserves a man from the illusions of personal preference or acquired prejudice, and enables him to judge things as they really are. Since prudence involves surrender to reality, it is a consequence of the complete surrender of self inherent in humility. Abandonment of illusion and surrender to reality enable a man to act as he ought.

For Cassian and St. Benedict, too, discretion is an intellectual virtue; but it is not only intellectual, for it is absorbed into the framework of supernatural charity that must rule the monk's entire outlook. Later on St. Thomas was to explain Augustine's assertion that prudence is love, by pointing out that "it is not love in its essence, but insofar as love inspires the act of prudence" (S.T. 2–2, q47, a 1, ad 1). The ancients did not make these distinctions, but they nevertheless understood the reality that lies behind them. St. Benedict's discretion is not the cold, calculating judgment of an executive, but the warm and loving concern of a father for his sons, who knows how to choose what is best for each of them and to teach them, in the spirit of Christian liberty, to make such wise choices themselves by developing a sensitivity to the invitations of divine grace.

3. COMPUNCTION

Sorrow Caused by Repentance

In seeking to define the attitude which the monk ought to assume in the spiritual ascent, the ancient monks had recourse to the concept of compunction which they found in the Scriptures. The Greeks called it *penthos*, which from the time of Cassian was rendered *compunctio* in Latin. Compunction is an attitude of profound grief, the psychological reaction produced in the soul by the many tribulations of the present life, whether adversities of various kinds or simply the fact of sin and its consequences. For the oriental monks it included the more emotional aspect of weeping over one's sins, which later became known as the gift of tears.

Compunction is grief over the loss of salvation, engendered by repentance. The monk must grieve over the loss of the only thing that can afford true joy; it is only sin and the effects of sin which can produce true sorrow in him. Compunction, then, is no morbid or cowardly grief indicating weakness of character; it is the attitude of the saint who fully realizes the depths of his own misery and the reality of the evil of sin.

St. Paul distinguished two kinds of grief: that which is "according to God" and that which is "according to the world" (2 Cor 7,10). The former alone is a virtuous and salutary sorrow, and it is that which he wished to stir up in the hearts of his converts. Worldly sorrow has no place in the life of the true Christian. Our Lord himself gave his blessing to authentic compunction in the Beatitudes, when he said, "Blessed are they who mourn, for they shall be comforted" (Mt 5,5). But it is only in the heavenly Jerusalem that "those that sow in tears shall reap rejoicing" (Ps 125,5) when the glorious Christ will overturn the world's scale of values and "God himself will be with them as their God. And God will wipe away every tear from their eyes. And death shall be no more; neither shall there be mourning, nor crying, nor pain any more, for the former things have passed away" (Apoc 21,3–4). The present life, when the Bridegroom is no longer among us (Mt 9,15), is the time for weeping.

Compunction in the Holy Rule

Ancient monasticism eagerly adopted the ideal of compunction, because it was the perfect expression of the habitual attitude of conversion which is the very basis of the monastic life. It was an axiom among the ancients that the principal task of the monk is to weep. In Syria monks were known simply as *penthikoi*, "mourners."

St. Benedict also recommends that the monk develop a lively sense of compunction. In speaking of prayer he says: "we shall not be heard for our much speaking, but for purity of heart and tears of compunction" (20,3). Both of these qualities of prayer were highly esteemed by his predecessors and occur frequently in Cassian. St. Benedict is not interested in a cold and speculative kind of prayer, which can too easily be sterile because it does not affect the will, but prefers an affective prayer in the form of a tender dialogue between God and the monk. Again he says that "if anyone wish to pray secretly, let him just go in and pray: not in a loud voice, but with tears and fervor of heart" (52,4).

Compunction is also one of the most fruitful activities of the Lenten season, when the monk should apply himself to "prayer with tears, to reading, to compunction of heart, and to abstinence" (49,4). Indeed, it should be a daily exercise, as one of the tools of good works prescribes: "daily in one's prayer, with tears and sighs, to confess one's past sins to God" (4,57).

Many of the other tools of good works are designed to nourish the attitude of compunction. The monk is to avoid excessive speech and laughter so as to preserve the silence in which he may profitably reflect upon his sins (4,52–54). He is to meditate upon the realities of death, judgment and hell as a stimulus to compunction (4,44.45.47). Especially he is to work constantly at the emendation of his life (4,58) and to be drawn onward by an intense "spiritual longing" for eternal life (4,46).

Compunction and Tears

Compunction goes further than penance. Even when a fault has been expiated, compunction cannot forget it, but continues to mourn it. It adds a psychological depth to penance, for in compunction the penitential spirit overflows into the sensible part of man and issues in tears. At least it was thus that the ancients conceived of it. This is not to say that compunction is a purely emotional thing. It is a profound attitude of soul, rooted in an intellectual appreciation of the horror of sin and in a movement of the will which, taking its point of departure from regret for the evil in one's life, overflows into the emotions and issues in an intense outpouring of love for God.

This emotional aspect of compunction is not likely to appeal to the modern Anglo-Saxon mind, especially in the form in which it is sometimes expressed by the Greek Fathers. National and individual temperaments will vary considerably on this point. Yet there is no reason why so profound a sentiment should not find exterior expression in a subject properly disposed. St. Benedict can scarcely be accused of emotionalism, and yet he prayed with tears (*Dial* 2, 17) and recommended such prayer to his monks (52,4). In any case, the emotional aspect is not the essence of compunction, though true compunction will ordinarily overflow into the sensible part of man.

A Profound Sense of Sin

What is important, however, is the interior disposition, the sorrow in the heart because one has strayed far from God. When God intervenes in a man's life with the grace of conversion, this conviction of the error of his past is the first movement that grace stirs up in his inmost heart. It is the action of the Spirit taking away the heart of stone and replacing it with a heart of flesh (cf Ez 36,26). The new spirit within him gives him for the first time a vital understanding of his existential situation before God: he is a sinner. It is a consciousness of sin itself and of his involvement in it, rather than any detailed cataloguing of individual past offenses, which makes him aware of his need for an interior re-creation. This awareness of his situation gives him a gravity and seriousness in facing life (cf *Rule* 7,62–66), though at the same time he experiences a profound peace in his realization that God has pardoned him.

When the ancients defined compunction as sorrow over the loss of salvation, they were not thinking merely of the complete loss of supernatural life through serious sin, but of the loss of its integrity. Any sin or fault, even if it be slight, impairs the totality of salvation. Anyone who has not achieved the highest degree of perfection possible for him at any given moment has suffered some loss of salvation and therefore has abundant cause to weep. The saints, who enjoy a special sensitivity to sin, find material for grief not only in the sins of their past, but in the inevitable weaknesses of human nature which no one can transcend in this life.

This profound sense of sin which is the basis for compunction is no morbid, pathological pessimism nor Freudian guilt complex, but an eminently realistic view of the fallen state of human nature and the actual fact of man's departure from God. Some modern currents of thought have rejected this sense of sin in favor of a false optimism about the goodness of human nature. Man has often sought to deny the reality of original sin and to find other scapegoats which might be blamed for the undeniable presence of evil in the universe. The texts of revelation, however, make no attempt to obscure the problem of evil, nor do they hesitate to attribute it to its real source, man himself and the kingdom of Satan to which he is subject so long as the power of Christ's redemption has not yet made a totally new creature of him. The monk must enter fully into the world of the supernatural and learn to envision reality from the point of view adopted by revelation. He will then be able to see the evil of sin in its proper perspective and appreciate the malice of his own personal sins.

Causes of Compunction

It is a sense of sin, therefore, that gives rise to the attitude of compunction. Aware that salvation is the only real value worth striving for and that it has been impaired and rendered uncertain by sin, the Christian is filled with profound sorrow. Mortal sin is of course the greatest evil, and the most powerful incentive to compunction. The monk must never cease to weep over the serious sins which he may have committed in his past life.

Even if one has never committed a serious sin, there is still sufficient reason to grieve. For we have all been infected by original sin, and who can claim that his daily life is not punctuated by numerous infidelities, faults and weaknesses of character? Few are so perfectly generous that they cannot find in themselves many reservoirs of selfishness through which the power of sin still operates. Even a lifetime of asceticism does not succeed in removing all the stains which impair the integrity of salvation. Further, no one can be sure what the future will hold. It is always possible that human weakness will fall into serious sins in the future, and we are certain that we shall one day have to face death, the penalty for sin, and the consequent judgment, which will mercilessly bring to light our innumerable infidelities.

The monk has reason to weep for the sins of others, too, as well as for himself. We are all united in the solidarity of our common misery, and the charity and apostolic zeal of the monk will urge him to grieve over the sins of others, especially those who are not conscious of their own miserable state. He will weep, too, over the outrage done to God's love by the innumerable sins of men, and thus his tears will permit him to grow in divine charity and in an ever closer union with God.

Stimuli to Compunction

Compunction, like conversion itself, is a grace. No one can be moved to tears for his sins unless God takes the initiative and inspires in him a realization of the misery of his own state. But the monk must cooperate with this grace and take advantage of the many opportunities which present themselves in his daily life to move him to grief for his sins. While the sinner in the world is often moved to a realization of his sins by the calamities which result from them, the monk is not terrified by any temporal adversities. But to him God's grace presents itself in many other ways.

The monk's reading and meditation upon the Sacred Scriptures constantly bring to his attention the fact of sin and the corruption of human nature which has resulted from it. In the repeated infidelities of the chosen people to the covenant he sees his own life reflected as in a mirror. Through meditation and self-examination he will come to know himself better, and will find hidden depths of perversity and unresponsiveness to grace which he had not previously suspected. His own temptations and his weakness in coping with them will make him realize how far from perfection he is, and how precarious his salvation remains. Only the saint sees himself as he really is, and that is why he is able to shed tears over his state and to recognize that he is the least of all.

All of the exercises of his monastic life will help the monk to enter into this mentality: silence, mortification, detachment from material things and distractions, spiritual exercises and the continual struggle against temptation. On the contrary, it is the neglect of these exercises and a surrender to dissipation which will render impossible the development of a true spirit of compunction.

Liturgy and Compunction

In the liturgy, too, the monk experiences a powerful stimulus to compunction. There the religious history of mankind is unrolled before his eyes: the fall and its consequences, the history of God's people with all its vicissitudes, the redemption and the summons to conversion. The liturgy sees reality as it really is, from the viewpoint of God, and through it the monk can learn to live in the real world and to understand his own state, the sublimity of his vocation and the misery of his failure to respond fully to it.

The liturgy never allows us to forget that we are sinners. In the Mass itself the Church places upon the lips of the priest many formulae which emphasize his unworthiness to approach the altar. The creature cannot take part in the divine mysteries without acknowledging his sinfulness. It is significant that the Roman liturgy, notwithstanding its customary sobriety, contains not only a Mass formulary *pro remissione peccatorum,* but also an oration *ad petendam compunctionem cordis.* Prayers for the grace of compunction occupy an even more important place in the oriental rites.

It is especially in the psalms of the divine office, however, that the monk presents himself as a sinner, identifying himself with the psalmist who acknowledges his poverty, his misery, his sin, his profound need of divine mercy and divine help. In prescribing the recitation of Psalm 4 at Compline every night, it was undoubtedly the thought of St. Benedict that the monk should end the day by placing himself in an attitude of compunction: *quae dicitis in cordibus vestris in cubilibus vestris compungimini.* Such was also the monastic interpretation of Psalm 6,7: "Every night I flood my bed with weeping; I drench my couch with my tears" (cf Cassian, *Conf* 20,6).

The monk's duty to weep is also given expression in the liturgy of monastic profession. In one of the orations of the profession rite the new monk is referred to as "your servant, whom you have withdrawn from the concerns of other men through the fire of holy compunction." And the Preface for solemn profession expresses the wish that the monk may "ceaselessly, with tears and sighs, acknowledge and wash away his sins."

Compunction and Union with God

We must guard against thinking that compunction is a purely negative thing, a preoccupation with sin. It is true that it is intended to effect the purification of the soul (the Greek Fathers considered it a kind of baptism, because the flow of tears washes away sin and cleanses the soul of evil desires), but it is precisely this purification from sin which leads the monk on to perfect love of God and thus to beatitude. Only when he is purified of sin can the monk arrive at that "perfect love of God which casts out all fear" (*Rule* 7,67).

The sorrow which is "according to God" is in no sense incompatible with spiritual joy. True peace can be found not in the denial of evil but only in a consciousness of God's sublime gifts despite the misery of one's own sins. Tears are the way to true joy. "Those that sow in tears shall reap rejoicing," says the Psalmist (Ps 125,5). The fullness of that beatitude will never be attained in this life, but the monk who cultivates compunction will have a foretaste of it. He will enjoy peace, because he will know his own place in relation to God, and his tears of compunction will lead him to the highest contemplation and most intimate union with his Creator. It is part of the paradox of Christianity: only those who weep can be truly joyful.

Nowhere can we find the positive aspect of compunction better emphasized than in the writings of St. Gregory the Great, from whom it passed to the entire monastic tradition of the Middle Ages. For Gregory compunction is a sorrow which arises from the consciousness of sin on the one hand and from a desire for God on the other. But it is the latter which he stresses. We already possess God, but only obscurely and for a time, and we must constantly seek to find him again. Compunction, which urges us on to the search, is a compunction of love. It is God acting within us, arousing us, stirring us up as with the pricks of a pin, through tribulations, temptations, even our own faults. Compunction makes the soul homesick for heaven, and it empties it of all its attachments to give it a greater capacity for God. And so it is fundamentally desire for God, and it leads to the union of beatitude.

4. HUMILITY

Importance of Humility

While St. Benedict incorporated into the *Rule* the traditional teaching of the monastic Fathers on compunction, it is not this concept which forms the basis of his doctrine of the spiritual ascent. For him the fundamental attitude of the monk is to be determined by humility. Like the teaching on compunction, this was traditional among his predecessors.

The sayings of the Fathers contain many references to the necessity of humility for the monk; their anecdotes recount examples of both the true humility of the saintly anchorites and the false humility of those whose pride vitiated the value of their ascetical efforts. Cassian devoted considerable space to the discussion of humility in the *Conferences*, where it is treated in numerous passages, and especially in the *Institutes* (4,39), where he draws up a list of ten indications which permit one to form a judgment on the humility of a monk.

It was undoubtedly from these sources that St. Benedict drew his teaching on humility, especially from Cassian, from whom he derived the inspiration for arranging the spiritual ascent of the monk according to degrees of humility. But he has made something quite new out of the teaching of his predecessors. For him humility is understood in a much broader sense than it was by the earlier monks or by later generations of theologians. His entire program of the spiritual life revolves about humility. It is no longer simply one virtue among many, but is a fundamental attitude which determines the relationship of man to God and consequently is the necessary foundation upon which all progress in virtue must be built.

What is Meant by Humility

St. Benedict strongly emphasized the part played by God in human perfection. It is God who invites the monk to perfection and to union with him, and it is his Holy Spirit whose power works within the monk to produce the fruit of virtue. St. Benedict's monks, "judging that they can do no good of themselves and that all cometh from God, magnify the Lord's work in them, using the word of the prophet, 'Not unto us, O Lord, not unto us, but unto thy name give the glory' " (Ps 113,9; Pr 29–30). And they are admonished "to attribute to God, and not to self, whatever good one sees in oneself. But to recognize always that the evil is one's own doing, and to impute it to oneself" (4,42–43).

God is the Creator, the Supreme Being, sufficient in himself; man is a mere creature, dependent upon him for everything, even his very existence. This is the fundamental and inescapable fact of human existence. Of himself man can accomplish absolutely nothing of supernatural value. All human striving must begin from this principle, and nothing in human life can ever abstract from the basic fact of man's unalterable relationship to God. Unless a man is conscious of the immensity of the gulf which separates him from God, he will never be able to see himself as he really is and to appreciate the magnitude of the debt which he owes to God and which can never be paid.

Now humility is precisely the attitude which man assumes in the face of these facts. It is the interior disposition by which he understands his own place in the hierarchy of being, sees his relationship to God as one between impotent creature and all-powerful Creator, freely accepts this situation, and makes it the basis of all his efforts to advance in the spiritual life. Through it the soul becomes conscious both of its own misery and of the wonderful things which God's grace can accomplish in it. In St. Benedict's conception, humility is the most fundamental disposition, because it is the only one which goes to the root of the problem of human existence.

The Vice of Pride

The importance of humility can more clearly be seen by comparison with the vice of pride, which is its opposite. St. Benedict never lists the eight principal vices, but such a catalogue was traditional in monastic circles, and Cassian devoted his entire fifth *Conference* to it, as well as the greater part of the *Institutes.* The last of the eight vices is that of pride. Cassian, who treats *ex professo* of pride in his twelfth *Institute*, declares that it is the origin of all vices and the worst of all because it destroys all virtues and robs man of all holiness. Other vices destroy only the virtues directly opposed to them, but pride is the negation of all spiritual progress, because it is directly opposed to God.

The proud man is not content with his status as creature, but wishes to appropriate to himself the prerogatives of God. Pride is the essence of all sin: it is ingratitude for the numberless benefits received from God, and rebellion against him. It is a claim to moral autonomy: no longer God, but man himself, becomes the norm according to which human actions are to be judged. This was precisely the attitude of Satan in his refusal to submit to God, and it was the essence of the sin of Adam, whatever may have been its outward form.

The proud man is simply unwilling to face reality. He wants to make of himself something that he is not and cannot be. He refuses to accept the fact that there is an infinite distance between himself and God, and thereby subverts the entire purpose of creation and attempts to rob God of the glory which is due to him. Since original sin itself was an act of pride, man's fallen nature is continually drawn toward this vice, which defeats man's purpose in life and the entire purpose of creation.

Biblical Basis for Humility

The only remedy for this situation is to overcome the vice of pride by its contrary, which is humility. Humility is simply the acceptance of things as they really are. The humble man freely acknowledges his place in creation, which is a very lowly place. In the sight of God he is as nothing: he was drawn from nothingness through God's mercy and owes everything that he has to his love. Knowing that he has nothing which he has not received, he does not attempt to attribute any good to his own merits (cf 1 Cor 4,7).

As usual, St. Benedict bases his teaching directly upon the Scriptures, choosing the words of the Lord, "Everyone that exalteth himself shall be humbled, and he that humbleth himself shall be exalted" (Lk 14,11; *Rule* 7,1). This is the principle upon which a man must base his attitude toward himself. It is utterly impossible for him to accomplish anything in the supernatural order by his own efforts. Consequently he can make progress only by admitting his total dependence upon God, and opening himself to the divine action, which alone is able to raise him up.

The Gospel teaching, which St. Benedict sees confirmed in the text of Psalm 130,1–2 (7,3–4), is simply another application of the paradox of Christianity. Just as the rich will find themselves dispossessed in the reversal of values which will take place in the eschatological times, and those who found joy in this world will have sorrow in the next, so the proud, who attempt to push themselves forward, are precisely the ones who will never arrive. It is the law of Christ's kingdom. Consequently humility is the most fundamental attitude which the Christian must assume in accepting the conversion which God offers to him, for only through humility can his soul be opened to the sanctifying power of God, who "resists the proud, but gives grace to the humble" (Jas 4,6; 1 Pt 5,6).

The Degrees of Humility

It is evident that the attitude of humility is closely related to compunction. They are two similar reactions to the basic truths of religion, and consequently St. Benedict is able to assimilate both into his spiritual teaching. Of the two, however, humility is the broader concept, if understood in the sense of St. Benedict. While compunction takes the reality of sin as its point of departure, humility goes further and begins with the ontological relationship of man to his Creator. While the two attitudes harmonize, they are not entirely coextensive. Since humility is the more basic concept, it is that which St. Benedict has chosen as the foundation upon which he builds his entire program of spirituality.

In constructing this program, he has recourse to an allegorical interpretation of the Scriptures. Jacob's ladder, which extended from earth to heaven, represents our life in this world; our body and our soul form the two upright sides of this ladder. Jacob saw angels descending and ascending on this ladder, who symbolize the descent of self-exaltation and the ascent of humility. The rungs of the ladder are degrees of humility—St. Benedict lists twelve—which enable us to climb up to heaven. While these degrees lower us progressively in our own estimation, it is precisely this descent, according to the terms of the paradox, which enables us to rise in the sight of God.

Doubtless, St. Benedict did not intend a too literal interpretation of these steps of humility. It is impossible to measure progress in virtue mathematically. Cassian did not speak of degrees of humility, but rather of signs (*indicia*). For St. Benedict they are something more than signs; they are true norms of conduct. But they are not to be understood as successive in a mutually exclusive sense, though they do progress from more general to more particularized norms. The first seven degrees are norms for the growth of the interior disposition of the monk; the last five specify the exterior conduct which should result from the attitude of humility.

The First Three Steps

The first degree of humility is that a man be possessed by the fear of God. In an extended treatment of this basic attitude, St. Benedict insists again and again that its prerequisite is to be ever aware of the omnipresence of God, its result the avoidance of evil. Certainly he does not intend that this should be a purely servile fear, for a filial love for God is often recommended in the *Rule;* but before we can truly love, we must fear. We have every reason to fear if we are truly aware of our creature-Creator relationship and of the fact of sin. The Scriptures never cease to remind us that God knows our inmost thoughts and that the man who truly fears God will strive to keep his conscience immaculate before him.

The man who fears God will be distrustful of his own will, an attitude which constitutes the second degree of humility. Man's free will is one of the greatest of God's gifts, yet it is his misuse of this faculty which has plunged him into sin. Since original sin has left his will with a strong inclination to evil, man can no longer safely pursue everything to which his own will directs him. This degree of humility invites the monk to adopt a higher and thoroughly reliable norm of action: the will of God. Christ is our model in this, for, as the Scriptures declare, he did not his own will, but the will of the Father who sent him (Jn 6,38; *Rule* 7,32). Christ is the guide who teaches the monk to make a total surrender of himself and who gently leads him up the ladder of humility.

The third degree of humility requires obedience to the monk's superiors. If, indeed, he wishes to make the will of God the supreme norm of his actions, he must be willing to see the divine will manifested for him in the commands of his superiors. In St. Benedict's sacramental view of the monastery, the abbot holds the place of Christ; he is for his monks the sacramental who prolongs the presence of Christ in their midst. This is a conclusion of supernatural faith, for we must *believe* that the abbot holds the place of Christ (2,2; 63,13), and the motive for obedience must be a supernatural one, not merely an attachment to the ideal of good order: "the obedience which is given to superiors is given to God" (5,15). Here again Christ is the model, he who "was made obedient even unto death" (Phil 2,8; *Rule* 7,34), and hence obedience "becometh those who hold nothing dearer to them than Christ" (5,2). We shall speak later of the qualities of obedience which the *Rule* requires.

The Fourth to Seventh Degrees

St. Benedict does not attempt to conceal the difficulties of perfect obedience. Not only is it repugnant to our fallen nature, but to this are added in practice innumerable circumstances which can make it a real psychological martyrdom. The fourth degree of humility is to endure all these difficulties with patience and perseverance. There is no logical solution to the problems of monastic obedience; there is only the solution of faith. Patience means suffering in reality as well as in etymology. The humble monk will not only endure this suffering, but will joyously embrace it. St. Benedict cites the

Scriptures again, texts which clearly put the monk's perseverance and hope upon an eschatological plane: "Let thy heart take courage, and wait thou for the Lord" (Ps 26,14; *Rule* 7,37).

The fifth degree of humility is manifestation of conscience. The monk is invited not only to submit his actions to the abbot in external obedience, but also to open to him the hidden depths of his heart, making known his evil thoughts and his secret sins. Thus no sphere of his life will any longer be subject to his own egoism; all of the evil will be brought out into the open where it can be healed. St. Benedict makes it clear that such manifestation is really a manifestation to God; once again, the abbot is only his instrument.

The sixth degree brings the monk to a state of great simplicity and joy. Now convinced of his own worthlessness, he is quite content to have the meanest and worst of everything. He has lost the desire for human advantages and favors; he sees quite clearly that he is not really worthy of such things, and that the worst is what becomes him best. He sees the defects in his own accomplishments and so has no desire to be praised for them. This state is one of joy, for it liberates the monk from the things that men most strive for, and leaves him with God alone, his real treasure.

The highest point in the interior disposition of humility is reached in the seventh degree. The monk is now so filled with the action of the Holy Spirit, so intent upon God alone, that he sees himself only in relation to the divine majesty. And from that point of view, he is himself at the other end of the abyss, so that he can envisage nothing lower than himself. He truly regards himself, in his inmost heart, as the least profitable of all God's creatures. In this state, due to the contemplation of God's perfections, he has lowered himself through humility as far as he can go.

Exterior Conduct

The remaining five degrees describe the exterior comportment of the monk who is animated by an interior disposition of humility. The eighth degree consists in external conformity to the common rule of the monastery and to the example of the elders. Singularity of behavior is a result of self-will, an attempt to exalt one's own views and preferences at the expense of the recognized customs of the community. Conformity in these matters is another step toward the totality of the monk's self-surrender.

The next three degrees have to do with the monk's speech: the ninth is the practice of taciturnity; the tenth is a seriousness of disposition which excludes unrestrained laughter and levity; the eleventh a certain gravity of manner and quiet dignity which manifests itself whenever the monk has reason to speak. All of these degrees are designed to exclude from the monk's life that spirit of dissipation which can only reveal that he has not yet made a total surrender of his self-love, which still shows itself in his desire to put himself forward in conversation and to cling to his old habits of self-exaltation. Certainly St. Benedict does not intend to exclude the cheerfulness and good sense of humor which are the mark of a man whose conscience is pure. What he does wish to banish is the worldly and frivolous conduct which shows that the roots of self-love have not yet been eradicated.

The twelfth and final degree is the manifestation of humility in all the monk's external behavior. When he has reached this stage, the profound spirituality of his interior disposition translates itself into action at every turn of his daily life. In whatever position he finds himself, he keeps his head bowed and his eyes downcast, for he is filled with the spirit of compunction. Ever mindful of the presence of his Creator and Judge, he expresses the humility of his heart in even the smallest actions of his everyday life. For the truly humble monk this is no feigned posture, nor is there exaggeration in it. He really believes himself to be the least of all, and he acts accordingly.

Growth in Divine Love

Such is the program laid down by St. Benedict for the monk who wishes to achieve perfection. Humility is for him identical with perfection itself, for the other virtues are nothing more than manifestations of humility. The degree of humility which the monk has achieved will determine the perfection of his motive, which is all important in the supernatural life. At the beginning he will act chiefly from fear, but when his soul has been purified by the ascent of the ladder of humility, he will come to "that perfect love of God which casts out all fear" (1 Jn 4,18; *Rule* 7,67), and he will then act "for love of Christ and through good habit and delight in virtue" (7,69). Then when he shall have been emptied of every egoistic desire to exalt himself in opposition to God, and shall have opened himself entirely to the workings of grace, the power of the Holy Spirit will be free to stir up in his heart that perfect love of God which brings about an anticipation in this life of the beatitude of the next.

Compunction and humility thus create an attitude of deepest reverence and of eager responsiveness which invites God to take the initiative and by his grace to accomplish the monk's complete conversion. These dispositions are nothing other than the attitudes required by the prophets and by our Lord himself. If conversion is a grace, then man's response to it can only be a readiness to follow instantly the invitation of God and to allow him to achieve what our fallen nature cannot achieve of itself. Thus monastic spirituality is simply the working out of the program laid down in the Scriptures and ceaselessly renewed in the liturgy: the change of heart, the turning away from sin, the turning toward God in compunction and humility, the eager acceptance of the gift of him who never ceases to summon us back to himself, our sole beatitude.

5. ASCETICISM

Christian Paradox: Life through Death

The mystery of Christ is a mystery of life through death. Here we come to grips with the inner core of the paradox of Christianity, applied in the Person of the Lord himself. "Unless the grain of wheat falls into the ground and dies, it remains alone. But if it dies, it brings forth much fruit. He who loves his life, loses it; and he who hates his life in this world, keeps it unto life everlasting" (Jn 12,24–25). Christ could not enter into his glory until he had first done battle with death, the last enemy. "Did not the Christ have to suffer these things before entering into his glory?" (Lk 24,26)

The law of the cross which Christ applied to himself holds equally for his followers. His Mystical Body must be united to him in suffering if it is to be united to him in glory. Through baptism each of his members enters into a mystical union with the crucified Christ in order to be able to rise with him from the death of sin. "Do you not know that all we who have been baptized into Christ Jesus have been baptized into his death? For we were buried with him by means of baptism into death, in order that, just as Christ has arisen from the dead through the glory of the Father, so we also may walk in newness of life. For if we have been united with him in the likeness of his death, we shall be so in the likeness of his resurrection also" (Rom 6,3–5).

While the death of the Christian's old self, a subject of Satan's kingdom, is essentially accomplished in the sacrament, not everything is done there. His entire life must be brought into conformity with the new supernatural relationship with God which he has acquired in baptism. The principle of life through death must be applied to his every action: it is only by dying to his sinful tendencies that he can live fully his new life with Christ. "If you live according to the flesh you will die; but if by the spirit you put to death the deeds of the flesh, you will live" (Rom 8,13). This is the basic principle of all Christian asceticism.

The Purpose of Mortification

It is the desire for complete union with Christ, then, which leads the Christian to the practice of asceticism. Authentic mortification does not proceed from the merely negative desire to punish human nature, but from the will to free oneself from the hold which evil still exercises so that the love of Christ may expand to embrace the person's entire being. Original sin has left behind it a concupiscence which seeks every occasion to express itself in actual sin. One who is aware of his own evil tendencies will realize the constant necessity for mortification of his natural appetites.

The purpose of mortification is not to kill the body nor the passions but to kill sin. St. Paul did not establish a dualism between body and soul, but between flesh and spirit. The flesh is not the body; it is the natural man, the part of man to which the influence of the redemption has not yet penetrated, still subject to the power of sin. The spirit, on the other hand, does not mean the soul, but the supernatural man, the person insofar as he has come under the influence of the new life in Christ which he has received radically in baptism.

In this kind of anthropology, there can obviously be no question of killing the body to free the soul, an idea which is not Christian but Platonic. What must be killed is the "flesh," the perverse tendencies through which sin is able to operate. The attachment to sin must be annihilated if grace is to have its full effect. The tendency to sin resides not only in the body, but in the whole person, and therefore mortification must be directed not only at man's physical nature, but at the principle of evil. And it must be inspired by charity.

Monastic Asceticism

The first monks were giants of corporal asceticism. Nothing is more striking in the early monastic literature than the emphasis upon extreme feats of mortification. They went to heroic lengths to submit the flesh to the spirit. Unfortunately, not all of their practices were in accord with the purest Christian teaching on the subject. In some of the eastern monks there is an unmistakable Platonic tendency to look down upon the body as a thing almost intrinsically evil and to attempt to suppress nature by sheer force.

Some practices betray a lack of discretion. There were monks who refused to take any measures to procure food for themselves, believing that God would come to their aid by a miracle. Others so weakened themselves by penitential practices that they were no longer able to pray or to serve God. Simeon the Stylite was once found nearly dead at the end of Lent, after having refused to eat or drink during the forty days. There was also an all too human rivalry among them, each trying to outdo the other in the matter of corporal penances. They tended to count perfection in terms of measurable quantities rather than paying attention to the interior growth of charity which cannot be seen.

The Role of Asceticism

The theorists of monastic life, however, taught a perfectly sound doctrine on the value of mortification. In the system of Evagrius and Cassian, the active life is a dynamic advance toward the attainment of purity of heart, the total purification of the spirit through complete detachment from everything created. Purity of heart is identical with sanctity and charity; yet this is not an end in itself, but only a condition for the attainment of the final end, eternal life. The heart is like a mirror: when it is clouded by impurities, it cannot give a clear and accurate reflection of God; but when cleansed of every stain, it reflects the image of God as he really is. "Blessed are the clean of heart, for they shall see God" (Mt 5,8).

It is in the phase of the active life, therefore, that asceticism makes its contribution of eradicating everything which is an obstacle to purity of heart. The monk, in the words of St. Paul, must "crucify his flesh with its passions and desires" (Gal 5,24) to give full scope to the life of Christ in him. Again the Apostle says, "With Christ I am nailed to the cross. It is now no longer I that live, but Christ lives in me. And the life that I now live in the flesh, I live in the faith of the Son of God, who loved me and gave himself up for me" (Gal 2,19–20).

Renunciation is the beginning of the monk's conversion, but it must continue throughout the active life. Cassian, again following his master Evagrius, sketches three stages in this continuing renunciation. The first stage is that of progressive detachment from external goods, riches and material possessions. The second penetrates into the monk himself, drawing him away from his own vices and passions and inordinate affections. The third phase is one of detachment from everything that is visible and palpable, from all that is earthly, in favor of the invisible realities of the world to come.

It is in order to attain purity of heart, not because they are evil in themselves, that the monk leaves behind the world, his family and friends, his material possessions and the legitimate pleasures of life. He seeks solitude, renounces comfort, deprives himself of food, sleep and conversation, submits to work, holy reading and the practice of virtue. But neither renunciation nor the practice of the various virtues constitutes sanctity. They are only so many means, *instrumenta perfectionis*, which are to be used in the ascent toward the proximate goal of purity of heart. When they are made ends in themselves, they cease to fulfill their purpose.

Mortification: St. Benedict

St. Benedict did not base his ascetical teaching upon Cassian's distinction of the two lives. Though the reality is the same, he has expressed it in different categories. The term "purity of heart" occurs only once in the *Rule*, and there defines the proper disposition for prayer (20,3). On the contrary, the entire ascetical effort of the monk is based upon humility and upon its primary manifestation, obedience. The spiritual ascent proceeds by degrees of humility rather than by progressive detachment from created goods. The goal of this ascent is divine charity, which the monk reaches at the top of the ladder of humility (7,67). This same charity Cassian had identified with purity of heart, it will be recalled, but St. Benedict's method of expressing it is more positive. The ultimate end, of course, is eternal life in the kingdom of heaven (Pr 50).

The place of mortification in St. Benedict's teaching is not, therefore, essentially different from its place in Cassian's. Solitude, chastity, detachment from material goods, the observance of the *Rule*, obedience, even humility itself are not ends. St. Benedict does not want formalism, nor does he want an inhuman kind of asceticism which would destroy the very faculties that must be perfected. All ascetical practices are nothing more than means, instruments designed to bring about the monk's attainment of charity. Once the reign of charity is assured, he finds himself accomplishing with ease what previously required an intense ascetical effort (7,68).

Authentic Value of Mortification

This does not mean that mortification can be dispensed with; it only means that it must be kept in its proper place. It is true that St. Benedict greatly mitigated the austerities which had become traditional in eastern monasticism. He knew that the way which leads to God is already filled with hardships and trials (58,8) and so he wished to add nothing harsh or burdensome in his school of the Lord's service (Pr 46). The discretion for which he is justly famous (*Dial* 2,36) is nowhere more evident than in the matter of corporal asceticism. In matters of food, drink, sleep, clothing and work he lessened the austerities of the eastern monks to put monastic life within the reach of a greater number of Christians, and the *Rule* knows nothing of the extreme and artificial penances which they sometimes practiced.

But it would be a mistake to conclude from this that St. Benedict's monastic ideal was different or that he rejected the value of mortification. He remains in the tradition of the great theorists of eastern monasticism. As a hermit at Subiaco, he practiced the most severe austerities himself, and the *Rule* shows clearly that he continued to maintain the superiority of the eremitical life (1,3–5). As the hermits mortified themselves in order "to fight against the temptations of mind and body" (1,5), so the cenobite also must practice mortification. The tools of good works admonish him "to deny himself, in order to follow Christ" (4,10), "to chastise the body" (4,11), "not to seek soft living" (4,12), "to love fasting" (4,13), "to avoid worldly conduct" (4,20), and not to allow himself too much food, drink, sleep or comfort (4,35–38).

Especially during Lent the monk is to practice mortification. The ideal is that his whole life "be lenten in its character" (49,1): St. Benedict himself, in his cave at Subiaco, did not even know when it was Easter (*Dial* 2,1). But making allowances for the weakness of his monks, he hopes that at least during Lent they will "expiate the negligences of other times" (49,3). The most important mortification is abstinence from sin itself, and increased devotion to prayer, sacred reading and compunction (49,4), but to this the monk should add some voluntary abstinence from "food, drink, sleep, talk and jesting" (49,7). But once again obedience is more important than acts of corporal asceticism, and hence the monk must ask his abbot's permission for whatever mortification he practices (49,8–10).

Avoiding Extremes

St. Benedict, therefore, recognizes the value of asceticism but does not erect it into an end in itself. In the Prologue he defines its purpose precisely: it is "for the amendment of evil habit or the preservation of charity" (Pr 47). It is a necessary means to eradicate the vicious habits which have been left in the monk by original sin and his own personal faults, to bring about the death of the old self, the flesh, so that, dying with Christ, he may rise to new life with him. And this new life is precisely the life of charity, which St. Benedict sees as the goal of all the monk's striving and the proximate end which is a condition for his entry into eternal life.

The monk must be careful to avoid formalism in his outlook, particularly when he is young and inexperienced. The *Rule* and monastic tradition prescribe certain mortifications and exterior observances, as well as the somewhat intricate demands of the rubrics in the daily celebration of the liturgy. It would be sheer formalism to believe that perfection has been attained when one has become perfectly observant. This is simply to mistake the means for the end. There are, in fact, certain types of temperament which delight in a perfectionist observance of all the rules. There are even abnormal temperaments which experience a masochistic pleasure in self-inflicted suffering. Mortification endured without love or sought for selfish reasons is both psychologically and spiritually unhealthy. St. Benedict clearly defines perfection in terms of charity, which is to be achieved through humility and obedience, and the various observances of the monastic life are only means toward growth in humility.

On the other hand, however, the opposite extreme must be avoided. The monk who believes that, under pretense of charity, he can safely neglect mortification and the various forms of observance which monastic tradition has sanctioned, labors under a serious illusion. It is true that these things do not constitute perfection, but the experience of centuries has taught that they are an efficacious means to obtain it, and that it can scarcely be achieved without them. A charity which is authentically supernatural will normally tend to express itself in corporal austerity. Real charity is love for the crucified Christ and it cannot escape an imitation of him in the body as well as in the soul. Any profound interior disposition will seek corporal expression; this is a law of human nature. It is self-deception to think that we can eradicate our self-love without doing violence to our flesh, which is the favorite breeding ground of egoism. A true humility and obedience will recognize the need for bodily asceticism. The end should never be lost sight of, but neither may the normal means to its attainment be neglected. To both must be accorded the correct place and the real value which they have in leading the monk to his end of eternal life.

The Struggle of the Active Life

At the beginning of the active life, corporal asceticism will be difficult. Although baptism is already the deliverance from the kingdom of Satan, the Holy Spirit dwells in the soul only as first fruits and as a pledge, and concupiscence still makes its power felt. The enticement to the pleasures of the world is still strong, and the voice of the

Spirit is but dimly heard. But the Spirit sweetly invites the soul to engage in the work of total conversion and instills in it an attraction to divine realities which renders possible a firm resistance to the seductions of the flesh.

In the early stages of his progress in the spiritual combat, the monk will be vividly conscious of the strength of his lower nature, which he will have to fight with the weapons of ascetical exercises. He will be less conscious of the interior working of the Spirit, buried in the depths of his heart and still obscured by the tumultuous rebellion of concupiscence. Consequently the combat will seem more like obedience to an exterior norm, meeting violence with violence, than conformity to interior prompting. But if he is faithful and generous in the struggle, despite the tenacity of the enemy and the discouragement engendered by his own failures, divine grace will gradually gain a firmer hold upon him.

It is then that the practice of virtue becomes second nature to him. His soul is filled with a profound peace and joy, he is more sensitive to the voice of the Spirit within, he accepts the work of grace with profound humility, conscious that what has happened to him is not the product of his own efforts, but a gratuitous gift of God. St. Benedict describes this state as the climax of the ascent of the ladder of humility: what the monk formerly did out of fear, he now performs effortlessly, "for love of Christ and through good habit and delight in virtue" (7,69). This is the goal of the *vita activa:* it is Cassian's purity of heart, St. Benedict's "perfect love of God which casts out all fear" (7,67).

Passive Penance

Once the spirit and purpose of mortification are understood, the different kinds of mortification must be discussed. Spiritual writers usually distinguish active and passive mortifications. The former term refers to those which are freely chosen by the individual; the latter to those which are sent by God and freely accepted by the individual.

Of the two, passive mortification is the more profitable. Active mortification always runs the risk of inducing the monk to exercise self-will in making the choice and to finish with a sense of personal accomplishment. But when it is simply a question of accepting the trials which God sends, then it is clear that it is he who is making the choice and accomplishing the work. Every trial is sent by God for a purpose: our Lord said that "my Father . . . will cleanse every branch that bears fruit, that it may bear more fruit" (Jn 15,2). Passive mortification is the free acceptance of this cleansing process which God effects for the monk's own purification.

It is clear that St. Benedict found the monk's acceptance of God's will to be the most valuable form of asceticism. For that reason he bases the whole ascetical life upon the principle of obedience. Obedience is submission to the will of God: "the obedience which is given to superiors is given to God, since he himself said, 'He who listens to you, listens to me' " (Lk 10,16; *Rule* 5,15). If the *Rule* greatly modified the penitential practices of eastern monasticism—active mortifications undertaken of the monk's own will and sometimes leading to bizarre and unprofitable excesses—it certainly did not reduce the exigencies of surrender of one's own will through humility and obedience.

One's Own Infirmities

There is ample opportunity in the life of every monk, indeed, of every individual in any state of life, to practice passive mortification. Especially for the monk, who has assumed additional obligations, the supreme mortification is simply to be faithful to these, to observe the *Rule* as it is interpreted for him by the will of his superiors. This is what it means to be satisfied with God: to accept monastic life wholeheartedly, with whatever it may bring, and not to seek elsewhere for extraneous satisfactions and for escape from its obligations. "Meeting in this obedience with difficulties and contradictions and even injustice, he should with a quiet mind hold fast to patience, and enduring neither tire nor run away." (7,35–36)

It is passive mortification to observe St. Benedict's admonition: "Let them bear with the greatest patience one another's infirmities, whether of body or character" (72,5). It will be a mortification for the monk simply to be patient with himself. Only by experience will he discover how weak he really is, how seemingly incorrigible, how deeply ingrained are his faults. He will have to learn to be patient with himself, to persevere even when it may seem that he is making no progress. Faith itself is the first mortification: really to believe that all the things he must endure under obedience are God's will for him.

First of all, the monk must be satisfied with what he has received from God, with his own temperament, his state of health and his talents. If his talents are few, he must not indulge in self-pity and useless comparison with others; if they are many, then he will have the problem of giving the credit for them to God and of using them well. Every period of life will bring its own problems: the disorganization of youth, the frustrations of middle age, the infirmity of senility. Defects of health must be borne patiently: not only real sickness, but also things like nervousness and exhaustion and sleeplessness which can plague a person throughout his life. One must submit to the outward circumstances of his life, too: it will be a real penance to perform some of the assignments that are given under obedience. The spiritual life has its own difficulties, for nothing can be more trying than desolation in prayer, delusion and doubt, and the feeling of failure.

Infirmities of Others

Nor is it only his own infirmities that the monk must bear patiently, but also those of his confreres. While the young monk may be enthusiastic and idealistic, he will find that others do not share his enthusiasm, and that his ideals receive little sympathy and fall short of realization. He must expect to meet with misunderstanding, indifference, ingratitude and open opposition.

It is scarcely possible for men to live as closely together as they do in community life without conflicts arising. Differences of opinion should be expected and need not be harmful to harmony, for peace consists in a union of wills rather than of minds. But there may also be conflicts of wills and of temperaments. It is impossible to have an equal affection for all and not to feel a distinct dislike for some.

There is plenty of material for mortification in bearing patiently with others. One can practice the good manners, common sense and considerateness which are careful not to offend. One can be meek and patient with those who bore, or boast, or antagonize. One can make an effort to show attention to those whom others despise, who withdraw into themselves, or whom sickness prevents from taking a full part in community life. Thoughtfulness and kindness can be shown to all.

Need of Active Mortification

In the case of all these passive mortifications, we are sure that they are God's will, and there is little danger of our own selfishness intervening to spoil them. They are his way of purifying us to lead us to perfect charity. Nor is there any danger of exaggerating such passive penances. Voluntary mortification of the body must always be performed within due measure, with regard to health and exterior circumstances. But there is really no limit to our acceptance of the trials sent by God.

Passive mortification alone, however, is not sufficient. The monk is gifted with free will and he must use it not only freely to accept but also freely to choose the way of penance. He must of his own accord share in the sufferings and death of Christ. Through active mortification he must wage war upon the impulses of the flesh which have not yet been subdued to the reign of Christ. Active mortification, like passive, can be both interior and exterior. It is a question of purifying and disciplining all of a man's faculties—his intellect, his will, his internal senses, his affections and his body—and of bringing them into a harmonious balance in the service of God.

Intellect, Memory and Imagination

The manner of discipline which must be imposed upon the intellect will depend upon the individual. The person who is intellectually lazy will find no better mortification than to force himself to use his mind to the best of his ability, to apply himself seriously to study and whatever other intellectual work is given him, and to gain a deeper appreciation of the truths of faith and of the nature of his vocation. On the other hand, the monk who is naturally interested in intellectual pursuits will need to purify his motives in order to exclude a purely human ambition and to direct his efforts toward the right end. He must avoid an intellectual pride which can vitiate all of his accomplishments and which often shows itself in an excessive attachment to his own opinions, with an unwillingness ever to admit an error and to retract or apologize.

Everyone must make a careful selection of worthwhile objects of knowledge and accordingly mortify his natural curiosity. It is scarcely consistent for those who have abandoned the world to be thirsting continually after purely secular affairs. Monks who are priests, especially if engaged in the active ministry to some degree, must be aware of the problems faced by the faithful, but this does not require them to spend a great deal of time with secular newspapers and magazines, radio, television and movies. Frequent exposure to these media can only deaden their sense of the supernatural. Nor should a monk cultivate purely natural friendships and associations with laymen or maintain an extensive correspondence which serves no apostolic purpose.

The memory and the imagination also provide abundant scope for mortification. By the recollection of past pleasures and the conjuring up of daydreams, a person can seek escape from his own problems and begin to live in a fanciful world of unreality in which everything is designed according to his own taste. The monk who is truly mortified will resolutely refuse such an indulgence in self-pity and will courageously face the real world without attempting to escape from its difficulties. Nor will he allow a useless recollection of past triumphs or of worldly amusements once enjoyed to interfere with the harsh necessity of his constant advance in the way of perfection.

Mortification of the Will

The problem of the proper disciplining of the will is, of course, the whole problem of human perfection. In the last analysis, perfection consists in charity, and charity resides in the will. Hence, when the will is properly directed toward its end, then the entire man is in order. The whole question of the mortification of the will, then, is a problem of fixing it upon its proper object. When it becomes completely identified with the will of God, perfection is achieved. But before we can adopt God's will as our own, we must renounce the *propria voluntas* which is the source of all straying from the path of virtue.

The will, then, must be re-educated and re-formed. St. Benedict's entire program of spirituality is based upon this disciplining of the will; that is why he insists so much upon humility and obedience, which go contrary to self-will. The will must form the habit of making virtuous choices. Every mortification that a man performs, in whatever faculty, is at the same time a mortification of the will, for it is there that the choice is made. But the formation of the will must not be looked at so much from the viewpoint of self-control and self-mastery as from that of self-surrender. For the proper activity of the will is to love; its perfection consists precisely in its love for God. If we surrender ourselves to him, he will do the rest.

The monk must be sure, however, that he has the right motive in all that he does. Here he has the opportunity to mortify the natural desire for human respect. One who measures his actions according to the impression they will make upon others is putting the opinions of men and his own desire for esteem above his love for God. There should be no illusions about the possibility that this may be a real temptation in the monastery. Others will criticize the monk who is observant, who refuses to join factions, who does not share majority opinions. It is difficult to stand one's ground alone against overwhelming odds. But the apostolic principle ever remains in force: "We must obey God rather than men" (Acts 5,29).

Mortification of the Passions

The monk can never relax his vigilance in regard to his passions. Here he must always be on the alert to exercise a sane control over the affections of the heart and the desires of the flesh. Mortification of the passions is not a question of suppressing them, but rather of sublimating them and subjecting them to the higher law of love. The monk will not cease to love created goods, but he will love them not in themselves but insofar as they are a faint reflection of the Supreme Good to whom he gives his heart completely. He will want to mortify his appetites precisely because he loves Christ more than anyone or anything else.

The basic purpose of all of St. Benedict's tools of good works is to lead the monk to a more ardent love for Christ. He is exhorted, indeed, "not to fulfill the desires of the flesh" (4,59), but if he must deny himself, it is "in order to follow Christ" (4,10), and the greatest of all the tools is "to prefer nothing to the love of Christ" (4,21). And Christ is the solution, too, to the unruly demands of his passions: "When evil thoughts come into one's heart, to dash them at once on the rock of Christ" (4,50).

The emotions will always clamor for attention. They must be kept in their proper place. The onrush of anger must be checked, the surge of impatience calmly moderated. Doubt and fear must be overcome by confidence and hope, melancholy and unhealthy sadness by Christian joy. Excessive hilarity must be countered by sobriety. Laziness can be cured by the energy which is inspired by love; the want of precision and punctuality and the wasting of time by a stiffening of resolve to achieve order. The excessive love of physical comfort needs the counterbalance of a sincere desire to share in the sufferings of Christ.

The Sense of Sight

The body, like the interior faculties, must be mortified if it is to be properly trained for the service of God. The body must be treated not only as a thing intrinsically good, but as a sacred thing deserving of reverence. The second Person of the Blessed Trinity did not shrink from assuming a human body, and his glorified body is now at the right hand of the Father in heaven, the first fruits and the guarantee of our own resurrection (cf 1 Cor 15,20; 2 Cor 5,1). But concupiscence operates in the body, and hence it must be disciplined and purified of its tendencies to evil.

The sense of sight, which produces such vivid representations of earthly reality, needs to be subjected to firm control. It is evident that a monk cannot allow himself to look without cause at things which are of such a nature as to excite the passions, whether these be persons, objects or pictures. But the custody of the eyes must insure more than the mere avoidance of sin and of dangerous occasions of sin. The monk who wishes to keep his attention fixed upon God and upon the requirements of his vocation will strive to shut out from his gaze, and thus from his mind, anything which can distract him from his purpose.

One who allows his eyes to wander about and who concerns himself with everyone else's business can scarcely concentrate upon his own duties and his own salvation. He will do well to take seriously the twelfth degree of humility: "that whether he is at the work of God, in the oratory, in the monastery, in the garden, on the road, in the fields, or anywhere else, and whether sitting, walking, or standing, he should always have his head bowed and his eyes downcast" (7,63).

The Sense of Hearing

The sense of hearing also needs control. Once again the basic mortification consists in refraining from willingly listening to anything which is in itself sinful, such as murmuring or detraction, or which can arouse the lower appetites. But beyond that, the monk must furthermore shut out the noise of secular and scurrilous conversation and amusement, and anything which can distract him from his real object. It is impossible to live in the world of the supernatural if one is constantly opening oneself to this kind of distraction. This problem is very closely related to the control of the tongue and the cultivation of the virtue of silence.

If there is a negative aspect to the mortification of sight and hearing, it is only in order to kill the evil so that the good may have a more vigorous life. When used for the purpose for which they are intended, these senses, too, can lead the monk to God. Beautiful sights and sounds, both of nature and of art and music, should inspire him to lift his heart to the Supreme Beauty whose reflection in them can be seen and heard by one who watches and listens rightly.

The Sense of Touch: Fasting

The most demanding of all the senses, and consequently the one which requires the firmest discipline, is that of touch. The passions which impel man to self-preservation and to reproduction are the most violent which he experiences. The latter of these will be treated in a later chapter, in which we shall speak of chastity. The principal weapon to be used against the former is fasting.

Of all Christian ascetical practices, fasting is the most ancient, having been in continuous use since Old Testament times, and the one which has proved the most effective over the centuries. The ancient monks practiced it with extreme rigor, and St. Benedict, while mitigating the measure of its observance, imposed it upon his monks, as the Church does upon all the faithful. It launches a direct attack upon the flesh in one of its most vulnerable spots, pacifies the passions and restores order and harmony to man's faculties. St. Leo the Great, in the magnificent sermons which St. Benedict knew and admired, and which the Church still reads in the divine office, presents a Christian theology of fasting which is both authentic and inspiring.

Our Lord sanctified fasting, already traditional in the Old Testament, by inaugurating his public ministry through a forty days' fast. In this respect, as in others, Christ did not destroy the old law, but fulfilled it. While accepting the practice, he purified it of Jewish legalism, and insisted that it be an interior act of repentance and submission to God.

The early Christians adopted fasting and, apparently in the third century, added the practice of abstinence, which is not of evangelical origin. In the liturgy, where *ieiunium* designates the sum total of mortifications, it is regarded as the act par excellence of Christian asceticism. "We will deserve to be mocked by unbelievers," says St. Leo, ". . . if while we fast our conduct should fall short of the purity of perfect self-restraint. For the essence of fasting does not consist merely in abstinence from food, nor is it of any value to deprive the body of food, unless the heart is restrained from evil-doing" (*Sermo* 42,2).

Fasting and Eschatology

Fasting, however, has another significance besides that of asceticism. Moses and Elijah fasted as a preparation for their encounter with God; hence the forty days of fast became a preparation for the eschatological times. Christ repeated this gesture to show that the time was finally at hand. He was about to establish the new covenant of the last days, as Moses had established the old covenant and Elijah had renewed it. During the time that elapses between Pentecost and the parousia, the Church must likewise wait in readiness for the final coming of Christ and the definitive eschatological times. This is the time for fasting, when the Bridegroom is absent and the wedding guests watch in readiness, awaiting his return (Mt 9,15; 25,1–13).

The Church fasts, therefore, in expectation of the return of the Lord. This is the significance particularly of the Eucharistic fast and of the fast of the paschal triduum, in which the ascetical aspect is secondary. Here fasting is symbolic of the Church's expectation of the imminent coming of Christ. In the Eucharist his coming takes place: not yet the definitive coming, but a real coming which foretells and in part already realizes the parousia. The early Christians expected the parousia with each celebration of the Eucharist, particularly that of the paschal vigil. The fast and the Eucharist represent the two poles of the Church's life in the present age: waiting and possession, future and realized eschatology, salvation yet to come and salvation already accomplished, means of grace and reality of grace.

Monasticism and Fasting

Both the ascetical and the eschatological aspect are present in every fast, though in varying proportions. If it is the former which has predominated in monasticism, it is nonetheless related to eschatology, because the very reason for which the monk wishes to purify himself is that he may be ready for the coming of the Lord. If fasting in the broad sense includes the whole of asceticism, in the strict sense it is the principal activity of asceticism. Accordingly the monk must conscientiously observe not only the law but also the spirit of fast and abstinence.

In our day the general laws of the Church have been considerably relaxed, nor do most monks any longer observe the letter of the *Rule,* which must have been considered extremely benign in the time of St. Benedict. This makes it even more urgent that monks be faithful to whatever observance they have retained. If they are faithful to their vocation, they must do more than is expected of the ordinary Christian in the world. "The life of a monk," says St. Benedict, "ought at all times to be lenten in its character" (49,1). Monasteries should and generally do have days of fast and abstinence in addition to those prescribed by the general law of the Church, nor is there any reason why monks should avail themselves of all the relaxations which the laity have been permitted in this regard.

The season of Lent, to which St. Benedict attributed such importance, should be a time of annual spiritual renewal for the monk. His observation that few have the strength to maintain the lenten observance throughout their life has been confirmed by the experience of the vast majority of his followers. But the monk who at least keeps Lent well can hope thereby to "expiate the negligences of other times" (49,3), and can hope, too, that his careful observance of that season will echo frequently in his heart throughout the year. But the monk who does not observe Lent well will probably not observe anything else well either.

Eating, Drinking, Physical Comfort

If the full lenten observance can be restricted to the forty days, however, that does not mean that mortification can be ignored at other times. In order to be fruitful, it must be habitual. Especially in matters of food and drink there is need of deliberate restraint for those who have grown up in a civilization that is affluent, comfort-loving and indulgent. The monk will have to struggle against habits of indulgence that he may have formed in the world.

The thing of first importance is that the monk be satisfied with what he receives in the monastery. This means taking the sixth degree of humility seriously. Continual complaining about the food and the living conditions is as harmful to the monk's own spirit of detachment as it is to the peace of the community. He should make no effort to obtain extra things, such as food or drink of better quality, on some spurious pretext, either within the monastery or from outside. Asceticism in matters of food and drink requires that he eat only as much as is necessary to maintain his strength and perform his duties; not more than this, "for there is nothing so unfitting for a Christian as surfeiting" (39,8). And it means that he refrain from eating outside the appointed times (43,18), following in this matter the custom of his monastery.

Mortification of the sense of touch requires furthermore that the monk willingly submit to the discomfort and inconvenience which are a natural result of his state in life, without trying to escape from them. Extremes of heat and cold, for example, should be patiently borne, without seeking air conditioning and electric fans. And the monk should wear his habit at all times when his work permits, regardless of the discomfort in hot weather.

Excessive concern about one's health is likewise contrary to a genuine spirit of detachment. A slight indisposition is not sufficient excuse for taking to bed and avoiding work. A monk who allows himself to be constantly concerned about his health can easily become a hypochondriac and use his supposed infirmity to escape from all the *dura et aspera* which are precisely the things that he ought to seek because they are the indispensable instruments for leading him to the goal of his monastic life.

Correct Choice and Motivation

St. Benedict insists that exterior penances voluntarily chosen must not be undertaken without the permission of the abbot (49,8–9). The type and amount of mortification chosen will necessarily vary from one individual to another, depending upon the generosity and the ability of each. Some will be prevented by health, work or other exterior circumstances from doing much in the way of corporal mortification. This does not mean that they need not or cannot advance in the ascetical life: the ordinary penances, after all, are generally the best, and if they are not practiced, extraordinary ones will be of little advantage. But even severe and extraordinary mortifications should not be ruled out a priori: they will be for the few rather than for the many, but for one who is impelled by the Holy Spirit they may be the authentic way to perfection.

It must be remembered that no permission is required for passive mortification or for active mortification that is interior, nor is there any limit to their exercise. And these are the best penances, for they work more directly upon the will. A monk can practice them at all times and in all circumstances, and thereby convert his entire life into a sharing in Christ's sufferings and an extension of the power of the resurrection to every corner of his being.

Interior penances, too, avoid the possibility of ostentation and false motives. Corporal mortifications so often involve the temptation to attribute one's supposed accomplishments to oneself and to exhibit them publicly with a feeling of pride. The fact that one's motives are still imperfect, of course, is no reason for abandoning mortification; the solution is rather to continue the mortification but to purify the motive. Nothing is better calculated to give the right atmosphere to acts of penance than a good sense of humor, which will prevent eccentricity and taking oneself too seriously. Mortification will be of little value unless it is performed in a spirit of joy and generosity: not, of course, the collegiate jocularity which does not really penetrate to the inside, but what St. Benedict calls "the joy of spiritual longing" (49,7).

Apatheia: *Effect of Ascetical Life*

The monk who is truly mortified will reap an abundant harvest from his efforts in his own spiritual life. The oriental monastic tradition expressed the results of the ascetical life in the term *apatheia*. This means a certain impassibility, an entire freedom from passion. But when the ancients spoke of extinguishing the passions through asceticism, they did not mean the destruction of nature, but only of the evil tendencies of the flesh. Cassian refers to this state, the goal of the ascetical life, as *inmobilis tranquillitas mentis* (*Conf* 9,2), a complete serenity in which the monk is no longer troubled by the stings of the flesh because he has achieved a total victory over them. St. Gregory tells us that St. Benedict achieved such a state through the ascetical efforts of his three years in the cave at Subiaco (*Dial* 2,2).

Apatheia is attained when one has arrived at perfect purity of heart. If the two states are not entirely synonymous, they are at least coterminous. In this state the monk is at perfect peace, with himself and with God; he is no longer disturbed by the desires of the flesh, for he has completely renounced all self-will in a total self-surrender, to enter into an intimate and all-pervading union with the risen Christ. In this state he is able to see everything from the viewpoint of God, and thereby gains a certain delicacy of perception in regard to himself and to the entire question of virtue. For Cassian, this state is identical with perfect charity, and it is this latter which is St. Benedict's ideal in the ascetical effort. This charity, which is God's love for him ardently reciprocated, will overflow into his entire life and mark all his dealings with his fellow men. Thus we see that the final goal of monastic asceticism, far from being negative, is the most intimate union with God: asceticism is not so much a question of giving as of receiving–receiving the gift which God makes of himself to those whom he loves.

6. POVERTY

The Paradox of Poverty

The abandonment of material goods was an essential ingredient of the renunciation involved in the monastic vocation from the very beginning. It was the Gospel invitation to sell all his goods and give the proceeds to the poor which first attracted the young Anthony to a life of renunciation (*Vita Antonii* 2). The practice of poverty in the concrete has differed considerably in the religious institutes that have arisen in the Church through the centuries, but the basic exigency of renouncing temporal goods for the greater good of the kingdom of heaven is common to them all. This is so because it is a question of a fundamental Christian attitude toward material creation.

The Christian virtue of poverty seems paradoxical. If material creation is good in itself, why should the Christian renounce it? If Christ teaches that it should be renounced, is this not an indication that it is evil? Both of these extreme views are erroneous; the truth lies somewhere between the two. Christianity has always maintained the intrinsic value of material creation. At the same time it has taught absolute renunciation as a counsel of perfection.

The Christian concept of poverty must incorporate both of these truths and maintain them in harmonious balance. It must avoid a false dualism which would lead to an attitude of contempt for or suspicion of material goods, but at the same time it must be careful not to spiritualize poverty to such an extent as to emasculate the concrete exigency of real renunciation. In order to be seen in proper focus, Christian poverty should be viewed against the background of sacred history.

Poverty in the Old Testament

Poverty appears in the Old Testament as a shocking social phenomenon, a thing which ought not to exist in Israel. Since the promise to the patriarchs was expressed in terms of abundance of material goods, the social fact of poverty seemed a contradiction to the expectations of the people of God. Thus it was natural for the Jews to interpret poverty as the result of sin. The ancient theory of temporal retribution held that observance of the law would result in temporal prosperity, while the sinner would be deprived of the blessings of this life.

In a parallel current of thought, the practical wisdom of the sages was faced with the dilemma that great riches often bring temptation, and yet poverty is a sign of God's disfavor. Therefore they concluded that neither riches nor poverty is the best condition for the cultivation of virtue, but an intermediate state in which the necessities of temporal life may be secured without excessive wealth.

The situation became clearer with the transposition of poverty to a more spiritual plane. The prophets, condemning the evils of avarice and injustice introduced into Israel by the prosperity of the golden age of the monarchy, taught that the deprivation of material riches could lead the nation back to a rediscovery of God. Israel had been faithful in the destitution of the desert, but apostatized as soon as she encountered the prosperity of the promised land. Therefore a return to poverty was needed to bring her back to God, to detach her affections from God's gifts and concentrate them once more upon the Giver. For the thing that was supremely important was her dependence on God.

Poverty therefore becomes the characteristic of the man who seeks God. If the prophets fulminate against the rich it is not because they have wealth but because they trust in their wealth instead of in God. And if they praise the poor it is not to exalt material destitution but to recognize the religious value of a state in which a man abandons himself entirely to God in faith and humility and patience. Lack of material goods is not an end in itself but a means to that spiritual poverty which puts a man completely in the hands of God.

Teaching of the Gospel

It is in this context that the teaching of Jesus must be understood, for he came not to destroy but to fulfill. "Blessed are you poor," he taught, "for yours is the kingdom of God" (Lk 6,20). St. Matthew, interpreting the words of the Master, reports the saying as: "Blessed are the poor *in spirit*" (Mt 5,3). For Jesus is not exalting material destitution. He recognized the existence of the poor as a social class —"for the poor you have always with you" (Mt 26,11)—and considered them as privileged. But the man who is poor in spirit is blessed because he is humble, detached, dependent on God for everything. He receives the kingdom of heaven because he puts no obstacle in its way.

Every Christian must be poor in spirit. He must make the kingdom of heaven his treasure, the pearl of great price for which he is willing to forego all else. But if he would be perfect, this is not enough. He must be actually poor, he must leave all earthly values behind to follow Christ. The invitation to the rich young man of the Gospel demands that he dispose of all that he has to be free for the exclusive following of Christ (cf Lk 18,22). For poverty is freedom—liberation from the obstacles imposed upon us by our temporal existence to enable us to devote ourselves exclusively to the one thing necessary. It is the freedom which Francis of Assisi found when he stripped himself of his clothes in the bishop's palace, cutting himself free of all earthly ties, so that he might truly say, "Our Father, who art in heaven."

Poverty and Eschatology

The basic justification for Christian poverty is the fact that the kingdom of God is not of this world. True, its beginning takes place in this world, as the kingdom in the hearts of men, but it will not be consummated until the Son of Man comes upon the clouds of heaven. Thus the treasure of a Christian cannot be found in this world, but only in the world to come. The call to poverty, like every other aspect of the kingdom, has a messianic and eschatological character. No one can be secure in this world, for the present age is about to pass away. A man who remains bound by earthly ties is not free to embrace the coming age wholeheartedly.

The paradox of poverty is the paradox of Christianity itself. The material world is God's creation, capable of leading us to the better world that is to come. But he who would devote himself entirely to the kingdom cannot be tied down by attachments to a transitory world. He must free himself from the treasures of this world to receive the treasure that will endure forever. Material possessions are good, if directed to the right end, but freedom from them is a more perfect state.

Poverty of the Ancient Monks

Poverty as a counsel of perfection found an immediate response among the early Christians. Soon after Pentecost we find Christ's teaching on the detachment required of an apostle concretely applied in the life of the Jerusalem community. Property was held in common so that the material resources of the community were directed to the needs of the Church and the poor, while the individual found himself free from material concerns to devote his energies to the spread of the kingdom.

The early monks did not intend anything other than a literal observance of the pure evangelical teaching when they stripped themselves of all earthly goods. So essential was this renunciation to the monastic vocation that monks were often called *apotaktikoi* or *renuntiantes*, "those who renounce." All the monastic writers insisted unceasingly upon the necessity of despoiling oneself of all temporal possessions. One of the sayings attributed to Macarius put it in trenchant form: "If anyone does not renounce all wordly goods, he cannot be a monk."

Yet the anchorite was still obstructed by a certain degree of temporal concern, for he was obliged to provide for his own subsistence, meager though it was. The origin of cenobitic life accentuated the monk's dependence upon the community for his material needs, removing all temptation to arbitrariness, giving occasion for the practice of social virtues and forming a more perfect image of the primitive Jerusalem community. This is the ideal of poverty which St. Benedict adopted for his monks.

St. Benedict and Poverty

The oft-praised moderation of the *Holy Rule* is not an invitation to mediocrity, but the guarantee of a spiritual freedom which may enable the monk to reach the heights of perfection. So in the matter of poverty there can be no hedging. The monk makes an absolute renunciation of everything, and he must know that henceforth he cannot own a single thing, however small or inconsequential. Private possession in a monastery is a vice which can give rise to any number of evils and therefore must be utterly rooted out (33,1). The principle is categoric: he may own nothing at all, *nihil omnino* (33,3). The stripping of his clothes from the novice during the profession ceremony (58,26), though it might offend modern sensibilities, is nonetheless profoundly significant. The monk, standing naked before God, breaks every bond of earthly affection and henceforth depends upon God alone.

His dependence on God is expressed concretely in his dependence on the monastery for his needs. He may hope to receive all that is necessary from the father of the monastery, who holds the place of Christ (33,5). The possession of wealth confers upon a man a certain power; his future depends upon his own resources. The monk, in stripping himself of all resources, places his future entirely in the hands of God. His treasure is not in earthly goods, but is God himself. His hope is not based upon the power that may come to him from his resources, but upon the power of God.

Here again we perceive that eschatological character of poverty which is so evident in the Gospel. The monastery is, in a sense, the kingdom of God already realized. The monk lays up his treasure in heaven, and the goods of the monastery are already associated with the wealth of heaven. They do not belong to a monastic corporation, but to God. Therefore even the ordinary material objects which the monk receives for use in his daily life have a sacramental character; they are, according to St. Benedict, to be regarded as the sacred vessels of the altar (31,10).

Communal Character of Benedictine Poverty

Benedictine poverty is not, therefore, destitution, but neither should it be a kind of corporate capitalism. The community may own property, but must never lose sight of the fact that everything that belongs to the monastery belongs to God. The monastic chapter is not an assembly of corporation stockholders; it is a group of men who have stripped themselves of all attachments in this world in order to bear communal witness to the ideal of evangelical poverty. Whenever community expenditures and building projects begin to establish deeper roots in this world rather than tending to the eschatological kingdom, they are veering away from the ideal of monastic poverty, and the individual poverty of the monks is likely to follow in the same direction.

Benedictine tradition has always sanctioned a certain magnificence in the matter of divine worship. What is spent on churches, vestments and sacred vessels is spent for God. Obviously, in this matter as in everything else, there is need for discretion and for a sane simplicity which is quite distinct from parsimony. The wealth of monastic churches has often been acquired through gifts made by fervent Christian laymen. It must be remembered that such gifts are made to God and not to the monks. When monks begin to regard themselves as the beneficiaries of such donations, they are forgetting the ideal of their poverty and concerning themselves with laying up treasures on earth rather than despoiling themselves of everything in view of the eschatological kingdom.

It is true that the individual monk can continue to live poorly even when his monastery has become large and wealthy. But individual poverty is not enough; the monastery itself should bear corporate witness to the Gospel ideal of detachment from things of this world. Institutionalized forms of monasticism always tend to consolidate their position in this world, to sink roots, and it cannot be disputed that a sound if frugal economy is essential to their survival. But a continual vigilance must be exercised to see that the institution does not swallow up the ideal. A balance must be achieved between legitimate concern for economic stability and the holy indifference to temporal goods which is essential to monastic ideology.

Monasteries do not exist in order to achieve this-worldly ends through the exercise of temporal power and influence. The time of feudalism is past. The contribution which monasteries can make to the Church in our time is to testify to the transitory character of this world and the primacy of the kingdom of God. This will be accomplished by the small, poor monastery rather than by the large, rich and powerful abbey which inevitably appears to many today as a relic of the triumphalism of the medieval Church. There must be real poverty, not merely a formalistic concern to see that canon law is not violated.

The Value of Poverty

Poverty, which is so contrary to the spirit of the world, always intent upon material values, can be meaningful only in the light of a profound faith. St. Paul says of our Lord: "being rich, he became poor for your sakes, that by his poverty you might become rich" (2 Cor 8,9). Poverty, therefore, introduces the Christian into the mystery of the Incarnation; it is only in the light of the divine economy manifested in sacred history that he can perceive the intrinsic values of renunciation of the goods of this world.

Poverty is an expression of confidence. Detached from all else, the monk has God alone as his treasure, and he trusts in him for all his needs, not in his own ingenuity or even in the resources of his monastery. It is an attitude of complete abandonment, and therefore a state of complete joy. No one can be as happy as the man who has given up everything, because in possessing God he possesses everything. It is the radiant joy of the Poverello of Assisi, bursting out into songs of praise for the beauty of his "Lady Poverty."

It is a continuation of the redemption. Christ elevated human poverty to make it a means of redemption. By sharing in the poverty of Christ, the monk continues his work of redemption, filling up in his flesh what is lacking of the sufferings of Christ (cf Col 1,24).

Through his poverty the monk shares profoundly in the mystery of the cross.

Poverty has a social value. Christ's work was to reunite a divided humanity into a community of love. When men insist on their rights, the people of God remain divided; only by voluntary renunciation can they become united in a bond of fraternal charity. The monastery is a small scale model of the kingdom of God. The poverty of the monk is a living testimony to the ideal Christian social order.

The Practice of Poverty

Poverty, in separating the monk from material goods, frees him from one of the principal obstacles to perfection. But poverty is a two-edged sword, for human nature reacts to it by craving all the more that of which it has been deprived. The tendency to acquire things is so deeply rooted in human nature that the observance of poverty requires a constant struggle. The monk may never relax his efforts. He must love his poverty, value it, seek it out, embrace it. He must realize that whenever he does not feel his poverty, then he is not fully observing it. It is a renunciation, and a renunciation must do violence to nature.

There must, then, be an element of privation in the monk's life. He must not allow himself to sink into a comfortable bourgeois existence. It is possible, even in a monastery, to acquire little things and to become attached to them. Renunciation of the greater pleasures of human life often makes the smaller ones seem more desirable. The monk must daily renew his intention to be detached from everything, to suffer privation for the sake of Christ. No matter how watchful superiors may be of the observance of poverty, only the individual monk can safeguard his own spirit of detachment. With a little examination of conscience, it is not difficult to tell when one is attached to something. The determining factor is: Am I willing to give it up? If this were taken from me, would I feel resentment? Would I be satisfied with another object instead of this one to which I have become accustomed? Or would I be willing to have none at all, if the abbot should so desire?

Acquisition and Care of Property

The monk may keep nothing which has not been given or permitted by the superior. St. Benedict is liberal in permitting him all that is necessary, and even gives a detailed list of objects that the abbot should provide for his use (55,19). This list may reasonably be interpreted in view of the change of times to include such useful objects as a fountain pen, a typewriter, a watch, an alarm clock, an electric razor. But a monk may acquire such things only through superiors, and may not keep the objects which are superfluous.

Sometimes it is possible to get permission for things which are not really necessary, if superiors are especially liberal or not sufficiently watchful. The monk must remember that, for his own conscience, it is not enough to have permission, especially if it has been obtained under false pretenses; he must also have a real need. Otherwise the object is superfluous. He should ask humbly for what he needs, make no effort to obtain what he does not need, and accept both a concession and a refusal with equal humility. Nor may objects be transferred from one monk to another without permission, unless it is a question of articles of common use.

Especially in the case of gifts, even if they are small and insignificant, he must always ask permission. Gifts are made to the monastery, not to the individual monk. St. Benedict is very severe on this point (54,1–5), and monastic discipline demands that personal gifts which consist of superfluities be rigorously excluded. In any case the monk must be conscientious about presenting every gift to the superior and accepting his decision as to whether it may be kept. It is better to ask permission to receive a gift before it has been given, whenever this is possible.

Poverty in the Cell

A monk's cell should give immediate evidence of the poverty which he has professed. The fundamental characteristic should be simplicity. A crucifix, a desk, a bed, one or two chairs, a lamp, a shelf to hold a few books—these should suffice. In any case, he must be satisfied with whatever furnishings are supplied and make no effort to better them, unless he has a real need, which he should present to the superior. As soon as a monk begins to fill his cell with keepsakes and various conveniences, it may be wondered what has become of his ideal of monastic poverty and simplicity. He should make a periodic checkup and immediately dispose of everything which he is not actually using. Nor is a possibility of future usefulness sufficient justification for collecting things; storing up treasures for the future is scarcely consonant with the ideal of those whose treasure is in heaven. Most constitutions wisely prescribe that such a checkup should be made annually and a list given to the abbot; the prescription should be literally observed.

A monk does not require a large wardrobe, for his clothing needs are simple: as many habits as is customary in his monastery, a suit if he has to go outside the cloister, a coat and hat for winter where the climate requires it, underclothing sufficient for reasonably frequent change, shoes, a few towels and handkerchiefs. He should not try to obtain things that he does not really need, and should be satisfied with what he receives, making no special requests or complaints regarding color or quality.

As for books, the fewer personal books he possesses, the better. Each monk should have the books necessary for choir use, a Bible, a Holy Rule, a dictionary, and whatever books he needs for the studies or teaching in which he is engaged. Anything else, and even these when no longer needed, should be catalogued in the common library. Every monk should frequently check his bookshelf and return to the library anything which he is not using.

Care of Property

The spirit of poverty demands not only that the monk have only what is necessary, but also that he take good care of what is given him for his use. St. Benedict states the principle clearly: since the property of the monastery really belongs to God, it must be treated like the sacred vessels of the altar (31,10). This means that the monk must have a sense of economy, being careful not to waste food, electricity, water, or anything else. Tools, machines, books and clothing must be handled carefully and made to last as long as possible. Common sense in these matters is the best way to avoid both wastefulness and miserliness, neither of which is consonant with poverty.

Poverty, however, is not to be identified with a certain economic shrewdness. The monk who is preoccupied with financial matters and is constantly finding ways in which the monastery could save money if the superiors would only have the good sense to put *him* in charge manifests an excessive concern for material things, which is rather the contrary of the spirit of detachment.

Poverty in no way implicates slovenliness. A monk should be scrupulously clean and neat about his personal appearance. St. Benedict prescribes that the monk's clothing should fit properly and that he should look decent especially when he goes outside the monastery (55,8.14). If the licentiousness of the sixth century put bathing in a bad light, this is no longer true today. Yet the monk must likewise avoid the false cult of physical cleanliness so prevalent in our society today. What some people in the world now regard as necessities in this matter scarcely seem compatible with the spirit of mortification and simplicity required of monks. In these matters, as in all else, discretion must determine the norm. The monk's cell, as well as his person, should be kept neat and be frequently cleaned.

If anything belonging to the monastery is lost or broken, the monk must acknowledge his fault and make culpa to the superior. Objects that belong to God cannot be treated lightly, and even if the monk has not been personally at fault, he must make reparation for the loss (cf *Rule* 32,4–5; 46,1–4).

Travel and Use of Money

There are no vacations from the life in which the monk has promised to persevere until death. Necessary trips outside the monastery, then, ought not to be considered as opportunities for temporary escape from religious discipline. The traditional saying that a monk suffers some loss whenever he leaves his cloister is still true today (cf *Rule* 66,7). St. Benedict prescribed that a monk should not eat outside the monastery if his journey was reasonably short (51,1–3). The letter of this prescription often cannot be observed, but its spirit can and should.

In any case, the monk must be mindful of his poverty while traveling. He should be content to suffer some inconvenience in the mode of travel, avoiding expensive and luxurious accommodations. It is often possible to get by with a sandwich until one's return to the monastery, rather than taking advantage of the opportunity to enjoy a fine dinner in a restaurant. A monk is out of place in first-class compartments of ships, trains or airplanes, as well as in luxury hotels and restaurants. He should go only to the places for which he has been given permission, and take the most direct route. Money which has been given him for his use is intended for necessities of travel and not for accessory entertainment.

Upon returning to the monastery, he should promptly return to the superior the money which he has left, with a clear itemization of his expenditures. He should not keep money on his person or in his room, except insofar as his duties may require it.

7. VIRGINITY

The Paradox of Virginity

Faithful to the teaching of the Gospel and of St. Paul, the early Christians were unanimous in their esteem for virginity. Already in apostolic times there were virgins of both sexes in the Christian communities. Before the rise of monasticism the ascetics who lived in their homes and devoted themselves to the pursuit of perfection were distinguished chiefly by their observance of continence. Virginity was the symbol par excellence of the absolute renunciation of the present world and total dedication to the world to come.

For St. Anthony and the other early monks, continence was simply taken for granted as essential to the monastic life. The desert Fathers frequently discoursed on the difficulties of its observance and regarded it as the principal sector in which the demons delighted in attacking the monk and attempting to entice him into sin (cf Cassian, *Conf* 8,16; *Inst* 6). In thus valuing virginity, the monks were conscious of being faithful to the Scriptures and the most authentic Christian tradition.

The question of virginity, like that of poverty, involves an element of paradox. It means the renunciation of an intrinsic value, one of the things which every man holds most precious. It is not because he regards marriage as somehow evil or tainted that the monk renounces it. If at some periods in the Church's history theologians have attempted to exalt virginity by depreciating marriage, this does not represent the authentic Christian attitude. While consistently teaching that consecrated virginity is in itself superior to marriage, the Church does not thereby imply that marriage is a regrettable concession to the weakness of human nature, but positively presents its nobility and supernatural value. The relative values inherent in virginity and marriage are a consequence of the paradox of Christianity itself. The Christian attitude on this point is the climax of the gradual revelation of the mystery of the divine economy as it unfolded in sacred history.

Marriage in the Old Testament

The current of Old Testament thought on this subject seems at first sight to be diametrically opposed to Christian practice. For the men of the Old Testament were passionately attached to marriage, which they never ceased to exalt. For them the greatest of God's gifts was a numerous progeny, children who would cause their name to live on after them. The just man is surrounded by a wife like a fruitful vine and children like young olive plants (cf Ps 127,3); he hopes to see his children's children to the third and fourth generation (cf Job 42,16). Fecundity is a blessing from the

Lord, his reward to those who keep his law. The men and women of the Old Testament were prepared to do almost anything to obtain children: Sarah gives Abraham her maidservant (cf Gen 16,2); Tamar contrives a plot (cf Gen 38,13–26); Rachel cries out in anguish, "Give me children, or I shall die!" (Gen 30,1). Sterility was thought to be a terrible curse.

Yet there is another current of thought, still timid, vague and ill-defined, through which the Holy Spirit sought to prepare his uncomprehending people for the greater revelation to come. For, paradoxically, it is the sterile ones who play the greatest role in the history of salvation. Isaac, Samson, Samuel, John the Baptist, are all born of women whose faith triumphs over the disgrace of their sterility. For the fecundity which is profitable in the sight of God is not rooted purely in the physical. These miraculous births are a mysterious foreshadowing of the virgin Christ who would be born of a virgin Mother and proclaim the mystery of virginity to his followers. "Raise a glad cry, you barren one," cries the prophet, ". . . for more numerous are the children of the deserted wife than the children of her who has a husband" (Is 54,1).

Teaching of the New Testament

The full justification of virginity appears only in the New Testament. Christ explicitly proposes it to his disciples as a counsel of perfection, not for all men, but only for those who are called. "There are eunuchs who have made themselves so for the sake of the kingdom of heaven. Let him accept it who can." (Mt 19,12)

This brief but profound text contains in germ the whole theology of virginity. It is, first of all, an ascetical practice, the value of which St. Paul explains when he writes: "I would have you free from care. He who is unmarried is concerned about the things of the Lord, how he may please God. Whereas he who is married is concerned about the things of the world, how he may please his wife, and he is divided" (1 Cor 7, 32–33). The unmarried state is better for the man who is devoted to God's work, because it leaves him free to attend to the duties of his calling.

But there is a more profound aspect. It is not the ascetical, but the eschatological value of virginity which is its primary justification. He who adopts it does so for the sake of the kingdom of heaven. Virginity is a sign that a man does not belong to this present age, that he looks forward rather to the world to come. For him there is no other union than his final union with the victorious Christ who will come on the clouds of heaven. "The time is short," says the Apostle. "It remains that those who have wives be as if they had none . . . for this world as we see it is passing away" (1 Cor 7,29–31). It is the virgins who are on hand with their lamps to greet the divine Bridegroom at his marriage feast (cf Mt 25,1–13). They watch for him; their chaste lives are a continual reminder of the eternal marriage that is coming.

Virginity as a Perfection

The marriage union is the most perfect possible realization of the human personality on the natural level. No man is complete in himself; the very fact that the human race is differentiated into two sexes shows that a man needs another complementary being for his own perfection. Through the total giving of himself to another, and the total receiving of the other's gift to him, a man realizes the ideal of the human personality.

Yet this union of two persons in one flesh places certain limitations upon the personalities of both. The physical aspect of the union may somewhat curtail the spiritual giving of self which is essential to the perfection of the personality. A union in which the same gift of self could be achieved without the limitations imposed by the flesh would be a more perfect realization of the human person.

Such a union exists in the supernatural order. The man who vows perfect chastity gives himself totally to God, reserving no part of himself for any creature; and in his gift there are involved none of the limitations of marriage. His gift is a complete assertion of his personality; in giving all that he is, he can give no more. This is the basic reason that the state of virginity is superior to the state of marriage: it is a more perfect way of obtaining the same ultimate object.

Value of Virginity: Spiritual Marriage

It is not the mere fact of marriage that is important, but the value which it achieves. For the union of marriage is only a means toward and a symbol of the greater and more perfect union of Christ with the Church and, through the Church, with the individual soul. The teaching of the prophet Hosea, who referred to the union of God with his chosen people under the symbolism of marriage, was developed by the great prophets who succeeded him, as well as by the psalmists and the author of the Canticle of Canticles. In the New Testament it reappears, fulfilled and perfected in the love of Christ for his Church. The wedding feast is the symbol of the consummation of the union which takes place in the coming of the Messianic kingdom (cf Mt 22,1–14). St. Paul develops the idea in two strikingly beautiful passages: "I betrothed you to one spouse, that I might present you a chaste virgin to Christ" (2 Cor 11,2); "This is a great mystery–I mean in reference to Christ and to the Church" (Eph 5,32).

The ultimate purpose of marriage, then, is to achieve union with Christ. Marriage is a means to an end. If that end can be achieved in another way, then marriage can be dispensed with. And this state will be a superior one, for it will attain the supreme value directly, without passing through the medium of a carnal union which is only a symbol and preparation for the eternal union.

Because virginity attains union with Christ directly, bypassing the means to it supplied by the natural order, the Fathers referred to the virgin as the bride of Christ. The virgin does not reject the value of marriage; he desires it even more than others, but he knows that the real value of marriage is in the supernatural sphere. He, too, is married, but with a spiritual marriage to Christ, without the need of a human intermediary. He cannot be satisfied with a symbolic union; he must have the union that is real.

Virginity in the Church

Virginity has an eschatological significance, therefore, but Christian eschatology is twofold. In one sense, it is already realized: the kingdom has come, we are living in the final age of the world. We already possess the supernatural realities of the future life. Thus the union of the virgin with the divine Bridegroom is already realized. But its realization is only inchoative, for the consummation of the kingdom is yet to come. Thus the virgin is a symbol of the Church's waiting for the Spouse. The union already realized is a symbol of the union to come, but a symbol which already contains the reality.

In her liturgy the Church lives the mystery of virginity. The Epiphany is the great feast of the union of the Church, the virgin bride, with her heavenly Spouse. Cleansed in the nuptial bath of the Jordan, she advances to meet her Bridegroom in the mystery of Cana, attended by the wise men bearing their wedding gifts. "Today the Church is united to her heavenly Bridegroom, for Christ has washed her clean of her sins in the Jordan: the Magi hasten with their gifts to the kingly wedding feast, the guests are regaled with water changed into wine" (*Ant ad Benedictus*).

The Liturgy of Virgins

It is obvious that the marriage symbolism finds its most appropriate application in the case of a woman, and in fact it was developed by the Fathers in connection with the consecration of feminine virginity. But in the supernatural sphere, where all are one in Christ, there is no differentiation of sex. The reality applies therefore with equal force to the monk, who enters into a spiritual marriage with Christ in the same way as the virgin. In fact, however, the Church proclaims her theology of virginity most especially in the case of feminine virginity, in the rite of consecration of virgins and in the festive liturgy of virgins, particularly of virgin martyrs, who have sealed their union with their blood.

The rite of consecration of virgins in the *Pontificale Romanum* is a profound exposition of the theology of virginity. The virgin proclaims her love for Christ in the following responsory: "I have despised the kingdom of this world and all its trappings out of love for our Lord Jesus Christ, whom I have seen, whom I have loved, in whom I have faith, and in whom I take delight." Then the bishop sings, in the solemn consecratory prayer: "While no prohibition has diminished the honor of marriage and the nuptial blessing reposes upon holy wedlock, yet there exist more noble souls, who forego the carnal union of man and woman and desire rather what it symbolizes, who do not practice what is performed in marriage, but love what is thereby signified."

Fecundity of Chastity

If virginity is a spiritual marriage, then it is essentially a matter of love. It is not a negative thing, simply the renunciation of carnal marriage, nor is it the repression of a valued human faculty. It is a positive act of love for Christ. It is not the rejection of something natural, but rather the wholehearted acceptance of the supernatural.

If chastity is love, then it must be fruitful. No one can love Christ without loving his fellow men, for it is in his Mystical Body that Christ lives among us now. The monk, who gives himself exclusively to no creature, is all the freer to become all things to all men. The fecundity of his chastity will not depend upon the extent of his exterior activities on behalf of others but upon the intensity of his charity. If he grows in love for Christ, then his love for men will grow equally, and the fruitfulness of his chastity will enrich the Mystical Body in the supernatural sphere, through the mutual sharing of merits which obtains among its members.

The monk's love will be a human love, for he does not seek to repress his affections. Rather he elevates them so that his love becomes more disinterested, more fervent, more universal. The love of the chaste, freed from the bonds of the flesh, remains human and yet is supernaturalized, like the love of Christ himself, who knew human affection though he was God. It is fruitful like the love of the Blessed Mother, who, while remaining a virgin, brought forth the Savior of the world.

It is this fruitful increase of love which is the goal of the monk's chastity. Without it, his chastity will be merely a negative thing, a renunciation, a repression, a life of sterility. It would be far better to marry than to become an egoistic bachelor.

Virginity in the Holy Rule

Faithful to the mainstream of the earlier monastic tradition, St. Benedict takes it for granted that the renunciation which the monk professes necessarily involves consecrated virginity. So obvious is this that he does not even mention it in the rubric which explains the content of profession, nor devote a chapter of the *Rule* to it. There are, however, two references to chastity in the *Holy Rule* which indicate the importance which St. Benedict attributed to virginity and his conformity with tradition.

Twice he affirms that the monk who has renounced everything no longer has power over his own body (33,4; 58,25). He is almost certainly alluding here to 1 Corinthians 7,4, where St. Paul says the same thing in regard to husband and wife, and is therefore implicitly affirming the theology of chastity which the Apostle had just developed in the previous chapter. For St. Paul an act of impurity is evil because it is a violation of one's own body, and the body belongs to the Lord. His reasoning is not based on any philosophical notion of the dignity of man as an absolute value, but upon the fact that man's dignity derives from his position as a member of Christ. Impurity is an injustice to Christ and to the Holy Spirit, because it is a violation of his temple; it robs him of a member whom he loves. If this is true of every Christian, how much more of the monk who has consecrated himself in a special way to God.

St. Benedict further manifests his profound understanding of chastity when he includes among the instruments of good works *castitatem amare* (4,64)—to *love* chastity; not merely to practice continence, or to avoid temptation and sin. No allusion is made to the negative aspect; it is the positive which is emphasized. Chastity is a matter of love. The monk must embrace it with his whole heart, dedicate himself, body and soul, to this supreme expression of his love for Christ. Chastity is a holocaust through which the monk offers himself completely, even to this most intimate sphere of his own body, upon the altar of sacrifice.

The Practice of Chastity

It is sometimes affirmed by non-believers that the practice of perfect continence is impossible to human nature. There is a great deal of truth in this statement: on the natural level it really is impossible. It becomes possible only in the supernatural sphere. Outside the context of the eschatological kingdom, it is not only impossible, but incomprehensible. Let there be no misunderstanding about it: if the monk does not understand the real nature of his chastity, if his motivation is not supernatural, if he does not regard his chastity as an expression of love for Christ, he will not be able to observe it.

There should be no minimizing of its difficulty. The monk must have a realistic knowledge of the place of sex in human life and realize that, no matter how intense his personal dedication to his monastic profession, he nevertheless remains a man, with a body and a fallen human nature. Chastity does not seek escape from sex; it seeks to dedicate the sexual faculty to a higher end. There can be, in fact, no such thing as an escape from sex, which is an integral part of human nature. Anyone who seeks to suppress it is doomed to failure. Sex occupies a central and deeply rooted position in a man's personality; it is a mysterious and sacred element in his make-up, firmly entrenched in the very core of his being, from which it can never be eradicated. Any attempt to do so can succeed only in stifling and mutilating his human personality.

What chastity seeks to do rather is to elevate, sublimate, direct this human faculty to a higher goal. It is a process that requires a constant effort. It is not enough to vow chastity once; the monk must daily renew his intention to give his heart entirely to God. And he must know himself, face the problem of sex frankly and humbly, measuring the magnitude of his renunciation against the depths of his own weakness, confident of the power of the love of Christ.

Physiological Renunciation

Chastity frees the monk entirely from all human bonds to dedicate himself completely to God. This involves the sacrifice of every aspect of sexual fulfillment, and therefore requires a threefold renunciation.

The first renunciation is physiological. In the sexual union the role of the male is active and aggressive. For him sex expresses itself as a physical urge, while in a woman it is more manifest in the affective sphere. The renunciation of the physical pleasure attached to the use of sex is therefore a real sacrifice for a monk, and one that will require a struggle. The flesh will rebel again and again, without warning and even without provocation. The sexual urge may appear in many different forms, which can seem innocent until it is too late, for sex is the basis of many of our instinctive activities.

Obviously, physical constitution plays a large part in this matter, and no two individuals are exactly alike. Some may be subject to constant temptations while others find continence relatively easy. It may happen that up to the time of his profession a young monk has never yet experienced the rebellion of the flesh. But during the years of his maturity he may encounter temptations more severe than he could ever have suspected. He must be prepared to cope with such crises and to direct his sexual powers to their transcendent spiritual end. At the same time he should not be surprised or disturbed by the occurrence of phenomena which are purely physiological and in no way implicate the consent of his will.

An Affective Renunciation

Sex, however, is not merely nor even primarily physical, but also involves the spiritual part of man. A married man gives his heart to his wife together with his body. The renunciation of human love is one of the greatest sacrifices that the monk is called upon to make. His life will always be one of solitude. There is no other human person who belongs to him, with whom he can share the most intimate depths of his being. In this most personal sphere he will always be alone with God.

This means an absolute detachment of the heart, detachment, that is, from all purely natural affections, but fervent and wholehearted attachment to Christ. It does not mean that the monk should seek to root out his affections and become an unfeeling, impersonal robot. He should not be a man without a heart, but rather a man whose heart is generous, pure and expanded, elevating all its human affections to center them upon Christ as the object of its love.

The monk must always be on guard vis-à-vis his affections. He needs to love, because he is human, and it is only too easy to begin loving creatures for their own sake. If his heart is not completely filled with the love of Christ, then there will be room in it for the growth of those human affections which he has renounced. It is true that the needs of his affective life can be somewhat compensated by certain aspects of monastic life, such as the opening of his soul to superiors and especially fraternal love for his confreres. But even here there is a danger of seeking the gratification of sensible affections. Friendships, while remaining human, must be supernaturalized. If they become exclusive or are based upon carnal attraction, then they are usurping the place in the monk's heart that belongs to God.

Procreative Renunciation

Perhaps the most painful of all the aspects of the monk's chastity is the renunciation of human fatherhood. One of the greatest gifts he has received from God is the ability to share in communicating his existence to others. In this respect man is pre-eminently the image of God, a Being who causes existence. The procreative faculty is the most meaningful of human activities because it reproduces a man's being in another equal to him and through the continuance of the race confers a quasi-eternity upon him. God is a Father, and man, in becoming a father, realizes to the full his human dignity.

The monk, therefore, in renouncing fatherhood, is renouncing one of his most precious possessions. Perhaps when he makes his profession the young monk will not yet have experienced the pain of this renunciation. Later on, in the years of his maturity, it will become more acute. If he does not fill this void in his life with an intense love for Christ and for the Church, he will become an impaired being, less fully a man than those who are happily married in the world. Works of the apostolate can fill a real need in this respect. But the monk must take care that his activities remain on the supernatural plane and that he is not deceived into taking back again the very thing which he sacrificed in the holocaust of his profession.

Importance of the Motivation

Many practical suggestions are made by spiritual writers for the avoidance of temptation and for the positive growth of the virtue of chastity. But vastly more important than the means employed is the motive, the orientation of the monk's entire life. Unless he has an integral understanding of the value and beauty of what he has renounced, and at the same time a clear concept of the supernatural motive for renouncing it, he will not be able to remain chaste regardless of the means he employs. A person who comes to the monastery with a kind of instinctive revulsion for everything connected with sex cannot ordinarily be considered a suitable candidate for monastic life. His renunciation must be dictated by love and be kept alive by love.

At the same time, he must not allow the problem of chastity to assume too large a place in his psychology. It is an important renunciation, but it is only one aspect of the general renunciation which monastic life involves. A kind of obsession with his observance of chastity may very often be merely a façade for the emergence of suppressed sexuality. The love of Christ must direct and inform his entire existence.

A Wise Use of Natural Means

A monk whose life is marked by this radical orientation to Christ will wisely make use of all the means canonized by monastic tradition for the observance of chastity. First of all he will not neglect the natural means at his disposal.

The first necessity is a sane hygiene. Because the subject of chastity is the body, physical well-being plays a considerable role in this renunciation. It is not a question of substituting physiology for grace, but of recognizing the composite nature of man and the fact that grace builds upon nature. A wise discretion will strike the proper balance between a Jansenistic angelism which despises the body and may even disguise an unconscious masochism, and the pursuit of sensuality under the guise of hygienic necessity. Diet should be adequate and nutritional, but simple; overeating and indulgence in food which is too rich or too highly seasoned can have serious effects in the realm of chastity. Cleanliness must be insisted upon; an unwise asceticism in this regard may do more harm than good. A good night's sleep and a regularity of daily schedule are indispensable. Sufficient physical exercise should be obtained, yet not so much as to cause an excessive fatigue that engenders a state of excitement rather than calm. Nervous and organic stability are closely related to the normal functioning of the sexual faculty.

Next comes a prudent modesty. This is a religious attitude, inspired by a sense of the sacredness of sex, which should permeate all the actions of a monk. It is by no means to be confused with prudery or a fear of sex, but is a respectful attitude of reserve in the presence of a mystery, and involves a delicacy of conscience in matters of purity which is quite distinct from scrupulosity. The licentiousness of our civilization makes this virtue a rarity today, and the candidate who comes to the monastery will often be obliged to alter his thinking on this point. The monk will find that cultivation of true modesty will spare him many difficulties in the practice of chastity.

Finally, the monk must avoid occasions of sin. Many problems can be averted by simply using common sense to avoid the occasions of temptation. "Idleness," says St. Benedict, "is the enemy of the soul" (48,1). The first thing to do is to keep busy and mortify one's curiosity. It is necessary to exercise a vigilant guard over the senses if one wishes to stay away from things that may prove dangerous. Imprudent reading of books and magazines of a worldly character, as well as the use of radio, television and the movies, tends to fill the mind with idle, if not dangerous thoughts which distract from the monastic ideal. Especially in regard to relationships with people outside the monastery, particularly women, there is need of a prudent reserve which may never be relaxed. Even with one's confreres such a reserve is not out of place, for the monk must be on his guard to keep his affection for them from degenerating into a purely sensual gratification.

The Employment of Supernatural Means

The monk also has at his disposal powerful supernatural means for the preservation of chastity. He must first of all have a profound conviction of his own weakness and a confident faith that God can and will give him the grace of continence. The whole question of chastity is a matter of faith, for outside that context it becomes unintelligible. The monk who is humble will experience no surprise at evidences of his own weakness, or even at his falls, but will attribute his success to God and his failures to himself (4,42–43). Only the humble are generous enough to give themselves completely.

Next, he must cultivate the spirit of penance. Chastity is impossible without a real asceticism. Mortification, therefore, accomplished in the spirit of faith, is essential: mortification of the imagination and affections, to ward off the deviations which can almost unconsciously penetrate into our psychic life; mortification of the external senses, to tame the sting of the flesh. The monk who observes the prescribed fasts conscientiously will find that they have a definite effect in reducing the violence of concupiscence. Penance also will lead the monk to open his soul to a spiritual father, within or outside of the sacrament, to expose the temptations which afflict his heart, knowing that such disclosure weakens the power of the devil and increases his own humility.

Finally, there is the fervent use of prayer and the sacraments. If the monk is convinced that chastity is a gift of God, then he will do all that he can to obtain it by fervent prayer and meditation on the example of Christ and the saints. Above all, he will seek to strengthen his chastity by fruitful participation in the liturgical and sacramental life of the Church, especially through the Eucharist. As the Eucharist is the great eschatological sign in the Church, so it is pre-eminently the nourishment of those who through their virginity are themselves a symbol of the advent of the kingdom of God.

8. OBEDIENCE

Return to Paradise through Obedience

In paradise man and the whole cosmos were perfectly subject to their Creator. The hierarchy of being was recognized and observed. Through the sin of Adam this harmony was destroyed. The salvation of fallen man consists in a return to paradise, that is, to a theological state in which man will once again accept submission to God. It is because of the disobedience of the whole human race in Adam that obedience is an essential element of Christian perfection. It is on this profound level that St. Benedict deals with the question of monastic perfection at the very beginning of the *Rule:* "That by the labor of obedience thou mayest return to him from whom thou hast strayed by the sloth of disobedience" (Pr 2).

The entire history of salvation is the story of man's disobedience and the repeated efforts of an ever-merciful God to recall him to the path of obedience. The summons to obedience resounds through the ages as God addresses his Word to his people and invites them to return. But like their father Adam they often refuse to pay heed to his Word and, forsaking the source of living waters, dig for themselves broken cisterns that hold no water (cf Jer 2,13). His Word is humbly received by the great men of the Old Testament, Noah, Abraham, Moses, David and the prophets. But these were outstanding members of a humanity still to be redeemed, in fact themselves powerless to rescue man from the slavery of sin and restore him to the liberty of full submission to the will of God.

Such a liberation could come only from one whose obedience was beyond reproach. Only the Christ who was born of human stock, made subject to the law, and bowed submissively before the will of the Father who sent him, could make mankind able to obey as he did himself. "Just as by the disobedience of the one man the many were constituted sinners, so also by the obedience of the one man the many will be constituted just" (Rom 5,19). Through the work of his redemption Christ has closed the gap caused by sin and placed the human race once more in a state of obedience toward God.

Christ's Call to Obedience

It is by the merits of Christ, then, that we are made obedient and placed in the state of salvation. Salvation has been won for us once and for all. But each individual Christian must be brought into contact with the power of Christ's redemption by assimilating his own life, in the possession of the Spirit, to that of Christ. Therefore the imitation of Christ is essential to the personal realization of salvation, not merely an ontological imitation based upon the possession of the Spirit of Christ, communicated through the sacramental life, but also the extension of this imitation onto the ethical plane.

St. Paul extols the obedience of Christ, saying that he "humbled himself, becoming obedient to death, even to death on a cross. Therefore God also has exalted him and has bestowed upon him the name that is above every name" (Phil 2,8–9). St. Benedict perceived clearly that human obedience is nothing more than an imitation of the obedience of Christ. "Assuredly," he says, "such as these imitate that saying of the Lord wherein he says, 'I came not to do my own will, but the will of him who sent me'" (Jn 6,38; *Rule* 5,13; 7,32). The third degree of humility is "that a man for the love of God subject himself to his superior in all obedience, imitating the Lord, of whom the apostle says, 'He was made obedient even unto death'" (Phil 2,8; *Rule* 7,34).

The Gospel contains no explicit counsel of obedience, as it does of poverty and virginity. Yet the Gospel is filled with obedience, for its whole ethic is conceived of as a response to the Word of God. Obedience is one aspect of the way of renunciation which our Lord himself trod and upon which he invites Christians to follow him: "If anyone wishes to come after me, let him deny himself, and take up his cross, and follow me. For he who would save his life will lose it; but he who loses his life for my sake will find it" (Mt 16,24–25). Renunciation of self in imitation of Christ is the means by which man is restored to a state of submission to the Father. Every Christian must share in the obedience of Christ.

Obedience to the Scripture

There is a gap, however, between the exigency of submission to God's will, which applies to every Christian, and the demands of obedience to a religious superior. It is a gap which can be crossed only by a leap of faith. When the early monks withdrew into the desert, they did so in obedience to the Gospel and in imitation of Christ, but without any concept of the obedience to superiors which later developed. We have seen how Anthony's vocation was an obedience to the Gospel summons to despoil himself of earthly goods for the sake of the kingdom. There was obedience in ancient monasticism, but it was obedience to the Scriptures and the will of God rather than obedience to superiors.

The early monks were intensely concerned to obey the will of God. How was his will to be made known to them if not through the Scriptures, which contain the very Word of God? This is why the ancient monastic literature is often little more than a tissue of scriptural citations. It is why St. Basil rejected the idea of writing a rule of his own and instead compiled a series of practical questions, searching the Scriptures to find the right answers to them. It is why he began the whole work with a discussion of "the order of the Lord's commandments" (*Longer Rules* 1), and the second part of it by asking whether a person may ever do what he judges right without the support of the Scriptures (*Shorter Rules* 1).

While the observances of monastic life may be derived from the Bible, there is, however, need for a living authority to make the many prudential decisions that are daily required in life situations. The Christian possesses such a living interpreter in the indwelling Spirit, who gently urges him from within to a course of action in accord with the divine will. But the beginner in the spiritual combat finds that the voice of the Spirit is often drowned out by the turbulent clamor of his own passions, and he is unable to distinguish the divine prompting from the selfish urgings of his own will. Hence the need for the art of discernment of spirits and, until this ability is acquired, the imperious necessity for placing oneself under the guidance of one who can discern the voice of the Spirit.

Function of the Ancient

This need gave rise in early monasticism to the prominent role of the spiritual father or ancient. The ancient is a man of experience who has himself passed through the stages of the spiritual ascent. He is a master of the evangelical doctrine and so is able to teach the beginner to recognize and to accomplish the will of God. Through his own experience he is able to judge the "thoughts" which the young monk confesses to him, to unmask the diabolical illusions and discern the promptings of the Spirit. The beginner cannot do these things for himself: still enslaved by the tyranny of sin, he is unskilled at hearing the Word of God and putting it into practice. He needs a master to interpret it and apply it to the concrete exigencies of his life.

Thus monastic obedience arose as a pedagogical necessity. The monk is obedient to a teacher who is more accomplished than he in the spiritual art, because there is no other way of being certain that what he does will be in obedience to God. The master's authority is not of the hierarchical order, however, but is essentially charismatic. It is because he is more directly in contact with the Spirit, more sensitive to his promptings, that he is a reliable guide. In this concept of obedience, everything depends upon the quality of the master. If he does not truly possess authentic doctrine and holiness of example, he cannot effectively guide the disciple, and the whole educative process will be frustrated.

Obedience is not, therefore, conceived of as a value in itself, but rather as a means to an end. It is a way of assuring that the monk's action will be in conformity with the law of God, not an exercise in renunciation possessing an independent value in its own right. Through obedience the monk comes into contact with the will of God, interpreted and mediated by the ancient in view of the monk's personal needs here and now. Therefore a monk can outgrow the need for obedience. If the sole reason for it is his inability to perceive the will of God by himself, it ceases to be necessary as soon as this defect has been overcome. The educative process ought to lead to the perfecting of the disciple in the art of discernment of spirits so that he can henceforth direct himself. When the goal has been reached, the means to it can be abandoned. At this point the monk ceases to be a disciple and can himself become the teacher of others.

Role of the Abbot in Cenobitic Life

This concept of obedience, common in the eremitical and semi-eremitical life, was inherited by the cenobitic founders. While Basil's idea of authority and obedience developed in a different way, the Pachomian and western cenobitic tradition, exclusive of the Augustinian current, derived mainly from Egyptian eremitism. In this concept the community was not so much a social organism as a group of individual disciples gathered about an outstanding teacher. This is not to deny that there was a true community life and sense of brotherhood in these monasteries, but merely to affirm that their point of departure was the abbot who grouped disciples about himself, that the social structure served the spiritual formation of the individual monks and not vice versa, and that the relationship of the individual disciple to the master was more significant than that of the monks to one another. This idea of cenobitic life exercised considerable influence upon St. Benedict, who knew it through Cassian and the western tradition which followed him.

The formation of the disciple by the abbot, who is a wise, holy and experienced teacher, is uppermost in the mind of Cassian, who says that the role of the abbot is to pass judgment upon the "thoughts" of the disciple and to distinguish the promptings of the Spirit from the illusions of the devil (*Inst* 4,9; *Conf* 2,10); that is, to form the monk in view of the spiritual combat. St. Benedict also emphasizes the teaching function of the abbot by his use of the Biblical text, "He who listens to you, listens to me" (Lk 10,16; *Rule* 5,6). The abbot therefore exercises a prophetic charism; he is the mediator who makes the will of God known to the disciple. Obedience means making contact with the divine will through the intermediary of a spiritual father whose authority is guaranteed by his personal sanctity and his possession of the charism which inspires him to teach.

This is not the only function of the abbot according to St. Benedict, however; he is also father of the monastic family and administrator of the affairs of the community. Nor are the relationships of master to disciples the only ones which exist in the monastery, for there are also fraternal relationships in charity of the monks to one another. The *Holy Rule* represents a convergence of the Egyptian tradition on the one hand with the Basilian and Augustinian on the other, so that the abbot's exclusively educative function and the individualistic cast of the monastic structure are modified by the demands of fraternal charity. Nevertheless the concept of obedience as submission to the direction of an experienced elder, through whom the disciple hearkens to the voice of Christ, is prominent in the *Rule*.

Obedience as Mortification

In addition to the educative function of obedience, the cenobitic founders also valued its ascetical aspect. In this understanding of obedience, Christ is regarded as the model insofar as he was himself obedient to the will of his Father. He is no longer the divine teacher who gives the command through the master, but is himself the perfect disciple, the one who obeys. The monk in obeying imitates the divine Lord who was obedient to his Father in everything, even to undergoing the cruel suffering of the crucifixion. Obedience in this sense is the way in which the monk shares in the redemptive suffering of Christ, renouncing his own desires to let others do with him as they wish. This is the monk's passion: to let others have their way with him, and thus to follow Christ to Calvary (cf Cassian, *Inst* 4,8).

This aspect of obedience is also based upon scriptural texts. The self-humiliation of Christ by way of obedience is brought out in the Pauline text, "He humbled himself, becoming obedient to death" (Phil 2,8), and the Johannine saying, "I have come . . . not to do my own will, but the will of him who sent me" (Jn 6,38). Cassian cites both of these passages (*Conf* 19,6; 24,26; *Inst* 12,28), as well as our Lord's words in his agony, "Not as I will, but as thou willest" (Mt 26,39; *Conf* 24,26). We have seen that St. Benedict likewise employs the texts from St. John and St. Paul (*Rule* 5,13; 7,32.34). Thus a scriptural justification for monastic obedience is constructed: if this was the way which the Savior took, the monk must follow him. He too must allow himself to be crucified by sacrificing his own will on the cross of obedience.

Justification of Obedience

Thus far the matter is clear: God must be obeyed, Christ is the perfect exemplar of submission to the divine will, and hence the monk must obey God as he did. But when the transfer to monastic obedience is made, it must be confessed that the reasoning no longer appears as compelling to the modern Christian as it apparently did to the ancients, unless it is completed by further considerations. Indeed, the monk must obey God and humbly accept suffering and contradictions from his hand, but what assurance is there that a monastic superior can speak for God? What guarantees that obedience to another *man* is an expression of obedience to God?

Christ can hardly be invoked as a model of *religious* obedience, since he did not in fact practice obedience to a human superior of his own choosing. While the New Testament offers ample justification for obedience to legitimately constituted authority, whether parental, ecclesiastical or civil, it contains no explicit recommendation that a man should freely submit to a human authority of his own choosing. This is the crucial question for religious obedience: how does one know that God wants him to subject himself to another man and will regard this submission as obedience to his own divine will?

The fulfillment of another person's will is not in itself meritorious: the fact that a thing is difficult does not automatically make it pleasing to God. Obedience cannot be fruitfully considered as long as it is regarded merely as the execution of commands. It must be seen in an ecclesiological context. Through obedience the monk binds himself to a whole form of life in which he gives himself unreservedly to the service of God. He sacrifices what is precious in this life in order to orientate his whole existence toward God in faith, without relying upon any human supports. It is this orientation which gives religious value to the submission of his will: it is to the entire form of life that he submits, rather than to this or that command. Obedience is a necessary element in this form of life because it is contained in the very existential situation of the Church. The monk in his obedience is a symbol of the Church, who by her very nature must be subject to her divine Bridegroom.

Obedience as a Value in Itself

In this context we can see the justification for the cenobitic tradition according to which obedience is valued as the crucifixion of the monk's self-will. When obedience is understood in this way, the abbot is no longer the inspired teacher, but merely the agent whose task it is to mortify the will of the monk. The quality of his judgment is no longer of supreme importance. In fact, the crucifixion of the disciple's will can come not only from the abbot, but from his brethren as well, or simply from the vicissitudes of daily life in the monastery. The monk must recognize in other men and in difficult situations the hand of Providence ministering his passion to him. It is for this reason that St. Benedict says that the monk must be obedient also to his brethren (71,1–5), for they too can help to crush his self-will by providing him with a cross.

Obedience as the crucifixion of one's self-will is not only for beginners, as is obedience understood as spiritual formation, but must be practiced even by those who are far advanced in the way of perfection. Seen in this light, it is not only a means to an end, but has a value in itself: St. Benedict can therefore call it *bonum oboedientiae* (71,1). This value is one of humility, which is indispensable to the whole progress of the spiritual ascent. The value of obedience is that it launches a frontal attack upon the vice of pride, the most insidious enemy of the monk. In the second, third and fourth degrees of humility St. Benedict explicitly connects this virtue with the abnegation of one's own will through obedience.

Obedience viewed from this aspect, and given not only to the superior but to all men, is the monastic implementation of a counsel implicitly contained in the whole ethic of the Gospel and in the example as well as the teaching of Jesus. The Christian is advised to prefer the last place, to want to be the least of all, to put himself at the disposition of others, to lower himself in the esteem of others, to be animated by a universal desire to give himself in service. It is a question of his being self-effacing, of humbly desiring his own abasement, of renouncing his own views to give in to those of others, of offering no resistance to injury, of turning his left cheek to one who has struck his right, of giving up his coat to the man who wishes to seize it and letting him have his cloak as well, of willingly going two miles with the man who compels him to go one, of giving anything he has to one who asks for it, without expecting him to pay it back (cf Mt 5,39-41; Lk 6,29-30). This is a counsel for every Christian; when the monastic legislators prescribe that the monk should assume such an attitude toward his abbot, they are merely narrowing down into one particular sphere a much more general policy of conduct.

Bonum Oboedientiae: *Virtue of Cenobites*

In this sense obedience is the key to the whole of renunciation. Self-will is the culmination of the element of "flesh" in man, the very type of the disorder which sin has produced in human nature. All of Christ's redemptive activity was summed up in his obedience, by which he overcame his own will, even though it was not corrupted by sin, and submitted to that of his Father. It is only by imitating him in this self-abnegation that the monk can triumph over the power of sin manifested in his lower nature. The abandonment of self-will which is involved in obedience sums up all of the renunciations of which the monastic observance is composed. It is the abbot's task to administer the program of mortification which the rule defines. The monk must realize that the way of obedience will lead him to God (cf *Rule* 71,2).

The advantage of cenobitic life is to be found precisely in the fact that it affords the *bonum oboedientiae.* Even the tradition which stemmed from Egypt and looked upon the *cenobium* as a training school for the desert was much impressed by the advantage of obedience available to the cenobite. The imitation of Christ through obedience is a value which cannot be otherwise supplied; in this respect the solitary life cannot compete with the *cenobium.* In Cassian there is a certain hesitation on this question. While he defends the primacy of the eremitical life as more perfect in itself and foresees the graduation of cenobites to the desert, yet he seems much impressed by the account of a monk who returned to the *cenobium* after twenty years in the desert because he regarded obedience as a perfection which he could not acquire as a hermit (*Conf* 19,6).

St. Benedict was likewise convinced of the value of cenobitic obedience, without thereby abandoning his esteem for the solitary life.

Interior Obedience in Faith and Love

The cenobite therefore obeys his abbot for two reasons: because he wishes to be a martyr, offering the sacrifice of his own will, and because he wishes to be directed by the voice of God, manifested in the commands of his superior. Obedience is pre-eminently an exercise of faith, because it is only through supernatural faith that the monk can perceive that "the obedience which is given to superiors is given to God" (5,15). St. Benedict clearly puts it upon the plane of faith when he says elsewhere that the abbot "is *believed* to hold the place of Christ" (63,13; cf 2,2). A living faith will be the decisive factor in overcoming the repugnance of nature to submit to the direction of another human being.

If faith is its foundation, the act of obedience must be accompanied and motivated by supernatural love. If the monk obeys merely because he likes the superior and is able to see the reasonableness of his commands, then his obedience remains upon the natural level. If his obedience is to be authentically supernatural, then he must obey out of love for Christ, whose will he sees concretely expressed in the command of the superior. St. Benedict insists upon the element of love when he says that obedience "becometh those who hold nothing dearer to them than Christ" (5,2); they are those "who are impelled by the desire of attaining life everlasting" (5,10; cf also 7,34; 68,5; 71,4).

Obedience, therefore, must proceed from the will. Unlike the obedience of the soldier, it is not merely a question of obeying orders in order to get a job done, but is essentially the interior acceptance of the will of another. In fact, St. Benedict insists: "if the disciple obey with an ill will, and murmur not only in words but even in his heart, then even though he fulfill the command, his work will not be acceptable to God, who sees that his heart is murmuring" (5,17–18). Obedience is the outward expression of the interior attitude of humility; it is because they want to submit to the will of God that monks "dwell in *cenobia* and desire to have an abbot over them" (5,12).

Promptness and Cheerfulness

Furthermore, an obedience which is interior and based upon supernatural motives will also be prompt. There will be no need for delay to consider, judge or weigh the command; it will be regarded as the voice of God calling directly and will be promptly heeded. St. Benedict is emphatic on this point; his chapter on obedience lists one qualification after another in reference to promptness: *sine mora, mox, moram pati nesciunt, statim, in velocitate, citius* (5,1–9). The Scriptures are also invoked: "He hath listened to me and hath obeyed me" (Ps 17,45; *Rule* 5,5). When the command has been given, the monk must immediately forego his own will and leave unfinished what he was doing, so that "in the same moment of time that the master's order is issued, is the disciple's work completed, in the swiftness of the fear of the Lord" (5,9). There is need for decisive action, lest in delaying the monk find reason for questioning, rationalizing or attenuating the command. The only way to avoid this is to permit oneself no hesitation whatever: "As soon as anything has been ordered by the superior, they receive it as a divine command and cannot suffer any delay in executing it" (5,4).

A truly interior obedience will also be generous and cheerful. Obedience will be "acceptable to God and pleasing to men," says St. Benedict, "if what is commanded be not done timorously, or tardily, or tepidly, nor with murmuring or the raising of objections . . . disciples should give their obedience with a good will, because 'God loveth a cheerful giver' " (2 Cor 9,7; *Rule* 5,14–16). Since obedience that is given reluctantly and unwillingly is valueless, the greatest evil in the monastery is the vice of murmuring. Nothing else is more directly opposed to the total renunciation which the monk has voluntarily made. Accordingly it is categorically condemned in the *Rule:* "Above all, let not the vice of murmuring show itself in any word or sign, for any reason whatever" (34,6); "above all things do we give this admonition, that they abstain from murmuring" (40,9). The truly obedient monk will surrender himself generously to his superior, as the disciple eager to hear the Word of God and the martyr anxious to take up his cross, for he knows that the way of obedience is the way to God and to eternal life.

The Function of Obedience

For St. Benedict, as for the earlier tradition, obedience has two functions: the spiritual formation of the individual monk and the mortification of his self-will. It is not conceived of as an administrative necessity. In this respect the ancient monastic tradition is sharply distinguished from a concept of religious obedience which is widespread today. According to this view, the purpose of obedience is to insure the common good of the society and provide for the efficient accomplishment of its apostolic undertakings. In order for a community to function smoothly, efficiently and as a unit, there must be a central authority which will dispose all things for the good of the whole body. The good of the individual must sometimes give way before the welfare of the group. In obeying, the religious is serving the common good.

On the other hand, what is predominant in St. Benedict's idea of obedience is the relationship of monk to abbot as representative of God. It is true that he has somewhat attenuated the rigor of this concept found among some of his predecessors by combining the perspective which stemmed from the desert with the concern for fraternal charity derived from Basil and Augustine: there is a certain concern for the common good in the *Rule*. But the principal emphasis is not upon the abbot as representative of the community, but as representative of Christ and minister of his cross to the monk. The purpose of obedience is to lead the monk along the spiritual ascent, both by instructing him in the divine law and training him in discretion, on the one hand, and by exercising him in the conquest of his self-will, on the other.

The collectivist theory which places the mystique of the community in the foreground is a more recent concept of cenobitism which does not correspond to the mind of the *Rule*, so intent upon the monk's personal effort to achieve sanctity. It is an abuse of obedience to use it merely as an instrument for securing the common good and achieving community goals. Obviously, the common good must be a factor in making decisions; what is abusive is to make it the principal factor, giving it preference over the spiritual growth of the monks. The adoption of organized apostolic efforts by monasteries has led to a concern for accomplishment and efficiency which is difficult to reconcile with the basic monastic exigency of the progress in virtue of each monk as a person. When this results in a command which deprives a monk more or less permanently of the whole structure of cenobitic life and the monastic tools normally used in the spiritual ascent, such a command goes directly counter to the principal purpose of monastic obedience. A superior does not have the right to use obedience outside the framework of its proper finality; he is authorized to use it only for the purpose specified by the *Rule*. But a superior's abuse of authority does not dispense his subjects from obeying, unless the command is manifestly immoral; the superior receives the benefit of the doubt.

The Function of the Abbot

Indeed, the monk's obligation to obey every order which is not contrary to faith or morals does not give the superior the correlative right to command anything not contrary to faith or morals. The obligation upon the superior to govern wisely is just as binding as the monk's obligation to obey scrupulously. The fact that he has authority does not mean that he has authority to do what he pleases. For St. Benedict as for his predecessors, the abbot is the keystone of the monastery: the spiritual father who engenders the community, the exemplary monk, the shepherd of the flock, the father of the family and the administrator of its affairs. But he has modified the prestige of the abbot by recognizing his limitations and sharing his authority, by making the community a true brotherhood cemented together by charity, which produces the abbot from its own ranks, and by insisting that the foundation of the whole cenobitic life is the *Rule*, to which even the abbot is subject (cf 3,7.11; 64,20).

Hence the abbot is not a tyrant with power to act arbitrarily: his authority is given him in view of specified ends which he is obliged to pursue. He is not free to substitute other ends in conflict with the spiritual formation of his own sons and disciples, nor to exclude or render more difficult the spiritual ascent of any of them in order to achieve some community goal. Nor is he free to identify the common good with his own projects, interests and prejudices. Like all Christian authority, that of the abbot is not domination, but service (cf *Rule* 64,8). No exercise of authority can be truly Christian unless it is based upon love.

In other words, the abbot is not the highest and absolute norm of authority; he is only the mediator of the law of Christ. He is a channel which must faithfully transmit the divine Word to his disciples without distortion. This Word of God which he conveys to his monks he must also obey himself. Monastic obedience is not *ultimately* obedience to an abbot; it is obedience to Christ the supreme teacher, to the Scriptures which contain his Word, to the Holy Spirit who stirs up in the heart of each monk the desire for eternal life. Whenever the abbot gives a command, he must be conscious that he is communicating the command of God, not injecting his own too human opinions. He is further obliged to follow the *Rule*, which is the concrete application of the scriptural precepts to the style of life of a cenobitic monastery. If the monk must subjectively regard the will of the abbot as the will of God, the abbot himself may not presume that this is automatically so: there is no guarantee that his every opinion or prejudice objectively represents the will of God. He must humbly search for the will of God with the same human means that the monk himself has to use. He must listen to the voice of the Spirit before he presumes to speak himself.

Modern Objections against Obedience

In the contemporary world obedience is often a stumbling block to the acceptance of monasticism as a way of life, and can be the most difficult exercise for young monks to endure. Perhaps this difficulty is even more acutely felt in other forms of religious life, which are committed to external apostolic activities and envisage obedience as the service of the common good. Today there is a feverish concern with personal values, particularly for the inalienable freedom of the human person and his intrinsic right to the full development of his personality. While some of its manifestations may be exaggerated, the concern itself is legitimate, and the problem cannot be solved simply by ignoring it or dismissing it as a thinly veiled pretext for evading the hardships inherent in the Christian commitment.

Obedience, if not positively rejected, is often found to be repellent because it is seen as a total surrender of personal liberty and personal responsibility. It is not merely the fact that Christians today have discovered that ecclesiastical superiors can sometimes be incompetent, arbitrary and uncompromisingly committed to perpetuating the past rather than providing for the future. It is rather the very concept of obedience itself which is questioned: is it right that a man should abdicate his freedom and submit himself entirely to the judgment of another human being? Is this not a process of dehumanization which arrests the development of the personality, frustrates, impoverishes and mutilates it?

The terms in which this objection is couched betray a false appreciation of what obedience really is. Nevertheless the concern which prompts the objection is a legitimate demand for authentic human values, and it is necessary to show that true obedience is not destructive of these values. If a caricature has too often been substituted for its authentic image, this is partially because superiors and subjects have themselves distorted it and turned it into a dehumanizing process. If St. Benedict's concept of monastic obedience is rightly understood, it will be seen that it does not destroy human liberty nor arrest the development of the person.

Maintaining the Balance

St. Benedict regards obedience from two distinct points of view: as the spiritual formation of the disciple by the experienced master whose charismatic gifts enable him to lead the other along the way to perfection; and as the mortification of the monk's own will by submission to the will of the abbot and of his brethren, that he may overcome the weight of his fallen nature by sharing in the redemptive act of Christ. These are distinct points of view, even if the *Rule* does not always keep them separate and in fact sometimes mixes them together quite indiscriminately. Both of them together are required to constitute the fullness of monastic obedience according to the mind of the *Rule,* and they must be kept in delicate balance. If either is forced at the expense of the other, the result will be a distortion which will dehumanize obedience or rob it of its ascetical and redemptive value.

The most evident distortion results if the second function is chosen to the exclusion of the first. The sole purpose of obedience, in that case, would be to crush the will of the monk, to mortify him so that he may share in the passion of Christ. Wise commands are not required to accomplish this purpose; anything that mortifies will do. Ancient monasticism knew trials of obedience in which the monk was deliberately given irrational commands in order to destroy his self-will. Nor is the abbot the only one who can accomplish this; it is for this function of obedience that the *Rule* prescribes submission of the monks to one another, in practice to the elders of the community. In fact, a thoroughly incompetent and irrational superior is more adept at inflicting mortification upon his monks than an able and prudent one.

Avoiding Excess in Mortifying the Will

However, even if this were the only consideration, there is a fallacy concealed in this approach to obedience. The human will is not evil in itself. Interior mortification is not intended to kill the will, any more than exterior mortification is intended to kill the body. Both are directed against the "flesh," that area within man, whether of body or soul, which is still unredeemed, still subject to the kingdom of Satan, in which sin exercises its corrosive influence. Obedience as mortification does not attack the will itself, but the evil inclinations to which it is subject, the power of sin which works upon it. To kill the will would be to mutilate the human being; to kill sin in the will is to free it from the degradation of slavery and restore it to the state of Christian freedom.

Obedience conceived of as crucifixion of the will has its limitations. In principle, the mortification of the evil tendencies of the will can be accomplished by any command that goes contrary to the monk's personal desires. But in practice not every such command will effect the desired result. In order to overcome his selfishness, the monk must accept the mortification interiorly. And if the command is irrational or infringes upon his human dignity, the monk most likely will not so accept it, and so it will do him no good. Here a man must be led gradually and with regard to his personal limitations. In the course of a normal monastic life there are enough *dura et aspera* to mortify a monk's self-will if he will accept them as a share in Christ's passion. It is not ordinarily necessary for the abbot deliberately to contrive them.

This aspect of obedience would indeed lead to excess if it were the only one. It would dispense the abbot from any concern about the wisdom of his commands: the more irrational, the better, because the more mortifying. To any protest from a monk the abbot need merely reply that the disciple never errs in obeying and urge him to be grateful for the opportunity of sharing in the suffering of Christ. He would not have to know any other principle of monastic life; there would never be need to mention that the abbot also has obligations other than that of seeing that every monk is properly mortified. This would be tyranny; it would be the systematic destruction of the monk's freedom, natural talents and sense of responsibility. And it would be merely a caricature of obedience.

The Development of Responsibility

The balance is restored by considering the other function of obedience, that of spiritual formation. Here the wisdom and prudence of the superior is of primordial importance, for his task is not to destroy but to educate. He must guide the monk along the difficult path of the spiritual ascent, help him to overcome his weakness, and form him in the virtue of discretion. Far from being destructive of personal responsibility, this process is meant to develop it.

At the end of the period of formation, the monk should be ready to stand upon his own initiative, and even be prepared to instruct others. For the cenobite, this period may last for many years, perhaps even his whole lifetime. While in principle the cenobitic life is geared only to the *vita activa* and finds its logical goal in eremitism, in practice many monks will never reach this stage. However, the formative process of itself tends to develop in the subject a measure of personal responsibility which can render obedience in the educative sense unnecessary, though as an ascetical exercise it will retain its value even for the perfect monk. The abbot's goal must be to develop responsibility and the faculty of making wise decisions in his subjects. If he regards those who always agree with him as his best monks and tries to produce well-behaved and subservient robots, he is abdicating one of his most important functions and creating a travesty of obedience.

In the process of spiritual formation there is no suppression of personal liberty, nor abdication of personal responsibility. The monk voluntarily follows the advice and commands of the master because he recognizes his proven competence and wishes to enjoy the advantage of reliable direction in an area where he is himself unskilled. The abbot may impose harsh and difficult exercises upon him, but he does so for the monk's own profit, explaining the principles of the ascetical life and helping him to make his own decisions. The monk recognizes in him the mouthpiece of God who mediates the divine teaching to him. The restrictions which the master places upon his personal desires have as their purpose to make war upon the power of sin. Obedience, then, far from being an infringement upon his liberty, is actually its guarantee. It liberates him from slavery to his own selfishness and gives him the freedom to respond to the Word of God. Obedience to the abbot is the guarantee of obedience to God, and to serve God is to rule.

Integration of Functions

Yet neither may this aspect of obedience be stressed to the exclusion of the other. To do so is to emasculate Christianity by excluding the cross from it. Without the ascetical aspect of obedience the process of spiritual formation would degenerate into purely theoretical instruction. The monk must not only learn from Christ the teacher, he must also imitate Christ crucified; and to imitate Christ is to carry the cross and to suffer one's sinful flesh to be stretched upon it.

To be precise, it is not enough to maintain a theoretical balance between these two aspects of obedience; they must be fully integrated in practice, as they are in the thought of St. Benedict. The ascetical exercise of obedience must itself be a part of the formative process, gradually weaning the monk away from his selfishness and teaching him to bear the cross courageously and voluntarily, freely and responsibly. The ascetical and redemptive value of obedience, when integrated into the formative process by which the disciple receives the divine Word from the master, does not lead to dehumanization, but itself contributes to the acquisition of true liberty and responsibility.

Obedience thus conceived is the free response of a fervent Christian who has *chosen* to let himself be led upon the harsh but rewarding path of monastic asceticism. It is not the imposition of an exterior mechanism upon the human personality as a substitute for responsible personal decision. Neither the will nor the talents of the monk are crushed and mutilated; his inner life suffers no impoverishment. Rather his potentialities are brought to fruitful development by contact with the divine will through his inspired teacher. He will experience suffering and mortification, but these will further his liberty by overcoming the tyranny of the flesh to which he is enslaved. In true obedience the abbot is not the enemy or rival of the monk, nor a brutal force which warps his personality. Rather he is his ally and his guide in making the spiritual ascent. The abbot and the monk together seek the will of God and learn to listen to the voice of the Spirit.

Humanization of Obedience

It is evident that the most delicate discretion is required of an abbot who would administer both the divine teaching and the cross to his monks in this ideal fashion. St. Benedict recognizes that the abbot will not be perfect. Some of the difficulties of obedience will arise from his own human weaknesses, many others from the imperfections of the monk. The *Rule* represents a notable advance over previous monastic legislation in explicitly recognizing the human difficulties of obedience, both from the abbot's viewpoint and from the monk's.

The monk will sometimes find it almost unbearably difficult to obey. In chapter 68, which manifests a remarkable insight into the psychological state of the subject, this problem is explicitly treated. There are no ready-made solutions to these human problems; they must be handled with tact and charity, in an intensely human fashion. The monk should humbly present his problem to the abbot, explaining that "the weight of the burden altogether exceeds the measure of his strength" (68,2). Perhaps the abbot will decide that it would be better, in view of the total picture of the monk's state of spiritual health, not to insist upon the command. But if he is convinced that his command represents the will of God for that monk here and now, then the monk must bear the cross. But he should do so "out of love," that divine charity which is greater than human weakness, and "trusting in the assistance of God" (68,5).

The abbot must be equally conscious of his own weakness and limitations: "let him always distrust his own frailty" (64,13). St. Benedict never supposes that he will be omniscient or infallible, and neither should the abbot himself. He is not to parade his own prerogatives, but is to render humble service (cf 64,8). His overriding concern must be the salvation of the souls committed to him (cf 2,33–34); to insure this, he must be certain that his teaching is in conformity with the divine law (cf 2,4–5). Conscious that he is only a channel of the Word of God, the abbot must always take care to keep in contact with its source. He must be attentive to the Spirit, anxious to discern what God's will is for each of his monks. He will recognize that the Spirit may speak through others than himself, and so he will be ready to pay heed to the legitimate representations of his sons; it may even happen that the youngest of all will receive the most authentic inspiration (cf 3,3).

Obedience is the supreme expression of the monk's readiness to deny himself and take up his cross out of love for Christ. There is no guarantee that it will be easy. But neither is anything else in the spiritual ascent.

9. STABILITY

Perseverance in Obedience

The constitutive principle of cenobitic life is the relationship of obedience which binds the monk to his spiritual father, the abbot. This relationship is of its nature permanent. Insofar as the function of obedience is spiritual formation, the relationship is relatively permanent, for the monk must remain subject to the abbot so long as he is in need of his direction. Insofar as its function is to administer mortification of the monk's selfish desires, it is absolutely permanent, for this exigency never ceases in the present life. Christ himself, according to St. Paul, became obedient "even to death" (Phil 2,8). Applying this text to the imitation of Christ by the monk, the monastic literature interpreted the phrase in a temporal sense: the monk must persevere in obedience until his own death (Cassian, *Conf* 19,6; *Rule* 7,34). This perseverance is what St. Benedict calls stability. The renunciation which a monk makes at profession includes not only obedience but also the intention to persevere in it (58,17; cf Pr 50).

There was nothing new about the idea. From the beginning of monasticism the profession of a monk was regarded as binding him for life. One of the most difficult trials for the desert monks was to remain quietly in their cells, going about the regular routine of the exercises of the spiritual ascent. They were constantly tempted to break the monotony by going elsewhere to seek some better form of life. This chronic temptation to instability, which Evagrius classified as one of the eight principal vices, was called *acedia*. Cassian has given a vivid description of it in the tenth book of his *Institutes*. It was called the "noonday devil" (cf Ps 90,6) because it generally attacked the monk around midday. Then he was overcome by dejection and discouragement, regarded the place he was in as unprofitable and his brethren as unspiritual, sought to overcome his restlessness by flinging himself into activities, and eventually, perhaps, entirely abandoned his cell and the life which he had professed.

Abuses of Wandering

The ancients were often called upon to console and fortify younger monks overcome by the affliction of *acedia*. The only cure for it was to remain quietly in the cell, concentrating upon one's work and spiritual exercises and resisting the temptation to go out visiting others and finding out what they were doing under pretext that thus one would be edified. Perseverance is a harsh discipline, for it requires that one marshal and control his thoughts, return continually to the ever-present necessity of warring against oneself, and be content with the slow and monotonous progress of the spiritual combat. But only this perseverance, the ancients believed, could put order into the monk's life.

There was, however, another current of thought in ancient monasticism which, far from insisting that the monk stay in his cell, recommended that he become a perpetual wanderer, an exile without a home. In this sense wandering from place to place was adopted as an ascetical practice, in imitation of Christ who had "nowhere to lay his head" (Mt 8,20; Lk 9,58), and in literal fulfillment of the Apostle's description of the Christian as an exile in this world, far from his heavenly country (2 Cor 5,6; Phil 3,20; cf Heb 11,37–38; 1 Pt 2,11). But this practice easily led to abuses, and some of the wandering monks degenerated into lax and licentious vagabonds who merited the condemnations which frequently occur in the ancient monastic literature. St. Benedict calls them *gyrovagues* and speaks disapprovingly of their shameless manner of life (1,10–11; cf *Regula Magistri* 1,13-74).

The cenobitic founders, who institutionalized the master-disciple relationship, naturally opted for the view of the solitaries that the monk must persevere in practicing the exercises of the spiritual combat; if the anchorite must stay in his cell, the cenobite must stay in his monastery. St. Pachomius insisted that the monk must remain in the monastery of his profession (*Rule* 136; 175), and St. Basil regarded a departure motivated by instability as an apostasy (*Longer Rules* 36). In the fifth and sixth centuries various councils passed legislation to prevent excessive monastic wandering, and St. Augustine protested vigorously against it. The most sensational protests were those of two extreme types of monks: the recluses, who walled themselves in, and the stylites, who spent their whole lives on top of a pillar.

St. Benedict and Stability

St. Benedict stands in the cenobitic tradition which had reacted against the abuses of wandering and insisted upon the necessity of patient application of the monk's energies to the harsh program of monastic asceticism. St. Benedict required that a monk who entered his monastery commit himself to persevere in obedience (cf 58,9; 60,9; 61,5), even when he found that it was fraught with "difficulties and contradictions and even injustices." It is then that "he should with a quiet mind hold fast to patience, and enduring neither tire nor run away; for the Scripture says, 'He that shall persevere to the end shall be saved' " (Mt 10,22; *Rule* 7,35–36). This is the classic means of defense against *acedia*, transposed to a cenobitic structure. The essence of stability is perseverance in obedience.

Such perseverance normally involves what later came to be called *stabilitas loci*, permanence in the same community and the same monastic enclosure. St. Benedict's injunction that the monks should not be required to go out of the enclosure, "for that is not at all expedient for their souls" (66,7), is reminiscent of the solitaries' insistence upon staying in the cell because a monk outside his cell is like a fish out of water (cf *Vita Antonii* 85). But the physical enclosure is not inviolable: the monks may go out of the monastery temporarily for valid reasons which are approved by the abbot (67,1–7). The emphasis is not upon the material dimension of stability, the permanence in a place, but upon its spiritual dimension, perseverance in the trials of obedience. In St. Benedict's thought stability is not the primary consideration: it is obedience which is primary, and stability is merely a consequence of it.

Hence the concept of stability, while it ordinarily involves permanence in the same monastery, does not exclude the passage of a monk to a higher form of life. St. Benedict's praise of the hermits (1,3–5) shows that he retains the esteem for the solitary life which was traditional in the Egyptian current of monastic ideology which passed through Cassian to the West. There is nothing to indicate that he abandoned the traditional idea that the solitary life is in itself more perfect and that the function of the *cenobium* is to serve as training school for the desert by leading the monk through the stages of the active life until he is prepared to advance to single combat. The monk must persevere in obedience until he is sufficiently formed to stand alone. Stability is not conceived of in the legal sense which later developed, as a "vow" which would bar not only his return to the world but even his passage to a higher form of life.

Perseverance and Local Stability

Of course, the monk who actually is ready to make the transfer to the desert will be the exception rather than the rule; St. Benedict did not expect that every cenobite would actually reach the end of the active life and be able to dispense with the guidance of a master. In fact, the *bonum oboedientiae*, the crucifixion of the monk's self-will, retains its value even for the monk who has ceased to need obedience in the sense of spiritual formation. Its ascetical value is permanent, and in this respect the *cenobium* can compete with the desert. Hence the cenobitic legislators can recommend obedience "even unto death" in the monastery, while at the same time they hold that the solitary life is the logical goal of the spiritual ascent which the *cenobium* exists to safeguard. Like Cassian, St. Benedict seems to be torn between two values: obedience in the *cenobium* and solitude with God in the desert.

In any case, stability is primarily a question of perseverance in the way of obedience within the structure of cenobitic life, and only secondarily of material permanence in a place. St. Benedict was incapable of the modern casuistry which can place a monk for life outside the monastery in conditions antithetic to the pursuit of cenobitic perfection without any violation of stability, because his juridical connection to the monastery of profession has not been broken, and yet consider it a breach of stability for a monk to request transfer to a higher form of monastic life. Legal categories do not always correspond to reality.

To the *stabilitas cordis et loci* of which the medieval monks spoke, canon law has added *stabilitas legis*. St. Benedict was primarily concerned with stability of the heart: real perseverance in the spiritual combat within the framework of cenobitic life. He was secondarily concerned with stability of place insofar as it is a normal consequence of the former: while it is no guarantee of perseverance in obedience, it is normally a *conditio sine qua non* for it. Of legal stability he knew nothing: he was willing to take monks from other monasteries, if they were good monks and had the consent of their abbot (61,8–14). There seems to have been no juridical bar to such transfers, though of course a son does not normally change fathers unless there are compelling reasons for him to seek adoption.

Acedia: *Temptation against Stability*

Every monk is himself responsible for preserving the interior constancy which is his best protection against that restlessness of spirit which he has abandoned once and for all in making his monastic profession. Perseverance is a constant, daily challenge. No monk can hope to be free from temptations to seek change. He has cast his lot permanently with an imperfect group of men in an imperfect monastery, and he will have to face many disappointments. He may find his own monastery unobservant, suffer the disillusionment of discovering that his ideals will never be attained, see his community embark upon a course of action which he sincerely believes to be disastrous. The monastery may be suffering from incompetent administration, may be clearly on the decline, even on the point of dying out. His own ideals may strike no chord of sympathy among his confreres, so that he becomes an outcast among his own.

In such circumstances it will be easy for the monk to conceive the idea that he is wasting his time where he is and that it would be better to go elsewhere. He will begin to cast envious glances toward other monasteries which are flourishing, observant, well-administered, peopled by a community zealous for an integral observance of the *Rule* and directed by superiors with well-defined notions of the function of monastic life. The monk may foresee that there he would be accepted, understood, freed from harassment, and not only enabled but positively encouraged to pursue his own eminently praiseworthy ideals. The temptation may take different forms in different circumstances, but basically it is the onslaught of *acedia*. Cassian had a remarkable insight into the whole psychology of it fifteen centuries ago.

Necessity for Trusting God

Acedia is a formidable adversary because on purely natural grounds its arguments are unassailable. If the value of obedience is the share in Christ's suffering that it offers the monk, then perseverance in this assimilation to his redemptive passion can reasonably be motivated only by a profound faith and an ardent love. The monk cannot see into the depths of God's providence and there discern what in the long run will be best for him. What God wants of him is obedience to his will, and in the normal course of cenobitic life this means obedience to the abbot, in spite of all the *dura et aspera* which accompany this very human situation. The monk must follow blindly along this path to perfection, in the obscurity of that faith which means complete trust in God who is leading and in the certitude of that hope which depends upon the power of God to accomplish what is humanly impossible.

Perfection does not consist in precise observance but in sincerely seeking God. God seems to have a sense of humor, for sometimes he wants to be sought in the most improbable ways. It may be his design that a monk should work out his salvation in an unobservant monastery rather than an ideal one, if there be any such. The monk does not know why, for he cannot penetrate the inscrutable designs of Providence. He only knows by faith that it was God's will that he should bind himself to obedience within a particular monastery and that he should stay there until God signifies otherwise. The monk's ideals may be impossible of realization, but perhaps God does not want them realized. He can inspire a praiseworthy hope without willing that it be fulfilled. Perhaps he knows a better way of bringing the monk to him, a way that leads to the cross. In his omniscience he may realize that the path of suffering will lead the monk to a higher degree of perfection than could the most perfect observance.

Stability not an End but a Means

This is not to say that there could never be a case which would justify a change of monastery. St. Benedict himself abandoned the community of Vicovaro when it became evident that his efforts there could bear no fruit (*Dial* 2,3), and many of his saintly followers, in similar circumstances, have done the same. There are sufficient precedents in the lives of Benedictine saints to show that a change of monastery may sometimes be what God wills for an individual monk. St. Basil already held that a brother should leave a community which is confirmed in evil ways, for then it would not be a case of abandoning brethren, but of separating from strangers (cf *Longer Rules* 36). Passage from the *cenobium* to the solitary life was widely regarded as the normal, if not the usual, culmination of the *vita activa.*

Stability has been variously interpreted in the course of Benedictine history, but it has generally been found that a strict local stability is best. Nevertheless, this should not be interpreted so rigidly that every departure of a monk from the monastery of his profession is looked upon as a kind of apostasy. Stability is not an end in itself, but only a means to the perfection of the monk. The legal view of it as a "vow" binding the monk to one monastery for life, and the collective interpretation of cenobitism, which places the common good ahead of the spiritual welfare of the individual monk, have contributed to erecting stability into an end in itself. But God cannot be bound by ecclesiastical laws. If a monastic vocation is a free response to a summons of the Spirit, the monk is obliged to follow his call wherever it may lead him. We cannot a priori rule out the possibility that the Spirit may call again and summon a particular monk to a higher form of life in another monastery or in solitude. He does not usually do so, but to make it a principle that he cannot is to run the risk of stifling the voice of the Spirit and of obeying men rather than God.

Obviously, a monk cannot easily suppose that he enjoys a special inspiration. In the absence of evidence to the contrary, the will of

God for a monk is that he persevere in the monastery of his profession. If the Spirit wishes to inform him of a change in his plans for him, he can find means of letting him know about it. Until he does so, the monk must suppose that God wants him to stay where he is. One must practice discernment of spirits to be sure that the desire for change arises from divine inspiration and not from discontent with the regime of the monastery or with one's confreres. Perseverance in obedience means that a monk is continually alert to perceive the will of God and to follow it out, in whatever way it may be manifested.

The Vice of Instability

The monk must be sure that his desire for change is really a response to God's will and is not prompted by an unwillingness to submit to adversities which are what God really wants. The *dura et aspera* are an essential ingredient in the life of every monk. They are for him the literal fulfillment of our Lord's invitation to take up the cross and follow him. His salvation lies in the direction of accepting them and even enthusiastically embracing them, not in trying to free himself from what God has sent him for his own good. Obedience is a *bonum,* a value, precisely because it means a share in the cross of Christ. It will be a real value for the monk only if he perseveres in it.

The unstable monk is the victim of his own delusions. To him the grass is always greener in the cloister garden of some other monastery. He is always anxious to try out some new experiment, to be sent to another monastery, to make new foundations where he can implement his ideals. He keeps looking forward to some new source of excitement in his life, something to interrupt the boredom of the unchanging routine of his own cloister. He schemes to be sent out on trips or to receive new assignments outside the monastery. He is not willing to face the dismal prospect of working out his salvation through the monotonous, unexciting routine of the life which he has embraced.

His real trouble is a lack of interior constancy. He wishes to run from one place to another to escape his troubles. But he cannot escape from himself, and that is where the real trouble lies. Cassian long ago analyzed the problem of such a man quite accurately. The elders of the desert would have told him simply to stay in his cell and be quiet.

Perseverance and Patience

In the final paragraph of the Prologue, where St. Benedict speaks of the "school of the Lord's service" as the place where the monk is to work out his salvation, he associates perseverance with patience in an uncompromising fashion. For St. Benedict, the word patience retains its original sense of *suffering*. Stability involves precisely that: suffering from day to day the inevitable trials and disappointments which are the vicissitudes of the monastic life and which unite the monk to the suffering of Christ. Perseverance in obedience "even to death" is the monk's passion.

Although actual physical presence in the monastery is only the material dimension of perseverance, in the normal course of events it is the framework which best helps to preserve the spiritual dimension. The stable monk will he happy to stay at home in his cloister, grateful for the protection it affords him. He will not seek excuses to go out, and when obliged to do so under obedience, will take steps to see that his interior spirit is not thereby weakened. St. Benedict's warnings against the dangers of going out into the world and bringing its spirit back into the cloister are as relevant today as they were in the sixth century.

But it is stability of the heart which the monk must be principally concerned to guard. It is possible for a monk to remain in the monastery all his life and still be unstable in this sense. His heart must be genuinely attached to his cenobitic vocation, or he will begin to seek diversions and amusements which will deflect him from his purpose. Modern technology has added an infinite variety of new distractions to the older ones, which consisted chiefly of going from cell to cell to seek diversion and disturb others. The monk who is serious about his vocation will realize that he must seek God here and now, in the place assigned to him, in the daily routine of an ordered life, and not waste his time dreaming about more ideal surroundings. "The workshop, wherein we shall diligently execute all these tasks," says St. Benedict, "is the enclosure of the monastery and stability in the community" (4,78).

NOTE ON THE MEANING OF *CONVERSATIO MORUM*

The State of the Question

The rubric of St. Benedict which refers to the content of the monk's profession (58,17) mentions, in addition to stability and obedience, *conversatio morum suorum.* There is no general agreement about the meaning of this phrase. It is not a question of decisive importance as far as the understanding of monastic profession is concerned, since the nature of the active life is sufficiently defined by the rest of the *Rule* and the tradition from which it emerged. In this note we wish only to explain the state of the question regarding *conversatio morum* and the principal interpretations of it which have been proposed.

For many centuries this second of the three elements in St. Benedict's rubric was translated "conversion of life," but this translation was based upon the false reading *conversio morum,* which appears in most of the manuscripts from the eighth century onward. The commentators understood it in this sense from Carolingian times down to the twentieth century. The phrase would thus mean the total process of monastic conversion by which the monk leaves behind his sinful habits and devotes himself untiringly to the acquisition of perfection. Since the three elements of St. Benedict's rubric have generally been taken to mean vows, this would mean that the monk must make a special vow to persevere in the effort to achieve perfection.

In the late nineteenth century a serious study of the text of the *Rule* was undertaken. In the effort to establish the original text, purged of the corrections which had crept into the manuscripts, it was discovered that the best manuscripts read *conversatio morum* instead of *conversio*. This difficult phrase, like other late Latin usages of St. Benedict, was no longer understood by the monks of the Carolingian period, who had returned to a more classical ideal of Latinity. Consequently they corrected the reading *conversatio* to *conversio*, which from that time on was generally accepted. Since Dom Cuthbert Butler demonstrated, early in the twentieth century, that the authentic reading is *conversatio*, this has been adopted by all modern critical editions. But the problem of what the phrase means has not yet been definitely solved.

Meaning of Conversatio

Certainly for the contemporaries of St. Benedict the expression could not have been difficult to understand. He makes no attempt to explain it, and uses the term in order to clarify for the prospective monk the content of monastic profession. In such a context its meaning must have been clear to those for whom it was intended. But it is not clear to us, for the living tradition has been lost. Since the tradition which interpreted it as "conversion of life" can be traced back only as far as the Carolingian period, when the text of the *Rule* had already undergone correction, we cannot be sure that this is an authentic tradition going back to the sixth century. The correction may have involved only the substitution of a more correct Latin equivalent, but it may also have involved a change of meaning.

Modern scholars, then, have sought to explain the meaning of the terms employed from an investigation of contemporary Latin literature. The expression *conversatio morum* has not yet been discovered elsewhere, except in a text of St. Ambrose which is not a true parallel and does not help to clarify the problem (*De Virginitate* 10,59). *Conversatio* alone is a word of rather frequent occurrence. Derived from the verb *conversari*, it meant "conduct" or "manner of life"; in monastic literature it took on the meaning of "ascetical life," serving to translate the Greek *askesis*, and specifically the "monastic life."

This is the sense in which St. Benedict uses it elsewhere in the *Rule* (Pr 49; 1,3.12; 21,1; 22,2; 58,1; 73,1.2; but cf 63,1).

Everyone agrees thus far; it is in determining the meaning of the whole phrase *conversatio morum suorum* that scholars differ, since the usual meaning of *conversatio* does not seem to fit in this phrase. Some scholars maintain that the later tradition has correctly interpreted St. Benedict's meaning by translating "conversion of life." The Carolingian scribes who substituted *conversio* in the text were merely using a more correct Latin synonym for a word which was then no longer employed in that sense. The most cogent argument in favor of this view is that *conversatio* sometimes appears in monastic texts with the meaning of "conversion." Quite distinct from the other usage of *conversatio,* it was derived from *conversare,* frequentative of *convertere.* Thus the usage of *conversatio* became confused, because the word had two meanings: "monastic life" and "conversion" or "entry into monastic life." In the latter sense it was equivalent to *conversio;* hence the substitution did not alter the meaning: *conversio morum* meant the same thing in the eighth century as *conversatio morum* in the sixth (Schmitz, Mohrmann). This view depends upon the extent of the evidence for the use of *conversatio* in the sense of "conversion" in monastic texts: very few can be cited at present, but it is probable that more will turn up as critical editions are published which get beyond the Carolingian corrections to the authentic text.

Other Suggested Interpretations

A second opinion maintains that the traditional translation must be abandoned, since there is not sufficient evidence that *conversatio* could mean "conversion." The method that must be followed is to study each of the component parts of the phrase *conversatio morum suorum* and to attempt to find the syntactical connection which links them together, so as to arrive at the over-all meaning of the entire expression. The scholars who approach the problem in this way have proposed various translations: "the conduct of his life" (Butler);

"monasticity of conduct" (Chapman); "monastic behavior and striving for virtue" (Steidle). Steidle maintains that the genitive is epexegetical and that the phrase is equivalent to *conversatio et mores sui.*

A third opinion holds that the meaning of the phrase cannot be determined by dissecting it into its component parts, but that it must be taken as an idiomatic expression, its sense to be elucidated by the general context of the *Rule* and the intention of the author. What St. Benedict felt compelled to mention in explaining the content of profession were those aspects of his monastic program which differed from other types of monasticism then in vogue. There is a striking parallel between the three elements mentioned and the types of monks of whom St. Benedict speaks in chapter 1, where he singles out the cenobites as the "strong race" (1,13). Stability therefore will distinguish his monks from the gyrovagues, and obedience from the sarabaites. It is likely, then, that the third element of the profession distinguishes them from the anchorites.

Conversatio morum would therefore mean life in community, *cenobitic life* as distinct from that of the hermits. The phrase cannot be literally translated, but it is possible that the idiom could have this meaning because the word *conversatio* is derived from *conversari*, to live with. This is a different meaning than the word has in its other occurrences in the *Rule*, but it is based upon the same root, and the resulting idiom could have been easily understandable at the time (Lottin).

This view can be accepted only if one supposes that St. Benedict deliberately opposed eremitism. However, his praise of the solitaries in chapter 1 and his general agreement with the western current represented by Cassian indicate that he accepted the traditional Egyptian view of the superiority of the eremitical life and regarded the *cenobium* as a training school for the desert. At present the first opinion seems the most likely, though it needs to be supported by further linguistic evidence. St. Benedict's definition of monastic profession as a conversion of life is simply a statement of the fundamental exigency of turning from sin to a new life with God which is implicit in the very nature of monasticism.

10. WORK

Work among the Ancient Monks

While the whole ascetical effort of the active life is in itself a work painful to nature, work in the sense of manual labor is one of the exercises which the monk employs to further his progress in the spiritual ascent. While the ancient monks were careful not to over-emphasize the role of work lest it compromise the monk's preoccupation with heavenly realities (cf Cassian, *Conf* 24,4), they generally recommended it as an ascetical practice. Since the weakness of human nature tires easily in the pursuit of an ideal so exalted as that of incessant prayer, work was found to be a valuable means of asceticism in the struggle against *acedia*, provided that its nature was not such as to disturb contemplative quiet. By disciplining the monk against inconstancy, work can promote his spirit of recollection and foster humility.

At the same time, it was a practical necessity for self-support and a testimony to the life of poverty. The authentic monks scorned those who lived upon the charity of others, and maintained that true followers of Christ should provide for their own needs, simple as they were. They had little patience with the visionaries who refused to work on the pretext that they were pure contemplatives, quoting the saying of St. Paul, "If any man will not work, neither let him eat" (2 Thess 3,10; cf *Vita Antonii* 3; Basil, *Longer Rules* 37; Cassian, *Inst* 1,5; *Conf* 24,12). St. Basil explains how the evangelical precept of continuous prayer is to be reconciled with that of work, and Cassian rejects the suggestion that a monk is better off to be free of the care of supporting himself by accepting contributions. The proceeds of their labors which were over and above their own needs were used for almsgiving: the monastic literature has preserved accounts of extensive charitable works carried on by the monks. The type of work chosen was one with a minimum of distractions, and the monks had the custom of reciting psalms while they worked, so that their prayer would not be interrupted.

St. Benedict's Concept of Work

St. Benedict was dependent upon oriental monasticism in the matter of work, as in so many other things. For him, too, the work of the community is in no sense an end in itself, but is entirely subject to the order of the monastery and to the spiritual and ascetical purposes of the monastic life. The motto "Prayer and Work" has been traditionally associated with Benedictine life, though it is nowhere found in the *Holy Rule*. It would be more correct to say that St. Benedict envisaged the monk's day as divided into three activities: prayer, *lectio divina* and work. Nor are the prayer and work of a monk to be considered as mutually exclusive, for the monk's work is merely a means to the all-embracing end of his sanctification.

St. Benedict begins his treatment of work in chapter forty-eight of the *Rule* with the statement, "Idleness is the enemy of the soul." It is the ascetical purpose, therefore, which he has primarily in mind. Cassian had recorded a saying of the desert Fathers that a busy monk is besieged by only one devil, while an idle one is attacked by innumerable evil spirits (*Inst* 10,23). This is again the familiar theme of overcoming the vice of *acedia* by keeping busy at some useful work. When the monk is not at prayer or at his *lectio divina*, he is to be busy working.

It is not merely to fill up the monastic day, however, that St. Benedict insists upon work. Like his predecessors, he wanted his monastery to be self-sufficient. The work of the monks should ordinarily suffice both for the support of the community and for the alleviation of the misery of others through almsgiving. "Then are they truly monks," St. Benedict says, "when they live by the labor of their hands, like our fathers and the apostles" (48,8). It is to the example of his predecessors in the monastic life that he refers here, based in turn upon the example of the apostles, especially of St. Paul, who vigorously insisted upon providing for his own needs, even though he had a right to live by the Gospel (1 Cor 9,7–16; 2 Cor 11,7–12). St. Gregory relates that St. Benedict gave to the poor the last bit of food or money which he had in his monastery (*Dial* 2,27.28).

Manual labor was the type of work which St. Benedict had in mind. In the *Rule* we have references to work in the fields and to the exercise of arts and crafts, and in the *Dialogues* St. Gregory has described the patriarch and his monks performing manual labor of various types at Monte Cassino. In this he was following the monastic tradition of both East and West. Since the monastic order had not yet become clericalized, there was little occasion for the performance of some of the types of work in which monks are often engaged today.

Theology of Work

Pope Pius XII has declared that one of St. Benedict's greatest contributions to the world was to teach it the dignity of labor.

> The author and lawgiver of the Benedictine Order has another lesson for us, which is, indeed, freely and widely proclaimed today but far too often not properly reduced to practice as it should be. It is that human labor is not without dignity; is not a distasteful and burdensome thing, but rather something to be esteemed, an honor and a joy. (Encyclical *Fulgens Radiatur*, March 21, 1947: AAS 39 (1947) 153)

It may be profitable to examine more closely the precise meaning of work for the Christian. In the frequent labor disputes of our times work has often been considered to be a commodity which can be bought and sold. In socialism we have the apotheosis of work, but its human value is obscured by an undue emphasis upon production, as though it were only the result of work which is worthy of consideration, and not the intrinsic value of the activity for the welfare of man himself. Our technological society continues to reduce working hours through automation to the point where it seems that they may eventually almost disappear, leaving all work to machines. In this context work appears merely as a necessary evil which technology may one day succeed in banishing from our lives.

Is human labor, then, a curse which has been placed upon mankind as a result of original sin, so that all work must necessarily be toilsome and unpleasant? Or is it an intrinsic human value, which develops and perfects the human person and should therefore be a source of joy to him? The fact is that in the present fallen state of human nature there is a measure of truth in both viewpoints. Work contains both the aspect of toil and that of joyful fulfillment.

Work was not excluded from the garden of paradise. Adam was put into the garden to till it and look after it, and was told to fill the earth and subdue it and enjoy dominion over all the lower creation (Gen 2,15; 1,28). All of this involved human activity to bring about the development and perfection of himself and the whole universe. But this work in the state of original justice would have been a pleasure for man. It was only after the fall that a curse was put upon man which struck him in his essential function of breadwinner for the human family: "In the sweat of your brow you shall eat bread" (Gen 3,19). This is the simple but profound teaching of Scripture on the nature of human work: in itself an intrinsic human value, it has become unpleasant and toilsome because of sin.

Dignity of Work

Man is made in the image and likeness of God. When he works, he is exercising a creative activity which is a reflection of that of God. For God himself is the first and supreme Workman, who fashioned the entire universe and continues to work in it through his conservation of all creatures and through his interventions in human history. While all creation reflects the perfections of God, it is only man who is able to imitate him in his creative activity by his free and intelligent cooperation in the work of perfecting and subduing the material universe.

Christ is the Divine Workman who appeared in the form of man, the incarnate manifestation of God in the world. He came to do the work of his Father: "My Father works even until now, and I work" (Jn 5,17). "I must do the works of him who sent me while it is day; night is coming, when no one can work" (Jn 9,4). The Son of God, who came to remake the world corrupted by sin, did not disdain human toil. During his hidden life he toiled like a common laborer in the carpenter shop at Nazareth. Then and later during his public life, when exhausted by the work of evangelization, he experienced the weariness which is the effect of hard work.

The Christian, then, is called to a life of work in the service of Christ. It is the members of his Mystical Body who must carry on the work of redemption which he inaugurated, by extending his kingdom and remaking the world according to his design. "Amen, amen, I say to you, he who believes in me, the works that I do he also shall do, and greater than these he shall do" (Jn 14,12). Human work therefore has a theological significance. It is the cooperation of man in the fulfillment of the divine plan, the undoing of the havoc wrought by sin through the progressive extension of the redemption to the city of man.

Misery of Work

Nevertheless, in the present fallen state of human nature, work has taken on an arduous and unpleasant aspect. The material universe resists the efforts of man to remake it according to his designs. Original sin, in destroying the primitive harmony of creation, has changed not only man himself, but the entire cosmos. The redemption, it is true, has cosmic proportions, but its effects have not yet been fully realized. Hence St. Paul says that "all creation groans and travails in pain until now," until it "will be delivered from its slavery to corruption into the freedom of the glory of the sons of God" (Rom 8,21–22).

Man has to struggle, therefore, to exercise his dominion over the lower creation. Whereas work in the state of original justice would have been a joyful realization of man's lordship, it has now become a harsh necessity. His body resists the effort; he experiences a certain subjection and feeling of oppression; fatigue and monotony create new hardships.

This can be overcome only by regarding work from a supernatural viewpoint. The hardship involved is a means of expiation, rendered necessary by man's disobedience to God. But its ascetic value is not a purely negative thing. It has the positive value of liberating man progressively from his state of subjection. By exercising his faculties through work, he perfects himself, realizes his own personality. And through the creativity of work he imposes something of himself upon the material creation, remakes it according to the design of God, and brings it to a fuller share in the redemption of the whole universe, until the coming of the new heavens and the new earth.

A Christian theology of work, therefore, includes not only the ascetical element which is for the benefit of the individual himself, but also the aspect of contributing to the remaking of human society according to the divine plan. This latter aspect, however, was outside the horizon of St. Benedict. The ancient monks had no intention of developing a complete Christian theology of work; they saw it as one of the exercises of asceticism which help the monk to overcome himself and make progress in the active life. It was valuable for combating *acedia* and disposing the soul for contemplation. But it was not required that it fulfill any useful purpose in the temporal order, except that of providing for the meager needs of the monk's subsistence. This is also St. Benedict's view.

Function of Work in the Monastery

Paradoxically, it is precisely the other aspect of work which has become popularly associated with Benedictine monasticism and consequently attributed to St. Benedict. It is, indeed, a fact of history that the work of monks was an important factor in the preservation of the civilizing values of the past and the building of a new Christian order of society. But it would be an anachronism to attribute any such intention to St. Benedict. The *Rule* envisages no such incarnational activity; it is fully in the oriental tradition of flight from the world to work out one's salvation in solitude. Work is merely one of the ascetical exercises; it is not supposed to "get things done."

The oriental monks were intensely aware of the danger to contemplative quiet and poverty that could come from involvement in work: Abbot Paul was renowned because he worked all year as a defense against *acedia* and then burned all the products of his labor (cf Cassian, *Inst* 10,24). St. Benedict did not go to such extremes, but neither did he inaugurate a campaign to rebuild western civilization.

As a by-product of their life, monks can make contributions to the Church and society without infidelity to their own *raison d'être*. This requires, however, that their work be in harmony with the contemplative orientation of their life and that the secondary aspect of making contributions to the temporal order always be subservient to its primary ascetical purpose. There is a danger that work which is extremely absorbing will imprison the monks in its inexorable rhythm and stifle the contemplative spirit. The passion for "getting things done" can seize control of a community's effort and quickly overshadow its primary purpose of seeking God in an atmosphere of calm recollection and generous self-abnegation. The exercises of the active life must be hierarchically ordered within the total structure of cenobitic life so that their over-all orientation will not be obscured.

In practice, a monastic community should provide a variety of occupations so that every monk can find scope for his talents. Manual labor retains its value as an exercise of humility and poverty, but it does not exclude intellectual work, which demands intense concentration and can therefore also be a suitable means of self-discipline. While every monk should gladly work with his hands in imitation of Christ, manual labor should not be exalted exclusively in a monastery to the extent of engendering an attitude of suspicion or hostility to intellectual values. The deciding factor in choosing work is not what it will accomplish externally but what it will do for the monk. The problems of economic subsistence and of providing alms for the needy should be solved in function of this basic exigency, not vice versa. The supernatural viewpoint must dominate: the monk's work is not primarily a means of production, but a share in the self-abasement of Christ.

6 The Active Life: II. The Apostolate

THE *vita activa* of the monk is a preparatory stage which leads him to purity of heart, the condition for contemplation. The exercises of this phase of the spiritual ascent are principally the traditional practices of monastic asceticism. But they also include the works of the apostolate. Far from being unconcerned about the welfare of their fellow men, the monks conceived of their life as a contribution to the good of the Church as a whole. No form of the Christian life can abstract from the apostolic mission of the Church; yet each will contribute to the apostolate in a manner which conforms to its own structure.

The apostolate of the monk is principally an apostolate of prayer and of personal asceticism, practiced in the context of the Church's effort to become ever more worthy of her divine Spouse and oriented toward the welfare of the entire people of God. This primacy of the interior life, however, does not exclude the performance of works of charity on behalf of others, so long as these remain subordinate to the constitutive structure of the monastic life. Even the eremitical life affords opportunity for acts of beneficence toward other men. The community context of cenobitic life offers an even greater scope for the spiritual and corporal works of mercy, both within the monastery itself and on behalf of those outside who come into contact with the community. The purpose of this chapter is to define the monastic apostolate, to examine the relationship between the monastic life and the priesthood, and to assess some of the principal activities which constitute the contribution of monasticism to the Church's apostolic effort.

1. THE APOSTOLATE OF MONKS

Mission of the Church

The monastic apostolate finds its place within the mission of the Church. This mission is twofold. The Church's primary function is to glorify God and bring the divine economy to realization by converting men, uniting them to herself and sanctifying them so as to lead them to the heavenly Jerusalem, the Church's final fulfillment. Her secondary mission is to exercise an influence upon the world in which she exists historically, so as to remake it according to the divine plan and thus turn it toward God. St. Pius X clearly included both of these functions in his program to restore all things in Christ: "To restore in Christ not only whatever is incumbent upon the Church by reason of her divine mission, which is to lead souls to God, but likewise that which springs naturally from this divine mission, Christian civilization in each and all of the elements that compose it" (Encyclical *Il fermo proposito,* June 11, 1905: Actes de Pie X 2,93).

This mission is nothing more than a continuation of the mission of Christ. He came to deliver men from the power of the Evil One and to reconcile them to God, indeed to deliver all creation from the slavery under which it groaned and bring it to a share in the redemption. Fulfilling the threefold office of priest, king and prophet, he directed all the activity of his public life toward the salvation of men and of the world. His ministry was directed chiefly to the sanctification of men, as he went about "doing good and healing all who were in the power of the devil" (Acts 10,38). But salvation is to have cosmic effects also, so that the entire universe will share in the redemption.

It is the function of the Church to continue this mission in the "in-between" time that extends from Pentecost to the parousia. However, salvation no longer needs to be achieved; the Church only communicates it to the individuals whom she welcomes into the congregation of God's people. The cosmic effects of salvation must await the final fulfillment, for the "in-between" time is marked by the duality of the Church and the world. Yet it belongs to the Church, secondarily and in the measure possible, to extend the fruits of the redemption progressively to all creation by turning the city of man toward God.

The Christian Apostolate

The mission of Christ was both internal and external. Justification and salvation are invisible realities; the effect of preaching is interior illumination; Christ exercises his reign over the minds and hearts of men. But the law of incarnation demanded that his work should not be confined to the internal sphere. Thus we find Christ healing the sick, driving out devils from the bodies of the possessed, raising the dead; in short, exercising the spiritual and corporal works of mercy.

The Church's mission follows the same pattern. Her object is to save the whole man, body as well as soul. Hence her activity includes the works of mercy as well as the properly spiritual functions. These works pertain principally to the Church's primary function of leading men to salvation, though some of them may also be closely related to her secondary function of remaking the world.

We may define the apostolate as any activity on the part of any of God's people which furthers the Church's primary mission, i.e., contributes to the "building up" of the Church (cf 1 Cor 10,23; 14,12). Since it is the duty of every Christian to contribute to the building up of the Church, we may say without qualification that every member of the Church shares in the apostolate.

The Second Vatican Council has clarified the nature of the apostolate in the following way:

> The Church was founded for the purpose of spreading the kingdom of Christ throughout the earth for the glory of God the Father, to enable all men to share in his saving redemption, and that through them the whole world might enter into a relationship with Christ. All activity in the Mystical Body directed to the attainment of this goal is called the apostolate, which the Church carries on in various ways through all her members. For the Christian vocation by its very nature is also a vocation to the apostolate. No part of the structure of a living body is merely passive but has a share in the functions as well as life of the body: so, too, in the Body of Christ, which is the Church, 'the whole body . . . in keeping with the proper activity of each part, derives its increase from its own internal development' (Eph 4,16).
> Indeed, the organic union in this Body and the structure of the members are so compact that the member who fails to make his proper contribution to the development of the Church must be said to be useful neither to the Church nor to himself (*Decree on the Apostolate of the Laity* 2).

Spheres of the Apostolate

Within the apostolate, however, there are different spheres of activity. Pope Pius XII distinguished between the apostolate in the broad sense and the apostolate in the strict sense (cf Allocution *De quelle consolation,* Oct 14, 1951: AAS 43 (1951) 787). These correspond to the internal and external aspects of the Church's mission. Every Christian is called to contribute to the Church's work of sanctifying her members by his prayer and good example. Not all are called to the apostolate in the strict sense, for the abilities and form of life of some Christians do not permit their participation in the external activities of the apostolate.

> In the Church there is a diversity of ministry but a oneness of mission. Christ conferred on the Apostles and their successors the duty of teaching, sanctifying and ruling in his name and power.

> But the laity likewise share in the priestly, prophetic and royal office of Christ and therefore have their own share in the mission of the whole people of God in the Church and in the world . . . They are consecrated for the royal priesthood and the holy people (cf 1 Pt 2,4–10), not only that they may offer spiritual sacrifices in everything they do, but also that they may witness to Christ throughout the world. The sacraments, however, especially the most Holy Eucharist, communicate and nourish that charity which is the soul of the entire apostolate.
>
> One engages in the apostolate through the faith, hope and charity which the Holy Spirit diffuses in the hearts of all members of the Church (*Decree on the Apostolate of the Laity* 2–3).

In addition to the duty of prayer and of bearing witness to Christ by example, the apostolate involves the exercise of the spiritual and corporal works of mercy, to which the laity as well as the clergy are called and for which they receive the appropriate charisms from the Holy Spirit. The Church's work in the world to promote social justice and Christian civilization is also closely related to the apostolate, and constitutes a field of action in which the laity have the dominant role.

> They exercise the apostolate in fact by their activity directed to the evangelization and sanctification of men and to the penetrating and perfecting of the temporal order through the spirit of the Gospel. In this way, their temporal activity openly bears witness to Christ and promotes the salvation of men. Since the laity, in accordance with their state of life, live in the midst of the world and its concerns, they are called by God to exercise their apostolate in the world like leaven, with the ardor of the spirit of Christ (*ibid* 2).
>
> The whole Church must work vigorously in order that men may become capable of rectifying the distortion of the temporal order and directing it to God through Christ . . . The laity must take up renewal of the temporal order as their own special obligation . . . Everywhere and in all things they must seek the justice of God's kingdom (*ibid* 7).

Religious and the Apostolate

What is the position of religious in regard to the Church's apostolate? We have seen that they are distinct from the rest of the faithful, if we consider the Church as reality of grace, by reason of the external form of life which they adopt, a form better calculated to achieve the reality which is contained in the Church. In regard to dispensing the means of grace, they belong not to the hierarchical structure of the Church, but to the laity.

The life of the religious is entirely devoted to the pursuit of divine charity. It is a life of total consecration, complete dedication of self to God, involving the renunciation of everything that could hinder the completeness of self-giving, publicly declared before the whole Church. What the religious seeks is the perfection of charity. Thus his aim is to realize the reality of the Church here on earth, a reality which consists in the mystery of grace and of divine charity.

A religious is therefore not selfishly intent upon his own perfection to the exclusion of the rest of the Church. By perfecting himself in charity he is making a signal contribution to the Church. For if the Church is the mystery of charity, and her primary mission is the sanctification of her members, then his effort enters into the total effort of the Body of which he is a cell and, in the context of the communion of saints, contributes to the perfection of the whole.

The Role of Religious

The Second Vatican Council explains the contribution of religious to the Church in the following way:

> The evangelical counsels which lead to charity join their followers to the Church and its mystery in a special way. Since this is so, the spiritual life of these people should then be devoted to the welfare of the whole Church. From this arises their duty of working to implant and strengthen the kingdom of Christ in souls and to extend that kingdom to every clime.
>
> This duty is to be undertaken to the extent of their capacities and in keeping with the proper type of their own vocation. This can

be realized through prayer or active works of the apostolate. It is for this reason that the Church preserves and fosters the special character of her various religious institutes (*Constitution on the Church* 44).

This means, of course, that the religious has a vital role in the Church's apostolate. First and most fundamentally, he shares in the apostolate in the broad sense, for by the sanctity of his life, his prayers and good example, he contributes to the building up of the Church. This is his essential contribution, for it intensifies the Church's love for her Divine Spouse.

Secondarily, he may also contribute to the apostolate in the strict sense by exercising the spiritual and corporal works of mercy in accordance with the particular form of religious life which he has adopted. All religious share in these apostolic works, though in varying degrees; traditionally, even the eremitical life has always found some occasion to exercise the apostolate in the strict sense. Because this involves the *means* of salvation, religious in this respect are the helpers of the hierarchy and the clergy. Indeed, Pius XII declared that religious men who are not priests and religious women are the most valuable collaborators of the clergy in this regard (cf Apostolic Letter *Ad Ecclesiam Christi*, June 29, 1955: AAS 47 (1955) 543).

Manifestations of Charity

The apostolate in the broad sense and the apostolate in the strict sense are not two separate functions, and the various works undertaken by religious are not really so different as they may appear at first sight. In the context of the Church's mission they are all one. For the Church's effort is directed toward the sanctification of her members, that is to say, toward the growth of charity within the Body of Christ. Charity for God and charity for oneself and one's fellow men derive from the same theological virtue, for all have the same formal object, the goodness of God in himself. It is the goodness of God which motivates our love, whether we see that goodness in God himself or as reflected in his rational creatures.

These creatures are supernaturally lovable because God loves them and his objective love in them makes them capable of becoming the material objects of our love. "Let us therefore love," says St. John, "because God first loved us" (1 Jn 4,19). Love of God and love of neighbor are the same divine charity.

Religious institutes, therefore, are not differentiated according to their essential element, which in every case is the pursuit of charity, but only according to the external manifestations of charity in practice. Within the vast spectrum of the possible manifestations of charity, some religious concentrate principally upon the love of God in himself and immediately attained, less upon manifesting this love for God through service of their fellow men. Others, on the contrary, practice the love of God by performing the spiritual and corporal works of mercy for the benefit of others. Within this sphere there is an immense range of possibilities and accordingly a multitude of religious institutes engaging in different activities.

These two broad classifications of religious institutes are commonly referred to as "contemplative" and "active." We shall see later that this terminology is misleading. The differences between them are of an accidental character. Every authentic religious life is directed to the love of God and neighbor; it is only the manner of manifesting this love which differs. From the viewpoint of the apostolate, the differentiation of religious institutes depends upon the varying proportion of these manifestations. No exterior apostolate can be fruitful unless it is based upon a solid interior life rooted in divine charity. On the other hand, an authentic interior life invariably seeks expression in the service of one's fellow men. These two aspects of every religious life, however, can be mixed in various proportions.

The Monk and the Apostolate

Where does the monk find his place among the different forms of religious life and the various activities of the apostolate which stem from them? Monastic life is, indeed, the original form of religious life and for many centuries remained the only form. The monastic order, consequently, was the only religious body available to assume the tasks of the apostolate during the early centuries of the Church's history.

When we distinguish the various religious institutes from one another according to the particular manifestations of charity which they exhibit, it is clear that the monastic state must be ranged on the "contemplative" side of the scale. It is of the essence of monasticism to seek God in himself, to consecrate oneself totally to this search, and to withdraw from the world in order to achieve an unobstructed union with him. It was this ideal which sent the early monastic Fathers to the desert and which St. Benedict wholeheartedly espoused. Renunciation of the world, which necessarily involves a distinct degree of physical separation, must always remain an essential characteristic of monasticism.

The monastic apostolate, consequently, will differ from that of other religious institutes. Monks have an apostolate, they share in the apostolic activity of the whole Church, but the forms which that apostolate assumes will be determined by the specific form of life which they have adopted. Since it is the love of God in himself which receives the primary emphasis in their form of life, it follows that their principal contribution to the Church will be in the sphere of the apostolate in the broad sense.

Paradoxically, however, according to the evidence of history, it is precisely those who have abandoned the world and seem to have left it to its own perdition who have contributed the most to its salvation. For the monastic order has made signal contributions not only to the apostolate in the strict sense, but even to the promotion of justice and civilization in the world, which falls outside of the Church's primary mission. But it remains for us to examine more closely what precise forms these contributions have taken and should take.

Apostolate in the Broad Sense

We have seen that the apostolate in the broad sense signifies the contribution of one's self-dedication and personal sanctity, one's prayer and example, to the mission of the Church. The bond which unites the personal efforts of an individual to the worship and work of the whole Church is not a hypothetical thing. The individual Christian is by the very nature of his status a member of the Body of Christ, a cell in the total organism, and the bond which unites him to the whole is a real one.

The monk's chief contribution to the apostolate will be in this sphere. Even if he never performs any external activity for the spiritual or corporal welfare of his fellow men, he is nevertheless making a contribution to the Church's apostolate if he is faithful to the essential features of his vocation. For by sanctifying himself and joining his prayers to the chorus of praise and thanksgiving which rises to the Father from the congregation of his holy people, the monk is furthering the sanctification of the Church and bringing her closer to her eschatological goal of definitive union with her Divine Spouse.

Indeed, this is not only *a* contribution to the apostolate, it is the primary and essential one. The Church is a divine-human reality, but in this complex it is the divine element which is predominant and superior, and to which the human is ordered. The means of grace exist only in relation to the reality of grace which is the Church's goal as well as her possession, though not yet in definitive form.

Accordingly, the Second Vatican Council has declared:

> Institutes whose whole purpose is contemplation, so that their members live for God alone in solitude and silence, in unflagging prayer and fervent penance, always retain an outstanding place in the Mystical Body of Christ, in which "all . . . the members do not have the same function" (Rom 12,4), notwithstanding the urgent needs of the active apostolate. For they offer God a worthy sacrifice of praise, adorn the people of God with abundant fruits of holiness, motivate it by their example, and give it increase by their intangible apostolic fruitfulness. Thus they are the Church's glory and source of heavenly graces (*Decree on the Renewal and Adaptation of Religious Life* 7).

The monk's function in the apostolate is to bear witness to the reality of the Church. He is a living sign that she is a supernatural reality manifested in human form. He bears testimony by his uninterrupted dialogue with God, by his dedication, by his life and his very existence, that what is transitory in the world and in the Church herself will pass away. He is essentially an eschatological figure, turned toward the consummation of the kingdom that is to come.

Apostolate in the Strict Sense

This does not mean that monks have not played and cannot play a certain role in the apostolate in the strict sense. It is one of the paradoxes of history that they are commonly known more for their contributions in the sphere of the spiritual and corporal works of mercy than in that of their essential role of maintaining the supernatural life of the Church. Even historians who misunderstand or despise their radically supernatural function have paid tribute to their accomplishments in alleviating human misery. It is to be expected that it should be so, for the external and the visible are always more readily recognized by men than the interior and invisible. The most essential things are not always the most obvious.

The external works of monks are simply an overflow of the supernatural strength which has been built up by their interior life. An intense love of God always tends to manifest itself in love of neighbor. The two are so closely connected that the first, if genuine, always produces the second and generally, in one form or the other, manifests it exteriorly. Hence monks have always been engaged in both manual and intellectual labors which redound to the benefit of the Church. These have often taken the form of teaching, the care of souls, missionary work, care for the poor, for the sick, for travelers. For many centuries the monks were almost the only ones who undertook such good works on a large scale. But even in the modern world, when many of these functions have been taken over by public welfare agencies or by other religious institutes, the need for the monks' benefactions has not ceased. There is always an apostolate open to them.

Neither historically nor theoretically is there any intrinsic contradiction between the cenobitic state and the exercise of the active apostolate. Not only St. Benedict's monks, but even the hermits of the Egyptian deserts, from whom he derived his basic inspiration, practiced works of charity toward their fellow men. The difficulty is to determine precisely what works of mercy monks may reasonably undertake, and to what extent. There is a difference between taking care of one's sick confreres in the monastery infirmary and conducting a modern hospital, as there is a difference between teaching a few novices or postulants within the monastery and operating a twentieth-century university. What seems indisputable to one who objectively evaluates the elements of the problem is that a *monastic* apostolate is one exercised by those who follow a *monastic* form of life. When an apostolic activity necessitates changes in the *form of life* so profound that they transform or seriously restrict the features which we have found to be essential to monasticism, it cannot reasonably be held that such an activity is a suitable monastic apostolate. Vatican II offers a precise statement of monks' contribution to the Church when it declares: "The principal duty of monks is to offer the divine Majesty a service which is humble but at the same time noble within the enclosure of the monastery, whether by devoting themselves wholly to divine worship in the hidden life, or by legitimately taking on certain works of the apostolate or of Christian charity" (*Decree on the Renewal*, etc. 9).

Work for the World

Finally, a word must be said about the contribution of the monks to civilization. Here, too, historians recognize the debt that the world owes to monasticism. It is those who withdrew from the world and renounced the temporal values inherent in it who have contributed the most to civilization.

St. Benedict himself lived during the dark days of chaos that accompanied the breakup of the Roman Empire in the West. During the perilous times that followed, it was principally his followers that kept alive the spark of civilization and handed it on to the men of the Middle Ages, from whom we in turn have inherited our culture. Neither medieval nor modern civilization could have existed without the contribution of the monks. For this reason Pope Pius XII referred to St. Benedict as "the Father of Europe" (Homily *Exsultent hodie*, Sept 18, 1947: AAS 39 (1947) 453).

Pope Paul VI, hailing St. Benedict as "messenger of peace, architect of unity, master of civilization," proclaimed him the principal patron of all Europe. Again the civilizing influence of the monks is the reason for this distinction:

> At the collapse of the decaying Roman Empire, while some regions of Europe appeared to be falling into darkness and others were still deprived of civilization and spiritual values, he was there with constant and untiring effort to make the dawn of a new era spring up on this continent. It was principally he and his sons who, with the cross, the book, and the plow, brought Christian progress to the peoples spread out from the Mediterranean to Scandinavia, from Ireland to the plains of Poland (Apostolic Letter *Pacis nuntius*, Oct 24, 1964: AAS 56 (1964) 965)

Monastic culture will be discussed later on. Suffice it to say here that this culture has never been and cannot be the goal of monastic life. It is a by-product, one which follows almost inevitably from the principles of the cenobitic institute properly implemented according to the mind of St. Benedict, but nevertheless it remains a by-product. It is rather a case of the fulfillment of the Gospel promise, "Seek first the kingdom of God and his justice, and all these things shall be given you besides" (Mt 6,33).

Priority of the Life of Prayer

The ideal of incessant prayer, the early monks thought, can be achieved only by the solitary, who is free to a large extent from the temporal cares of life. The cenobitic life by its nature requires a certain attention to temporal needs and care for the orderly functioning of the monastery. This is accentuated in the large abbeys which have grown up over the centuries, for in them the institutional elements have developed to the point of requiring complex administration. But even in small monasteries which have reduced this institutional complexity to a minimum in order to recover the primitive simplicity of monasticism, there is still need for attention to temporal affairs and to human needs. These requirements must be met in such a way as not to disturb the radically contemplative orientation of the life of the community.

Here differences in temperament will be significant. Some men are by nature drawn to expressing their love for God in the humble tasks by which they serve the needs of the community; others are drawn rather to the interior service of prayer. Superiors must wisely dispose all things so that both can realize their talents in the varied forms of the apostolate. They must be vigilant to see that the rhythm of activity does not stifle the contemplative spirit of the community, but at the same time provide for the human needs of the monks, and sometimes, for the good of the community, demand the sacrifice of moderate activity from those who are more drawn to contemplation. In the last analysis, each monk must solve for himself the problem of conciliating his life of prayer with the duties which may be assigned him by obedience. He must be convinced of the priority of contemplation in his life. Even though he is not able to spend the greater part of his time quantitatively in prayer, he must realize that this is his most important contribution to the Church's apostolate and that whatever else he undertakes will be unfruitful unless he has a solid interior life.

The monk's day should not be divided into prayer and action as if into two separate and mutually exclusive compartments. Modern religious congregations, established in view of particular good works, have instituted special periods of time to be given over to mental prayer. While in practice the monk will also have to devise a schedule to ensure that his prayer does not give way before pressing duties, nevertheless the principle behind the arrangement is somewhat different. For him the entire day must be a prayer, he must strive to live always in the presence of God, and, if he must be temporarily distracted by active works, he must always return from them to his habitual attitude of recollection. His normal frame of mind must be contemplative, even though this be interrupted from time to time by necessary duties. The quiet of the monastery, the daily performance of the liturgy, and a type of work which is conducive to recollection will all help him to advance daily in the love of God.

Contemplation as Source of Action

Since all works of the active apostolate are simply exterior manifestations of the monk's love for God, they cannot be fruitfully pursued unless this divine charity is kept alive and growing in his heart. True zeal must be genuinely supernatural, not simply the overflow of natural energies. If it is not continually fed by an intense interior life, it will die from lack of nourishment and there will remain only a seeking of purely natural goals.

Every monk engaged in the active apostolate must be on his guard against becoming overly fascinated by the purely exterior aspects of his work. In every accomplishment there is the danger of pride, of attributing success to one's own abilities and one's own work. A man can become so absorbed in his work, so convinced of its importance, that he throws himself into it more and more and progressively neglects his interior life.

He ought to remind himself frequently that God does not really need his efforts. God's work is a supernatural work and it is only he who can supply the means to accomplish it. Throughout the history of salvation he has accomplished his designs by the most paradoxical means, choosing the weakest, least talented and least likely subjects as the instruments to accomplish his will. "The foolish things of the world has God chosen to put to shame the 'wise,' and the weak things of the world has God chosen to put to shame the strong, and the base things of the world and the despised has God chosen, and the things that are not, to bring to naught the things that are; lest any flesh should pride itself before him" (1 Cor 1,27–28).

The monk must be convinced that he is a weak and unworthy instrument, incapable of accomplishing any good unless God works through him. He should apply to himself St. Benedict's tools of good works: "To attribute to God, and not to self, whatever good one sees in oneself; but to recognize always that the evil is one's own doing, and to impute it to oneself" (*Rule* 4,42–43). Thus the monk will not cease to strive for a closer union with God, to attribute his successes to the divine strength working within him, and his failures to his own lack of cooperation with it.

If he does this, his contemplation and his action will react beneficially upon one another. His apostolic activities will convince him more and more of his need to rely upon divine help and will accordingly deepen his interior life. And as this life grows deeper and more intense, its effects on his action will be more fruitful because performed out of a more radically supernatural motive.

2. THE MONK AND THE PRIESTHOOD

Monks and Priesthood: The Present Situation

In treating of the apostolate of monks, we cannot abstract from the fact that today choir monks, as a general rule, are also priests. The present legislation of the Church does not permit a superior, without a special indult from the Holy See, to receive the profession of a monk destined for the choir, unless he also possesses the qualities required for ordination to the priesthood and desires to receive sacred orders. In practice, the apostolic work of many monasteries has become largely a clerical function rather than a strictly monastic one, and is often exercised outside of the monastery. The present situation is a fact which must be taken into consideration in assessing the apostolate of the monastic order.

At the same time, however, this present situation is of relatively recent origin, and is neither essential to the monastic order nor irreformable. In order to assess it properly, we must understand how it came into being, and what was the relationship between monasticism and priesthood in other periods of history. In its origins, monasticism was a lay movement. This is the situation which is presupposed by the Benedictine *Rule* and which endured for a long period of Benedictine tradition. The generalization of the priesthood of monks was the result of a complex historical evolution which brought about profound changes in the monastic order, not only in the sphere of the apostolic activities of the monks, but in their whole attitude toward the monastic life. This evolution must be taken into account in an examination of the contemporary situation and in any attempt to determine whether a revision of the present practice is in order.

Monasticism and the Apostolic Community

The first Christian communities were clearly apostolic in character. It was upon the apostles that Christ built his Church, and to them he gave the commission to preach the Gospel and to establish new churches. Without the apostolic succession, there could be no true Church. The early Christian communities were congregations of the faithful grouped about a bishop, in whose person they recognized the presence of Christ in their midst, in fulfillment of his promise, "Where two or three are gathered together for my sake, there am I in the midst of them" (Mt 18,20). Despite this universal conviction that one could belong to the society of the elect only by union with the visible hierarchical structure of the Church, the first monks deliberately withdrew, in a physical sense, from the apostolic community. We have seen that the reasons for the flight to the desert are not entirely clear to the historian; probably several factors were involved. But it is clear that the monks did not regard their distance from the local community as a separation from the Church.

In reality, the severance was not as complete as it seemed. The monks withdrew physically from the community only in order to belong to it in a more perfect way; for the Church is primarily a supernatural reality, and it was to this aspect of total dedication to God that they wished to bear witness. They saw no opposition between their charismatic function in the Church and her hierarchical structure. They had no intention of dispensing with all human intermediaries. They withdrew with the full approval of the apostolic community; the bishops were, in fact, among the most enthusiastic patrons and eulogizers of the monastic life. Later on the theorists of cenobitism were able to find a clear analogy between the abbatial and episcopal functions, and between the monastic community and the local church.

While remaining subject to the authority of the apostolic community, the monks also depended upon it for their sacramental life. As laymen, they were dependent upon the clergy for the means of grace. We have seen that even the solitaries in remote recesses of the desert maintained contact with the sacramental system. Groups of hermits and communities of cenobites summoned a priest to celebrate the divine mysteries for them. There was a distinct separation between the monks and the clergy. It would never have occurred to anyone to identify or confuse the two, as the faithful often do today. As a general rule, to be a monk meant to be a layman.

Attitude of Monks to the Priesthood

Nevertheless there were some cases of the ordination of monks even in ancient times. Bishops sometimes insisted upon the ordination of saintly monks, even against their opposition. In other cases the monks themselves took the initiative in presenting one of their number for ordination in order to provide for their sacramental needs. Some of the great bishops of the patristic period had been monks before their elevation to the priesthood and the episcopacy. Priests, with the permission of their bishop, sometimes embraced the monastic life. A priest could occasionally be found even among the anchorites.

In general, however, the monks were fiercely opposed to the reception of sacred orders. Cassian insists that the two classes of persons that a monk must be most careful to avoid are women and bishops—the latter because of the danger of their wanting to ordain him priest (*Inst* 11,18). Pachomius admitted priests into his monastery, though he was generally opposed to allowing his monks to be ordained. Numerous other examples of priest-monks can be found in the early monastic literature. Despite their opposition to the ordination of monks, the early monasteries seem generally to have included some priests. It is impossible to say how many—probably a very small proportion. Not infrequently the superior was a priest.

The reason for the monks' opposition to reception of sacred orders was not any lack of respect for the priesthood. On the contrary, they had the greatest reverence for the priesthood, as for the other sacraments. It was simply that they regarded it as a supreme honor, incompatible with the humility and simplicity which a monk ought to cultivate. And they feared that the exercise of the priesthood might remove them from the seclusion and retirement of their solitary life. When a group of monks did decide to have one of their number ordained, they held a council in order to choose the one most worthy of the office.

The fact that this was sometimes done, even if it was exceptional, seems to indicate that they did not see any *intrinsic* incompatibility between the two states. There is no indication that they ever worked out any theoretical understanding of the relationship between priesthood and monasticism; they generally opposed the ordination of monks, but sometimes made an exception in order to supply their own need, and in this they apparently saw no intrinsic contradiction. There are even a few exceptional examples of monks receiving ordination not to supply the spiritual needs of a community but simply out of devotion.

Priesthood and the Monastic Apostolate

While the early monks emphasized the ideal of complete solitude, in practice their isolation was rarely an absolute one. St. Anthony, despite his long sojourns in the wilderness, exercised a considerable activity of healing the sick, preaching and combating heresy. St. Pachomius engaged in similar activities and so, it seems, did the other famous Egyptian monks. Furthermore, the ancient literature speaks frequently of guests coming to visit the monks for instruction, spiritual direction and edification. The monks not only preached the Word of God to them, but also cared for their other spiritual and corporal needs. Thus the monastic institute wielded an important influence upon the Church. The historian Sozomen, commenting on the advanced age of some of the Syrian monks, speculates that God granted them such a long life for the benefit of religion, so much good did they accomplish in converting men to God (*Historia* 6,34).

It is clear from this that the ancient monks did not perceive any contradiction between their form of life and a certain exercise of the active apostolate, in which, as a rule, it was the people who came to them, not vice versa. Later many abuses developed, when monks began to wander from place to place and to engage in violent theological controversy. It was to eradicate these abuses that cenobitic rules insisted upon enclosure. A certain restricted exercise of the apostolate, however, does not stem from such deviations, but goes back to the purest sources of early monasticism. In addition to the bond of authority and that of the sacramental life, the monks' participation in the apostolate constituted a third bond of union between them and the hierarchical Church.

This apostolic activity, however, was quite independent of the priesthood. It was carried on by the monks, ordinarily, without any departure from the normal conditions of monastic life. Those monks who were priests did, no doubt, on occasion exercise their ministry on behalf of the faithful who came to visit them. Generally, however, it was exercised solely for the benefit of their brethren in the monastery, as a convenient means of providing liturgical services for the monks without requiring that a priest be called in from outside. If there was more than one priest in the community, it seems that only one, the elder, celebrated the liturgy. There are even examples of monk-priests who never exercised their priesthood at all, because it had been conferred on them against their will and they feared that its use would withdraw them from their monastic life. The best known case of this extreme position is that of St. Jerome. The priesthood was looked upon as a state which necessarily involved ministerial functions. As long as these were confined to the monastery, the priesthood could be conciliated with monastic life, but an exterior ministry was held to be incompatible. The apostolate proper to the monk was of a different type.

The Priest-Monk in the Holy Rule

In two separate passages of the *Rule*, chapters 60 and 62, St. Benedict speaks of priests in the monastery. His attitude toward the question appears with remarkable clarity when seen against the background of oriental monasticism. He envisages the same two possible sources of priests in the monastery: the case of a man who is already a priest entering the community, and the case of the abbot's having a monk ordained to supply the needs of the monastery. The priest who wishes to enter must in effect renounce his priesthood when he becomes a monk. He is to have no special prerogative because of his ordination. He may not even exercise his priesthood unless the abbot bids him to do so. From now on he is to be a monk and must practice absolute submission to his superiors. The monk who is ordained for the community, too, thereby acquires no special prerogative. He has received the priesthood for the purely pragmatic reason that the monastery needs someone who can dispense the sacraments to the monks. In every other respect he is no different from the rest.

In either case, according to the *Rule,* it is not the priesthood which provides the primary orientation in the life of a priest-monk. He is, in short, merely a monk whose job in the community is to celebrate the liturgy and administer the sacraments. His ideal remains the same as that of his lay confreres: the virtues he must develop are those proper to a monk, there being no mention of any kind of "priestly spirituality." It is evident that St. Benedict had no interest in constructing a theology of monastic priesthood or in creating a special spirituality for the priest-monk. The theoretical question of the reconciliation of these two distinct vocations in the same subject probably never occurred to him.

Neither did St. Benedict elaborate any program for conducting an active apostolate outside the monastery. He insists, in fact, that the monks shall go out as seldom as possible, because it is not good for them to do so (66,7). While St. Gregory pictures him sending his monks out to preach to nuns in the vicinity, and himself converting the country people of the environs, there is nothing in the *Rule* about this kind of activity. It does, of course, enjoin the traditional monastic apostolate of receiving guests and visitors at the monastery, and exercising the spiritual and corporal works of mercy on their behalf. It is in this eminently traditional way that the influence of the monastery is to benefit the Church. Without theorizing about it, St. Benedict acted exactly as the oriental monks had done.

Monks and Priesthood in the Sixth Century

The *Rule*, therefore, tolerates priests in the monastery to serve the needs of the community, but does not admit that the clerical state, i.e., the active ministry outside the cloister, is compatible with monastic life. Such a position was adopted, however, by the so-called urban monks in the West. These communities were composed entirely of clerics who, together with their bishop, pledged themselves to strive for sanctity in the framework of the common life, and at the same time performed the duties of the clerical apostolate. They assured the service of the liturgy in the cathedral or in parish churches, preached and instructed the faithful, and could be sent out to serve parishes or take care of other work in the diocese. These were not monks who adopted the priesthood and the active ministry; they were clerics who adopted the common life. But as monasteries had influenced them to adopt a quasi-cenobitic life, so they in turn exercised a reverse influence upon the monks.

It was not until the Middle Ages that this reciprocal influence became so extensive as to confuse the two forms of life. But already at the time of St. Benedict there was a certain influence of the urban monks upon the monasteries in regard to liturgical practice. It is from the practice of the basilicas that St. Benedict derived the predominance of the liturgy, which is much more significant in the *Rule* than in eastern monasticism. The *Rule* explicitly refers to the borrowing of liturgical practices from the Roman Church (13, 10). In the basilical monasteries of Rome in the early Middle Ages, it often happened that communities of monks gradually evolved into choirs of canons.

However, at the end of the sixth century, the distinction between the monastic and clerical states was firmly maintained by St. Gregory the Great. A monk himself, he yearned for the peace and solitude of the cloister amid the pastoral cares which had been thrust upon him. While it has often been affirmed that Gregory was responsible for assigning the monks to the care of souls, his letters show, on the contrary, that he had no intention of innovating in this regard. Priests within the monastery were to have no exterior ministry (*Epist* 7,40; 5,1). If a monk was ordained for the exercise of the ministry, he had to abandon definitively the monastic state (*ibid* 7,40; 8,17); and, conversely, a cleric who entered the monastery had to renounce the exercise of the ministry outside the cloister (*ibid* 1,40; 4,11; 5,1; 9,157). A clear distinction between the clerical and monastic states was accepted by the canon law of the time, and Gregory made no effort to change it. The manner in which the Anglo-Saxon mission was conducted did not constitute a real exception to this principle.

Clerical Invasion of the Monasteries

In the course of the Middle Ages, the distinction between monk and cleric was gradually obscured and the number of priests in monastic communities gradually increased. As the gulf between clergy and laity widened, the monks were gradually transposed, in the popular mind, to the category of the clergy. It was not so much that the monks became more like clerics, as that the clerics became more like monks. Their dress, their manner of life, their culture all became different from those of the ordinary faithful. As the people lost their contact with the Bible and ceased to participate actively in the liturgy, the sacred rites became the business of the clergy. Since the monks, too, had a distinct culture, dress and manner of life, and were actors rather than spectators in the liturgy, they gradually became identified with the clerics.

This identification in the popular mind had its effects upon the outlook of the monks themselves. During the early Middle Ages the number of monks raised to sacred orders gradually increased. While no precise statistics are available, the figures for some localities which have been assembled from the monastic literature of the period clearly testify to a constant increase. The phenomenon was closely associated with ritualistic developments, which demanded a greater number of sacred ministers, and with the direction taken by the theology of the Eucharist, with the consequent multiplication of private Masses. Yet many of the monks raised to sacred orders were deacons rather than priests, a fact which shows that the object in mind was the development of the liturgical services within the monastery, rather than any exterior apostolate.

Such an exterior apostolate did, however, make its appearance among the missionary monks of the early Middle Ages. Yet the studies made of this movement indicate that it was not simply a matter of monks abandoning their cloisters to do active apostolic work. The leaders were bishops who had once been monks but who no longer lived the monastic life because it was held to be incompatible with the episcopacy, according to the traditional jurisprudence. Their helpers were often diocesan clerics. The monk-bishops established monasteries, but the collaboration of the monks in the apostolate seems to have been a function of the community rather than of individual monks, and the traditional contemplative orientation of the monastic life was generally preserved, according to the wish of the bishops themselves. Nor did monastic cooperation in the apostolate necessarily involve the exercise of the priesthood, for laymen were still permitted to preach.

Developments in the Middle Ages

Under the feudal system the monasteries often possessed vast holdings, among which were many incorporated parishes. It would be wrong to suppose, however, that these parishes were always served by priest-monks; ordinarily the monasteries engaged secular priests for this purpose. It was only in the high Middle Ages that the monks themselves assumed the care of souls in parishes, and then on a small scale. The reason for this development was not any theory about the compatibility of monastic life and the active ministry, but rather a concern to receive the revenues from the incorporated parishes. The increased number of priest-monks and their apostolic activities gave rise to many controversies with the bishops and the diocesan clergy in the twelfth century. In these polemics the monks insisted that the priesthood was not incompatible with their state and defended their right to receive revenues from their holdings, but there was no attempt to justify theoretically a monastic participation in the active ministry which would have been contrary to the entire tradition.

There was, in fact, no idea of a necessary connection between the ordination of a monk and his exercise of an active ministry. On the contrary, the priesthood was sometimes conferred on those who had already departed from the company even of their brethren to lead the solitary life, or those who did so shortly after their ordination. In these cases sacred orders were thought to crown a life of exceptional sanctity. These men often protested their unworthiness and sought to escape ordination, a sign that their humility was sufficient to offset the dangers against which the ancient tradition warned. They not only exercised no active ministry, even in their own monastery, but perhaps even their celebration of Mass was restricted to rare occasions.

Monks Equated with Clerical Religious

It was only from the fourteenth century onward that the priesthood was more and more regularly conferred upon choir monks generally. This led eventually to the widespread assumption of the priestly ministry outside the monastery, though this phenomenon remained sporadic until post-Tridentine times, when it was promoted by factors quite extrinsic to the monastic life. By this time a change had taken place in the very concept of monasticism, and monks had been assimilated to clerical religious. If a monk is looked upon merely as a man who has the "vows of religion," he can be considered to observe his vows in the situation of the active apostolate as well as in the monastery. Thus the ancient idea of a basic incompatibility between monastic life and active priestly ministry was lost.

There is a certain formalism in this concept of monk, for it supposes that a man can be a monk merely by having a certain ideal, without actually living in a monastic framework of life designed for the realization of the ideal. Hence discussions have arisen as to how a man can be a good monk when he is a pastor or a university professor. For the ancients such a problem would have been simply unthinkable—evidently a man is not really a monk at all unless he is living as a monk. Solitude, poverty, asceticism, continuous prayer, are things not to be discussed but to be lived. A monk is a man who actually follows a certain form of life sanctioned by a centuries-old tradition.

Thus the generalization of the priesthood of monks was brought about by various complex factors. In this long history there is no constant tradition on the subject of the priesthood except on one point: that there is no intrinsic incompatibility between the two states. There have, in fact, been different realizations of the priesthood in monasticism. It was originally conferred in order to provide for the sacramental needs of the monks; only later was the exercise of the priestly ministry extended to others. In the Middle Ages there was what Jean Leclercq has called an "ascetical priesthood," conferred on monks of outstanding virtue without involving any ministry. Only in recent times has there been an institutionalized priesthood, in which the monks are equated with clerical religious and every choir monk is ordained, often for the exercise of the active ministry to some degree.

Excessive Emphasis upon the Priesthood

The present generalized and institutionalized priesthood of choir monks has undeniable disadvantages which in our time have brought the whole question of monastic priesthood to a point of crisis. In the first place, the emphasis given to the priesthood has obscured the essential character of monastic life. Whereas St. Benedict insisted upon the primacy of the monastic state in the life of every monk, including monk-priests, the priesthood often holds the primacy today in the thinking of Catholic people and of many aspirants to the monastery, as well as among the monks themselves. Candidates sometimes come to the monastery primarily to study for the priesthood, distinct from the diocesan priesthood only by the circumstances of the additional obligations assumed, the common life and the type of activity pursued. Some enter the monastery quite frankly with the intention of becoming parish priests, teachers or missionaries.

It must be confessed that the efforts made by some monasteries to stir up vocations often do not adequately dissipate such misunderstandings. Small boys are subjected to explanations of the difference between a diocesan priest and a "Benedictine priest" in terms of superficialities which never approach the real finality of the monastic life. This is hardly surprising in view of the fact that the same confusion has been introduced even in very recent times into the monastic legislation of some congregations, e.g., the unfortunate provision in some declarations which excludes solemnly professed monks from the monastic chapter until they have been ordained priests. This can only give the false impression that the priesthood is an essential requirement for one to be a monk in the full sense of the term.

Problems of Recruitment

Another difficulty is that the universal priesthood of choir monks places severe limitations upon the recruitment of monastic vocations.

There are many young men who do not have the ability or the scholastic background required for theological studies and yet may desire to live the monastic life. Particularly in our times, because of the cultural transformation which has taken place, young men may have received considerable technical education and yet be quite unprepared for philosophical and theological studies because they have not been trained in the humanities.

The clerical training which choir monks now receive is scarcely different from that given to clerical religious or to diocesan seminarians, another indication that there is now nothing specifically monastic about the priesthood of monks. In this respect the Holy See assimilates them to clerical religious, for whom it justly insists upon an adequate formation. For small monasteries the provision of such formation entails real difficulties, and its demands exclude candidates who may otherwise be judged to have a sincere monastic vocation. What is more serious is that the whole formation of young monks suffers from this emphasis upon clerical training. During their formative years their education is almost entirely clerical and their energies and interests directed primarily toward the priesthood and the ministry. While this situation could be alleviated by a revision of the training program, the emphasis upon the priesthood inevitably tends to deflect the attention of the young monk from the primacy of the monastic state in his life.

In addition to those who are not qualified for clerical studies, there are other potential candidates who do not wish to become priests. The renewed understanding of monasticism and the emergence of the laity in our time have called attention to the value of the monastic life itself as a distinct vocation, and some wish to avoid the tension which the priesthood in its present realization almost always creates in a monk's life. The renewal of the liturgy has given prominence to the value of the worshiping community quite independently of the exercise of ministerial functions. No disrespect for the priesthood is implied in the choice of another vocation which has its own distinct value in the Church, and the legitimate aspirations of youth should not be simply dismissed.

Problem of the Lay Brotherhood

The lay brotherhood is not an adequate solution for candidates who do not have the desire or the qualifications to become priests. It was not until recent times that brothers were considered real monks; originally they had a kind of oblate status. In fact, in spite of various attempts to alleviate the situation, the brotherhood does not permit a full participation in the monastic life and often tends to create a dichotomy within the community. The introduction of brothers in the Middle Ages served to accentuate the distinction between lay and clerical religious in the community and historically the two classes have been based upon class distinctions quite extrinsic to the monastic life itself.

The evolution of society has brought with it a leveling of the distinctions between social classes and an intense thirst for freedom and equality. A monastic organization based upon such obsolete distinctions cannot fail to appear anachronistic today, and in fact many monasteries have for some time experienced a crisis of vocations to the brotherhood. Reluctance to become a second-class citizen is not to be attributed to a lack of humility among candidates, but to a legitimate desire to share in the full conventual life of the community to a degree which is not possible for lay brothers in the present arrangement. If the contribution of the monastic order in mission lands is to be effective, it is not evident what advantage there can be in the perpetuation of a system which is the obsolete residue of a foreign culture.

Problems of Tension in Life of Priest-Monks

A further difficulty in the assimilation of choir monks to clerical religious is the ambiguity which this system projects in practice into the life of the priest-monk in view of the two vocations which he holds simultaneously. As a monk, he must strive to develop the specifically monastic virtues, and hence he will be anxious for solitude, recollection, humility, separation from the world, contemplation. The contemporary theological understanding of the priesthood, however, associates the reception of Holy Orders with a certain involvement in the ministry. To be sure, there are various modalities in the exercise of the sacerdotal apostolate, but almost any form of the ministry exercised outside the cloister will remove the priest-monk to some extent from the solitude required for a fruitful monastic life. Every priest who shares in the modern appreciation of the priestly vocation will want to be in some manner an instrument for the sanctification of others.

This is not to say that there is a necessary contradiction between the priesthood and the monastic life, for the entire tradition shows that they are intrinsically compatible. Their harmonization in practice, however, has differed in some periods of the Church's life, and what was not a problem in other times may yet legitimately be a problem today. The two vocations, which represent different aspects of the Church's life, do not move in entirely parallel directions. The priest-monk who values both of his vocations may easily feel that a certain tension has been introduced into his life by his desire for withdrawal on the one hand and for participation in the ministry on the other.

The generalization of the priesthood also poses some practical problems in determining the activities of the community. When all of the choir monks are destined for the priesthood, it is inevitable that demands will be made upon them to participate in the active ministry, especially in view of the shortage of clergy which prevails in many areas. On the one hand, it is extremely difficult to draw up limits to such activity which will respect the demands of the monastic life. On the other hand, however, the presence of large numbers of priests who never participate in the ministry is difficult to justify theologically, and perhaps still more difficult to justify on a practical level to the satisfaction of clergy and faithful who do not perceive the entire complexity of the problem.

Theological Explanations

In modern times attempts have been made to elaborate a theoretical justification of the priesthood of monks. It has been pointed out that the priesthood fits harmoniously into the monk's program of striving for sanctity. Of its nature the priesthood requires a high degree of perfection. The priest is another Christ, and the monk pledges himself to guide his efforts toward the imitation of Christ. Thus each vocation exercises a beneficial influence upon the other. However, since the priesthood is directed toward the ministry and not toward the personal perfection of the subject, this consideration is inadequate.

It has also been argued that the sacramental character of the priest confers a new dignity upon the worship which he offers to God. He is in a special way the representative of the Church, and the monastic liturgy is thereby vested with a superior quality due to its performance by priests. Again, however, this consideration alone does not suffice to justify the large-scale ordination of monks, especially since the performance of the liturgy is not the principal finality of the monastic life.

It is also alleged that, since the offering of the Eucharistic sacrifice is the essential and primary function of the priest, a priest who does only this is fulfilling the purpose of his ordination and no further justification is required. It is theologically correct that the sacerdotal ministry must be envisaged on a supernatural plane, centered about the Eucharist, and is not to be measured by the quantity of the priest's external activities. By celebrating the Eucharist he is truly providing the means of grace and thereby contributing, in a distinctly sacerdotal manner, to the building up of the Church.

However, while this justifies the limitations put upon the exercise of the ministry by a priest-monk, it is quite another question whether it justifies the large-scale ordination of priests who will engage only in the essential act of the ministry and not also to some measure in the other activities that flow from it. Attempts have accordingly been made to show that the Mass of a priest-monk, precisely because he is a monk, has some special significance in the Church. But it cannot be said that these endeavors have succeeded in making out a convincing case for such a theory. Contemporary sacramental theology tends rather to require that every priest, in addition to the power of celebrating the Eucharist, also have some mandate for the exercise of the ministry.

The Ministry of the Priest-Monk

In monastic tradition there is, indeed, no question about the legitimacy of ordaining a monk. His mandate for the ministry is sufficiently constituted by the need for a priest to exercise liturgical functions within his own monastery, as is explicitly envisaged by the *Holy Rule*. Every monastery needs priests and deacons to celebrate the Eucharist, administer other sacraments, preach and give spiritual direction. In modern times the reservation to priests of functions formerly permitted to laymen increases the need for ordained ministers. It is true that the ministry of such a priest-monk is quite restricted as far as external activity is concerned, though there will be occasion for him to exercise it on behalf of guests and others who come to the monastery as well as for the benefit of his confreres. But a priest who celebrates the Eucharist, his essential function, and who also has a specific apostolic ministry, even though restricted in scope, is fulfilling all the integral features of the sacerdotal vocation, and no further justification of his ordination is required.

Indeed, it is not the ordination of monks that is being called into question in modern times, but only the *universal* ordination of choir monks. The needs of the monastery do not require that all monks be priests, even though they do demand that there be some priests in the community. The evolution of sacramental practice over the centuries requires more ordained ministers in monasteries today than were necessary in St. Benedict's time, and in this there is no deviation from tradition. But it does not require that choir monks be assimilated to clerical religious. In view of the contemporary return to sources, it would seem more reasonable today that the ordination of a monk be the exception rather than the rule.

At present, an indult from the Holy See is required for a monk to make solemn profession without advancing to major orders. While some recent foundations have received a blanket permission to accept non-priest choir monks, in the case of older abbeys the indult has been granted only with many cautions and qualifications. While it is evidently necessary to proceed slowly in making major changes from established practice, the limitations placed upon the experiment have often hindered its effectiveness. The introduction of non-priest choir monks in some abbeys has had the effect of creating a third category, alongside the priests and the lay brothers, and this can create a psychological difficulty for the new group. It would seem that the whole problem of monastic priesthood must be approached from a broader basis. It may be hoped that some welcome clarifications in this area will be provided in the coming revision of the canon law.

3. THE CORPORAL WORKS OF MERCY

Apostolate of Works of Mercy

In the *Holy Rule*, as in the earlier monastic tradition, the principal apostolic work in which the monks are to engage is the practice of the corporal works of mercy within the monastery itself. Among the members of the monastic community there is ample scope for the performance of works of charity. The *Rule* is particularly concerned about those who are in need of special consideration because of youth, old age or sickness. Discretion is the characteristic of St. Benedict's legislation which has made it so universally adaptable through the centuries, and nowhere does he manifest this quality more abundantly than in his tender concern for those in special need.

Such too was the attitude of his predecessors in the cenobitic life, especially St. Pachomius, though none equaled St. Benedict in his application of the principle of discretion. It must be recognized that fraternal charity which expresses itself in works of mercy toward one's confreres in the monastery is a true exercise of the Church's apostolate. If the monastery is the Church in miniature, the building up of the community through the increase of charity is a real contribution to the building up of the Church.

The exercise of charity, however, is not limited to the members of the community, but extends its influence to outsiders as well. While the ancient monks, including St. Benedict, did not in principle engage in an active apostolate outside the monastery, they did exercise such an apostolate on behalf of those who came to them. This was, in fact, practically the only contact which enabled them to influence the world, and this influence was not insignificant. From the earliest times, even in the remotest recesses of the desert, the monks received innumerable guests and travelers, and through these contacts left an indelible imprint upon the Church. Since this is the primary and most traditional apostolate of monks, which retains its full validity today, it is the form of apostolic work which we shall consider first.

Care for the Sick Brothers

St. Benedict is especially anxious that charity be practiced on behalf of those who have some special need. In chapter 36 of the *Rule* he gives instructions on the care of the sick brothers. That he regards the matter from a supernatural viewpoint is immediately evident from the fact that he stresses the sacramentalism of service to the sick. Care given to the sick is really care for Christ. Like his predecessors, he bases this teaching upon the Gospel: "I was sick and you visited me"; and, "what you did to one of these least ones, you did unto me" (Mt 25,36.40; *Rule* 36,2–3). By healing the wounds of a member of Christ's Body, the monk is truly contributing to the Church's apostolate.

The care of the sick is the special responsibility of the abbot. He must, therefore, look upon the sick monk not as a useless member who causes annoyance and inconvenience, but rather as a blessing from God. Instead of regretting the extra care required and the loss of the sick monk's services, he will be grateful for the opportunity for the greater growth of charity in the community. He will see that the sick are properly cared for, principally by appointing a conscientious monk as infirmarian, who is to be chosen not only for his professional ability, but also for his supernatural qualities: he must be God-fearing, diligent and careful (36,7). In our day it is helpful if the infirmarian also has some professional training in the care of the sick. St. Benedict would surely approve of this, for he is always insistent that people be competent for the tasks assigned to them (38,12; 47,3; 53,22).

The Sick, the Old and the Very Young

While the principal responsibility for care of the sick falls upon the abbot, the infirmarian and the cellarer, this does not mean that the other monks are relieved of all obligation in their regard. One of the tools of good works is to visit the sick (4,16). It is the duty of every monk to visit his sick confreres, attend to their needs and do what he can to make their hardship easier to bear. It is the obligation of all to exercise supernatural charity, and they should be grateful for the opportunity to contribute in this way to the apostolate.

The sick themselves are not exempt from the duty of charity. If they are to be treated like Christ, they must also act as Christ would, and not annoy their confreres by excessive complaints and demands. They must accept their suffering as a gift of God. While they are allowed certain concessions because of their illness, they are not to take advantage of this special consideration, but should rather be humbled by the knowledge that unusual provisions have been made in their behalf. Each of the cells, whatever his function in the Body of Christ, must contribute his share to the building up of the whole.

Similar provisions are made in chapter 37 for the care of the aged members of the community and of the very young. Like the sick, they are to be treated with special care as their needs may require, and the full rigor of the *Rule* is to be relaxed for them. On their behalf, too, the monks will find many opportunities to practice charity.

The Apostolate of Receiving Guests

In chapter 53 of the *Rule* St. Benedict makes provisions for the reception of guests. He supposes that there will always be guests at the monastery and is clearly pleased that this is so, thus following the example of the oriental monks, who came trooping out in great numbers to welcome visitors. St. Benedict takes prudent measures to ensure that the frequent reception of guests should not unduly disturb the order and quiet of the monastery and the regular discipline, but beyond that he is prepared to go to almost any inconvenience to take proper care of guests, even allowing the breaking of the night silence (42,10) and of the superior's fast (53,10). Cassian had justified this usage by the Gospel: the guest is Christ, and the disciples cannot fast when the Bridegroom is with them (Mk 2,19; cf *Inst* 5,24; *Conf* 21,14).

The reason for this concern is again a supernatural one: the guest, like the sick, represents Christ. Here again St. Benedict refers to the Gospel: "I was a stranger and you took me in" (Mt 25,35), and reminds his monks that Christ will repeat these words to them at the judgment (53,1). Consequently the cellarer must see that they are not neglected (31,9), a monk who is filled with the fear of God is to look after them (53,21), the porter is to welcome anyone who comes to the door (66,3-4). All of the monks will have some part in the care of visitors. It is emphasized that the treatment of guests is to have a distinctly religious character—prayer, the kiss of peace, *lectio divina*—so that he may share in the supernatural goods of the monastery.

The care of visitors, then, was clearly looked upon as an authentic apostolate. It not only contributed to the increase of charity in the community, but had a positive apostolic value for those who enjoyed the hospitality of the monastery. The monastery was a kind of spiritual powerhouse which exerted an influence upon the Church and the world, not by dispersing its strength in exterior works, but by ministering its supernatural gifts to those who came to seek them at their source. It would be difficult to underestimate the influence that a monastery can have in this way. Monasteries are the only places where most Christians can go to find the Gospel lived in all its integrity and to see the liturgy performed with solemnity. The profound impression which is left upon people from the world who have witnessed this for the first time and have been welcomed with the charity of Christ is of no small apostolic value. Every monastery should have a guest house and should consider the reception of guests to be one of the most fruitful forms of its apostolate. Far from being looked upon as an inconvenience or as a way of making money, it should be regarded as a unique opportunity to give to others what only a monastery has to give.

Monastic Hospitality and Ecumenism

In our times monastic hospitality also has a role to play in promoting Church unity. The Fathers of Vatican II have called upon all Christians to contribute to the ecumenical task of the Church, each in a way suited to his own situation. The monastic orders have an irreplaceable role to fulfill in this apostolate, especially in regard to the Eastern Churches, with whom they have so much in common, as was pointed out by Pope Pius XI in his apostolic letter *Equidem verba* of March 21, 1924.

The eastern origin of monasticism has left an imprint upon the monks of the West which provides them with many points of contact with the Eastern Church. Both share a deep appreciation for the liturgy, an emphasis upon the life of prayer, a preference for decentralization, a love for solitude and peace. The Council Fathers have declared:

> In the East are to be found the riches of those spiritual traditions which are given expression especially in monastic life. From the glorious times of the holy Fathers, monastic spirituality flourished in the East, then later flowed over into the western world, and there provided the source from which Latin monastic life took its rise and has drawn fresh vigor ever since. Catholics there are earnestly recommended to avail themselves of the spiritual riches of the eastern Fathers which lift up the whole man to the contemplation of the divine (*Decree on Ecumenism* 15).

There is doubtless less background for fruitful contact with Protestants. Yet in recent years a notable development has taken place in the Protestant attitude toward monasticism. While the revival of monasticism in the Anglican Church dates back as far as the 19th century, the present century has seen a similar revival, still on a small scale but nevertheless important in its influence, in the Lutheran and Reformed traditions. Those monasteries which have especially devoted themselves to ecumenical work have established cordial and fruitful relations with Anglican and Protestant Christians, and much good can be done in this area.

The task of monks will be principally to make Christian unity an object of their prayer, to cultivate a serious interest in and adequate knowledge of ecumenical developments, and to provide an atmosphere of hospitality in which fruitful ecumenical encounters can take place. Whether received individually or in organized groups for conferences and discussions, the separated brethren who are welcomed in an attitude of true Christian charity and in the best tradition of monastic hospitality will be enabled to enter more rapidly into that meeting of minds and hearts which is indispensable to a profitable encounter of Christians in search of unity.

Care of the Poor

There is no chapter in the *Holy Rule* devoted especially to the care of the poor, but St. Benedict's concern for them is evident in a number of passages. To relieve the poor is one of the tools of good works (4,14). It is the cellarer's responsibility to look after their needs and to see that they are not neglected (31,9). The poor who come to the monastery should be received with even greater care than others "because in them is Christ more truly welcomed" (53, 15). Used clothing is to be saved for the poor (55,9) and the novice may bestow his belongings upon them before he makes profession (58,24).

In St. Gregory's portrait of St. Benedict in the *Dialogues* we see the holy patriarch putting these principles into practice. Whatever may be the value of these accounts for reconstructing the historical outline of St. Benedict's life, they are an authentic testimony to the concern of ancient monasticism for the poor. Unwilling to turn the poor from his door, St. Benedict gave them whatever he could find in the monastery, even though there should be nothing left for the community (*Dial* 2,27–28). St. Gregory remarks: "He wanted to distribute everything he had to the poor and thus store up riches in heaven" (*ibid* 28; cf Lk 18,22). In this brief comment is contained both the evangelical motivation and the eschatological outlook of ancient monasticism.

Monastic tradition has been a faithful interpreter of the patriarch's mind on this subject. In the Middle Ages the almoner was one of the most important officials in the monastery. It was his duty to distribute alms to the poor who came to the monastery each day, to provide food and clothing for the destitute and look after all those who recommended themselves to the charity of the monastery. In those days religious houses were the only places to which the needy could turn for help, and they willingly assumed the burden of charity and continued to minister to the indigent down to modern times.

Responsibility of Monasteries

Today charitable works have been largely taken over by other agencies. But while public welfare agencies can give material assistance, they cannot always supply the spirit and atmosphere of Christian love which is the principle behind St. Benedict's legislation. It is true that the distribution of charity should be discerning, lest it tend to confirm the unworthy in their laziness. But it is better to give to some unworthy recipients than to withhold charity from those who are really in need. The inevitable incidence of occasional abuses is no excuse for not fulfilling the duty of charity.

Today as in past ages, therefore, monks must have a genuine concern about those classes of society which, even in our affluent civilization, have reason to recommend themselves to our charity. The poor will always be with us, and it is a basic duty of monasteries to look to their relief. Modern accounting methods may sometimes create the impression that the monastery, from a financial viewpoint, is merely a legal corporation in which the profit motive takes first place. The supernatural viewpoint must not be lost sight of by the individual monk as well as by those who are especially charged with the material resources of the community.

In the last analysis, the monk's concern for the poor must flow from his own love of poverty and from his conviction that the poor hold a privileged place in the kingdom of God. A monastery should not be a corporation of wealthy landowners, magnanimously assigning some of their excess profits to works of philanthropy. Monks must give alms to the poor because they themselves know what it is to be poor, and they wish for love of Christ to distribute what little they have to the members of his Body who are in need. A monk should have a real sense of solidarity with the poor, the unfortunate, the outcasts: it was these with whom our Lord ate and drank, to whom he preached the good news of the kingdom, whom he proclaimed blessed.

4. MONASTIC CULTURE

Civilizing Influence

We have seen that the work of civilizing and perfecting the social order pertains to the secondary mission of the Church, and does not therefore directly concern the apostolate. It does not contribute directly to the building up of the Church, but only indirectly, insofar as it creates conditions in which the Church can effectively operate. Nevertheless monastic culture should come in for consideration here because of the immense role which monasteries have played in the formation of western civilization. Though not strictly apostolic, the preservation and transmission of culture has been one of the principal works of monks.

The contribution of the monastic order to European civilization in the Middle Ages is sufficiently well known. Cardinal Newman has characterized it as follows:

> St. Benedict found the world, physical and social, in ruins, and his mission was to restore it in the way, not of science, but of nature, not as if setting about to do it, not professing to do it by any set

time or by any rare specific or by any series of strokes, but so quietly, patiently, gradually, that often, till the work was done, it was not known to be doing. . . . There was no one that 'contended, or cried out,' or drew attention to what was going on; but by degrees the woody swamp became a hermitage, a religious house, a farm, an abbey, a village, a seminary, a school of learning, and a city. Roads and bridges connected it with other abbeys and cities, which had similarly grown up; and what the haughty Alaric or fierce Attila had broken to pieces, these patient meditative men had brought together and made to live again (*Historical Sketches*, vol 2: Mission of St. Benedict 9).

Testimony of Recent Popes

Pope Pius XII also paid tribute to the work of the monks:

Besides the fact . . . that the sons of Benedict were almost alone in the dark age of profound ignorance and turmoil, in preserving the codices of literature and learning, in translating them most faithfully and commenting on them, they were also among the pioneers in practicing and promoting the arts, science, and teaching. . . . It can be asserted that the Benedictine Institute and its flourishing monasteries were raised up not without divine guidance and assistance in order that, while the Roman empire was tottering, and barbarous tribes goaded by warlike fury were attacking on all sides, Christian civilization might make good its losses, and after civilizing nations by the truth and charity of the Gospels, would lead them skillfully and tirelessly to fraternal harmony, fruitful labor, and to a virtuous life ruled by the precepts of our Redeemer and guided by his grace (Encyclical *Fulgens radiatur*, March 21, 1947: AAS 39 (1947) 149).

More recently, Pope Paul VI has reiterated that the world has need of the values preserved in monastic life:

You Benedictines know this, especially from your history; and the world knows it, when it wishes to remember what it owes you and what it can still gain from you. The fact is so impressive and significant that it affects the existence and stability of this old society of ours, still alive but today so much in need of producing new sap at its roots from which to draw its vitality and its splendor: those Christian roots which in large measure St. Benedict gave it and nourished with his spirit. This is a fact so magnificent that it deserves our recognition, our homage, and our confidence (Allocution *Quale saluto*, Oct 24, 1964: AAS 56 (1964) 988).

Oriental Attitude to Earthly Values

The fact that western monasticism is held in esteem chiefly because of its contributions to civilization is a paradox of history, for cultural activity is at most a by-product of monastic life. Its real purpose lies in quite another sphere. If culture can be defined as a general appreciation of the world and of life and the cultivation of means of expressing this appreciation, then it cannot be asserted that culture played any significant role in monastic life at its origins. The early Egyptian monks were quite indifferent to it, when not positively opposed. They adopted rather the viewpoint of pure eschatology, the complete abandonment of the world, together with all human values, in order to seek God alone. Their ideal was not to Christianize temporal values so as to make them means of sanctification capable of leading men to God, but rather totally to abandon them, leaving the means aside so as to attain the end directly.

When the original Copts were succeeded by Greek-speaking monks in the Egyptian deserts, a certain cultural refinement entered the monastic milieux. However, these men maintained the eschatological orientation of monasticism, expressing it in terms of the popular Platonism which they inherited from the Alexandrian theologians. They considered temporal values as imperfect, transitory, mere shadows of the enduring values of eternity. In order to devote themselves entirely to attaining the latter, they were anxious to dispense completely with the former. Any concessions made to the values of this world were likely to endanger the monastic ideal. Hence reading and writing and the cultivation of the arts and the liturgy had relatively little importance in their lives.

There were exceptions, however, even among the Egyptian monks, and a more pronounced intellectual element in the Cappadocian and Augustinian traditions. Furthermore, even the simplest of the desert monks possessed a certain biblical culture. Like most men who do not read, they had phenomenal memories: some of them had memorized the entire Bible. While professing to despise human culture, they nevertheless drew a deeper wisdom from the inspired Word of God. The Bible was the foundation and source of their entire formation.

St. Benedict and Culture

St. Benedict began his monastic life as a faithful follower of his oriental predecessors. St. Gregory tells us how, when still a student at Rome, he saw others falling into vice and decided to flee from the world and all its values to save himself from a similar fate. "For he was afraid that if he acquired any of its learning he, too, would later plunge, body and soul, into the dread abyss. In his desire to please God alone, he turned his back on further studies, gave up home and inheritance and resolved to embrace the religious life" (*Dial* 2, Pr). And Gregory concludes that he went off into the wilderness *scienter nescius et sapienter indoctus.*

Nothing could be more like the desert Fathers than the vocation of St. Benedict. Having received the habit from one who was already a monk and thus become a charismatic, he dwelt alone in a cave for three years, completely cut off from all worldly values. He so lost track of time that he did not even know when it was Easter Sunday. Like St. Anthony, struck by the words of the Gospel, he abandoned everything to dwell alone with God.

It was only later, when disciples had come to him, that he established a form of cenobitic life. He did this not because he had in any way changed his monastic ideals, but merely to meet the requests of those who wished to share his life. Several passages of the *Rule* show that he kept his esteem for the eremitical life, and the vast majority of the observances laid down for his monks are derived from eastern monasticism. He had no intention of establishing a new form of monastic life, but merely of adapting the old traditions to his own locality and circumstances. His personal attitude toward culture and worldly values cannot have been radically different from that of his predecessors.

Culture in the Holy Rule

Nevertheless, some of the provisions of the *Rule* are such as to require a certain degree of culture of the monks. The liturgy assumes a place of importance in the life of the community, and its fitting celebration will require at least a minimum degree of cultural achievement. The *lectio divina* plays a prominent part in the daily life of the monk; together with prayer and work it is one of his principal activities. Reading is constantly performed in the choir and the refectory, and hence the monastery must have possessed some kind of library of the Sacred Scriptures and the works of the Fathers. The monks must have been able to read, or obliged to learn; they must have procured books or copied them themselves; they must have taught the boys who were admitted to the monastery. And through the continual *lectio divina* they must have acquired a considerable degree of religious culture.

In prescribing these things St. Benedict certainly was not conscious of making any innovation in monastic life. He had no intention of converting his monastery into a seat of learning, as seems to have been the ideal of his contemporary, Cassiodorus. It was simply that the exigencies of cenobitic life and the proper development of spirituality required a certain degree of intellectual activity, most of which could be dispensed with in the life of a hermit. But, for that matter, it is supposed that the hermit should have had the previous training of a monastery (1,3–5). Yet the introduction of these elements into the monastery certainly left the door open for cultural pursuits of wider scope than the *Rule* directly envisages. The subsequent growth of monastic literature sprang from a seed that was planted by St. Benedict himself.

His admission into the monastery of a considerable activity of reading and writing, however, does not mean that he was a humanist. Culture, even religious culture—which is the only kind envisaged—is not considered as a value for its own sake, nor is there any social or civilizing purpose in view. The sole purpose of monastic life is to seek God; the sole value in the monk's life is God himself. Everything else in his life can only be a means to the attainment of this supreme end. Culture, like everything else, can lead the monk to God; if it leads him in any other direction, it is an evil. The monk is not a humanist, but he can use human values as means to elevate his mind toward supernatural realities.

Monastic Culture in the Middle Ages

The flowering of monastic culture enjoyed a tremendous growth and vitality during the Middle Ages, particularly from the eighth to the twelfth centuries. The numerous painstaking studies of Dom Jean Leclercq have brought us into intimate contact with the monasteries of this remote period and have enabled us to follow the development of the culture, the theology and the spirituality of the monks who lived in these Benedictine centuries. He has shown how it was the *opus Dei* and the *lectio divina* which gave rise to the studies of monks, entirely centered upon the Bible and the liturgy. Their intellectual life was always merely a means to an end. It was a question of renouncing culture for the sake of God, then finding it again on a higher level in the course of one's search for God—for to him who seeks the kingdom of heaven everything else shall be given besides (Mt 6,33).

Thus in the course of the development of St. Benedict's concept of the monastic life, the ideal of pure eschatology which marked the origins of monasticism became an ideal of eschatological humanism. But eschatological it remained. The monks were contemplatives, their attention was fixed upon the goal of eternal life, and all their intellectual and artistic pursuits were made to serve this end. Human values were absorbed in the divine.

The monks of the Middle Ages developed a true monastic culture, distinct from other branches of medieval culture. It was characterized by certain constants which are proper to monasticism and serve to distinguish it from the scholastic culture which was developing at the same time, as well as from secular learning. The place occupied by the liturgy is one of the most important of these constants, for it was the liturgy which gave the monks their vision of reality, their general outlook upon things, and determined both the content and the style of their literary productions. Together with this went their devotion to the Bible, which supplied the substance of both their liturgical texts and their *lectio divina* and determined their religious mentality. Then there was a profound sense of tradition which linked them to their monastic ancestors and to the patristic period. Finally, monastic culture was strongly tinged with an ascetical and spiritual tendency which gave it a markedly religious character and made it devotional and contemplative rather than dialectical and scientific.

Everything in the life of these monks was made to serve their monastic ideal. They studied to bring themselves closer to God; they wrote books, composed music and created works of art in order to beautify the house of God, illumine the minds of men and contribute to the fitting service of God in the liturgy. They placed the supernatural first; human values could never be sought for themselves, but only as a means.

Contemporary Challenge

The question of the place of intellectual and artistic pursuits in monastic life is one of those perennial problems which can receive no absolute and enduringly valid solution. Each epoch and each monastery must solve it anew in accord with the circumstances of its own time and place. Every monk must, in fact, arrive at his own solution, for it is also an individual problem, involving the subordination of all human values in his life to his striving for the one thing necessary.

In our day there is no unified monastic culture. Monasteries no longer retain their intellectual leadership; monks are no longer the sole or even the principal guardians of cultural values. Learning has become positivist, fragmented, extremely specialized, extended to the masses. In many fields of learning, monks cannot hope to compete with others, nor is it necessary or desirable that they should do so.

This does not mean that monks no longer have a contribution to make. While aware of the changed conditions of modern times, they nevertheless can still profit from the example of their medieval ancestors. The monks of the Middle Ages did not attempt to compete with the rising scholasticism. They were broad-minded enough to realize its value, but they also realized that it was not their proper field of activity and that it should be left to others, while they confined themselves to traditional pursuits more suited to their form of life.

Monastic Culture in Modern Times

The situation today is an analogous one. The task of monks is to maintain a genuine religious culture in the face of the increasing secularization and materialism of modern society. Their contribution is to bear witness to an authentic hierarchy of values, to put first things first, to cultivate the real values of the mind and the spirit, to show by their own example that human achievements are of value only if directed to man's ultimate end. Their culture must be based upon the Bible and the liturgy and nourished by the pure sources of tradition and authentic Christian spirituality. A culture which is not based upon these foundations and is not directed toward the seeking of God may be a form of humanism, but it is not a monastic culture. And if they are to maintain a monastic culture, they must safeguard their holy leisure for the *vacare Deo*, the authentic contemplative peace which alone can make this possible.

Monastic culture does not mean that monks must be great scholars, great theologians, great artists. The few examples in monastic history of the attainment of such an ideal indicate that it is difficult to achieve without sacrificing important elements of monastic life and organization. As a by-product of the general culture of the mass of monks, it is to be expected that some will occasionally excel in different pursuits. But that is not the purpose. The purpose is to fill the minds of monks with the beauty and nobility of their ideal, to generate a profound sense of the hierarchy of values, the human in the service of the divine, and to bear witness before the world to the true, the good and the beautiful, which are reflections of the perfections of God.

5. MONASTIC SCHOOLS

Monastic Teaching

A form of work which has occupied monks for many centuries and in which the majority of Benedictine monasteries in this country are engaged today is that of conducting schools. In some countries, in fact, Benedictines are popularly thought of as a "teaching order." How misleading this idea is should be evident from all that we have said before. Nevertheless, educational work has played an important part in the history of Benedictine monasticism.

St. Benedict admitted boys to his monastery as candidates for the monastic life, who lived as monks insofar as their age permitted. According to St. Gregory, Placid was only a small boy when brought to him at Subiaco. We know that Bede entered the abbey of Wearmouth at the age of seven, and the Pseudo Paul the Deacon, in the ninth century, speaks of boys as young as four and five. These boys had to be taught. The *Rule* makes no detailed provisions for their education, though it does legislate for their discipline. But it is evident that they, even more than the older monks, had to learn what was necessary for them to take part in the *opus Dei* and the *lectio divina.* Their studies were principally centered about *grammatica,* which meant Latin grammar and composition, with an intense study of the classical authors, who were regarded as the finest models.

All of the early monasteries must have had such internal schools for monks and for boys destined to become monks. At the beginning of the Carolingian renaissance we find the monastic schools attended also by secular clerics and young men studying for the clerical state, and sometimes by lay students. Charlemagne, in order to promote his cultural program, decreed that all monasteries should have external schools, but this decree was revoked by the reform of Benedict of Aniane, which attempted to limit the schools to monks. This ruling was not always observed, and we find external schools in some monasteries throughout the Middle Ages, though reform movements usually sought to eliminate them. Sometimes the monasteries merely promoted such schools, but located them at a distance from the abbey and employed seculars to do the teaching.

The students admitted to the external schools were usually clerics and boys from the vicinity. They were admitted regardless of social class; even the sons of serfs attended, and without payment if their parents did not have the means. They received the same education as the candidates for the monastery.

Advantages and Drawbacks

There was always a certain opposition to conducting external schools, as it was widely recognized that they frequently presented obstacles to the full observance of the regular discipline. Although the growth of the urban schools rendered them less necessary, there seems never to have been a time when some monasteries did not have such schools. In modern times, schools for secondary and even higher education have become quite common among Benedictines.

Such a development is an understandable phenomenon in view of the cultural leadership which was so long enjoyed by the monasteries. Truth and beauty are self-diffusive, and it is natural that the monk should be inclined to communicate to others what he himself has acquired. It is even necessary that he should do so within the monastery itself, if the tradition is to be passed on from one generation to the next. And it is natural that outsiders should seek to learn from him. Schoolwork has the advantage of being generally limited to the confines of the cloister and therefore seems compatible with the communal life.

At the same time, it must be recognized that the operation of external schools in modern times is not without its disadvantages to the monastery. Monasteries are no longer the principal guardians of culture, and the function of teaching can now be carried on by others. Given the nature of their life, monks can scarcely operate a modern school with as much competence and efficiency as modern congregations especially organized for such work, without serious compromises of their ideal. Any school will necessarily interfere to some extent with the regular life and the order of the day, and some types of school will interfere a great deal. A number of monks will have to be absent from common exercises a good part of the time and some may have to be frequently absent from the monastery for one reason or another. The constant pressure of schoolwork makes it difficult to safeguard the holy leisure so necessary for spiritual growth and tends to crowd out other activities more intimately related to the monastic apostolate.

Difficulties of School Operation

As state requirements become more exacting, monasteries find themselves obliged to make more sacrifices in order to keep their schools up to standard. Monks must study outside the monastery for long periods of time in order to qualify for teaching. While this may result in enrichment for some, in other cases it has unfortunate results. The pressure of providing teachers and administrative officials sometimes leads superiors to place burdens upon subjects who cannot bear them without serious damage to their monastic life, and the complexity of the organization makes it difficult for superiors to make changes which may be indicated on other grounds. School pressures also tempt superiors to neglect the monastic and even clerical training of young monks in favor of more directly utilitarian training. The monk who is also a priest and a teacher must live three vocations simultaneously. It is not easy to do so.

Furthermore, modern schools have become very expensive undertakings. Any monastery will find it difficult to make the financial outlay necessary to keep in competition with others. Once it has succumbed to the temptation to indulge in fund-raising schemes, it may well be launched upon the uncontrollable spiral of expanding resources. From that point onward Parkinson's Law is in full operation. All this increases the burdens of administration and takes monks out of the monastery for reasons which continue to expand without limit: student recruiting, alumni meetings, fund-raising dinners, athletic and social events, vocation drives, public relations affairs of various kinds. The quiet apostolate is then overshadowed by fiscal machinery and bureaucratic "efficiency."

If a monastery is going to operate a school, therefore, it should at least be very careful about the type of school it undertakes. Monks cannot hope to compete with large universities either in personnel or in financial resources. Any attempt to do so is guaranteed to spell monastic suicide. Ventures into such institutions, with their specialized professional schools, highly organized activities and myriad social programs, can only bury the simplicity of the monastic ideal under an avalanche of other preoccupations.

The Function of Monastic Schools

Primary and secondary schools present fewer problems, as they ordinarily require less in the way of facilities and trained personnel. Real difficulties may be felt, however, even with these institutions; much depends upon the size and type of school. A day school, for instance, will ordinarily involve fewer inconveniences for the monastic routine than a boarding school. In any case, monasteries should remain free from the temptation to indulge in mass production. A school is not necessarily better because it is larger. A smaller school will involve less interference with the monastic life and should also make it possible to give better quality of instruction.

If there is any justification for monks operating schools today when there are so many others to do this work, it can only be because they have something to offer which others cannot or do not achieve as well. Contemporary monks must, therefore, have a real sense of educational values. On the one hand, to conform to educational fads which are not based upon sound principle is to obstruct the advancement of culture. On the other hand, however, to bask in the glories of monastic achievements in the past without making any attempt to meet the valid scholastic standards which secular educators justly insist upon today, is to commit the fatal error of supposing that teaching will be good simply because it is done by religious personnel. Piety and good intentions are no substitute for competence.

If monks are serious about continuing the traditions of the monastic culture of the past, they must first be sure that they have acquired it themselves so that they may have something to pass on to others. They must have a clear concept of the nature of the school, of its role in society and of their own mandate as teachers. They must aim to train the intellect, to provide an atmosphere conducive to the development of intellectual virtue for subjects who are qualified to receive such training, regardless of their social or economic status. This must be accomplished within a Christian intellectual context and hierarchy of values in a monastic environment which should be a living exemplification of Christian truth and values.

6. THE CARE OF SOULS

Exercise of the External Ministry

The exercise of the ministry by monks has already been treated in connection with monastic priesthood. The two questions are closely related, for the exercise of the ministry, at least in our time, is permitted as a rule only to those who have received sacred orders. The ancient monastic tradition held the exercise of the priestly ministry outside the cloister to be incompatible with monastic life. The *Holy Rule* is clearly in this tradition, nor is this contradicted by St. Gregory's portrait of St. Benedict undertaking the conversion of the people who lived near Monte Cassino (*Dial* 2,8), or occasionally sending his monks to care for the spiritual needs of nuns who lived nearby (*ibid* 2,19). While the influence of the urban monks led to the undertaking of certain ministerial functions at an early period, the tradition of incompatibility was generally maintained all through the Middle Ages. Some priestly work outside the monastery was done throughout the Middle Ages, but there was always a certain opposition to it and a recognition that it was not an ideal work for monks and could be justified only temporarily in view of the urgent need of the Church. It is only in quite modern times that monasteries have engaged in such work on a large scale.

At the present time the care of souls outside the monastery is one of the principal activities of monks in some of the Benedictine and Cistercian congregations, though rejected in whole or in part by others. This work takes on various forms: the operation of parishes; chaplaincies in hospitals, convents, schools and other institutions; the preaching of retreats, missions and occasional conferences; temporary parish assistance; and individual mission work in territories where the Church is struggling to become established. This development was not intended by the monastic founders and, at least when conducted on a large scale, can scarcely be reconciled with their principles. The judgment to be passed upon the diverse forms of the care of souls as exercised today must, however, be carefully nuanced, for some forms of this work can be carried on with less inconvenience to the monastery than others.

Permanent Assignments Outside the Monastery

It is difficult to see how the permanent operation by monks of parishes distant from the monastery can be justified. In some places monks are assigned to parish work immediately after their ordination and remain there for the rest of their lives. Their monastic life is reduced to the few years which they had spent at the abbey before their ordination. They live, and begin to think, like diocesan priests; sometimes they lose contact to a great extent with their monastery. It is not unusual for them to be all alone in a parish; legal provisions intended to prevent this are sometimes ignored or rendered inoperative through casuistry. None of the elements most characteristic of monastic spirituality can be realized in such circumstances.

Surely this is the negation of almost everything that monasticism originally stood for, and it is hard to see how it can be justified by the considerations which are usually advanced. In the case of a truly urgent need of the Church which cannot be otherwise met, it might be justifiable on a temporary basis. But there must be an effort to keep temporary situations temporary and not extend them indefinitely. Especially to erect the practice of serving parishes into a deliberate and permanent policy is not easy to justify on any grounds, and it can only serve to confuse and obscure the real nature of monasticism for the laity, the clergy and the monks themselves.

The same judgment must be passed upon permanent chaplaincies, as their case is not substantially different from that of parishes. They have the same effect upon the observance of the common life and the monastic liturgy, and often upon the individual monk, who can no longer preserve his separation from the world. An exception would have to be made, however, in the case of chaplaincies to convents of Benedictine nuns and sisters. Though he will not be participating in the full life of his own monastery, a monk in such a position will be living in a monastic environment. It is, furthermore, the obligation of monks to care for the spiritual needs of their sisters in religion—an obligation which, according to St. Gregory, was recognized by St. Benedict, and has recently been emphasized by the Holy See (*S. Cong. of Religious*, November 5, 1957). The ideal solution would be to locate convents of nuns in close proximity to monasteries, so that a monk resident at the monastery would easily be able to go to the convent for the daily exercise of the ministry among the nuns.

Occasional Ministry

Much less harmful to the monastic life are those forms of work for the care of souls which are conducted on a temporary and occasional basis. The monk who is sent out to other religious communities to give a conference or conduct a retreat, or to a parish for a mission or forty hours' devotion, will be absent only briefly from his monastery and will be performing an apostolic work which can contribute to the deepening of his own religious life.

The same may be said in general of occasional assistance in parishes. There is a demand in many parts of our country for the help of religious priests to celebrate Mass, hear confessions and preach, especially on Sundays and feast days. The monk who is assigned to such work will be able to reside in his own monastery and follow the full monastic observance, and will go out only on occasion for definitely assigned tasks in the ministry.

In principle this seems to do little harm to the monastery and to provide the priest-monk with an opportunity to exercise his priesthood, which should redound to his own supernatural benefit as well as that of the faithful to whom he ministers. But the practice is susceptible of exaggeration, and when carried on beyond just limits can certainly be harmful to the monastery. If the monastery is regularly emptied every Sunday and feast day of all its able-bodied priests, who ordinarily constitute the bulk of the community, this means that it will be impossible to carry on the monastic liturgy with fitting solemnity. First things will no longer be put in first place, for the active apostolate will take precedence over the essential features of monastic life.

Harmful Results of Frequent Absences

This practice can also be harmful to the monks themselves. Sometimes monks are assigned to the work of preaching retreats and missions on such a regular basis that they are practically always absent from the monastery. There is little difference between this kind of life and permanent assignment to a parish. Or they are assigned to replace pastors who are absent for a considerable length of time, or sent out so frequently for assistance in a parish that it becomes more regular than occasional, with resultant harm to themselves as well as to the monastery.

It is certainly unrealistic to pretend that frequent trips outside the cloister are not at all harmful to monks. St. Benedict thought differently about it when he wrote that there should be no necessity for monks to go outside, "for that is not at all expedient for their souls" (66,7), and insisted that those who had been outside are not to tell others what they had seen and heard there, "because this causes very great harm" (67,5). St. Anthony said that a monk outside his monastery was like a fish out of water (*Vita Antonii* 85). All this remains true today. At best, a parish cannot provide a suitable monastic environment, and frequent absences from the community exercises mean so much loss to the monk.

The less frequent and closer to the monastery these activities are kept, the better it will be for the monastery as well as for the individual monk. The monastic apostolate should be exercised principally on behalf of those who come to the monastery, rather than for those whom the monks must go outside to seek.

7. THE MISSIONARY ROLE OF MONASTICISM

Monastic Activity in Mission Fields

The tradition of monastic collaboration in the missionary effort of the Church is usually traced back to the initiative of St. Gregory the Great, who conceived of the monastic order as an instrument of evangelization when he sent forty monks, under Augustine's leadership, to undertake the conversion of England. From England the movement returned to the Continent, animated by the great monk bishops such as Boniface, who were the architects of the mission to the barbarian tribes. Thus the Christianization of Europe was to a large extent the work of monks, who became the creators of the Christian civilization of the Middle Ages. In modern times the needs of the Church have again called forth the collaboration of monasteries. Today monastic centers have been established on every inhabited continent of the globe and many new foundations are now being made as part of the Church's effort to become truly universal.

In the nineteenth and twentieth centuries, the work of monks in the mission fields has often been scarcely distinguishable from that of other missionaries, conceived of as a participation by more or less isolated individuals in the work of the active apostolate. According to this system, a central house is established in which the entire monastic regime is maintained by at least a skeleton community. From it priests are sent out to found mission stations and to remain in residence there in order to evangelize and care for the needs of the native population. They are usually accompanied by brothers, who perform many material services. The monasteries or their dependencies often conduct seminaries or other schools and engage in many types of active apostolic work.

This is basically the system employed by modern religious and diocesan congregations, especially organized in view of such work, and it has proved effective. Basically this is a clerical apostolate. The type of work performed is that of priests and their lay auxiliaries; there is nothing specifically monastic about such an apostolate. The fundamental question is whether monks do not have a distinct role to play which cannot be filled by others, a specifically monastic contribution to make to the Church's missionary effort, which is the effect not of the priestly ministry but of the monastic life itself.

The Purpose of Missionary Work

This specific role of monks will be determined by two factors: the goal of the Church's missionary activity, on the one hand, and the function of monasticism in the life of the Church, on the other. The purpose of the Church in her missionary work is not merely to promote individual conversions, still less to detach the indigenous people from their own culture and way of life so as to bring them to the faith by initiating them into the cultural context of the Christianity of other regions. It is rather to plant the Church, in all the fullness of her life, in a new environment, so that it may there develop according to the laws of growth proper to that territory and express itself in outward forms drawn from the native culture of the region.

> The Church fulfills its mission when, in obedience to the command of Christ and moved by the grace and love of the Holy Spirit, it becomes actively present to all men and all peoples to bring them to the faith, to liberty and to the peace of Christ by living example, by preaching, by the sacraments and the other channels of grace. In all this, its purpose shall be to open to all peoples the broad and reliable road leading to full participation in the mystery of Christ (*Decree on the Church's Missionary Activity* 5). The particular efforts of the Gospel preachers sent by the Church throughout the whole world, to announce the Gospel message and plant the Church among peoples and groups which do not yet believe in Christ, are commonly called "missions" (*ibid* 6).
> Mission work is no more and no less than the epiphany or manifestation of God's plan, and its fulfillment in the world and in history. In this history God openly concludes the story of salvation through mission work . . . Thus mission work tends to an eschatological fullness . . . By missionary activity the Mystical Body is increased to the measure of the fullness of Christ (cf Eph 4,13); and that spiritual temple where God is adored in spirit and in truth (cf Jn 4,23) grows and is built up upon the foundation of the apostles and prophets, with Christ himself as the chief cornerstone (Eph 2,20) (*ibid* 9).

This was the aim of the apostles in their missionary work. St. Paul's efforts were directed not only to leading men to faith in Christ, but to the *plantatio Ecclesiae*, the establishment of local churches within the unity of the Church universal. To do this he set up the entire organization of his churches so that the Holy Spirit could function effectively through their organs. This means that the goal of missionary work must be to establish the Church in all her manifold functions of sanctifying, teaching and governing so that she may be in every place an apt organ for the outpouring of the Spirit. Missionary efforts should lead to the eventual establishment of a native hierarchy and clergy and of indigenous forms of all the institutions through which the Church accomplishes her mission. So long as some of her vital organs are lacking, something is still wanting to the fullness of her life.

This process demands that the foreign missionary make no attempt to impose his own culture and thought patterns, but rather that he enter into the mentality of the people and allow the Church to assume an outward form in accord with the genius of the native culture. This opens up the whole problem of the adaptation of the Church to various forms of civilization and to local needs. It can be successfully carried out only by those who are willing to make the sacrifice of stripping themselves of their own acquired mentality and making the effort to understand that of the region in which they work. Profound study and sound judgment are required to produce an adaptation which conserves essentials and remains within the great stream of Catholic tradition while still responding to the demands of the concrete situation.

Role of Monks in the Church's Life

It is in this context of the missionary Church's purpose that the contribution of monasticism must be situated. The apostolic function of monks is not primarily to carry on the works of the active ministry, but to represent the reality of grace in the Church. It is primarily the eschatological element of the Church's life which receives expression in the monastic community, this group of Christians gathered together to constitute the place of encounter with God, and by their prayer and austere lives to prepare for his coming. The monk testifies to the enduring truth that the kingdom of God is not of this world, that it cannot be brought about by natural means, that man must prepare himself for it by living in humility and poverty, contemplating the perfection of God and seeking him perseveringly.

The Church is not complete without this contemplative element of her life. It must, indeed, exist in the life of every Christian, but it must be established, too, in the Church's organic structure. Some of her organs must be devoted primarily to this task, while others perform the many varied functions which go to make up the totality of her life. It is a question of emphasis, not of exclusiveness. Religious who devote themselves to the pressing pastoral tasks which always face the Church are not lacking this element, but for them it is secondary. For the monk it is primary, while the active ministry is secondary. When the Church encourages the establishment of contemplative religious houses in missionary lands, she does not do so in the hope that these religious will abandon or profoundly modify their way of life in order to contribute to the needs of the active apostolate, but because she realizes that their own proper contribution is essential to the fullness of her life in these regions.

It is in this sense that Vatican II has declared:

> Institutes of the contemplative life have by their prayers, works of penance and tribulations a most important role in the conversion of souls. It is, after all, God who responds to prayer by sending laborers into his harvest (cf Mt 9,38), by opening the minds of non-Christians to hear the Gospel (cf Acts 16,14), and by making fruitful the Word of salvation in their hearts (cf 1 Cor 3,7). Indeed these institutes are implored to found houses in mission places, as many have already done, so that leading their life in a way suited to the genuinely religious traditions of the people, they may bear outstanding witness to the majesty and charity of God and of union in Christ among non-Christians (*ibid* 40).

The Task of the Monk-Missionary

A monastery in mission territory therefore has a distinct contribution to make to the Church in that area, quite apart from the incidental services which it may render to the needs of the surrounding populace. It cannot fulfill its purpose by dissipating its energies in external works, but only by being faithful to the inner logic of its own structure. An integral monastic life is itself an apostolic work, because it contributes to the vitality and growth of the Church. This apostolic function would be accomplished even if the monastery's external apostolate were so reduced that many were unaware of its presence, for it is the inner, invisible life of the Church which is affected by the monastic apostolate of prayer and asceticism.

The essential task of monks in the mission fields, therefore, is simply to be monks. It is not what they do so much as what they are that is decisive. The inner life of the Church cannot be measured by external norms. The monastic community must be a fervent cell of the Mystical Body of Christ, testifying that the Church is here present. The monk is a witness, not because he preaches and converts, but because his own life manifests what Christianity truly stands for.

A monastic community in mission territory must neither be nor appear to be a foreign importation. It is essential that it grow out of the native soil, that it be adapted to the social and economic conditions of the region and to the native mentality and culture. Otherwise it cannot be truly a part of the Church indigenous to that region, but will always appear to be a transplantation which has not really taken root. The monks will therefore be obliged to study the conditions of the region and the culture of the people so that they may evolve a form of monastic life which, far from suppressing any of its essentials, will make them stand out all the more clearly by clothing them in forms which are meaningful in that context.

> They must attentively consider how to assimilate into the Christian religious life those ascetical and contemplative traditions, whose origins were placed by God in the ancient culture, sometimes even before the preaching of the Gospel . . . The various efforts to establish the contemplative life are worthy of special mention. In some such cases, the members of an institute seek to implant the rich traditions of their order while retaining the essential elements of the monastic institute. Others try by returning to the simpler forms of ancient monasticism. But in all cases a genuine adaptation to local conditions must be carried out. Since the contemplative life is part of the fullness of the Church's presence, it should be established in the newer churches everywhere (*ibid* 18).

Statement of the Bouaké Conference

The role of monastic foundations in missionary countries was studied in detail by the Panafrican Monastic Council, which assembled at the monastery of Bouaké, Ivory Coast, West Africa, from May 21 to 26, 1964. Representatives were present from some thirty foundations which have already been established in Africa by Benedictines, Cistercians and the Brothers of the Virgin of the Poor. The declarations of this conference represent an excellent statement on the mission of monasticism in Africa today, which can be applied, *mutatis mutandis*, to monastic missionary work in general.

The superiors of the monasteries of Africa, gathered together in fraternal assembly, have taken note of their unanimous desire to present to Africans a monastic life open to their own genius and, at the same time, in conformity with the place of monasticism in the Church and with its traditional ideal.

This ideal, as it has been lived since its origin on African soil, is that of a humble and hidden life, entirely oriented toward the search for God. Aiming at the perfect realization of evangelical charity, through an effective separation from the world and a common life of the brethren, 'forming but one heart and one soul,' the monastery will be a witness to the demands of the kingdom of God and to his presence among men. Through prayer, penance and work, the monk joins himself intimately to Christ's sacrifice, and cooperates in his adoration and redemptive work. Through poverty according to the Beatitudes, which awakens in him a desire for the eternal realities on account of which he has left everything behind, he helps to hasten the coming of the kingdom.

The primary goal of monastic foundations in Africa is to allow those African souls who feel drawn thereto by the Spirit to realize this contemplative ideal in a state of life consecrated by the Church and thus to bring about its firm establishment in their native land.

Since the monastic life represents a state of humility in the Church, it does not of itself tend to prepare its members for hierarchical functions: its goal normally excludes all pastoral offices. The monks in no way intend to be unconcerned about the influence which monasteries, through their life of prayer and charity, cannot fail to exercise upon the surrounding population. The traditional practice of hospitality allows them to take care of the spiritual and corporal needs of those who come to them in search of peace, help and encouragement, without prejudice to the essential conditions of silence and recollection without which an authentic monastic life cannot flourish.

The Missionary Challenge Today

The potential of this monastic contribution to the Church's missionary effort should not be underestimated. Monks have a function to perform in the mission fields which cannot be adequately accomplished by other organs of the Church. While others work tirelessly to care for the spiritual and material needs of the populace and thus demonstrate the Church's concern for men, the monks must testify to her absorption in God and to her complete disinterestedness in living out the concrete demands of the Gospel. In our times, when the era of colonialism is passing and new nations are seeking to emerge as independent masters of their own destiny, there is a compelling urgency about the complete and lasting establishment of an indigenous Church in these regions.

The serious crisis which now faces the Church in the non-Christian areas of the world, as well as in nominally Christian regions now subject to new pressures, presents a challenge to the monastic orders. The established monasteries of Europe and America must be willing to make sacrifices to respond to the need of the Church. They must have the foresight and apostolic zeal to give preference to this need over local and ephemeral interests, which should not be permitted to monopolize the entire horizon of their concern. The monk's separation from the world should broaden rather than restrict his concern for the welfare of the universal Church and make him anxious to widen the scope of monastic influence, rather than merely consolidating positions already won. The present missionary challenge provides an unlimited opportunity for monks to employ their traditional spirituality in the service of the Church's apostolate.

8. THE APOSTOLATE OF THE LITURGY

The Monks and the Liturgy

In the past century Benedictines have become identified with the liturgical movement. It was largely due to the study and popularization of the liturgy by the revived monasticism of the nineteenth century that the groundwork for the modern liturgical movement was laid, and the origins of the movement itself in the twentieth century were to a great extent the work of Benedictine monks. This was somewhat of an innovation in monastic history. While divine worship always played an important role in monastic life in the Benedictine tradition, it is only in modern times that monks have been looked upon as leaders of a liturgical apostolate.

The earliest monks, as we have seen, were scarcely interested in the liturgy, since they looked upon the ascetical exercises of their life as a form of divine worship in itself. St. Benedict, influenced by the liturgical customs of the Roman basilicas of his time, attributed a greater importance to the place of the liturgy in monastic life. But the prominence which St. Benedict accords to the divine office is rather the spontaneous consequence of the communal character of the cenobitic institute, as he conceived it, than a conscious emphasis upon the values of the Church's liturgical life, for in his idea of monastic spirituality he is still the faithful follower of the eastern tradition. He was not a promoter of the liturgy in the modern sense.

It was in Carolingian times that monks began to develop the liturgical aspect of their lives, influenced by their contact with the canons. This tendency reached its apogee in the Cluniac movement, while the Cistercian reform marked a return to simplicity of liturgical observance. Throughout the Middle Ages it was the liturgy which constituted the dominant influence in forming the spirituality of monks. The subsequent period was a time of liturgical decadence, in monasteries as elsewhere, which lasted right down to the time of Dom Gueranger, who from the beginning joined the cultivation of the liturgy to his revival of monasticism.

Benedictines and the Liturgical Movement

If the contemporary promotion of the liturgy by Benedictines is a recent development in monastic history, however, it nevertheless falls quite logically within their tradition. The liturgical emphasis in their spirituality has always been maintained, even if it has undergone periods of decadence in the course of history. It is in harmony with the communal character of cenobitic life, with the original Biblical inspiration of monasticism and with the Church's sense of a proper hierarchy of values in maintaining the delicate balance between individual and community in the life of prayer.

The close association of monks with the origins of the modern liturgical movement gave rise in some circles to the bizarre idea that the liturgy is a kind of Benedictine monopoly. Liturgical spirituality was sometimes depicted as the distinctive spirituality of Benedictine monks, in somewhat the same way as certain "devotions" are promoted by other religious orders, and was thought to consist principally in the esthetic element of worship: rubrical precision, Gregorian chant, "gothic" chasubles, "liturgical" altars, albs and Christmas cards. In the early days of the liturgical movement, these misconceptions were perhaps unavoidable, due to the undeveloped stage of theological penetration, deficient popularization and the inevitable presence of a lunatic fringe. Such false ideas did their share of harm to the liturgical apostolate, for they convinced some people that the liturgy had nothing to do with the mass of the faithful, but concerned only an esoteric group closely associated with monasteries and attracted by esthetic values.

Fortunately these misconceptions have now been almost entirely dissipated. Since the Second World War it has been widely recognized that the apostolate of the liturgy has immense pastoral consequences, and it is largely men of action in the Church, imbued with apostolic zeal for the spiritual welfare of the faithful, who have assumed the leadership of the liturgical movement. The efforts of the Holy See to reform the liturgy and to encourage popular participation in it have reached a dramatic climax in the pronouncements of the Second Vatican Council and the liturgical renewal whose first fruits are already in evidence. Today it is impossible for anyone who has a minimum of good will and even the most limited access to journals of public opinion to remain under the illusion that the liturgy is of concern only to a few monks in their secluded cloisters, who pass their time measuring the cut of vestments and discussing the execution of medieval music. Monks can only rejoice that the liturgical movement has largely passed out of their hands and now occupies the place where it belongs, at the very center of the Church's life. It means that their efforts in laying the foundations have borne fruit.

Primary Contribution of Monastic Community

This is not to say that monks no longer have any role to play in the apostolate of the liturgy. The recent development of the liturgical movement and its adoption by the Fathers of the Council as the business of the whole Church, in fact, helps to clarify the role of monks to a degree which was not previously possible. If the liturgy is "the outstanding means whereby the fatihful may express in their lives, and manifest to others, the mystery of Christ and the real nature of the true Church" (*Constitution* 2), then the liturgical apostolate is the concern of all the Church's organs, but each must contribute to it in a manner which corresponds to its own nature and type of activity. The contribution which is incumbent upon monks can be easily discovered if one examines the place of the liturgy in the apostolate of the Church and the nature of the monastic apostolate.

There can be no question that for a monastic community the first and essential contribution to the liturgical apostolate is the very celebration of the daily liturgy in the fullest and most perfect manner possible. Prayer is the monk's only essential duty: he has separated himself from the world and submitted to the discipline of monastic life precisely in order to facilitate prayer. This is his job. In the liturgy he participates in the Church's own worship of God, the prayer of Christ united with his members. If the liturgy is "the summit towards which the activity of the Church is directed . . . the fount from which all her power flows" (*Constitution* 10), then it is the Church's primary apostolic means: "No other action of the Church can equal its efficacy by the same title and to the same degree" (*ibid* 7). A monastic community is one of the organs of the Church which is able to devote itself to carrying out this apostolate in a complete and relatively exclusive manner. Pope John XXIII said of the divine office that it "nourishes the life of monks in a special way, and should be the primary form of their apostolate" (Allocution *Vos paterno animo*, Sept 25, 1959: AAS 51 (1959) 707).

Apostolic Value of Liturgical Worship

Whatever active measures a monastery may take to further understanding of the liturgy and participation in it by the faithful, this form of the liturgical apostolate remains essentially subordinate to the community's primary apostolate of prayer, which is always centered in the celebration of the liturgy. For a monastery to engage in external activities to promote the liturgical movement while at the same time neglecting this essential aspect of the liturgical apostolate would not only be an inversion of values, but would even vitiate the exterior apostolate itself by depriving it of its real source of supernatural life. The life of solitude, prayer and asceticism, flowing from the liturgy and returning to it, is the primary contribution of monks to the apostolate by the very nature of their life and role in the Church.

It is not always sufficiently understood that the celebration of the liturgy is itself an apostolic work. Those who separate themselves from the ordinary circumstances of human life to devote themselves to prayer and asceticism cannot thereby dispense themselves from love of neighbor or separate themselves from the redemptive mission of the Church. They only contribute to it in another way. Their separation from the world unites them all the more closely to their fellow men. Thus Pope Pius XII could affirm that contemplatives "cannot be considered strangers to society, but rather . . . contributors to its spiritual welfare" (Encyclical *Sacra virginitas*, March 25, 1954: AAS 46 (1954) 178), and that they "participate in the apostolate of love of neighbor under the three forms of example, prayer and penance" (Radio address *Lorsque Nous*, Aug 2, 1958: AAS 50 (1958) 585). On another occasion the same pontiff declared: "Their vocation is fully and wholly apostolic, in no way restricted by limits of place, circumstances, or time" (Apostolic Constitution *Sponsa Christi*, Nov 21, 1950: AAS 43 (1951) 14).

It has been the constant teaching of the Church that the life of prayer, even to the total exclusion of external activities, is not only fully legitimate, but even more valuable to the Church's mission than the works of the active ministry. This is true because the Church's primary duty is the worship of God, to which her mission of sanctifying men remains subordinate. The Second Vatican Council reaffirms this truth when it declares that in the Church "the human is directed and subordinated to the divine, the visible likewise to the invisible, action to contemplation, and this present world to that city yet to come, which we seek" (*Constitution on the Sacred Liturgy* 2). Pope John XXIII affirmed categorically "the pre-eminence of the duties of worship and of total consecration to a life of prayer over any other form of apostolate" (Allocution *Gli innumerevoli ceri*, Feb 2, 1961: The Pope Speaks 7 (1961) 8).

Exemplary Value of the Monks' Liturgy

This contribution to the spiritual welfare of the whole Church is realized simply by the fact that the monastery is living the life of the liturgy as prayerfully as possible, even if others are not aware of it or not consciously influenced by it. In our times, however, monasteries are usually accessible to the faithful, who are drawn to them precisely by the attraction of the liturgy. Thus by their example monks can offer a further contribution to the liturgical apostolate. This has, in fact, been one of the principal factors in the influence which Benedictine monasteries have exercised upon the renewal of the liturgy in the past hundred years.

While the liturgy should provide the primary orientation of the spirituality of every Christian, the layman in the world is not able to live the life of the liturgy to the same quantitative extent as the monk. The monk's life is structured precisely to permit him to participate in the liturgy on a full and comprehensive scale. He is specifically trained in the execution of ritual and chant, and should contribute his best efforts to this essential duty, so that the monastic liturgy may reasonably be expected to excel in a sober solemnity and precision.

Thus a monastic community should present to the faithful a living example of what a worshiping community should be. It is a benefit to the faithful to provide them with a place of refuge where they may temporarily lay aside the cares and turmoil of their daily life in the world, and find peace, order and an atmosphere of recollection. They are anxious to drink from the spring of monastic prayer, to subordinate all other concerns to the worship of God, and be edified by the devotion of the monks to their primary duty of glorifying God and interceding for the needs of their fellow men. A monastery's liturgical observance can thus become an effective apostolic influence.

Active Promotion of Liturgical Renewal

A further area of influence which monks can have upon liturgical renewal in the Church is that of activity to promote the liturgical formation of the faithful. There are many ways in which they can accomplish this, through the spoken and written word, without leaving the monastery to enter the active ministry. This apostolate, however extensive it may be, always remains subordinate to the primary monastic apostolate of living the full life of the liturgy. Not only is it subordinate in the very nature of things, but it also depends for its effectiveness upon the primary apostolate, for unless the community itself is soundly formed in the liturgy and actually living a prayerful liturgical life, it will not be able to exercise a fruitful influence upon others.

If the liturgical renewal is to prosper, it must be based upon sound studies. In these times of transition and change, practice must be based upon the assured results of historical and theological investigations. Monks should be eminently qualified to undertake this task, as their own authentic liturgical life should give them a proper sense of values and perspective. There is great need in our country for scholarship in the field of liturgical theology, as well as for skillful popularization of the conclusions of scholarship.

Not only the liturgy itself, but also other fields connected with it, should form the object of the researches of monks. Given the place which the Bible occupies in relation to the liturgy, liturgical renewal cannot proceed confidently without sound scriptural studies, both on the scientific level and on that of popularization. Likewise the study of sacred music, sacred art and the exercise of the crafts associated with it, editions and translations of patristic texts, and work in theology, philosophy, history and canon law will contribute to the renewal of the life of the Church in our times. For the monk such study is an extension of the *lectio divina*, proceeding from his own life of prayer. While on the one hand it can bring him closer to God and to the truth and beauty of heavenly realities, on the other hand, as an apostolic work, it can enable him to share these experiences with others and thus make God better known and loved by his fellow Christians.

7 The Contemplative Life

IN THE SYSTEM of Evagrius and Cassian, the exercises of the active life lead the monk to the second phase of the spiritual ascent, the contemplative life. Purity of heart introduces him to a state of intimacy with God, a continuing dialogue in which the monk listens to the Word of God and is enabled to reply to it through the working of the Spirit within him. The goal of this phase of the spiritual ascent is the contemplation of God, the experience in this life which most closely resembles the activity of the blessed. While the actual experience of the spiritual ascent does not proceed in as rigorous a fashion as this systematization suggests, nevertheless the purification of the heart, the uprooting of vices and cultivation of virtue by means of the exercises of the ascetical combat is the condition for union with God in love and contemplation. This state has traditionally been compared to the life of Adam in paradise and of the angels in heaven.

1. THE MONK AS A MAN OF PRAYER

The Duty of Praise

The universe was created for the glory of God. The purpose of all creatures is to give glory to their Creator. Every creature glorifies

God objectively by the very fact of its existence and its tendency toward its final end. For this reason the Bible can represent the entire universe as an immense orchestra engaged in a symphony of praise to its Creator. It is from this common purpose that the unity of the cosmos in Christian thought is derived, an idea which is developed in the hymns of the Psalter and in the canticle *Benedicite.*

In addition to this objective glorification of God, however, there is also a formal praise of him, proceeding from a conscious and voluntary act. Of all the creatures in the material universe, man alone is capable of this glorification of God. This ability to give conscious praise to God as the spokesman for the whole cosmos is for man his highest dignity and at the same time his sacred duty. Adoration, indeed, which is an act of homage to God as Creator, is the primary and essential duty of the creature.

It has been further determined by the positive will of God that this adoration should ascend to the Father through Christ. Christ is the Head, not only of the Mystical Body, but of all creation (cf Col 1,15–20), and he alone, the supreme High Priest, can offer adequate worship to God the Father (cf Heb 9,11–14). It is "through him and with him and in him" that all honor and glory is rendered to the Father by men whom the Holy Spirit has drawn into unity. Our ideal upon earth must be to imitate the eternal liturgy of the heavenly Jerusalem, where the choirs of angels and men sing praise to the Father seated upon the throne and to the Lamb (cf Apoc 5,11–14).

The Role of Monks

While all men are obliged to join in the chorus of praise ascending to the heavenly Father, there are some whose state of life permits them to achieve a fuller share in it. Not all of the members of the Body have the same function: "The eye cannot say to the hand, 'I do not need thy help'; nor again the head to the feet, 'I have no need of you' " (1 Cor 12,21). Each member has his own particular contribution to make to the welfare of the whole Body. Some writers, elaborating on the metaphor of St. Paul, have observed that monks are the lips of the Mystical Body, entrusted with the duty of praise.

Every metaphor has its limitations, and this one should not be pressed so far as to pretend that praise is the only duty of monks, or that it is not also the duty of other members of the Body. Rightly understood, however, it conveys the truth that monks devote themselves in a special way to the adoration of God, speaking not only for themselves but for the whole Church.

From its very beginnings, monasticism has filled this role in the Church. The monastery is a symbol of the heavenly Jerusalem in which the divine liturgy is carried on ceaselessly. But it is a symbol that already contains the reality, though to an imperfect degree, for the praise which it offers to God is the worship of Christ and his members, which is radically the same glorification that is accomplished by the heavenly choirs. In ancient times some monasteries attempted a more perfect anticipation of the ceaseless adoration of heaven through the use of alternating choirs, so arranged that the choir service was always in progress. While this is no longer possible today, it has been observed that the combined efforts of all the monasteries around the globe result in an uninterrupted chorus of praise, the *laus perennis.*

The Monastic Ideal of Incessant Prayer

The ideal of the first monks was to carry on incessant prayer. Here again we see the radically evangelical orientation of primitive monasticism, for in their continuous prayer the monks saw a fulfillment of our Lord's recommendation to "pray always" (cf Lk 18,1), and of the precept of St. Paul, "pray without ceasing" (1 Thes 5,17). Incessant prayer was an imitation of the prayer of the primitive Christian community (cf Acts 12,5). At the same time, it was thought to be a return to the blessed state of Adam in paradise before the fall, when he was on intimate terms with God and continually mindful of the divine presence.

The anchorite's ideal was a renunciation of the world so complete that all thought of the world and its cares would be totally banished from his mind, leaving him free to fill his mind and heart with God alone. In order to maintain this continual remembrance of God even during the few occupations which were necessary in their simple life, the anchorites recited psalms or mediated upon passages of Scripture throughout the day. Fixed hours of prayer during the day and also by night served to concentrate their attention even more upon an uninterrupted communication with God.

The prayer with which the monks occupied themselves did not consist solely of praise. While this is the principal element of prayer, other types are rightly distinguished. Thanksgiving is closely related to the prayer of adoration, for it glorifies God on account of his many benefactions. The prayer of compunction glorifies God for the mercy which he continues to show despite repeated human infidelities. The prayer of petition begs his continuing aid to sustain his children in the spiritual and corporal necessities of life. Far from being purely selfish, it glorifies God by giving expression to man's dependence upon him. All these types of prayer have this in common, that they are a form of dialogue with God. Through the Word of his revelation he has spoken to man. Through the word of his prayer man replies.

The Monk as a Man of Prayer

The monk is pre-eminently a man of God, a charismatic who constantly strives to be filled with the presence of God and to maintain constant intercourse with him. He is consequently a man of prayer, for prayer is nothing other than communication, dialogue, with God. Clement of Alexandria, from whom the early theorists of monasticism partially derived their doctrine on prayer, defined it as "conversation with God." "Though whispering and not opening the lips we speak in silence, yet we cry out inwardly. For God continually hears our inward conversation" (*Stromata* 7,39,6).

Prayer, therefore, is not a monologue, but a dialogue. The monk must first listen to God before he can speak to him. His own words are only a reply to the Word which God has first addressed to him. Furthermore, God himself enables the monk to pray, for it is the divine Spirit within him who moves him to prayer: "The Spirit also helps our weakness. For we do not know what we should pray for as we ought, but the Spirit himself pleads for us with unutterable groanings. And he who searches the hearts knows what the Spirit desires, that he pleads for the saints according to God" (Rom 8, 26–27).

The exercise of prayer has therefore a Trinitarian significance. Christ, who is the Word par excellence which the Father has addressed to us, is also the Mediator and High Priest who brings our prayer before the Father. And our prayer is in reality the voice of the Spirit speaking within us, expressing our sentiments of love and obedience to the Father's will. The three divine Persons are therefore involved in the prayer of the monk: it is the supreme expression of his response to the initiative which God has taken on his behalf.

St. Benedict: Man of Prayer

St. Benedict himself represents the highest ideal of the monk as a man of prayer. Just as St. Athanasius wrote his *Life of Anthony* to present a model of a life consecrated to the service of God, so St. Gregory wished to present St. Benedict as the ideal man of God, the incarnation of all the virtues which had hitherto been associated with the monastic state. Above all, he is the model of Christian prayer.

For three years the youthful Benedict in his cave at Subiaco shut himself off from all communication with men in order to enjoy uninterrupted intercourse with God. Through the practice of a rigorous asceticism, he achieved the state of *apatheia*, perfect purity of heart, the condition for the practice of "pure prayer." Gradually he began to communicate to those who came to visit him the fruits of his exalted contemplation of heavenly realities (cf *Dial* 2,2). As the father of a community, both at Subiaco and later at Monte Cassino, he was still the man of prayer par excellence.

The *Dialogues* represent St. Benedict at prayer so frequently that it seems he was always engaged in divine contemplation when free from community exercises and the government of the monastery. He prayed in his cell, completely absorbed in God and shedding tears of compunction. His intercession with God was so powerful that it resulted in the gift of miracles (*Dial* 2, 1.6.7.21.26.27.28.29. 31.38), even the raising of the dead to life (*Dial* 2, 11.32). His intimacy with God was so great that he enjoyed the gift of foreknowledge (*Dial* 2, 5.8.15.17.37) and of reading the thoughts of others (*Dial* 2, 3.12.13.14.18.19.20). The power of his prayer, like that of the Egyptian solitaries, repeatedly overcame the devil (*Dial* 2, 4.8.9.10.11.16.30). The heights of contemplation to which he attained are best expressed in the great vision in which he saw the entire universe gathered up in a single ray of light (*Dial* 2, 35), a vision which acquired great importance in later theological discussion of the gift of contemplation.

Place of Prayer in the Holy Rule

Devoted to prayer himself, St. Benedict wished that his monks should also become men of prayer. The amount of space devoted to prayer in the *Rule,* while considerable, is nevertheless not a sufficient indication of the importance which St. Benedict attributed to it in the lives of his monks, for in this respect he was quite in line with the traditions of eastern monasticism. The distinctions which are made in modern times between common and private prayer, and between vocal and mental prayer, were entirely unknown to him. For St. Benedict, as for the entire preceding tradition, these types of prayer were not to be separated and opposed to one another, but unified in a single movement of the soul toward God.

Quantitatively speaking, the *Rule* accords more space to the detailed arrangement of the divine office than to what we would call private prayer. That this does not signify any lack of esteem for the latter is evident from the brief but pertinent statements of chapters 20 and 52. Nor is there the slightest suggestion that the praying of the divine office was to be merely a formal and official exercise which could dispense with the qualities of true prayer. On the contrary, chapter 19 explicitly points out that the divine office is a participation in the liturgy of the heavenly Jerusalem, carried on "in the presence of God and his angels" (19,6), and that it must proceed from the heart, in such a fashion "that mind and voice may be in harmony" (19,7).

Chapter 20, which treats of reverence at prayer, lays down the basic qualities of authentic prayer. We see here that the prayer of the individual monk, whether alone or in community, forms an indissoluble unity with the divine office, for it is both the necessary preparation for the office and the fervent prolongation of it. The monk's prayer, both in the psalms and in his private efforts, is the praise of a devoted child who fears and loves his Father.

St. Benedict is more concerned with the basic dispositions than with laying down any hard and fast rules about how to pray. The prayer of cenobites, who are merely on the way to a perfection which can be achieved only in the solitary life, is less perfect than that of the anchorites. Hence St. Benedict wishes to lay the foundations rather than to discourse upon the heights of mystical prayer. Yet his foundations are such as to open the door to the ascent to the highest degree of union with God.

Qualities of Prayer

The characteristics of prayer which St. Benedict enumerates are those which we can observe in his own prayer. The first is humility: if we do not presume to approach men of high rank without showing respect for their station, a fortiori our approach to God should reflect our consciousness of our own nothingness in his presence. We have seen the close connection between humility and compunction: a true sense of humility will produce tears of compunction.

Since the spontaneous movement of the soul cannot long be sustained by those who are not yet far advanced in the way of prayer, it should ordinarily be short, "unless . . . prolonged by the impulse and inspiration of divine grace" (20,4). Short but frequent prayer is better than prolonged periods in which the soul cannot sustain its attention. This rule applies especially to those prayers which were said in common, probably intercalated in the divine office, as have recently been restored to the liturgy.

Above all, prayer should be pure. Pure prayer is the work of a pure heart, one which the asceticism of the *vita activa* has liberated from attachments to the world, from passion, from the power of the devil to entice into sin. The further the monk has advanced in renunciation, the purer his prayer will be. A pure heart is capable of abandoning itself to God without restriction, of fixing its gaze uninterruptedly upon God and adoring him in silence and love. This is the prayer of the monk who has climbed the ladder of humility and now acts no longer from fear but from love of Christ (cf 7,69), who, with heart enlarged, runs "with unspeakable sweetness of love in the way of God's commandments" (cf Prol 49). His contact with God is personal and intimate; it has become natural for him to cry "Abba! Father!" with simplicity and spontaneity.

Lectio Divina *and* Opus Dei

The prayer of the monk, then, is to be spontaneous and free, the loving approach of a son to his Father, unencumbered by details of method which might serve more to focus attention upon his own psychological state than to direct the soul toward its object, the divine Partner in the dialogue. St. Benedict did not prescribe any particular method of prayer, because for him the life of prayer was a unified whole. His monks had a living liturgy and a living *lectio divina*, and the entire life of prayer flowed spontaneously from these two sources. If excessive attention has been paid to method in modern times, it is largely because these sources of prayer have ceased to be functional.

The *opus Dei* and the *lectio divina* are, indeed, the two poles between which the prayer of the monk must be situated. Prayer, we have said, is dialogue with God. If it is to be nourished at its source, then the monk must listen to God's voice. This he does in the *lectio divina*, whether in those parts of the liturgy where the Word of God is proclaimed in the context of the Church's life or in the privacy of his cell. His response to that Word is contained in the *opus Dei*, where, together with all the members of Christ's Body, he joins the Head in praising the Father with the words which the Holy Spirit places in his heart and in his mouth. His personal efforts outside of these exercises will be a hearkening to the Word of God and a prolongation of the prayer of the psalms. It remains for us, then, to speak of the *lectio divina*, of the *opus Dei* and of the prayer of contemplation.

2. LECTIO DIVINA

The Word of God to the Chosen People

Lectio divina is the assimilation of the Word of God through reading. God's Word has been proclaimed to us in the Sacred Scriptures, which recount the history of God's intervention in human affairs. Our hearkening to his Word, however, cannot be conceived of outside the living context of the Church which he has provided for it. This is not an artificial context, the fruit of later speculation. On the contrary, the Word of God was given to mankind in the context of the people of God, which was gathered together precisely to receive it.

In the great deliverance of the exodus, God formed a people for himself through Moses, to listen to his Word proclaimed from the heights of Sinai and to accept the covenant which he offered to them. The people's response to this Word of God was to hearken, to accept it, to assimilate it vitally as the charter of their common purpose and the norm which should govern their lives, to offer sacrifice symbolic of the offering of themselves. The Word of God was proclaimed again, after the entry into the promised land, each time the covenant was renewed, in a ceremony which was probably performed annually during the period of the tribal confederacy.

In a later period of their history, the chosen people continued the proclamation of God's Word in their synagogue service. They read and reread the law and the teaching of their prophets, who had been new instruments of God's revelation, speaking in his name and making known his Word. In these public liturgical readings, the Jews drew forth the treasures of the Scriptures, perceiving their moral significance and its demands upon their lives, looking forward to the eschatological times when the final fulfillment of God's promises would be achieved.

The Written Word of God

The early Christians were no less conscious than their Jewish ancestors of the primacy of God's Word in their lives. It was proclaimed again, and pre-eminently, in the teaching of Jesus, the Messiah sent to them from the Father, then in the living instruction of the apostles. They were conscious of being the new people of God, gathered together around the long-awaited Messiah, vivified as a community by the Holy Spirit who dwelt in them, the fulfillment of God's promises from of old. The whole of revelation was meaningful to them, for it was in them that this entire succession of living experiences came to a climax. God had intervened once again, and this time definitively: it was for them to hearken to his voice and now, in the end-time, assimilate his Word into their lives.

When the first generation of Christians had passed on and the voice of revelation was stilled, the written Word of God assumed a new prominence. Revelation was complete and could no longer be added to; but God's Word had been recorded by inspired writers and could be proclaimed again and again. In their liturgical assemblies, the early Christians read the law, the prophets and the writings of the old covenant as the record of the experiences of the people of God and the prefiguration of what had now been accomplished in them. Christ's proclamation of the divine Word was prepetuated in the reading of the Gospels; the teaching of the apostles in the reading of the apostolic writings. The Roman Mass seems originally to have had three readings in the liturgy of the Word: one from the Old Testament, one from the apostolic writings (still called an "apostle" in the Eastern Church) and one from the Gospels.

Although God's Word was now preserved in written form, it was not forgotten that it had originally been an oral communication, made to the entire people of God by men chosen to be his mouthpiece. The reading of God's Word, therefore, could not be envisaged outside the context of the life of the Church, the new people of God. In the liturgy of the community, it served as a reproclamation of the divine Word to the redeemed people gathered together to offer the response of their worship. Thus the liturgy of the Word, in which God addresses his people, is the prelude to the sacrifice, in which that people offers itself to him.

The Word of God in the Liturgy

Among the early Latin Fathers, the term *lectio divina* primarily means this liturgical proclamation of the Word of God contained in the Scriptures. Since, with few exceptions, nothing other than the Bible was read in the liturgy, the term *lectio divina* became a technical designation of the Bible itself. In fulfillment of St. Paul's command (1 Tim 4,13), it was the task of the clergy to proclaim the Scriptures to the faithful in the liturgical assembly, as a herald proclaims the decrees of his sovereign.

The spoken word has a special effectiveness. Even now, we prefer to hear our president address the nation over radio or television rather than simply to read his speech in tomorrow's newspaper. But we have lost the significance of the vocal proclamation of God's Word in church, since the liturgical language has for many centuries been incomprehensible to the people. The introduction of the vernacular should help to re-establish the contact of the faithful with the continuity of God's pronouncements through the Church.

In the early Church the voice of God addressing his people was still a living reality. When God spoke, man was silent and listened. In the Church he continued to speak through divinely appointed representatives, as he had done throughout the entire history of the people of God. The lector in church is the mouthpiece of God, just as the prophets were for the chosen people, and the apostles for the Christians of the first generation. We have already noted the tremendous impact which was made upon the early monks by the proclamation of the Gospel in the liturgy. The words of Christ which they heard there they took to be addressed to them personally; and upon his command, they sold all that they had, gave the proceeds to the poor, and withdrew to the desert to follow him literally.

The Monks and the Divine Word

It was natural, then, that the monks should continue the exercise of the reading of the Scriptures which lay at the root of their vocation. On Sundays and feast days the solitaries assembled at the church to hear the solemn proclamation of the divine Word. In the quiet of their cells they continued to read the Scriptures, to reflect upon them, to assimilate the Word of God which associated them with the sacred history of his people. Those who were unable to read memorized the Scriptures so that they could recall the sacred text to mind to meditate upon it: we hear of some who committed to memory the entire Bible.

Their reading was simply the prolongation of the liturgical proclamation of the divine Word. They had few books; the *lectio divina* was almost entirely restricted to the reading of the Scriptures. They looked upon themselves as the continuation of the lives of the prophets, the apostles and the martyrs; hence the reading of the prophetic and apostolic writings assumed an unparalleled significance and actuality for them. They were to experience in their own lives all the stages of the sacred history recounted in the record of God's dealings with his chosen people.

Furthermore, their reading of the Scriptures remained basically an audible reading. The liturgical proclamation of the Bible was the standard to such an extent that it influenced even the private reading of the Scriptures. This oral character of monastic *lectio divina* can still be discerned in the *Holy Rule*, where public reading is prescribed in the refectory (38,1) and before Compline (42,3). The tools of good works do not prescribe that the monk be anxious to read to himself, but rather that he "*listen* gladly to holy reading" (4,55). The principal subject matter of this reading was the Bible, other works being admitted only insofar as they were considered to be commentaries upon Scripture (48,15; 73,3–6). Hence the great responsibility of the reader, who has a quasi-liturgical function: he is not to perform this function unless he is truly capable (38,12; 47,3); he is to receive a liturgical blessing to preserve him from the spirit of pride (38,2); he is to be given the closest attention in perfect silence, out of reverence for the Word of God (38,5).

Lectio Divina *and* Meditatio

The monks of the Middle Ages had a profound understanding of the importance of the *lectio divina* in their lives. Throughout this period, as in antiquity, the concept of audible reading was maintained. Private reading was done aloud, at least by moving the lips and pronouncing the words to oneself, so as to fix them in the mind. St. Benedict presupposes this when he prescribes that during the siesta anyone who wants to read rather than rest should do so in such a way as not to disturb anyone else (48,5). In this case, by way of exception, reading was not to be done aloud.

The term *meditatio* in the writings of St. Benedict and the medieval authors denotes an analogous exercise, which is the complement of reading. *Meditatio* is the principal exercise of the novices (58, 5) and is performed in association with the *lectio divina* (48,23). It added something more to the exercise of reading: an intense reflection upon the text directed principally toward practical application, and a memorization of the text to imprint it firmly upon the mind so that it could be recalled later. Memorization of scriptural passages, especially the psalms, accounts for the remarkable facility of ancient writers to form mosaics of scriptural passages in their works. They did not conceive of meditation as a separate exercise, a reflection in the abstract upon ideas, as is done today; it always had its basis in a text, which was the Word of God. St. Benedict clearly equates the exercise of *meditatio* with the memorization of texts, when he prescribes that those who still have a part of the psalter or the lessons to learn should devote the time remaining after vigils to *meditatio* (8,3).

Lectio Divina *and* Opus Dei

For St. Benedict the *lectio divina,* combined with *meditatio,* is one of the principal exercises of the monastic life. The hours of the day not devoted to work were divided between *lectio* and the *opus Dei* in such a fashion that, on the average, about four hours a day were assigned to *lectio.* It was a spiritual exercise, for, as we have seen, its purpose was to imprint the divine Word upon the mind and heart of the monk.

This means that it was not intended to serve merely as an intellectual stimulant; it is distinct from study in the modern sense. It required an intense intellectual activity, but involved the other faculties as well: the will especially, but also the physical faculties. It was the whole man who engaged in reading, and its purpose was the proper formation of the whole man. It provided the nourishment necessary for the interior life to grow and develop, and kept alive an enthusiasm for spiritual advancement.

Lectio is the indispensable preparation for the *opus Dei,* and at the same time its prolongation. Through reading the monk receives the Word of God and accepts it into his heart; in the psalmody he replies to God's Word with his own personal response, phrased in the words of Scripture which the Holy Spirit stirs up in his heart. But the two exercises are not mutually exclusive. Each in a sense includes the other, so that the monk's life is a continual passage from *lectio* to *opus Dei* and back again. *Lectio* is included in the *opus Dei* in the lessons of vigils and the short readings from Scripture at the other hours; and prayer spontaneously issues forth in the course of reading. Thus there is created a marvelous unity in the monk's whole interior life.

The Purpose of Reading

How, then, should a monk approach the reading of the Bible? In this respect he can scarcely do better than to imitate the practice of the monks of antiquity and the Middle Ages. Rather than considering his "spiritual reading" as merely one of the many exercises into which the monastic day is divided, the monk should regard a vital contact with the Word of God as the principal food of his soul and the unifying principle of his interior life. If performed in this spirit, it can lead him to an authentic prayer life and reduce all of his striving for perfection to a unity focused upon essentials.

To begin with, his reading must be intelligent. The ancients regarded the literal, historical sense of the Bible as the indispensable foundation. The monk must know what the text itself means and not despise even the "dry bones" of biblical criticism, for the edifice of his spiritual life must be built on a solid foundation, lest it degenerate into purely subjective reverie. In this regard we are better off than the ancients, for the achievements of modern biblical scholarship have immensely widened our knowledge and brought an understanding of the Bible down to the level of the faithful in general. But the Bible itself must receive the primary emphasis, rather than books about the Bible: it is only by reading and rereading the sacred text again and again that one can hope to gain that familiarity with it which is essential to developing a biblical mentality.

The monk's reading, however, must not stop with the acquisition of knowledge. The Bible's value for him is not only in what he learns from it, but rather in what it makes him become. The truth has been revealed not for speculative knowledge, but for life. The purpose of reading must be existential. The letter must lead us to the spirit. Therefore it is essential that the monk enter into it with the proper dispositions. His ascetic life disposes him for the reception of God's Word, which can mean little to the carnal man. Humility and generosity are required in order to penetrate the spiritual meaning of the Scriptures.

Lectio: *A Personal and Interior Message*

Reading properly performed should bring the monk to an understanding and an appreciation of the unity of revelation. He should see in the Bible the total history of God's relationships with mankind, culminating in Christ. Everything in sacred history is an aspect of the mystery of Christ. In the history of Israel, the history of Christ and the history of the Church, the monk must see the great themes which run throughout the story of salvation: the election and formation of the people of God, the exodus, the desert, the promised land, the Messianic King, Jerusalem the city of the elect, the dwelling of God among men.

It is not enough, however, to view this sacred history as from afar: the monk must identify himself with it, reliving the experiences of God's people, adapting himself to what is written. There is so much variety in the Bible that everyone can find something especially suited to his needs. He must not approach it passively, but must actively participate in what he reads, realizing it vitally in himself. For this reason the *lectio divina* is an exercise of intense spiritual activity. One cannot remain indifferent before the Bible; one must take sides, placing oneself within the context of the sacred history.

This means that the *lectio divina* is an intensely personal activity: the Bible is a message intended for all God's people, but each individual must perceive its special application to him. It is a mirror in which he strives to see his own reflection, and if his image is distorted or out of conformity with the norm that he finds there, then he must revise it to bring it into harmony with objective truth. The Word of God must be individualized and interiorized by every reader. His reading must tend to become a dialogue: he must not only listen to the divine voice, but also respond to it.

A Method of Reading Based on the Liturgy

Profiting from the reading of the Bible is not merely a question of absorbing truths and moral principles, but of evoking an atmosphere. The result of the *lectio divina* properly performed is a biblical mentality. The categories and images of the Scriptures become a part of the psychological outlook of the reader; the Bible becomes so much a part of him that he unconsciously thinks in its terms. It is this mentality which we find in St. Benedict and in his followers during the Middle Ages, who had completely absorbed the psychology of the Word of God into their lives, were totally formed by it, and made of their whole lives an actualization of sacred history.

If the monk is to achieve this goal, he must read and meditate upon the Bible continually. At this point we come back again to the liturgical proclamation of the Word of God, for it is the liturgy which teaches the method to be followed. In the divine office the Church proclaims the Word of God to us incessantly in the *lectio continua* of the Scriptures. The abbreviated lessons in the present breviary are a remnant of the reading of the whole Bible which formerly was comprised in an annual cycle. The Church reads the Bible throughout the year, arranging the various parts of the Scripture to correspond to the liturgical seasons.

The monk may profitably follow this same practice in his private reading, thus completing the truncated lessons of the modern breviary. He will thus live in the spirit of the Church and penetrate ever more deeply into the mystery of Christ. No hard and fast schedule need be followed in the choice of reading, but no part of the Bible should be neglected, for everything in it fits into the unity of revelation. One may at times concentrate on a single book or group of books, or one may follow a particular theme throughout revelation. It is important both to assimilate the various parts and at the same time to acquire a view of the unity of the whole.

The liturgy also teaches us how to assimilate these texts and to proceed from them naturally into prayer. The scriptural readings in the liturgy are combined so as to trace a theme throughout the Bible, showing both prophecy and fulfillment. They are followed by responsorial chants, which are a meditation upon the lessons. Then comes the silent prayer of all the worshipers, followed by a public prayer in which the priest, speaking in the name of all, sums up the sentiments of the congregation. Similarly, private reading should also provoke the response of prayer.

Broader Concept of Lectio Divina

So far we have spoken only of the reading of the Sacred Scriptures, which is the original sense of the *lectio divina.* The meaning of the term gradually evolved to include other works as well. This was already true in the time of the Fathers and the early monks, and is clearly indicated in the *Holy Rule.* In modern times "spiritual reading" is taken to mean any edifying reading that can contribute something to the spiritual life.

In antiquity, however, other works were never conceived of as constituting a category separate from the Bible. The works of the Fathers were primarily commentaries upon Holy Scripture. Everything that they wrote was intended merely to illustrate and explain the Word of God. God continued to speak through them as he had through the inspired writers of the Old and New Testaments.

We must distinguish properly scriptural inspiration from this inspiration in the broad sense, but in antiquity there was a persistent conviction that the Fathers were the mouthpiece of God. An eloquent witness to this view is the legend that St. Gregory's works were dictated by the Holy Spirit, sitting on his shoulder in the form of a dove. The *Holy Rule,* too, was considered to be, in a sense, an inspired document. If the purpose of the *lectio divina* was to listen to the voice of God speaking through the *voces paginarum,* then whatever medium he used for his communications was inseparable from the Word of God par excellence contained in the Scriptures.

The Fathers and Monastic Writings

St. Benedict states clearly what he considers suitable material for the *lectio divina* in addition to the Sacred Scriptures. First come the works of the Fathers, which serve as explanations of the Bible, and are "manifestly devoted to teaching us the straight road to our Creator" (73,4). Next in importance is the monastic literature, which exposes the principles of monastic life. Explicitly mentioned are the principal works in this category: the *Conferences* and *Institutes* of Cassian; the *Vitae Patrum,* which included lives of the early anchorites, the *Historia Monachorum in Aegypto,* long attributed to Rufinus, and various collections of sayings of the desert Fathers; and the *Rule* of St. Basil. St. Benedict says that these works are "tools of virtue for good-living and obedient monks" (73,6).

We know from the *Rule* that St. Benedict himself was well versed in all this literature as well as in the Scriptures. A glance at a table of sources and parallel passages in a critical edition of the *Rule* will show the extent of his familiarity with the Fathers and the monastic writings. He draws the most from Cassian, then from the Latin Fathers, especially Augustine, Jerome, Ambrose, Cyprian and Leo the Great. There is little that suggests an acquaintance with the Greek Fathers, which he could have known only in translation.

He drew extensively, however, upon the monastic literature of the East, which had already been translated into Latin: the *Verba Seniorum,* the lives of the Fathers and histories of the Egyptian monks, the rules of Pseudo Macarius, Pachomius and Basil. The sources of the *Rule* doubtless do not show the full extent of his learning, but they reveal that it was entirely biblical and patristic in character, and of a type which was acquired not by frequenting schools but by a long practice of the *lectio divina.* It is not unlikely, however, that St. Benedict's knowledge of the Fathers was partially derived from secondary sources rather than from a direct acquaintance with their works, since the monastic writers of this period freely made use of citations that were already current in the monastic literature.

Other Sources for Reading

In our own day, the materials prescribed by the *Rule* must remain the principal object of the monk's *lectio divina.* Monastic life cannot remain true to its origins unless it is nourished at the authentic sources of its spirituality. The individual monk cannot acquire an understanding and appreciation of his vocation unless he enters into the mentality of the Bible and the Fathers and seeks knowledge and inspiration in the monastic theorists to whom St. Benedict himself was so much indebted.

Evidently this does not mean that later works cannot be of value for the *lectio divina.* If St. Benedict were living today, his list of recommended readings would no doubt be much longer. Since his time the libraries of monasteries have been enriched with countless works from the pens of spiritual writers, Benedictine saints and commentators on the *Rule,* whose work can be of immense value in leading the monk toward the perfection of the interior life. These should not be neglected, for they can help the monk to penetrate more deeply into the inexhaustible riches of the Word of God.

The monastic literature of the Middle Ages provides especially fruitful material for the *lectio divina.* At that time it was still a living exercise, in close connection with the *opus Dei* and enjoying the unity of a life entirely centered upon God. The literature of the period is itself a product of the *lectio divina,* and manifests the degree of authentic religious experience that the monks acquired through this exercise.

Value and Use of Modern Works

In modern times literature on the spiritual life, as in every other field, has multiplied to an almost unbelievable extent. This is not entirely an unmixed blessing. It is possible to lose one's orientation in the maze of books available, and what is gained in breadth may be lost in depth. Techniques of speed-reading which have been introduced to meet the problem of quantity, while of undoubted usefulness for certain types of reading, are not applicable to the *lectio divina,* which of its nature must be meditative. Because the ancients had few books, they prized more what they had, rejected a superficial approach and went straight to essentials.

Nevertheless, for the monk who is discerning, the abundance of literature available today can be an advantage. Our own times, which have rediscovered the value of a return to sources, have brought about a tremendous progress in biblical, patristic, liturgical and monastic studies. The modern monk has at his disposal the tools for penetrating more deeply into the inexhaustible riches of the Word of God.

A wise use of the excellent books produced by the modern biblical movement can help to a better understanding of the Sacred Scriptures. Modern translations of the Fathers are available equipped with introductions and notes which help to clarify the text. The liturgical movement has produced an abundance of literature explaining the liturgical texts and their theological significance for the Christian life. The renewal of monastic studies has clarified the nature of monasticism and its role in the Church, has provided modern editions of the classics of monastic spirituality, and is producing many other works which can assist the monk to a deeper appreciation of his vocation.

Lectio Divina: *Way to Prayer*

All of these works can provide a valuable supplement to the Bible and the Fathers for the *lectio divina*. But they must be used discerningly. The *lectio divina* must be maintained as an exercise distinct from study; its purpose is not merely the formation of the intellect, but the formation of the whole man: to teach one how to live. The monk must bear in mind that it is essentially the proclamation of the Word of God in the Church, and that its effect must be the deeper penetration of God's Word into his mind and his heart. Then he will be able to maintain a hierarchy of values in his reading and reject what is merely superficial and destined to satisfy curiosity. Anything that has real value need not be spurned, but its value must be seen in relation to the Word of God to which it remains subordinate by way of commentary.

He must be careful, too, to see that his *lectio divina* does not degenerate into just one spiritual exercise among many. It must be an integral and vital part of the totality of his monastic life, closely associated with his participation in the *opus Dei* and with his personal prayer. Fidelity to the *lectio divina* is an indispensable condition for progress in the interior life. A day must not be allowed to pass in which the monk does not nourish himself at the sources of his spirituality. Along with the *opus Dei,* it is an essential activity of monastic life, and no other practice can substitute for it. It must be done in an atmosphere of leisure and in a spirit of humility and prayerfulness. If properly performed, it will tend to convert itself into prayer. The activity of the *lectio divina* is perhaps best summed up in a medieval saying which has been brought to light by Dom Jean Leclercq: *Legendo oro, orando contemplor.*

3. OPUS DEI

Meaning of the Term Opus Dei

We have already spoken sufficiently of prayer in general and of the place of the liturgy in monastic life. It is not our intention to repeat these observations here, but only to emphasize the specific importance of the *opus Dei* for the monk.

The term *opus Dei* occurs already in the oriental monastic writings, but is used in a very general sense. It signifies the totality of the monk's spiritual exercises and his ascetical life. It is to be understood as an objective genitive, the monk's "work for God," and has the connotation of something requiring effort and exertion. The entire life of the monk is work; he exerts himself as a slave in the service of the Lord. All the exercises of the monastic life are a service of God. The ancient monastic literature often referred this concept to the expression *opus Domini* which appears in the Latin version of Jeremiah: "Cursed be he who does the Lord's work remissly" (Jer 48,10), thus encouraging the monk to persevere in the fulfillment of his divine service (cf Cassian, *Inst* 4,33; *Conf* 21,22).

The term, however, can also be taken as a subjective genitive, and

St. Benedict probably included this sense in his understanding of it. Whatever the monk does is not so much his own accomplishment as that of God working within him. This meaning became clearer when the term was applied exclusively to the common prayer service of the cenobite. It appears in this sense already in the *Vitae Patrum* and is thus commonly used by Caesarius of Arles and other writers who were influenced by the monastic movement of Lerins. St. Benedict uses it fifteen times in the *Rule*, always to signify the divine office. The office is the monk's "work for God" insofar as it is the principal activity of the monastic program in the service of God; but it is also "God's work" in the monk, for it is the Holy Spirit who stirs up in his heart the words of praise which he addresses to God in the divine office.

The Opus Dei *in the* Holy Rule

The importance which St. Benedict attributes to the *opus Dei* can be seen not only from the amount of space which he devotes to it in the *Rule* (chapters 8–19) but also from the place of pre-eminence which he assigns to it among all the activities of the monk. He refers to it also as *opus divinum* (19,2), *officium divinum* (43,1), *servitutis officia* (16,2), *servitius pensum* (50,4). These latter terms recall the idea of the ancients that the monk's prayer is a work for God, the proper fulfillment of which requires the maximum of his attention and effort. St. Benedict's esteem for the divine office is summed up in his well-known phrase: *Nihil operi Dei praeponatur* (43,3). It is significant that on the only other occasions when he uses a similar expression, its object is Christ: to prefer nothing to the love of Christ (4,21); those who hold nothing dearer to them than Christ (5,2); let them prefer nothing whatever to Christ (72,11).

The monks must show eagerness for the performance of the divine office. "As soon as the signal for the divine office has been heard, let them abandon what they have in hand and assemble with the greatest speed, yet soberly, so that no occasion be given for levity" (43,1–2). Those who come late must make public satisfaction for their fault (43,4–12). When they awaken for the night office they should hasten to be among the first to arrive in choir (22,6). They are even allowed to break the night silence in order to encourage the sleepy ones to rise for the work of God (22,8). When they are working in the fields far from the oratory, or are on a journey, they are nevertheless to stop where they are and perform the divine office at the proper time (50,1–4).

This zeal for the work of God is one of the principal factors in determining whether a novice really has a vocation to monastic life (58,7). Prayer is the culmination of all the exercises of monastic life, and one who shows little aptitude for it can scarcely be considered to have a monastic vocation. A monk's zeal for the *opus Dei* will impel him to prepare himself well for this supreme work and to make the effort to perform it as well as he can: St. Benedict insists that no one should be permitted to sing or read in choir unless he can do so in such a way as to edify (47,3). The greatest punishment that can be imposed upon a monk is to deprive him of participation in this supreme act of the community (25,1). Thus he is effectively cut off from the spiritual life of the community and from one of the primary sources of his sanctification.

Official Prayer of the Church

The importance of the divine office in the life of monks should not, however, be exaggerated. In later times the characterization, *propter chorum fundati*, was sometimes applied to monks. Originally this phrase referred to the canons, who were deputed by the Church to assure the choir service in a particular church. There was in the Middle Ages a reciprocal influence of monks on canons and vice versa, with the result that the proper finality of the two became confused.

The ritual performance of the *opus Dei* cannot be considered the end of monastic life; even for the canons, it can only be a secondary end of the community. The end of the monk is to seek God; his praying of the divine office is a means to this end. The actual exterior performance of the office does not acquit him of his duty, for he is also obliged to take part in it interiorly. The purpose of the office is not automatically achieved by the very fact that it is performed according to the directives of the Church. It must be a human act, and must influence the life of the monk if it is to be an effective means to the attainment of his end.

To say that the office is the official prayer of the Church, therefore, does not mean that the mere external performance of it guarantees its efficacy. It means rather that its efficacy proceeds *ex opere operantis Ecclesiae*, that it is the common prayer of the members of the Mystical Body together with their Head, and the type which the Church recommends as the model of all prayer. But each individual who takes part in it must make this common prayer his own.

Deputation of Monks to Perform Opus Dei

In theory this official prayer of the Church ought to be one in which all the members of the Church are able to join, not only ideally, but actually. In the beginning it was such a prayer of the people, but the effect of a long and complex development of the liturgy has been to make it impossible for the majority of Christians to take an active part in it in practice. As a minimum, the Church now requires that clerics in major orders and religious in solemn vows assure the daily performance of the divine office, but this obligation can now be fulfilled by private recitation. The public performance of the *opus Dei* is now generally restricted to monks, nuns and chapters of canons.

Monks, however, are not deputed by the Church to the performance of the divine office in the same sense as the clergy. Originally the office was the prayer of all the faithful, and the clerics were deputed by the Church to conduct it for their communities. From the very beginning it was the function of the priests and other ministers to preside at the common public prayer of Christians. The monks, on the other hand, were laymen without any such ecclesiastical commission. The solitaries prayed privately and sought to pray incessantly. When they began to pray in common, they gradually developed fixed hours of prayer and some fixed formulae. But this prayer, while common, was not strictly liturgical; it was not the official prayer of the Church, but the private creation of a charismatic movement.

Later the monastic office was largely taken over by the Church and was itself influenced by the practices of the clergy and faithful, so that the two currents were fused. The distinction between monks and clergy in regard to the office was further obscured by the adoption of the custom of raising monks to the priesthood. Today the distinction between the monastic and clerical states is not generally perceived by the faithful. Canon law has further assimilated monks to solemnly professed religious. Consequently, from a legal viewpoint, as priests and as solemnly professed religious, they are deputed by the Church to perform the divine office; but insofar as they are monks, their *opus Dei* is rather the common expression of the prayer life of a group of charismatics.

Origins of the Office

The early development of the divine office was very complex, and historians of the liturgy have scarcely begun to solve the intricate problems connected with it. We are certain that there were two traditions, the one cathedral and the other monastic. The first was especially concerned with prayer in the morning and the evening, which eventually became our hours of Lauds and Vespers. These were perhaps influenced by the Jewish service of praise in the morning and the evening, both in the temple and in the synagogue.

The monastic practice consisted of the recitation of the Psalter, especially in the evening and during the hours of the night. To this was added readings from the Scriptures, a practice which later grew into the *lectio continua* of the Bible. In the early Church a vigil service had been held on Saturday night, in preparation for the celebration of the Eucharist on Sunday, and especially during the night preceding Easter. While this developed into the liturgy of the Word, the monks separated the vigil from the Eucharist and celebrated it every night. The number of twelve psalms was fixed by the Pachomian tradition and retained by St. Benedict.

The little hours are of monastic origin. As private prayers, they perhaps go back to apostolic times. The monks, who were, as always, conscious of continuing the biblical traditions, seem to have made common prayers of these hours already in the fourth century. Compline was introduced in the East sometime during the fourth century. Prime did not appear until the beginning of the sixth century and originated in the West, probably in the circle of Lerins. St. Benedict adopted it, but it did not become universal until several centuries later. This hour, which is to be totally suppressed in the forthcoming revision of the Roman office (*Constitution on the Sacred Liturgy* 89d), has recently been made optional for choral recitation in both the Roman and monastic offices, at the discretion of the superiors of each institute or congregation, and with the approval of the *Consilium* for the implementation of the *Constitution* (cf *Notitiae* 1 (1965) 272).

Distribution of the Hours

When the monks began to take part in the divine services of the basilicas, the two traditions were fused. In the West the monastic practice has left a strong imprint upon the organization of the office. By the time of St. Benedict all of the hours which we have at present were in use, because of his adoption of Prime: seven during the day, and vigils during the night. The monks saw in this a fulfillment of Ps 118,164: "Seven times a day I praise you for your just ordinances." St. Benedict applies this verse only to the day hours, and adds another text from Scripture for the justification of vigils: "At midnight I rise to give you thanks" (Ps 118, 62; cf *Rule* 16,1–4).

The monks saw in the distribution of the office throughout the day and night a fulfillment of the scriptural precept of continuous prayer. The hours of the office sanctify the different times of the day as they succeed one another, so that the soul is lifted to God in every circumstance of daily life. It is clear that the later practice of bunching hours together so as to get them out of the way can only serve to defeat the original purpose for which they were instituted. Modern liturgical reforms have succeeded to some degree in restoring to the hours of the office the functional meaning which they were originally intended to have in the sanctification of the day. An ideal monastic horarium will respect the character proper to each hour and will thus enable the monk to base his own incessant prayer upon the liturgical model through which he joins his brethren in sanctifying the successive times of day. Whether further reform is needed in the structure of the office is a question now under discussion.

The Symbolism of the Hours

The monks, who were prompted by a concern for biblical literalism, sought to find precedents in the Bible itself for each of the hours. Thus, for example, Lauds was related to the morning sacrifice of the Jews and to the morning prayer referred to in the psalms employed at this hour (Ps 5,4; 62,2.7); Terce to the prayer of the apostles assembled in the upper room when the Holy Spirit descended (Acts 2,15); Sext to the prayer of Peter upon the rooftop at Joppa (Acts 10,9); None to the prayer of Peter and John in the temple (Acts 3,1); Vespers to the evening sacrifice of the temple service (Ps 140,2) and to the Last Supper. Different monastic writers gave various interpretations of this symbolism of the hours (cf Cassian, *Inst* 3,3; Basil, *Longer Rules* 37). In the present office the symbolism of the hours is interpreted chiefly by the corresponding hymns.

Lauds and Vespers are the hours of praise, a glorification of God and of his wonderful works throughout the course of sacred history. Like the morning and evening service of the temple, they chiefly employ psalms of hymnic character: the *Laudate* psalms daily at Lauds, the psalms of the Hallel at Vespers. Lauds praises God chiefly for his work of creation, Vespers for his interventions in the history of his people.

The little hours mark the day off into periods and concentrate upon the character of the hour at which they are said. Terce marks a pause in the morning to recall the soul to the contemplation of God; Sext prays for strength in the combat at the heat of day; None is more restful, at the decline of day. These three hours are quite stereotyped so that they can easily be recited from memory. Prime, a preparation for the day's work, and Compline, a preparation for the night's rest, stress the needs of man more than the glory of God. The latter especially is introspective. Vigils is chiefly meditative, alternating between psalms and readings, as is fitting for the night time when it is said.

Difficulties of the Psalms

The principal element in the divine office is the psalmody. While in the East many ecclesiastical compositions have been introduced into the office, the Roman and western monastic liturgies are constructed almost exclusively from scriptural texts. This tradition goes back to the origins of monasticism, when the vigils of the monks alternated between the reading of the Word of God and the recitation of psalms. The incessant prayer of the monks consisted of the meditative recitation of the psalms, for they could hope to find no better prayers than those which the Holy Spirit had himself composed and given them for their use. Through the repeated use of the psalms they reached the heights of contemplative prayer.

The modern mind is inclined to find the psalms difficult. Aside from the initial difficulties of text and language, the novice who first begins to recite the psalms may feel that he simply does not understand what he is saying. He will feel that he has entered an entirely different world from that to which his previous prayers have accustomed him. The sentiments expressed will appear strange, the imagery and allusions products of a culture and mentality foreign to his habitual mode of thought and expression.

These difficulties can be resolved only if the monk undertakes a serious study of the psalms. Knowledge is indispensable, but it is not enough. His study must be more a question of acquiring a mentality, of learning to live in the religious world which produced the psalms. This can be effected only through persevering application to the *lectio divina*, whence appears once more the intimate connection between *lectio* and *opus Dei.* The psalms are a summary of the entire Bible: one cannot understand the summary unless he is thoroughly acquainted with the whole.

Study of the Literal Sense

Study is first of all required to understand the literal sense of the psalms, which is the indispensable foundation for their religious value. Modern progress in biblical studies has contributed enormously to the scientific understanding of the psalms and the place they occupied in the religious life of the chosen people. Excellent books are now available which put this information at the disposal of the beginner, unencumbered by the technicalities which often serve to discourage one who is not yet ready for them.

It is necessary first of all to acquire some clear ideas about the Psalter as a whole. One must understand the literary and poetic character of these religious works and their relationship to the concrete circumstances of the life of Israel. They must be replaced in the context of the liturgy of the temple, for which some of them were specifically composed and in which all of them were used.

The modern investigation of the psalms according to their literary types has facilitated this task. Exegetes have succeeded in classifying the psalms, though not yet with complete agreement, into such types as hymns, individual and national thanksgiving psalms, individual and national psalms of supplication, royal psalms, pilgrimage psalms, psalms of congratulation, sapiential psalms, and other minor categories. Their study according to these groupings enables us to discover the origin and life-situation of these religious poems.

Religious Value of the Psalms

This is, however, only a first step, which remains upon the level of literary criticism. Once it is accomplished, one must advance further and penetrate into the theology of the psalms. The ancients saw in the Psalter a summary of the entire Old Testament. Prayer is the finest expression of the religious beliefs of a people, and in the Psalter we find occurring again and again the great themes of sacred history, both of God's past interventions on behalf of his people and of their expectations of a glorious future.

The study of these themes necessitates a classification of the psalms according to their content rather than according to their literary form. It also involves the relationships between the psalms and the rest of the Bible, for these themes run like a thread through the whole of sacred history. Obscure at the beginning, they are gradually developed through progressive revelation and the increasing consciousness of the sacred writers, until they find their fulfillment in the New Testament.

This means that the psalms are not only a witness to the religious history of the past, but also a prophecy of the future, a prophecy of Christ, of the Church, and of all the mysteries of salvation which have now been realized. The Fathers saw Christ everywhere in the psalms: for them the value of the Psalter was principally prophetic. In this they were only following the example of Christ himself, who told the disciples on the road to Emmaus: "All things must be fulfilled that are written in the Law of Moses and the Prophets and the Psalms concerning me" (Lk 24,44). He explained the Scriptures to them as prophecies of himself, and the apostles followed his example, frequently citing the psalms in the primitive catechesis as examples of realized prophecy.

Use of the Psalms as Christian Prayer

Such is the Christian sense of the psalms, and it is to this that the monk must advance. It is not enough for him to pray the psalms in their literal sense, to see in them an expression of Old Testament theology. The themes of this theology are not complete unless viewed from the aspect of their fulfillment. Revelation is dynamic and progressive: it is entirely centered upon the mystery of Christ, who is everywhere present in the indissoluble unity of the two testaments. The psalms can now be seen in the light of their fulfillment, and thereby become an authentic Christian prayer, indeed, the noblest of all prayers, for they are the words which the Holy Spirit himself puts into our mouths.

The early Church knew two methods of praying the psalms. The first is represented chiefly by St. Augustine, who understood the psalms in an allegorical sense. Convinced that the psalms speak everywhere of Christ, he interpreted every detail allegorically as applying to some aspect of the mystery of Christ. The psalms thus become the voice of Christ praying to the Father. They are the prayer of Christians insofar as all the members of Christ's Body associate themselves with their Head, praying through and with Christ to the Father.

St. Benedict, who cites the psalms more than any other book of the Bible, was almost completely uninfluenced by the Augustinian method. Instead, he follows a current of piety that can be traced back to Origen, according to which the psalms are not the prayer of Christ to the Father, but of the Christian to Christ. The "I" of the psalms is the monk himself; the Lord is Christ, to whom he expresses his sentiments of praise, thanksgiving and supplication in the inspired words of the psalmist. The Psalter thus becomes the prayerbook of the Church and of the individual Christian, addressed to Christ the Lord. This prayer to Jesus is traditional in monastic piety. That these two methods of praying the psalms are neither contradictory nor mutually exclusive is evident from the liturgy, which employs both of them.

Assisting at the Opus Dei

If some of the techniques of patristic exegesis no longer appeal to the contemporary mind, the purpose which inspired them is nevertheless sound. The modern monk must assimilate the riches of the Christological sense of the psalms, and allow it to form his habits of thought and of prayer. The prayer of the psalms in the context of the *opus Dei* is a powerful means of achieving the purpose of monastic life, union with God. The psalms are the monk's school of prayer, because they are the model of all true prayer, centered as they are upon the mystery of Christ. At the same time, the divine office is not only a means to the end, but is already, in a sense, the attainment of it. It is in the *opus Dei* that the monk achieves an anticipated realization of union with God, for there he associates himself with the divine liturgy by sharing in the first fruits of the eternal praise of the heavenly Jerusalem.

This can be achieved if the monk conscientiously follows the directions which St. Benedict gives in chapter 19 on how to sing the divine office. Basing his advice upon Scripture, he asserts that the monk is never so literally in the divine presence as when he assists at the *opus Dei.* He draws a magnificent sketch of the monastic choir, gathered together in a spirit of faith and profound reverence together with the angels who stand before the throne of God: an anticipation of the choir of the heavenly liturgy. It is a matter of common observation that the spiritual level of a monastery can be accurately judged by the manner in which the monks perform the divine office. If they realize what they are doing, it is evident with what faith and sincere devotion they must approach so exalted a task.

Respect and reverence which proceed from the fear of God, attention and the total dedication of self which are a mark of true divine wisdom, a consciousness that he is moving in the world of the supernatural: these must be the qualities of the monk at prayer. Then his prayer will truly arise from the heart, so that "mind and voice may be in harmony" (19,7). Everything must add up to a perfect unity: the details of the sacred chant, the minutiae of the rubrical gestures, the words of the psalms, and the sentiments of the heart which all of these externals are meant to express. The praying of the divine office must be a fully human activity, the work of a man who is completely absorbed in the majesty of God and responds in a spirit of fervent simplicity with the expression of those sentiments of respect and love which the Holy Spirit stirs up in his heart. Such prayer will be truly worthy to be called a "work for God."

4. CONTEMPLATION

Pure Prayer the Goal of the Monk

The ancient monks identified the perfection of monastic life with the perfection of prayer. We have seen that Cassian distinguished the goal of monastic life, purity of heart, from the end, eternal life, which consists in union with God through perfect charity and the unending contemplation of the divinity. The end can be attained only partially in this life, insofar as the monk advances to the perfection of pure prayer, which is a foretaste of the eternal contemplation of heaven.

Cassian says:

> The whole purpose of the monk and the perfection of his heart is directed toward a continual and uninterrupted perseverance in prayer. Insofar as it is possible for human frailty, he strives for immovable tranquillity of mind and perpetual purity. For this reason we tirelessly seek and continually practice both bodily labor and contrition of heart: between the two there is a reciprocal and indissoluble bond. For since the entire edifice of the virtues is directed toward the perfection of prayer, the whole structure will not be firm and durable, unless all the parts are brought together and held fast by this keystone (*Conf* 9,2).

The soul which has attained purity of heart becomes like a mirror wiped clean of every stain, so that the vision of God is clearly reflected in it, and all other things in him. This highest stage of prayer, which Cassian calls *oratio ignea,* is reached by an ascending series of degrees of prayer. The monk must climb to the top of Mt. Tabor where, like the three favored disciples, he can enjoy the contemplation of the divinity. This cannot be achieved by purely human effort, but is the gift of the Holy Spirit to those properly prepared by the works of the *vita activa.* Cassian thought that it could be attained only in the solitary life, which alone was sufficiently free of distractions to permit uninterrupted contemplation.

Origin of a Terminology

It is evident, then, that monastic life was originally considered to be contemplative. The term contemplation, however, has taken on a specialized meaning in recent centuries and hence lends itself to ambiguity. We must see, therefore, what meaning this term had for the ancients and particularly what position St. Benedict adopted on the question of contemplation in the cenobitic life which he organized for his followers.

The terms contemplative life and active life were derived from the Greek philosophers. By contemplative life Plato and Aristotle meant the life of a philosopher, entirely devoted to the study and contemplation of truth for its own sake. The active life was that of free men who devoted themselves to the activities of civil life, such as politics, law and commerce. The active life provided occasion for the practice of virtue, and was not a truly human life unless governed by virtue.

This terminology was adopted by the Fathers, first by Clement and Origen, from whom it passed into the entire patristic tradition. For them the active life meant the practice of virtues, the ascetical life, which is a preparation for contemplation. The contemplative life is the life of pure prayer, attainable only after the active life has been brought to perfection. This doctrine was taken over by Evagrius of Pontus, who constructed his theory of monastic life upon it. Cassian came into contact with this system during his sojourn in Egypt; we have already seen that his concept of the *vita activa* and the *vita theoretica* is the same as that of Evagrius.

"Action" versus "Contemplation"

It is clear from this that the Fathers had no intention of making the active and contemplative lives into two separate vocations or two distinct forms of the Christian life which would be pursued by different individuals. Rather they are two aspects of the one Christian life which exist side by side in the vocation of every Christian. The contemplative life is not the private property of a small elite group, but is open to all. The life of every Christian must be contemplative to some degree; in fact, the act of contemplation is germinally present in every act of faith.

St. Augustine and St. Gregory restricted the exercises of the active life to the practice of the spiritual and corporal works of mercy, but both maintained that every Christian must practice both lives. The latter had an especially profound influence upon the Middle Ages. By the time we come down to St. Thomas, however, the two lives have been separated into distinct careers. Contemplative life now means a distinct form of the Christian life, in which an individual organizes his whole manner of living in view of the pursuit of divine contemplation. The active life is one entirely devoted to exterior activities, particularly works of mercy. An attempt is made to obviate the evident difficulties of such a division by the introduction of a medium category called the "mixed life."

With the growth of new religious orders alongside the traditional monasticism, these terms were applied to religious life. But it is ambiguous to speak of "contemplative orders" and "active orders" as if the two were mutually exclusive. Every form of religious life must be contemplative by reason of its end, for the ultimate end of all religious is the same: union with God. At the same time, it is active by reason of the means which it uses to attain the end: these means are all the practices of the ascetical life, including works of charity.

Benedictine Life "Contemplative"

St. Benedict wholeheartedly adopted the ideal of monastic life proposed by his predecessors. He is clearly in the patristic tradition of the unity between contemplation and action in the life of the same individual. It is true that he tempered somewhat the ideal of Cassian to make it accessible to a greater number of people and cast it in the mold of the occidental mentality. But he did not depart from the basic concept of monastic life as propounded by the oriental theorists.

For St. Benedict the active life consists in the ascent of the ladder of humility. This leads the monk to the perfection of charity, which is equivalent to Cassian's purity of heart, and opens the way to the exercise of pure prayer. St. Benedict's ideal is that of oriental cenobitic life, which somewhat modified the concept of the solitaries. But the search for God is still the end which he holds before them, and the characteristics of prayer which he names are those of ancient monasticism. If the cenobite cannot attain to the perfection of prayer reached by the anchorite, he can nevertheless rise to an exalted degree of charity, which opens the door to the highest form of prayer. Further, the monk who has reached this stage through the practice of cenobitic life can advance from there to the solitary life: a solution which St. Benedict himself envisaged, which was practiced by Benedictine monasteries in the Middle Ages, and which has aroused a new interest in our times.

It is correct, therefore, to say that monastic life as conceived by St. Benedict is contemplative, provided the term is properly understood. According to the ancient terminology, this meant that the end of monastic life is an uninterrupted contemplation of divine realities, and that the works of the active life are directed toward the attainment of this end. In the modern terminology, to classify Benedictine life as contemplative means that the institute as such has no secondary purpose in addition to the purpose of the sanctication of its members, though it may on occasion undertake works of charity which are one form of the ascetical exercises that contribute to its end. It is evident that solitude and leisure are indispensable for a monk to pursue the search for God in the sense intended by St. Benedict.

Fragmentation of the Spiritual Life

The modern Christian is so accustomed to think of "contemplation" and "action" as two separate forms of the Christian life that he finds it difficult to conceive of an existence in which the two are harmoniously united. This was no problem for St. Benedict, because for him all the activities of the spiritual life were unified in a single movement of the soul toward God. Works of charity, ascetical exercises, *lectio divina*, *meditatio*, *opus Dei*, and what is now called contemplative prayer were not conceived of as distinct activities, but as so many phases of a life which was entirely centered upon the contemplation of heavenly realities.

The loss of a vital contact with the Scriptures and the liturgy, which gradually came about in the late Middle Ages, was responsible for the breakdown of this unity. The Christian of the sixteenth century had little contact with the Word of God, because the Bible had become largely a closed book, and the liturgy, which had become fossilized, had ceased to perform its function of proclaiming the divine Word. Consequently the imagination was used to supply food for the soul which had previously been provided by these living sources. Meditation was then conceived of as an exercise of discursive reasoning operating upon some object of faith and designed to stir up images in the imagination which would give rise to affective acts.

The effect of this development was to oppose meditation to contemplative prayer. An attempt was made to link the two by defining an intermediary state, called "acquired contemplation," in which the soul would so perfect its meditation as to enter naturally into the phase of contemplative prayer. The controversy as to whether such a state really exists still continues. The emphasis upon the psychological state of the subject which grew out of these distinctions, while it resulted in valuable analyses of the psychology of prayer and in methods of prayer which are not without their utility, has nevertheless tended to rupture the unity of the spiritual life still further and to stress the activity of the subject rather than the action of divine grace in a soul which has acquired tranquillity through the exercise of the *vita activa*.

Unity in the Spiritual Life

A re-examination of the viewpoint of the ancients can be a valuable aid to a recovery of the unity of the spiritual life. While it is helpful for us to make distinctions which the ancients did not perceive, with a view toward achieving greater clarity, it can only be harmful to allow these distinctions to grow into separation and even opposition between elements which must harmoniously contribute toward the unity of the spiritual life. The rediscovery of the Bible can restore our contact with the living Word of God; a renewal of active participation in the liturgy will give us the divine Word in the vital context which the Church has designed for it. Pure prayer, which is the end product of both together in combination with the *vita activa*, should flow naturally from these sources and not have to be artificially contrived.

The ancient monks saw no opposition between vocal and mental prayer. Vocal prayer, in fact, was the springboard from which the soul could soar aloft to the noblest heights of contemplative prayer. In commenting on the Lord's prayer, Cassian says that the fervent recitation of the *Pater* can lead to the loftiest stages of prayer:

> This prayer . . . lifts those who are devoted to it to that higher degree of which we spoke above and leads them on through a loftier stage to that *oratio ignea* which is known and experienced by only a few and is properly called ineffable. This prayer, which transcends all human thought, is marked by no sound of the voice nor even by a movement of the tongue or the pronunciation of a word. The soul, illumined by heavenly light, is not tied down to the narrow confines of human speech, but generously pours forth its thoughts, flowing out as from an abundant fountain, and directs them ineffably to God. In that brief moment of time it pours forth so many sentiments that, when it has returned to itself, it cannot easily relate or even recall them (*Conf* 9,25).

The Psalms as a Source of Prayer

The same is true of the prayer of the psalms. The oriental monks had assimilated the words of the Psalter so perfectly that when they prayed they spoke in biblical language. They chose verses of the psalms to be used continually as ejaculatory prayers, as they thought the inspired Word of God to be suitable for all occasions and needs. Their favorite ejaculation was the verse, "Deign, O God, to rescue me; O Lord, make haste to help me" (Ps 69,2), which St. Benedict adopted for the beginning of the hours of the divine office, a custom retained by the Roman liturgy ever since.

After commenting at length on the usefulness of this verse, Cassian explains how the psalms lead the monk to the heights of pure prayer:

> Penetrating into all the sentiments of the psalms, he will begin to sing them in such a way that he pours them forth with the deepest compunction of heart, not as words composed by the psalmist, but as if he had written them himself as his own prayer. At least he feels that they are meant directly for him and knows that what they express was not only fulfilled in the psalmist, but finds its fulfillment every day in his own life. . . . Penetrating into the same state of mind in which each psalm was sung or written, we become its author, so to speak, and rather than following its meaning, we anticipate it, so that we perceive the significance of what it says even before we understand the letter.
>
> We find all our own sentiments expressed in the psalms. Seeing all the things that occur in them as if in a clean mirror, we gain a deeper understanding of them. Instructed by our own reaction to them, we perceive these things not merely as something we have heard, but things we have actually seen. They are not merely something we have memorized, but we give birth to them from the depths of our heart as something arising from our own nature, so that we penetrate their meaning not from the act of reading but by our own former experience.
>
> Thus our soul will arrive at that state of pure prayer . . . which does not depend upon the consideration of any image, is not expressed through the sound of the voice or in any words, but is poured forth in a fiery upward surge of the soul, an ineffable transport of the heart, an impetuosity of spirit which cannot be satisfied. Ravished beyond the senses and beyond everything visible, the soul pours itself out to God with inexpressible yearnings and sighs (*Conf* 10,11).

Liturgy and Contemplation

The disjunction of contemplative prayer from the other phases of the spiritual life has given rise in modern times to the idea that participation in the liturgy is opposed to contemplation and even a hindrance to it. The external conformity required by the liturgical action would constitute a distraction which would prevent the true contemplative from entering into an intimate union with God. This leads to the absurd notion that a religious can really begin to pray only after he has satisfied the obligations imposed by his rule by finishing his office, his meditation and the other required spiritual exercises.

This specious difficulty rests upon a false understanding of the nature of liturgical worship, to which we have already referred. It is conceived of as a merely external participation in the liturgical rites. In reality true liturgical worship must be both external and internal: it is not authentic worship unless, in the words of St. Benedict, "the mind is in harmony with the voice" (19,7). Contemplation and liturgy are not two mutually exclusive forms of prayer; rather contemplation is the internal aspect of a liturgical worship which has reached the stage of perfection, and the continuation of this outside the liturgical action. Liturgical worship is not perfect until the interior conformity of the mind and the will which accompanies the exterior participation reaches the stage of contemplation.

The possibility of reconciling even the higher stages of mystical prayer with an intense participation in the liturgy and the *lectio divina* is demonstrated by the experiences of certain mystics who enjoyed an extraordinary degree of union with God and at the same time faithfully took part in the traditional exercises of monastic spirituality. The best known example is that of St. Gertrude. Her writings reveal that it was precisely while assisting at the performance of the *opus Dei* and the celebration of Mass that she was seized by mystical transports. Her genuine mystical experiences are entirely colored by the liturgy and the traditional practices of monastic spirituality. All prayer was for her either a preparation for or a continuation of liturgical prayer, and her spiritual life was formed by a harmonious combination of ascetical exercises, *lectio divina*, *meditatio*, *opus Dei*, sacramental life and authentic mystical prayer.

Experience of God in Purity of Heart

Prayer must proceed from an attitude of simplicity of soul. This is another way of saying that purity of heart or charity constitutes the gateway to the contemplative life. The ancients often spoke of prayer in terms of the Beatitude, "Blessed are the clean of heart, for they shall see God" (Mt 5,8). Prayer is not a question of intellectual knowledge, but rather a sense of connaturality with God and the things of God. It is an experience: an awareness of the presence of the Holy Spirit in the soul. When charity has flooded one's heart so as to become a vital influence in every aspect of one's life, there comes with it a kind of intuitive experience of God himself. This is the point of departure for contemplation.

This experience of God through indwelling charity gives a man a new outlook upon the universe. Nothing appears to him any longer as purely profane; he sees, as it were, the footprints of God everywhere in his creation. Creatures no longer attract him, as they do the carnal man, in view of the sensible pleasure they can afford; they become sacraments which proclaim the presence of God everywhere and testify to his love for man. Everything becomes meaningful because it speaks to him of God's love. The universe is seen as a vast symphony of praise to the Creator. Creation no longer "groans and travails in pain," but seems to be already vibrant with the cosmic redemption for which it eagerly longs (cf Rom 8,18–22).

It is above all in his fellow men that the monk whose heart is pure will recognize God. Prayer is not a purely individual relationship to God; the monk prays as a member of Christ's Body, indissolubly linked to the destiny of the whole people of God. He experiences the misery that the Israelites, the early Christians and his contemporaries have felt at their total incapacity to achieve salvation on their own terms; with them he surrenders himself to God as the sole source of happiness; with them he feels an intense joy in abandonment to the Father. The monk does not pray alone, but in union with all his brothers. His prayer, like theirs, is not his own, but is the voice of the Spirit within him, who "pleads for us with unutterable groanings" (Rom 8,26).

Beginning in Prayer

While all prayer is due to the presence of the Holy Spirit within the soul, the monk who is beginning on the way of perfection will find it difficult to be aware of the Spirit's interior workings. He will be too much occupied with the level of the senses to have acquired a deeper spiritual perception. At this stage prayer will be a constant effort to free oneself from slavery to the senses and to concentrate upon God. While he may at times feel a sensible fervor, this experience is still on the level of the emotions and not yet entirely free of self. It cannot be depended upon, for it comes and goes, and is at best but an imperfect crutch which the Spirit uses only temporarily to sustain his faltering steps.

The monk beginning in the way of prayer is like a child learning to walk. The new skill does not come spontaneously, but has to be learned gradually through efforts which go contrary to the comfortable inactivity to which he has been accustomed. These first efforts will seem artificially contrived rather than springing from his inner nature, and he will be overconscious of them. It is only later, when praying, like walking, has become natural and effortless, that he will be able to pray without concentrating on the technique of praying.

It is important from the very beginning, however, that he be able to distinguish the essentials of prayer from the efforts which are necessary to stimulate it in its earlier stages. It will be necessary to employ intellectual considerations, acts of the will and practical resolutions, but these are only an approach to prayer, not prayer itself. It is only when these efforts have led him deep within himself, and he finds there an authentic thirst for God and delight in his presence, that he will have reached the reality of prayer. It is neither in the discursive reason nor in sensible emotions that he will come to an awareness of the attractions of the Spirit, but in the "heart," the most profound and intimate depths of his being.

Progress in Prayer

This inner attraction may at first be very feeble. It will grow stronger only in proportion as the monk progressively detaches himself, through asceticism, from material things and sensible pleasures. Then grace seizes a firmer hold upon his being, and the thirst for God and for divine things becomes stronger. Once it is recognized as the real essence of prayer, the monk will give it free reign and be content to walk without his crutches.

This does not mean that he will experience a sensible delight in prayer. On the contrary, his attraction to God may be accompanied by a spiritual dryness which robs him of any kind of consolation. He will, however, experience a sense of peace and sober joy at the same time as he retains a clear perception of his own imperfection and emptiness before God. He will in principle be suspicious of sensible delights, knowing that what he must seek in prayer is not his own consolation, but an encounter with God in the depths of his heart.

The fact that he has once become attentive to the interior attraction of the Spirit does not mean that all his prayer will be effortless from that time on. It is not easy to keep the heart fixed upon God. There will be many distractions in prayer, and the enticement of sensible pleasure will still prove attractive to the passions. At this juncture the monk must keep a close guard over his heart, and prevent the storms raging outside from disturbing the peace of that inner sanctuary where his gaze is fixed upon God.

The Monastic Ideal of Continuous Prayer

When this guard over his heart becomes habitual and the monk is effectively detached from sensible affections, he can make progress toward continuous prayer. The ancients looked upon *oratio continua* as the summit of the monastic life. It was not only a fulfillment of the evangelical precept to "pray always," but also an anticipation of the eternal liturgy of heaven. Cassian, we have seen, speaks of "continual and uninterrupted perseverance in prayer" as the purpose of the monk and the standard by which his growth in perfection may be measured (*Conf* 9,2).

If such an ideal seems unrealizable, it is only because we too often look upon prayer as a series of acts of the will and the discursive reason. Obviously, one cannot always be making such acts explicitly, even in the relatively undisturbed atmosphere of monastic life. But prayer essentially resides in the "heart"; on this deeper level of one's being God can always be present to the inner self. This is a matter of being always receptive to the movement of grace within the soul. It means seeking to please God in everything, doing nothing for the gratification of self. One who has become thoroughly attuned to the interior inspiration of the Spirit will follow his direction in everything without stopping to analyze what he is doing. This is the fruit of a connaturality with divine grace, a spontaneous acquiescence to the promptings of the Spirit.

Such a state can be achieved only by the monk whose heart is purified. Only the monk who has been freed from all attachments to created things, by the asceticism of the triple renunciation, can always seek God with no interposition of self to obscure the divine presence in his heart. The heart that is still divided prays only from time to time; the pure heart keeps its gaze fixed upon God regardless of what else it is about. Only a vigilant custody of the heart can preserve this uninterrupted gaze.

Monastic Life and Progress in Prayer

While the monk should know something about the theology and psychology of contemplative prayer, he need not be a specialist in the theory of mysticism. But he must be convinced that the monastic vocation carries with it the obligation to strive untiringly to advance toward the perfection of prayer. The numerous exercises of the monastic life to which his profession binds him are not ends in themselves but only means. The progressive purification of the ascetical life must lead him to a state in which God takes complete possession of him, in which he becomes ever more conscious of the divine action within him, and responds by participating wholeheartedly in the dialogue with God.

The life of prayer is not an isolated aspect or distinct exercise of the monastic life. It is the keystone of a structure in which every element must play its part and contribute to the unity and finality of the whole. Progress in prayer is not a matter of a more intense psychological concentration, but of growth in faith and charity, and a progressive conformity between one's faith and the rest of one's life. It cannot be separated from the practices of monastic spirituality which we have outlined above: the monk's response to the Word of God through interior conversion, the practice of penance and virtue; the exercises of *lectio divina* and *meditatio;* the *opus Dei* and the sacramental life—all these draw him onward to pure prayer, the dialogue between a son of God, cleansed of vice and glowing with the ardor of charity, and his heavenly Father.

5. THE MONASTERY AS PARADISE

Paradisus Claustri

Monastic tradition has enthusiastically compared the union with God which the monk experiences in the contemplative phase of the spiritual ascent to the life of Adam in paradise and of the angels in heaven. The monastery a paradise, the monk an angel: these are bold metaphors indeed, but nonetheless pregnant expressions of some of the essential features of the monastic state. These features pertain to the mystical phase of monastic life, but are to be found to some degree in the life of every monk—indeed, in the life of every Christian.

The expression *paradisus claustri,* which was frequently applied to the monastery by the monks of the Middle Ages but is really the continuation of a theme that is much older, may seem strange to the contemporary mind. The term paradise brings to mind a utopia, a place of ideal happiness, where all is delight and pleasure, unmarred by the imperfection, pain and unhappiness which everywhere accompany human existence. Whatever may be said for monastic life, no monastery is a paradise in this sense.

On the contrary, the monk will not require a very long experience of the monastic life to discover that his return to God is beset with difficulties. The ancients rightly conceived of it as an *agon,* a constant and bitter struggle against the evil tendencies of one's own nature. By its very definition it involves renunciation, which is painful to human nature, for through it the monk turns his back upon those same legitimate pleasures which are usually associated with a utopian existence. Monastic life does, indeed, bring joy to those who live it seriously, but this is a spiritual experience, not a delight for the senses.

St. Benedict recognized this clearly when he said that monks "choose the narrow way," according to the Lord's words, "Narrow is the way which leadeth unto life" (Mt 7,14; *Rule* 5,11). And he would have the novice under no illusions about this, for he warns him at the outset: "If, for good reason . . . there be some strictness of discipline, do not be at once dismayed and run away from the way of salvation, of which the entrance must needs be narrow" (Pr 47–48). The monastery, then, is anything but a garden of sensible delights.

Theological Significance

It was not this which the ancient monks had in mind when they spoke of their cloister as paradise. What, then, is the meaning of this comparison? First of all, it is a metaphor, a comparison between two apparently dissimilar realities based upon features which are common to both. The monastery is called paradise because there is an analogy between certain features of monastic life and important elements of the paradisiacal state. The meaning is not a psychological one: it is not that the monastery makes the same impression upon the senses as does paradise.

On the contrary, sensible delights are not the essence of paradise, even though they may come first to the imagination of the average person who encounters the term. Paradise is essentially a certain religious state of man which situates him in reference to God and to other creatures. It is this religious reality which provides the basis for the analogy. It is a question not of psychology but of theology.

Threefold Level of Comparison

The essential feature of this theological state is that man is at peace with both God and creation. The paradisiacal man is endowed with exalted gifts of nature and grace, which he uses to glorify God, not to defy him. Within himself there is peace, for his faculties are in order, undisturbed by the ravages of sin. He is master of the lower creation, which joins him in offering a symphony of praise to the Creator. In paradise man enjoys a state of harmony and familiarity with God, his fellows and the entire universe: he lives the life of God.

The primary analogate in this comparison is the earthly paradise of Adam. Following the lead of the Bible itself, the Fathers and monastic writers saw in it a type of the Church, the new garden of spiritual delights which the new Adam, Christ, has reopened for mankind. But the Church is a reality which belongs to the in-between time and, while itself a fulfillment, it at the same time points forward to the further reality of salvation definitely achieved. The analogy, therefore, moves on three separate levels of type and fulfillment: the earthly paradise as the first level, the heavenly paradise as the third and final one, with the paradise of the Church in the middle. It is on this second level that the theme of the monastery as paradise finds its point of insertion.

The paradise theme is a rich comparison, playing upon the diverse symbolic elements which characterized the earthly paradise and sounding their overtones in the stages of fulfillment. These elements recur at every level, but with a progressive spiritualization and enrichment of meaning. They are symbolic elements, drawn from the imaginative but meaningful account which the Bible gives us of the earthly paradise. But this is no mere literary artifice: it is the poetic expression of profound religious truths. It depicts man's share in the divine life at successive stages of sacred history, from the creation to the parousia.

Paradise in Eden

The earthly paradise is described in the second creation account of Genesis. It was a verdant garden, or rather an oriental park, such as ancient Mesopotamian monarchs used to construct for themselves, a fertile oasis in the midst of forbidding desert. It was watered by a river. The garden was filled with a luxuriant growth of trees which supplied both beauty and nourishment. Pre-eminent among these trees was the tree of life, which conferred immortality upon those who ate of its fruit.

God placed man in this garden to care for it and to live there in idyllic peace and joy. Man was free to eat of the tree of life, and hence enjoyed the gift of immortality. He was on terms of intimate familiarity with God. He was at peace within himself, for as yet nothing had disturbed the integrity of his own nature. Men lived in harmony with each other: the man was content with the woman whom God gave to him as a companion. All of nature enjoyed the same harmony, for the animals were subject to the man, who displayed his dominion over them by giving them their names.

It is in this vivid, symbolic language that the biblical author has represented for us the ideal state of man. It is a supernatural state, for in addition to the extraordinary gifts of nature that were his, he also enjoyed a relationship of friendship and intimacy with God. This theological state of man, which God had originally intended for the human race, was disrupted by the invasion of sin. The ground was cursed, man was subjected to toil and suffering, the woman to the pangs of childbirth. They were condemned to a continual conflict with the forces of evil until such a time as God would give them victory. They were ejected from the garden so that they could no longer approach the tree of life, and the entrance was blocked by the cherubim wielding the fiery sword.

The Quest for Paradise

Such is the Bible's explanation of the original state of mankind and the cause of all human misery, which can be expressed in one word: sin. Sunk in the depths of his own wretchedness, man could do nothing to regain his lost state. His continual quest for happiness is really nothing but a search for the lost paradise, an attempt to regain his friendship with God. Such is the aim of all the religions and philosophies which have developed in human history and which offer to regain the lost paradise for their adherents through some sort of esoteric experience.

But man of himself can find no remedy for his sickness. He is powerless to recapture paradise, which is a free gift of God and can be restored only by his liberality. God, however, held out hope from the beginning that he would one day readmit his erring sons to the paradise which they had forfeited. Upon his initiative, the process was begun by which man might be led back once again to his idyllic state of friendship with God. God went in search of man, and throughout the successive phases of sacred history arranged events through his intervention in man's life to bring him gradually to the definitive restoration of the lost paradise.

The great works of God on behalf of his people were not only stages of preparation for the future redemption, they were also types of it. The prophets looked upon God's past benefactions as symbols of what he would do in the future when the day of the Lord would come to inaugurate the Messianic era. They recalled the wonders of the past only to stir up faith in greater wonders to come. Thus they evoked features of the earthly paradise to point forward to the new paradise that God would establish in eschatological times.

It is not a question of a return to the old paradise, but of a new creation that God was preparing, which could be pictured in the colors of the paradise of Adam.

Looking Toward A New Paradise

The prophets visualized the paradise of the new creation in terms of the original Eden. Amos and Hosea foresee the Messianic era as a time of wonderful fertility and productivity of the soil (Am 9,13; Hos 2,23–24). Isaiah pictures it as a time when the peace and harmony of the original paradise will be restored. Men will beat their swords into plowshares and war will be banished (Is 2,2–5; 11,6–9).

Ezechiel speaks of the stream of water flowing from the temple and making the desert bloom down to the Dead Sea, like the river which flowed through Eden. Its waters would teem with fish, and would even sweeten the waters of the Salt Sea. On the banks of the stream trees would grow in wonderful profusion and would provide food unfailingly. Their leaves would never drop off, and they would produce a fresh crop of fruit every month (Ez 47,1–12; cf Zech 14,8).

The Jewish apocrypha of the intertestamental period reveal an exuberant flowering of the paradisiacal symbols to represent Messianic times. Further developing the themes of the prophets, they speak of a restoration of the tree of life, which would confer upon the just a long life without toil or pain (Hen 25,1–6). The fertility of paradise would be restored (Hen 10,19). Women would give birth painlessly (2 Bar 73,7) and would bring forth thousands of children (Hen 10,17). Peace would reign everywhere among men (Hen 52,8; Jub 23,29), and the animals, rendered tame and amiable, would again be subject to them (2 Bar 73,6). The gate to paradise would be reopened, the fiery sword sheathed (Test Lev 18,10).

The Paradise of Christ

The prophets did not have a clear vision of Messianic times. We misunderstand them if we look for a mathematical equivalence between their prophecies and the reality of the fulfillment. They did not know when or how God would bring to fulfillment what he had promised; they only had the certainty of faith that he would do so. In fact, fulfillment was to come about in a way which they doubtless never suspected, and the reality would far surpass the horizon of their hopes. In place of the old paradise God would bring about a new creation.

It is the essence of the New Testament message that Messianic times have arrived with Christ. Accordingly the new paradise foretold by the prophets is here: the paradise of Christ is the Church. Paradise regained is not identical with the one lost, but far surpasses it. Through Christ man has regained his familiarity with God, but to a far greater degree than that enjoyed by Adam. The grace of Christ is a more intimate share in the divine life than what was given to our first parents.

The New Testament, with the exception of the Apocalypse, does not exploit the paradisiacal themes of fertility, the tree of life, submission of animals, and universal peace, to the same extent as the prophets. Rather the accent is upon the person of Christ, who is himself the source of salvation. Here we encounter the theme of the new Adam. It seems to be present already in the episode of the temptation, where Christ undoes the work of the old Adam by rejecting the suggestions of the tempter. By his victory over Satan he restores the paradisiacal state of mankind forfeited by the old Adam. St. Mark here mentions that Jesus was "with wild beasts" and that "angels waited on him" (Mk 1,13), apparently allusions to the restoration of paradisiacal conditions of dominion over the animals and friendship with the angels.

The New Adam in St. Paul

It is St. Paul, however, who principally develops the theme of the new Adam. Adam, he says, is "a type of him who was to come." Then he introduces a contrast between the work of the old Adam and that of the new:

> If by the offense of the one the many died, much more has the grace of God, and the gift in the grace of one man, Jesus Christ, abounded unto the many. . . . For if by reason of the one man's offense death reigned through the one man, much more will they who receive the abundance of the grace and of the gift of holiness reign in life through the one Jesus Christ. Therefore as from the offense of the one man the result was unto condemnation to all men, so from the justice of the one the result is unto justification of life to all men (Rom 5,15–18).

St. Paul here insists that Christ is the source of our justification under the new covenant. The paradise theme therefore becomes centered upon the person of the new Adam, who has overcome the sin of the first man and, through his resurrection, the death which is its consequence. Elsewhere he says: "Since by a man came death, by a man also comes resurrection of the dead. For as in Adam all die, so in Christ all will be made to live" (1 Cor 15,21–22). St. Paul emphasizes the superiority of the new state of the Christian over that of man in the earthly paradise, when he refers to "the abundance of the grace and of the gift of justice" (Rom 5,17). The Church is a new creation, the new people of God gathered together by the Messiah and restored to the divine life by being grafted into his Body.

The Church, the New Eve

St. Paul treats another paradise theme in the epistle to the Ephesians, where he speaks of the Church as a new Eve. The prophets had already spoken of Israel as the Bride of Yahweh, comparing his love for the chosen people to that of an injured husband for his unfaithful spouse. The Canticle of Canticles celebrates this divine love in language which is reminiscent of the paradise themes of the prophets. St. Paul transposes the theme to the love of Christ for his Bride, the Church. The words of Genesis referring to Adam and Eve, "For this cause a man shall leave his father and mother, and cleave to his wife; and the two shall become one flesh" (Gen 2,24; Eph 5,31), he declares to be a great mystery, which he understands in reference to Christ and to the Church (Eph 5,32). The Church, in the new economy, corresponds to the old Eve as Christ corresponds to the old Adam.

Christ has conferred upon the Church an integrity comparable to that of Eve in paradise: "Christ also loved the Church, and delivered himself up for her, that he might sanctify her, cleansing her in the bath of water by means of the word, in order that he might present to himself the Church in all her glory, not having spot or wrinkle or any such thing, but that she might be holy and without blemish" (Eph 5,25–27). The new paradise consists in this, therefore, that Christ through his salvific work has sanctified the Church, has given her the divine life and supernatural gifts surpassing those of the paradise of Eden, and thus united her to himself in a union more intimate than the familiarity which our first parents enjoyed with God. The nuptial bath which cleanses Christ's members of every stain and clothes them in the paradisiacal gifts is baptism.

The Gateway to Paradise

Baptism, then, is the door to the new paradise. Developing the baptismal doctrine of St. Paul, the liturgy and the Fathers built up a rich typological explanation of the rites of Christian initiation, in which the paradise theme recurs frequently. The neophyte turned toward the west to renounce Satan, then to the east to profess his faith in Christ. While the original reason for this orientation may have been the expectation of Christ's glorious return in the east, the Fathers often explain that the neophyte faces east because paradise was "a garden in Eden, to the east" (Gen 2,8). The gesture therefore is an expression of nostalgia for paradise. When the catechumen has renounced the covenant of Adam with Satan, paradise opens before him and, facing it, he enters a new covenant with Christ.

This done, he enters the baptistry, an act which symbolizes his admission into the paradise of the Church. For this reason baptistries in ancient times were decorated with paradisiacal motifs. Christ the

Good Shepherd stands among his sheep in a garden filled with a lush growth of trees and flowers. Through this garden flows the bubbling river of paradise: the waters of baptism. Deer with serpents in their mouths are quenching their thirst in the water, according to a belief of the ancients that these animals devoured serpents and thereby acquired an intense thirst. It is an allusion to Psalm 41,1: "As the hind longs for the running waters, so my soul longs for you, O God." The neophyte, who has vanquished the serpent of the paradise of Adam, thirsts for the baptismal water of the new paradise.

The baptismal ceremony itself contains further allusions to paradise. The catechumen is stripped of his garments, which represent sin and corruption, for it was only after their sin that Adam and Eve were clothed in the garments of skin that the Lord made for them (Gen 3,21). The neophyte thereby sheds the corruptibility in which he shared as long as he was in the realm of Satan. He descends into the font completely naked, as Adam was in the earthly paradise, for through baptism he recovers the primitive innocence which Adam forfeited. The Fathers observe that the shame which Adam and Eve felt in their nudity after their sin is banished for the baptized Christian, for the filial confidence and intimate friendship with God of the first paradise are now restored to him.

Additional Typology

The Fathers push further the typology of the Church as the new paradise. Particularly in connection with the paschal mystery, they find a detailed parallelism between the fall of man and his restoration to innocence. As the fall occurred in a garden, so also the act of redemption. As the tree of life stood in the first paradise, so the new tree of life, the cross, stands in the midst of the new paradise to vanquish sin. Just as God cast our first parents out of paradise in the afternoon, so in the afternoon Christ announced to the thief that it was once again open. The origin of Eve from the side of Adam during his sleep is a type of the birth of the Church from the side of the new Adam in his sleep of death upon the cross.

The new paradise, then, is the Church. The trees which contribute to its splendor are the saints who inhabit it. In the midst of them is the new tree of life, Christ, who is the source of divine life for those who are nourished by his fruit. The glory of Adam reappears in the new Adam, and it is his glorious humanity which becomes the source of glory for all who attach themselves to him by faith and baptism. The four rivers of paradise are the four Gospels; their water is baptism. St. Cyprian sums it up in the following passage: "The Church, which reproduces the likeness of paradise, contains within her walls fruit-bearing trees, any one of which does not bring forth good fruit is cut down and thrown into the fire. These trees she waters with four streams, which are the four Gospels, by which she bestows the grace of baptism in a heavenly and salutary stream" (*Epist* 73,10).

What is realized in the Church is also realized in the individual Christian. The Fathers also drew out the significance of the paradise themes on the personal level: the theme of the paradise of the soul. The soul of the Christian, like the Church, is a new garden of paradise; irrigated by the flow of baptism, it produces a rich growth of virtues. The new creation of baptism reproduces the new Adam, Christ, in each of his members. Every Christian life contains in itself the interior regeneration which the paschal mystery has worked within the Church. Hence the paradise of Christ is reproduced in everyone who is incorporated into his Body.

Paradise of the End-Time

The Church is the eschatological kingdom. She looks forward to the complete manifestation of Christ's victory over the forces of sin. The total return to the conditions of paradise will be realized only when Christ "has put all his enemies under his feet" (cf 1 Cor 15,26) and handed over the kingdom to his Father. The two terms of sacred history, therefore, are the paradise of Eden at the beginning and the paradise of heaven at the end. The second is the antitype of the first.

The Apocalypse, which presents a magnificent vision of the final triumph of Christ and the glorification of the Church, his Bride, describes the eschatological paradise in figures derived from the paradise of Eden. The ancient serpent is chained up so that he can no longer do harm to men (Apoc 20,2). The tree of life, symbolizing the gift of immortality, is once again available to those who have achieved victory with Christ: "Him who overcomes I will permit to eat of the tree of life, which is in the paradise of my God" (Apoc 2,7; cf 22,2.14.19).

This paradise, to which the faithful Christian will be admitted after his triumph over the forces of evil, is described in the coloring of Eden in the final vision of the Seer, in which he combines the traditional paradise themes with his representation of the new Jerusalem. While originally distinct, the two themes had been fused already by Ezechiel. The river is there, containing the water of life, flowing from the throne of God and of the Lamb (22,1). The tree of life stands in the midst of the new city and produces twelve fruits, one for each month, and leaves which "had a healing power for the nations" (22,2). In this blessed city the peace and happiness and immortality of the original paradise shall be restored: "God will wipe away every tear from their eyes. And death shall be no more; neither shall there be mourning, nor crying, nor pain any more, for the former things have passed away" (21,4).

Monasticism as Paradise

Between the paradise of Eden and the final paradise of the endtime stands the Church, caught in the tension between them. The Church and her members are in a transitory state, waiting for "the former things" to pass away and give way to the definitive manifestation of the kingdom. But even now paradise is a reality. Like the paradise of Eden and that of eschatological times, the paradise of the Church and of the soul is neither a place nor a time, but a state of man, a state of friendship with God and of restoration of the goods of paradise through incorporation in Christ, the new Adam. But it is a hidden paradise, a state which is not yet manifest to all: "For the eager longing of creation awaits the revelation of the sons of God" (Rom 8,19).

The reality of paradise finds expression to a varying degree in the different states of life within the Church. It is one aspect of the life of every Christian: the aspect of salvation already achieved *in germine*, of the goods of paradise restored. This aspect finds its most perfect expression in the monastic life. The monk, because he has left the world even through physical separation, is in a sense outside of space and time. He is already in the state of paradise, a restoration of the first paradise and anticipation of the final one. Monasticism, by reason of its separation from the world, its cultivation of virginity, its dedication to divine worship, is a dimension of the Christian life which most perfectly realizes its eschatological aspect. It is the Church's area of paradise par excellence.

Paradisus Solitudinis

From the earliest times monastic writers developed the idea that the monastic state was a realization of paradise. The themes of *paradisus solitudinis* and *paradisus cellae* appeared in the fourth and fifth centuries and thereafter became a common element in the monastic tradition. The monks loved to picture the forbidding desert of Egypt as a flowering garden of delights because of the fruits of virtue which were produced there. The comparison with paradise is based upon the supernatural state in which the monks lived, but this is expressed in the traditional paradisiacal symbols of the Bible and the liturgy.

The first point of comparison is the monk's recovery of integrity. Integrity is the consequence of the monk's mastery of himself, achieved through a rigorous asceticism. It is the quality of *apatheia*, a perfect domination of the passions. The monk who has achieved this state through the practice of chastity, fasting, vigils, poverty and the continual struggle against the demons, regains the integrity which Adam enjoyed in paradise. His interior tranquillity cannot be shaken by external pressures, nor by the persuasions of the devil, nor by the enticements of his own appetites. His passions are completely under the control of the divine life which dwells in him by reason of the intimate union with God to which his *apatheia* has brought him.

Qualities of Adam

The traditional paradise themes are pressed into service to illustrate the recovery of the integrity of Adam. Thus the tranquillity of soul which the ascetics had achieved overflowed into their bodily appearance. St. Athanasius tells us that Anthony was of striking appearance, so that men were naturally drawn to him. His countenance manifested the purity of his soul, so that from the appearance of his body one could recognize his interior state. The calmness of his soul prevented him from ever feeling any agitation, while the supernatural joy in which he lived kept him from ever experiencing any sadness (*Vita Antonii* 67).

Furthermore, Anthony is represented as enjoying a quasi-immortality. So complete was the integrity of his bodily strength and of his faculties that he preserved a kind of perpetual youth. Even when he was more than one hundred years old, his eyesight was still unimpaired and he had all of his teeth. At the time of his death he was more vigorous than younger men who had lived a much easier life. His death was a quiet passage into the heavenly paradise rather than a dissolution (*Vita Antonii* 93). We hear also of solitaries who wore no clothing at all in imitation of Adam before the fall.

Some of the celebrated monks also suggested the primitive state of innocence by their patriarchal appearance. Their long white hair and beard were comparable to Jacob's, the glory of their countenance like that of Moses, but usually it is said that their appearance was "angelic." Some of them were resplendent with a heavenly brilliance. This theme appears in the liturgy of St. Benedict, in an antiphon for March 21, which attributes various paradisiacal qualities to the holy patriarch: "Benedict the man of God had a tranquil countenance, adorned with angelic virtues, and such a striking brilliance radiated from him that while he was still on earth, he was already living in heaven" (*Breviarium Monasticum*, 4th antiphon at Lauds).

The Reign of Peace

It was not only the person of the monks, however, but the entire environment which they created, which constituted a restoration of paradise. Appropriately, the ancient versions of the *Apophthegmata* sometimes bear the title *The Paradise of the Fathers.* St. Athanasius tells us that the cells of the solitaries who grouped themselves around Anthony were like "tents filled with heavenly choirs," as their inhabitants occupied themselves ceaselessly with prayer, work, holy reading and fasting, and were filled with joy in expectation of eternal life. The observer, marveling at the sight, was inspired to cry out the words of the oracle of Balaam: "How beautiful your dwellings, O Jacob, your tents, O Israel! Like shady groves and like gardens by the rivers, and like tents which the Lord has pitched, like cedars by the waters" (Num 24,5–6; *Vita Antonii* 44).

In this paradisiacal milieu, conditions of universal peace were restored, not only among men, but also with the lower creation. The wild animals obeyed St. Anthony and refrained from doing him any harm (*Vita Antonii* 50). When the devil sent vicious hyenas to attack him, he dismissed them by proclaiming himself the servant of Christ (*ibid* 52). The theme of the subservience of the beasts to men of God becomes a commonplace in monastic hagiography. Two lions are said to have dug the grave of St. Paul the Hermit; a wolf became devoted to St. Odo of Cluny. The raven who befriended St. Benedict and faithfully served him is an elaboration of this paradise theme (*Dial* 2,8). Whatever may be said of the *genus litterarium* of these stories, their theological import is clear.

The Medieval Developments

The medieval monastic literature contains a prolongation of the paradise themes of the Fathers. While the Fathers employed these themes to illustrate the mysteries of Christian initiation, the monks placed the accent rather upon the claustral life. While the sacraments of initiation always remain supposed, the application of the themes becomes more directly monastic. The return to paradise is accomplished by the second baptism of monastic profession; the restored goods of paradise are benefits of an ascetical and mystical order which are realized in monastic life. There is a great variety in the application of the themes to monasticism, which lends rich coloring to the paradisiacal aspect of the claustral life.

The monk is a new Adam because the baptism of his profession has restored in him the obedience of the first parent. The monk experiences a joy akin to that of Adam because the peace of God dwells in him. The monastery effectively prepares a man to become a fit stone for the construction of the heavenly Jerusalem.

From the theological viewpoint, the monastery is a garden of delights. Like the original Eden, it is watered by a river, which is the harmony of unanimity in the monastic body. Fraternal charity is an essential condition for a monastery to become a true paradise, for it alone can produce unity and thus peace. This river divides into four branches, which are the fruits of charity: prayer, meditation, reading and the practices of virtue. The names of the four rivers of Genesis provide an occasion for flights of allegorism.

The tree of life in the monastic paradise is the cross of Christ. As the first tree was associated with the disobedience of Adam, the second was the scene of the obedience of Christ. Just as this tree opened the gates of paradise to the good thief, so the monk's obedience in imitation of Christ will open paradise to him. The tree is surrounded by other plants of great variety and beauty: these are the virtues which spring up in paradise. The monk must seek the true paradise of virtue, not that of transitory pleasures. The virtues, and the fruits of the heart which they produce, are the sources of true joy, the spiritual joy which flows from monastic observance and an authentic interior life.

The Desire for Heaven

The paradise theme is essentially eschatological. It is because monasticism is the fullest expression of the eschatological longing of the Church that it has chosen the symbolism of paradise as the preferred expression of its inner reality. The monks of all ages have been convinced that their life is a restoration of the goods of Eden. Prayer, intimacy with God, the domination of concupiscence, the work of cultivating the garden, delight in virtue, peace with oneself, harmony with the rest of creation: these are characteristic of the paradisiacal state. The monk comes into possession of these goods in proportion as he gives himself to the demands of his vocation. Above all, he enjoys them in the fullest measure possible in this life when he has reached the heights of contemplation. For paradise essentially, as a theological state of man, is union and friendship with God. The paradise of the cloister, the satisfaction of the monk's spiritual striving, is nothing else than the hundredfold promised already in this life to those who abandon everything for Christ.

But even this state, sublime though it may be, is only an anticipation of the definitive paradise still to come. The monk knows that the paradise of the cloister is only a transitory state which looks forward to the paradise of the heavenly Jerusalem. It is already an anticipation of that final paradise, a germinal sharing in the same goods which will be fully enjoyed there. So the monk adds his voice to the groaning of all creation which waits for the final deliverance, inspired by an intense longing for the eschatological paradise. He is already with the Lord, but he looks forward to the day when his union will become irreversible and face to face. Evagrius of Pontus, the great theologian of ancient monasticism, wrote: "The just are still on this side of the city which is the inheritance of the perfect; but the perfect are already with our Lord in Eden and in the heavenly Jerusalem, because they are like unto him" (*De justis et perfectis* 13).

6. THE MONK AND THE ANGELS

The Theme of Angelic Life

Another theme which is closely associated with that of paradise is the comparison of monastic life to the life of the angels, of the monk himself to an angel. While this is distinct from the paradise theme, it expresses a similar theological truth, and the two have had a parallel development in monastic tradition.

Once again, we are here dealing with a metaphor. The monk is not an angel, but he can be called one, because he is in some respects *like* an angel. The comparison is not one of nature, but of function. The monk does not cease to possess an integral human nature, he does not become a purely spiritual being. But the theological state in which he finds himself by reason of his profession is comparable to the state of the angels in heaven. He has an angelic vocation.

The theological state of the angels is like that of Adam in paradise. The angels are in heaven, they constantly enjoy the vision of God. They already possess the good which the Christian in this life is striving to attain. Monastic life already anticipates this state: it is a heavenly condition, for it is free of every purely temporal preoccupation. The angelic state is a dimension of the life of every Christian, for the life of grace is already the life of heaven in a germinal state. But it is more fully realized in the life of a monk, for he has more radically separated himself from the concerns of the world. He lives only for heaven. The fullness of redemption which is being brought to maturity in his life is the first fruits of the eternal vision of God which will crown his efforts. Hence various aspects of monastic life are analogous to the vocation of the angels.

St. Luke and Angelic Life

The foundation for the traditional theme of angelic life is to be found in the New Testament. The principal text is contained in the Gospel of St. Luke, where Jesus replies to the crafty question of the Saducees about the resurrection: "The children of this world marry and are given in marriage. But those who shall be accounted worthy of that world and of the resurrection from the dead, neither marry nor take wives. For neither shall they be able to die any more, for they are equal to the angels, and are sons of God, being sons of the resurrection" (Lk 20,34–36).

Several observations may be made about this passage. First of all, it provided the terminology for the comparison of the Christian life, and especially monastic life, with that of the angels. Unlike the other evangelists, Luke uses the term *isaggelos*—"like an angel"—the only occurrence of this word in the entire Bible. It was later adopted by the Fathers and applied to the Christian and to the monk. Further, this text brings out the relationship between the angelic life and virginity. Neither the angels nor those who share their society in heaven marry or are given in marriage. Consequently, for those who are still in this life, the state of virginity constitutes one of the principal elements in the imitation of the life of the angels.

Finally, the full eschatological content of the theme of angelic life is rooted in this text, which is concerned with the resurrection of the body and the heavenly state to which the resurrection opens the door. Heaven is a state which entirely transcends this world, a state of "being with the Father." Jesus entered this state with his resurrection and now sits enthroned at the right hand of his Father. The salvation which he accomplished makes it possible for us to join him there, but only after we have traversed the same path through suffering to glory. Our definitive entrance into that world will come only at our own resurrection. But the state of glory is anticipated here below in the life of grace, which is an initial realization of the fruits of salvation. Hence the Christian who lives with the fullness of Christ's life here below is already living the life of the angels in heaven, and is on the way to a definitive entrance into their eternal city.

Living with the Angels

Another New Testament text which the Fathers utilized for the theme of angelic life is Matthew's saying about the angels in our

Lord's ecclesiastical discourse. This sermon (ch 18) identifies the true members of his kingdom on earth as the "little ones" who manifest the simplicity and guilelessness of children. "See that you do not despise one of these little ones; for I tell you, their angels in heaven always behold the face of my Father in heaven" (Mt 18,10). From here it is but a step to associate the life of Christ's true follower with that of the angels. The Fathers discovered the theme also in the parable of the lost sheep, which they interpreted allegorically, usually following the text of Luke (15,4–7), which lends itself more easily to a Christological interpretation.

The hundred sheep represent all intelligent creatures, angels and men alike, who were originally created to enjoy the life of heaven. The lost sheep is the human race, who left the flock and the shepherd and wandered away through sin. The good shepherd, Christ, tenderly concerned about the fate of his erring sheep, leaves the ninety-nine, who represent the myriads of angelic beings, in heaven —Matthew says the mountains, Luke the desert—and goes in search. Finding the lost sheep, Christ puts it upon his shoulders—for he bore the burden of our sins—and carries it home. The joy in heaven that results is the rejoicing of the angels over the return of their erring human brother. Thus through the Redemption man is readmitted to the society of the angels, enabled once more to live their life. St. Benedict knew this Christological interpretation (*Rule* 27,8–9), though he makes no reference here to the angels.

Our Citizenship with the Angels

Frequently in the New Testament the Christian life is associated with the life of heaven. "Our citizenship is in heaven," says St. Paul, "from which also we eagerly await a Savior, our Lord Jesus Christ, who will refashion the body of our lowliness, conforming it to the body of his glory by exerting the power by which he is able also to subject all things to himself" (Phil 3,20–21). The Christian has no permanent dwelling place in this world; his home is not in the city of man, but in the city of God, that society of the angels to which the resurrection will admit him, when at the parousia all things become subject to Christ, who will turn the kingdom over to his Father (cf 1 Cor 15,24–28).

In this world, then, the Christian is a stranger and a pilgrim (1 Pt 2,11), a wayfarer on the way to his permanent home. The present life is an "exile from the Lord" (2 Cor 5,6). The theme of exile and pilgrimage runs through both the Old and the New Testaments, from the very beginning of the history of the chosen people. Abraham was the first pilgrim, summoned from his native land to go into a country which God would show him. His descendants are likewise pilgrims, wandering in the forbidding wastes of the desert in search of the promised land. When they reach it and mistake the symbol for the reality, they are sent again into exile, where they learn that their coveted land is only a symbol of their real and lasting home. In the post-exilic period Jerusalem becomes the figure of the eternal city of God, and their pilgrimages to it are symbolic of man's journey toward that final dwelling.

In the New Testament, the epistle to the Hebrews develops the theme at some length. "Here we have no permanent city, but we seek for the city that is to come" (Heb 13,14). Abraham is the type of the Christian "looking for the city with fixed foundations, of which city the architect and the builder is God" (11,10). He and the other great men of the Old Testament lived by their faith in that city that was to come, regarding themselves as pilgrims here on earth. "They seek after a better, that is, a heavenly country. Therefore God is not ashamed to be called their God, for he has prepared for them a city" (11,16). Every Christian enters through baptism upon a spiritual journey which will take him to his final goal, the city of the angels.

The Monk as Pilgrim

The way to reach this city is by following Christ, who has declared himself to be the way to the Father (Jn 14,6). The monk is the perfect follower of Christ. On the journey he marches at the front of the ranks, following as closely as possible behind the Master. He is an exile par excellence, for by abandoning the world and fleeing into solitude he shows that he does not look upon any place in this world as his home. His life is a constant pilgrimage, a striving to advance. The monastic state is not a "state" in the sense of a static condition, for the monk can never stand still. On the contrary, it is a dynamic movement forward toward the final goal. This is a prominent theme for St. Benedict (Pr 20–25).

During the period of monastic origins and down into the Middle Ages, many monks took a literal view of their vocation to be a pilgrim. Frequently they left their native land to live elsewhere, practicing a voluntary exile. The purpose of this was to effect a more complete renunciation, to tear up the roots that attach a man to his home, his family, his native soil. It was sometimes joined with the preaching of the Gospel, sometimes with the search for martyrdom. At times the practice degenerated into abuses, which St. Benedict took steps to correct. Yet it continued after his time, not, indeed, as a characteristic element of monasticism itself, but as a practice undertaken by many monks.

Its theological significance was well in the logic of the renunciation proper to monastic life, faithful to its biblical inspiration. In the twelfth century the theme of pilgrimage was transposed to a more spiritual plane: an abandonment of self rather than an abandonment of one's native land. The real exile demanded by renunciation was seen to be an exile from self, one which could be realized within the monastery. Thus was resolved the paradox of the simultaneous demands of stability and exile in monastic spirituality. In the solitude of his cloister the monk could continue his journey toward the city of the angels.

Angels and Men in the New Jerusalem

The epistle to the Hebrews vividly represents the city of the angels to which the Christian, especially the monk, is advancing. "You have come to Mount Sion, and to the city of the living God, the heavenly

Jerusalem, and to the company of many thousands of angels, and to the church of the first-born who are enrolled in the heavens" (Heb 12,22–23). Here the entire redeemed community of angels and men is pictured, assembled together to offer worship to the Father. It is a cultic assembly, in which men redeemed by the blood of Jesus are joined to the angels in the liturgy of heaven.

The same vision of the union of angels and men in a great assembly of divine worship is presented in the last two chapters of the Apocalypse. The holy city, the new Jerusalem, is made ready like a bride adorned for her husband (21,2). This is the place where God dwells with men, so that the prophetic saying receives its final fulfillment: "They will be his people, and God himself will be with them as their God" (21,3). There is no temple there, for the Lord God and the Lamb are the temple; no sun or moon, for the glory of God illumines it, and the Lamb is the lamp thereof (21,22–23). His servants shall serve him, shall see his face, and his name shall be on their foreheads. And they shall reign forever and ever (22, 3–5).

In these descriptions men are joined with heavenly beings in a single city of God, and together offer him their praise and adoration. It is the intercommunion of the world of the angels, the Church triumphant, and the world of men, the Church militant. Man is admitted to the angelic life. The new Jerusalem is a description of heaven, but it also applies to the Church on earth. In the Church we enjoy the same heavenly gifts of God's own life, we participate in the liturgy of heaven. Thus the life of a Christian in this world, to the extent that he conforms himself to the exigencies of Christianity, is an angelic life. Monastic life, which is the most complete and logical expression of the Christian vocation, is therefore angelic life par excellence.

Angelic Life in the Liturgy

The unity of men and angels is a cultic unity. All of creation is directed toward a single finality, the consummation of the kingdom of God, a purpose which creates a solidarity among the various classes of creatures. This cosmic unity is expressed in the common worship which they offer to the Father, the lower classes of beings by fulfilling the purpose for which they were made, men and angels by consciously and intelligently contributing to the glorification of God. It is only sin that has disrupted the unity of the cosmos, as symbolized by the hostility of the cherubim who prevented fallen man from re-entering paradise to reach the tree of life.

This rupture has been healed by the salvific work of Christ. It was, says St. Paul, the mystery of God's will according to his good pleasure that "he purposed in him to be dispensed in the fullness of the times; to re-establish all things in Christ, both those in the heavens and those on the earth" (Eph 1,9–10); "therefore, you are now no longer strangers and foreigners, but you are citizens with the saints and members of God's household" (Eph 2,19). This re-established unity of the cosmos is already a reality in the Church. It finds its highest expression in the liturgy, where angels and men join together to offer their common praise to God.

This is the firm conviction of all of the Christian liturgies, which frequently refer to the role of the angels in the sacraments, the divine office and especially the celebration of the Eucharist, the mystery through which heaven and earth are united. The description of the liturgy of the heavenly Jerusalem in the Apocalypse is no doubt influenced by liturgical practices of the early Christians familiar to the author. There we already find the *Sanctus* (Apoc 4,8), the song of the seraphim, which later appears in all the liturgies. St. Benedict was intensely aware of the unity of heaven and earth in the celebration of the divine office. For him, the *opus Dei* is not merely an imitation of what the angels do in heaven; the angels are really present at the monastic liturgy and it is in their presence that the monks perform their daily service. It is from Scripture that he derives this teaching: "In the sight of the angels will I sing to thee," says the psalm (137,1); "let us then consider how we ought to behave ourselves in the presence of God and his angels, and so sing the psalms that mind and voice may be in harmony" (*Rule* 19,5–7).

The liturgy is the meeting place of heaven and earth; the point of convergence of the entire cosmos.

The Kingdom of Darkness

There is one class of creatures, however, who do not belong to the city of God: the demons, who have forever excluded themselves from the society of the blessed. Since the monk is an ally of the angels and a member of their society, he is pitted against the forces of Satan, who wage a ceaseless war against the city of God. Hence the monk is engaged in combat with the demons, and demonology occupies a prominent place in the ancient monastic literature.

Already in the earliest sources the demons appear on almost every page. In the *Vita Antonii*, Anthony engages in mortal combat with them from the very beginning of his withdrawal into solitude. At every successive stage of his further withdrawals deeper into the desert, the struggle becomes fiercer. It is especially the anchorite who is the object of their attack: the further he separates himself from human society, the more he encounters the forces of evil. The desert is, indeed, their special dwelling place, their last refuge, since an expanding Christianity has driven them from the strongholds which they formerly occupied in a world dominated by paganism.

The demons, the ancients believed, live in the air. Normally they are invisible, but at times they attack the monk in visible form. At first they attempt to dissuade him from his purpose by the suggestion of evil thoughts. If this tactic fails, then they attack openly through hallucinations intended to deceive him and lead him into sin. They terrify him with visions of wild, ravenous beasts of enormous size, or they tempt him to gluttony or fornication with visions of delicate foods or attractive women. Even more deceptively, they sometimes assume the form of men or good angels and pretend to give sound advice, even prophesying, quoting Scripture and chanting psalms, in order to deceive the monk and bring him to ruin. But they can do nothing to harm the faithful monk who combats them with prayer and asceticism, and who is able to unmask their trickery with the charismatic gift of discernment of spirits, which prevents him from being deceived.

These elements of demonology, which appear in the earliest lives, were organized into a theological synthesis by Evagrius, who devoted much speculation to the nature and activity of the demons, and to their classification according to the stages of the spiritual life and the different vices.

Significance of Demonology

This omnipresence of demons and speculation about them may seem unrealistic to the contemporary mind. The preoccupation of the ancient monks with demons can no doubt be explained in part by the cultural atmosphere of the times. Unable to explain many natural phenomena scientifically, the ancients concluded to the action of spirits upon the human body and the elements of the material universe. The monks were children of their time in accepting such speculation.

This factor, however, must not blind us to the theological significance of their demonology, which is of lasting value. Whatever they may owe to Jewish and Greek speculation, their belief in the activity of Satan and his forces is essentially Biblical. The New Testament is filled with the struggle against Satan. The source of sin and death, he has reigned over creation since the fall of Adam. He resolutely opposes Christ, who has come to despoil him of his kingdom. Our Lord defeats him in the hand-to-hand combat of the temptations of the desert, but Satan returns to the attack. The miracles are a means of vanquishing his power, for sickness and death are the consequences of sin. The Passion is the crucial hour of the combat: the crucifixion, which Satan believes to be his victory, is precisely the dramatic moment when his kingdom is definitively overturned.

Yet Satan is only despoiled; he is not yet completely annihilated. Hence he continues to wage war upon the followers of Christ. The Christian renounces him in baptism, but must be prepared to withstand his continual onslaught. The ascetical life is the art of combating the devil. In this combat the Christian, the monk, is not alone; he takes part in the battle of the whole Church. It is a conflict between two kingdoms, two cities, a combat which achieves cosmic proportions. The whole of history between Pentecost and the parousia is the story of this gigantic warfare between the kingdom of God and the kingdom of Satan.

In this combat the angels fight at our side. The Apocalypse represents them, drawn up in battle array, overcoming the forces of Satan (Apoc 12,7–9; 20,1–3). The liturgy often refers to this cosmic battle, and the monastic literature is full of references to the thousands of angels who protect the monk against the enemy hordes. Monastic life means enrolling in the angelic legions to combat the powers of darkness. The monk is a soldier in the heavenly armies; as he advances in the angelic life he becomes more and more impregnable to the attacks of the enemy. Finally he will enter the definitive city of the angels, where he will occupy one of the places left vacant by the defection of the bad angels.

The Fuga Saeculi *and Renunciation*

The theme of angelic life is, we have said, based upon analogies with the life of the angels. The monk is not called an angel because he has the same nature, but because he has the same vocation. What, then, are those constitutive elements of monastic life which have been singled out by tradition as making it comparable to the life of the angels in heaven? They may be conveniently divided into ascetical and mystical features. Both in the *praktike,* the exercises of the *vita activa* by which the monk advances toward *apatheia,* and in the *theoretike,* the state of union with God through contemplative prayer, the monk is comparable to the angels.

The first ascetical feature is that of flight from the world. Every Christian must separate himself from the world, understood in the sense of the evil world which is under the dominion of Satan and hostile to the kingdom of God and his angels. The monk dramatizes his radical opposition to the world and his citizenship in heaven by a real physical separation. Like the angels, he is *extra mundum positus*. We have seen that it is flight from the world which stood at the origin of monasticism and constitutes its most distinctive feature. The flight to the desert is a dramatic manner of witnessing to the truth that this world is transitory, that we have no permanent home here below, that our real citizenship is with the angels in heaven. The monk, who is already outside the world, is an eschatological figure. By analogy he is an angel.

The *fuga saeculi* leads him to a new form of life in his solitude. It involves the renunciation of all the goods of this world. Those who are already citizens of heaven have no need for temporal goods. They by-pass the relative values of material creation to give themselves entirely to the absolute values of eternity. Hence the monk's poverty has an eschatological meaning. Through it he imitates the angels, who have no need for temporal goods and are not weighted down with earthly cares.

Asceticism as Angelic

The asceticism of the desert is likewise an imitation of the angels. These heavenly beings require neither food nor sleep, wherefore the fasting and watching of traditional monastic practice makes the monk comparable to them. The monk's fast is a visible testimony that he has a better form of food and drink, the Word of God, for "not by bread alone does man live, but by every word that comes forth from the mouth of God" (Mt 4,4; cf Dt 8,3). His vigils seek to reproduce the continual watching of the angels, who praise God day and night. In the past, some monks, called the *acemetae* or "sleepless ones," took this feature so seriously as to arrange a continuous choir service around the clock. The denial of food and sleep may seem a purely superficial resemblance to the angels and one based on their nature rather than their function. Actually, the angelic quality of mortification goes much deeper. Its purpose is not to destroy nature but to destroy sin. Consequently asceticism is an angelic exercise, not because it makes the monk a spiritual being, but because it helps to make him a sinless one. It is in this sense that he becomes an angel.

Obedience, too, is a quality of the angels. Their name is derived not from their primary function of glorifying God, but from their secondary function of acting as his messengers. In this respect they manifest a perfect obedience; they are the ideal servants of God, entirely dependent upon his will. The monk, therefore, in making God's will the norm which determines everything in his life, is imitating the virtue of the angels.

The angelic virtue par excellence, however, is virginity. Our Lord himself lends his authority to this, when he compares those who neither marry nor are given in marriage to the angels in heaven. Once again this analogy is not based upon nature, but upon religious realities. Virginity is of value not because it is a negation of the body, but because it is an anticipation of the life to come. Chastity, far from merely repressing natural instincts which in themselves are good, is an eschatological sign of the kingdom that is coming in its fullness. The monk shows by his life of virginity that he already lives in this kingdom of the future; he is already a citizen of heaven with the angels.

Angelism or Eschatology

All of these ascetical practices, traditionally features of monastic spirituality, are means which the monk employs for the attainment of *apatheia*, the goal of the *vita activa* and its ultimate perfection. The monk who has arrived at this point shares in the fullness of the angelic life. The angels are impassible: their being is entirely unified and fixed upon God. The monk becomes like them when he enters a similar state of domination over passion and perfect tranquillity of spirit. We have seen that St. Benedict expresses this reality in terms of the ladder of humility leading to perfect charity. The monk's goal must be this charity which confers a perfect unity upon the spiritual life, a state of simplicity in which his entire being is unified in an over-all direction toward God. At this point his ascetical life is no longer merely a means, but is a symbol, a sign of his freedom from the trammels of earthly existence and of his total belonging, together with the angels, to the heavenly Jerusalem.

This assimilation of monasticism to the angelic life must be properly understood. It is not a question of angelism in the sense of a false spirituality marked by a disdain for the body and a misunderstanding of the proper place of temporal values in the supernatural order. To live the angelic life does not mean to become something less than a man; it means to be fully a man—a man living out his Christian vocation to the ultimate degree. There is no question here of a Platonic dualism that would regard the body as the enemy of the soul. It may be that some formulations of the angelic ideal in tradition have been infelicitous, for patristic thought was influenced by Platonic categories. Basically, however, its inspiration was profoundly biblical. Closer examination will usually reveal that the vesture of Platonic terminology is only a vehicle of expression for a thought that is authentically Christian. In the last analysis, the theme of angelic life is an eloquent expression of the eschatological dimension of the monastic vocation.

The Climax of Angelic Life

This becomes still clearer when we turn to the mystical aspects of monasticism. Asceticism is by no means a negative exercise; the monk despoils himself of everything on earth only to possess God more completely. If he is like the angels in the spoliation, he resembles them even more in the possession. The contemplation of God is the very essence of the vocation of the angels, who behold his face continually in heaven. Here we come back to the New Testament roots of the theme of angelic life, for the contemplation of the Father is our Lord's own definition of the angels' activity. To act as heavenly messengers is only a secondary function of the angels, who continue to behold the face of God even when occupied with his messages. "*Nihil sunt angeli,*" says St. Augustine, "*nisi videndo te*" (*En in Ps* 34,1,13): an angel can be defined only in terms of his constant vision of God.

The contemplation of God is also the highest ideal of the Christian. The supreme happiness of heaven will consist in the beatific vision. For the monk, however, it is not sufficient to aspire to this blessed state in the life to come; he wishes to achieve it in this life, to occupy himself here below with what will be his permanent activity in the heavenly Jerusalem. This is the one thing necessary for which he makes all the renunciations which are comprised in the gradual ascent of the ascetic life. At the top of the ladder he finds the promised land, which is the goal of his earthly pilgrimage, the blessed *theoria* which is the constant occupation of the angels. In this life contemplation is obscure, through faith, yet it is germinally the same supernatural reality as the contemplation through vision in heaven.

It is in the higher states of prayer that the monk realizes the fullness of the angelic life. He knows through faith that the angels are present at the celebration of the Eucharist and the divine office. But it is only after a gradual purification has led him to the heights of *theoria* that he becomes aware of their presence and consciously lives and praises with the angels. St. Bernard is said to have seen the angels in the choir at Clairvaux, one standing next to each monk and keeping a record of the care with which he sang the office. The contemplative is conscious of the angelic presence, for he has already entered into his true home, the world of the angels, and is totally absorbed in their activity of seeing and praising the Creator.

7. FREEDOM AND SIMPLICITY

Confidence of the Christian

Numerous practical consequences flow from the fact that the monastery is a paradise in the theological sense and that monastic life is the life of the angels anticipated upon earth. The monk's attitudes toward God, his fellow men, and toward all of reality depend upon this theological state in which he finds himself. Here we wish to consider some of these attitudes which are characteristic of the monk who lives the angelic life in the paradise of the cloister.

The first of these qualities is that of confidence. In Christian terminology this quality signifies the assurance which the Christian enjoys in his relationship with God as a result of the divine sonship which he has received through baptism. Since the monk has, to a greater extent than other Christians, carried his baptismal commitment through to its logical conclusions, confidence is especially predicated of him in the monastic literature and is directly associated with the paradise theme.

In treating of the confidence of the Christian, the Fathers were merely developing a theme which already appears in the New Testament. The Greek word which expresses this reality, and which already occurs in the Septuagint, is *parresia.* The term derives from political usage in the city-state of Athens, where it signified the citizen's right of freedom of speech. The citizen was entitled to stand up in the assembly of free men and boldly proclaim whatever was on his mind. Thus the concept of *parresia* included the aspects of freedom, boldness and frankness.

Parresia *in the New Testament*

The New Testament took over the terminology of *parresia* to express the freedom of the Christian before God. This theme occurs in the first epistle of St. John. The Christian's confidence is based upon his faith in Christ and his fulfillment of the commandments of Christ, especially the precept of love of neighbor. In such a man the Holy Spirit takes up his dwelling. It is the divine principle within us, a certain connaturality with God himself, which gives us confidence. *Parresia* comes into being when God dwells through his Spirit in those who keep his commandments. This confidence has an eschatological reference: it is especially on the day of judgment that it will be manifest. "Abide in him, so that when he appears we may have confidence, and may not shrink ashamed from him at his coming." (1 Jn 2,28)

Parresia is especially significant in relation to prayer. The Christian who is united to God through his obedience to the commands of

Jesus is instructed by the Holy Spirit. The Spirit within him enables him to open himself to God in prayer with perfect freedom, and gives him the right and power to speak frankly to God, together with a firm confidence that he will be heard. "Beloved, if our heart does not condemn us, we have confidence towards God, and whatever we ask, we shall receive from him, because we keep his commandments and do those things that are pleasing in his sight." (1 Jn 3,21–22)

For St. Paul, *parresia* is pre-eminently the quality of an apostle, who speaks his message boldly, enjoying confidence both before God and before men. He asks the Ephesians to pray that "when I open my mouth, utterance may be granted to me fearlessly to make known the mystery of the Gospel . . . so that therein I may dare to speak as I ought" (Eph 6, 19–20). The freedom and confidence of the Christian stand in sharp contrast to the fear and servitude of the old law (cf 2 Cor 3,12–18). Whoever has been grafted on to Christ finds himself in a state of true freedom before God and can approach him with perfect confidence. "In Christ Jesus our Lord . . . we have assurance and confident access through faith in him" (Eph 3,11–12).

The Parresia *of the Monk*

The Fathers enthusiastically took up the theme of *parresia.* They applied it particularly to the martyrs, who in the moment of their torment looked confidently toward God in the hope that he would give them victory. With the peace of the Church and the development of monasticism, it was the monks who took over the role formerly occupied by the martyrs. Accordingly *parresia* became pre-eminently a quality of the monk. It was especially applied to the power of working miracles, which plays such a prominent role in monastic hagiography. The monk enjoyed the privilege of *parresia* to such a degree that he could ask God for anything and be assured of receiving it.

We find this theme already in the *Vita Antonii.* In connection with the miracles worked by his hero, St. Athanasius points out that these were in accord with the promise of Christ: "If you have faith like a mustard seed, you will say to this mountain, 'Remove from here!' and it will remove; and nothing will be impossible to you" (Mt 17,19); "Amen, amen, I say to you, if you ask the Father anything in my name, he will give it to you. . . . Ask and you shall receive" (Jn 16,23–24). In connection with these scriptural promises, Athanasius comments: "For Anthony did not heal by issuing commands, but by praying and calling upon the name of Christ, so that it was evident to everyone that it was not he who did this, but the Lord manifesting his compassion to men and, through Anthony, healing those who suffered" (*Vita Antonii* 83–84).

St. Gregory likewise presents St. Benedict as a great miracle worker. If he is able to accomplish so many prodigies, it is because he is completely filled with the Spirit and therefore possesses the gift of confidence in prayer. When asked to raise a boy from the dead, he declines on the plea that only the apostles have *parresia* sufficient to ask such a gift from God. But when urged further, he raises his hands to heaven in prayer, and soon the boy is restored to life (*Dial* 2,32). The same is true of his sister Scholastica, who obtained a thunderstorm in answer to her prayer (*Dial* 2,33). The miracles of monastic hagiography are not idle tales, but a proof of the perfect possession of the Spirit of God by one who is in the fullest sense a *vir Dei.*

The Freedom of Apatheia

Consequently, the Fathers connected the gift of *parresia* with the attainment of *apatheia.* When the soul has been purified by the practices of the ascetical life it regains that perfect freedom which was characteristic of Adam's relationship with God in paradise and can dare to stand before God with confidence of being heard. *Parresia* is therefore achieved when the monk enters into the blessed state of *theoria,* a share in the life of the angels. It is opposed to shame and fear, results of original sin; when these are banished by the indwelling

Spirit they are replaced in the new life of paradise by freedom and confidence to approach God, just as Adam was on terms of familiarity with him in the first paradise.

The monk is delivered from servitude to sin and enjoys "the freedom wherewith Christ has made us free" (Gal 4,31), "the freedom of the glory of the sons of God" (Rom 8,21). No longer a slave to sin, he is now a slave in the service of God, sensitive to the promptings of the Spirit within him: *servus Dei.* This condition, far from being degrading, is actually a great perfection, for it is simply the recognition of his ontological relationship to God. The twelfth degree of humility is a description of the attitude of the monk who recognizes his position as a slave in the service of God. But under the new law the Christian passes from fear in God's service to love. "No longer do I call you servants . . . but I have called you friends" (Jn 15,15), for "you have not received a spirit of bondage so as to be again in fear, but you have received a spirit of adoption as sons" (Rom 8,15).

Parresia makes its appearance when the monk passes from the *praktike* into the *theoretike,* because it indicates a higher stage of the supernatural life. It is contrasted not only with the shame which is characteristic of the servitude of sin, but also with the fear which marked the old law. It is the mark of Adam in paradise and of the angels in heaven, and thus belongs to the monk who, freed from both sin and fear in the ascent of the ascetical life, enjoys the perfection of the angelic life in the paradise of the cloister. It is significant that St. Benedict says of the monk who has climbed the ladder of humility that he arrives at "that perfect love of God which casts out all fear" (7,67), precisely the quality which St. John attributes to the Christian who has "perfect confidence" (1 Jn 4,17–18).

Parresia *in Prayer Life*

It is in relation to prayer that the monk's *parresia* is especially important. Christian prayer is essentially conversation with God as a

Father. This demands an objective foundation, a real participation in the divine life which we receive through the indwelling of the Holy Spirit. Origen pointed out that prayer to God as a Father was lacking in the Old Testament because the divine sonship was lacking (*De Orat* 22,1–2). St. Paul tells us that it is our consciousness of adoption as sons that enables us to cry out "Abba, Father!" (Rom 8,15). "The Spirit himself gives testimony to our spirit that we are sons of God" (Rom 8,16), and "pleads for us with unutterable groanings" (Rom 8,26).

Thus the recitation of the Lord's prayer is the supreme expression of the *parresia* of the Christian. It is because the Spirit within us makes us sons of God that we have the right to pray, "Our Father." In the words of the Roman Mass, "we dare" to say this; we dare to speak to God as sons to a Father, in perfect freedom and confidence of being heard. Formerly the Our Father was said immediately after baptism, because it is the reception of the Spirit which gives the Christian the right to address God in this bold fashion. For St. Benedict the expression, "Abba, Father," refers to Christ, in accord with his practice of addressing prayer to Christ (2,3).

The posture of prayer in the early Church was itself a manifestation of the *parresia* of the Christian: standing, eyes raised toward heaven, arms extended. This is the familiar position of the *orantes* in the iconography of the early Church, fortunately restored by the recent revision of the rubrics of the Roman missal from the truncated form to which it had been reduced. It is, in the monastic literature, the position of the *vir Dei* addressing God. This was the way St. Benedict died: "supporting his weakened body on the arms of his disciples, he stood erect with his hands raised towards heaven, and breathed forth his spirit together with words of prayer" (*Dial* 2,37).

Freedom in the Monastic Life

A sense of freedom is pre-eminently characteristic of the monk who has been restored to the theological condition of paradise. For St. Paul this freedom affects not only the Christian's relationship with God, but also his dealings with men. He is free not only to speak boldly to God, but also to express himself with frankness before men (2 Cor 3,12; Eph 6,19–20). "Where the Spirit of the Lord is, there is freedom" (2 Cor 3,17). "Making known the truth, we commend ourselves to every man's conscience in the sight of God." (2 Cor 4,2)

The monk must in practice be conscious of his freedom. His obedience to superiors and subjection to a form of life which regulates every detail of his existence, far from engendering a cramped and narrow attitude, ought to make him all the more conscious of his essential freedom. It is the possession of the Spirit, not any purely human device, which makes him free. The service of God is the highest form of liberty. As a man and as a Christian, he must strive to preserve "the glorious freedom of the sons of God" (Rom 8,21) in the face of everything which threatens to reduce or destroy it.

Freedom can be threatened by influences outside the monk himself, by the inevitable imperfections of ecclesiastical institutions. But we are here concerned with the threats to freedom which arise from the individual's own imperfections. Basically, they can all be reduced to egocentricity, which can take on various forms. Whatever form it may assume in the concrete, it is fundamentally a false attitude toward oneself in relationship to the rest of reality. Man must first be aware of his real metaphysical situation: he is neither an angel nor a brute animal. Beyond this, he must recognize his place in the supernatural order: a creature, endowed with noble gifts, wounded by sin, capable of restoration through incorporation in Christ. This is another way of saying with St. Benedict that humility must be the keystone of the monk's ascetical life.

Abdication of Freedom

Egocentric attitudes can only go counter to this sane outlook upon reality and restrict the monk's essential freedom by imprisoning him within himself. An excessive independence, an exaggerated sensitivity or an overzealous defense of what he contends to be his rights can only hamper the activity of the Spirit and prevent him from taking possession of all conscious thought and activity. Self-indulgence has a similar effect, for it tends to set up the individual's own desires as the supreme norm of his activity and thus implicitly reject the higher norm of the Holy Spirit.

On the other hand, a false compliance is an even more subtle threat to freedom. If the monk enslaves himself to convention, to inherited or acquired prejudices, to habits from which he is unwilling to make the effort to free himself, or to a vague fear of appearing singular, he renounces the "glorious freedom of the sons of God" (Rom 8,21). The man who cherishes the "freedom with which Christ has made us free" (Gal 4,31) must be prepared to do his own thinking, to make his own decisions, to stand upon his own feet. The greatest enemy to this authentic freedom is human respect, which can threaten to shape men's decisions in the monastery as well as in the world. To permit the views of others and the fear of their disapproval to rule one's life means in effect to place one's personal popularity before considerations of objective supernatural value. Though this may be done only in relatively minor matters, it is nevertheless an infringement of one's freedom.

Catholicity of Outlook

The monk must also be prepared to respect the freedom of others, who enjoy the same essential liberty as himself. Nothing is more contrary to the true monastic spirit than a narrowness of mind which would seek to force everyone else into a single mold. This is basically an egocentric attitude, for it reflects a wish to impose one's own standards, opinions and prejudices upon others. The humble man, on the contrary, who is acutely aware of his own limitations, will be more generous in his estimate of others, without in any way compromising his own principles.

A monk should be characterized by an habitual open-mindedness. If he takes freedom seriously, he must be prepared to welcome the diversity that is everywhere present in human affairs. He will recognize that no one person or community realizes all the potentialities of human nature, and will be happy to pay tribute to good wherever it may be found. He will be able to see the value of other customs, other viewpoints, other modes of life, other systems of thought, and will be marked by a certain ecumenicity of outlook in his judgments. The wish to impose a rigid uniformity upon everyone else is a manifestation of that bitter zeal which St. Benedict energetically condemns as destructive of peace and charity (72,1).

Monasticism, due to its links with the past, always tends to be conservative, in the best sense of the term, insofar as it has a wholesome respect for authentic traditions. This is in no sense incompatible, however, with an openness to change where nonessentials are concerned and with an ability to see the value of other approaches. The variety of forms which monasticism has taken on in the past and the many accidental differences among monasteries today are the result of a liberty of spirit which has always been a Benedictine characteristic. Breadth of view is basically a question of allowing the Spirit to breathe where he wills, rather than attempting to stifle his working by imposing preconceived norms upon it.

Simplicity: An Angelic Virtue

The reason that a monk can be tolerant is that he learns through prayer to look upon reality from the viewpoint of God: variety and multiplicity are not divisive if they are transcended by unity. It is the monk's union with God in his angelic state which enables him to go beyond all multiplicity, to rise above diversity. As a citizen of heaven he can survey the universe with understanding and tolerance. This is the virtue of simplicity.

Simplicity is often praised in the Scriptures. In the beautiful prayer of Chronicles, David exclaims: "I know, my God, that you test hearts and love simplicity; wherefore I too, in the simplicity of my heart, have joyously offered you all this" (1 Chr 29,17). The book of Wisdom opens with the admonition, "Think of the Lord in goodness, and seek him in simplicity of heart." Modern translations usually render this word as "integrity" or "uprightness," already an indication of its resonance. It refers to the sincere man who serves God in a forthright and undivided manner, without deceit.

Our Lord recommended the same virtue to his disciples: "Be therefore wise as serpents, and simple as doves" (Mt 10,16). While there may be a reference here to the natural meekness of the dove, the comparison seems rather to be based upon the use of the dove for sacrifice in Jewish ritual practice, and thus to express wholeheartedness and integrity in the service of God. St. Paul repeatedly mentions the virtue of simplicity in the sense of sincerity, single-mindedness and generosity in giving of oneself. Thus he exhorts the Corinthians to a single-minded generosity in contributing to his collection for the Jerusalem church (2 Cor 8,2; 9,11.13). He encourages slaves to offer their masters the same wholehearted service which they give to Christ (Eph 6,5; Col 3,22).

Monastic Simplicity

Simplicity is a property of God, and was characteristic of Adam in his paradisiacal state. His integrity was such that he served God with undivided mind and heart, as the angels in heaven do. This simplicity was lost with the introduction of sin; it can be regained only through the difficult process of the return to paradise. Insofar as the Christian is already a citizen of the rediscovered paradise, he possesses the simplicity of Adam.

The monk, in whom the paradisiacal element of the Christian life is especially manifest, should cultivate the virtue of simplicity. The monk's life should be one of simplicity because he is dedicated to a single-minded search for God. He renounces everything in this world to free himself for the search. The word *monk* was often interpreted by the Fathers in the sense of unity: unity of purpose, unity of conduct, undivided effort to be drawn into the unity of God himself. The monk in this sense is one who is totally devoted to his supernatural ideal, so that his whole life is orientated about a single pursuit from which it derives its simplicity.

This simplicity is closely associated with *apatheia,* the goal of the ascetical combat. It is the labor of the *vita activa,* with its continuing renunciation, which gradually frees the monk from the multiplicity of his attachments and concentrates his efforts solely upon God. He becomes undivided only in proportion as he is purified of worldly concerns and of self. Only the pure heart is totally dedicated to seeking God alone. Growth in simplicity therefore proceeds apace with progress in prayer, for it is the man who has attained *apatheia* who is capable of offering pure prayer. The authentic contemplative is a man of true simplicity, for he is totally concentrated upon God alone.

The Witness of Simplicity

Simplicity is a state of liberty, because it belongs to the soul which has been freed through asceticism from those ties of divisive self-love which restrict freedom. It is often referred to as spiritual childhood. The comparison is based not upon the child's unawareness of evil but rather on his total dependence upon his father. It was this recognition of one's own incapacity and willingness to depend for everything upon another rather than upon one's own resources which our Lord singled out in children and recommended to his disciples. "Whoever does not accept the kingdom of God as a little child will not enter into it" (Lk 18,17). The child is single-minded because he has no pretensions of his own worth and so is not divided. He is quite content to be wholly dependent upon his father. The monk likewise must be satisfied to be wholly dependent upon his Father in heaven.

Far from being an impoverishment, this attitude vastly enriches one's life. It leaves behind the good only to attain the better, the relative to attain the absolute. The virtue of simplicity is a share in the attribute of God, who is one in spite of the Trinity of Persons. It means becoming one with God by transcending the multiplicity of the present life with all its complexity and division. The principle of this divine unity is our share in God's life through the Holy Spirit dwelling within the soul. By virtue of simplicity the monk becomes a witness to the reality of the world of the absolute, of the transcendence of the kingdom of God. He manifests to the world the life of Adam in the restored paradise and of the angels in heaven. Like them, he has no treasure except God.

Epilogue: The Relevance of Monastic Spirituality

THIS BOOK has attempted to introduce the reader into the riches of monastic spirituality: to situate it in its historical context and its place in the life of the Church, to define and describe the elements which compose it. In spite of the richness and complexity of the themes which have been indicated, representing the flowering of a centuries-old tradition, the dominant characteristic of monasticism remains its simplicity: the search for God in solitude, apart from the anxiety and turmoil of the world, according to the purest evangelical doctrine.

At the end of this investigation the question must be asked: does monastic spirituality still have a place in the modern world? Does it still have a contribution to make to the Church of today, in which conditions are so different from the time of its origins? Is it still a vital factor in Christian life, or merely a curious, if interesting, relic of the past?

At the present time the Church stands in a period of renewal which has stirred the Christian world to a degree unparalleled for many centuries. There are some elements in this renewal which parallel the traditional approach of monasticism and thus are quite in harmony with monastic spirituality. The renewal is based upon a return to sources. This means that there is an intense concern in modern times to recover the Church's authentic tradition beyond the deviations which have sometimes intruded themselves at a more recent epoch. This process involves a careful study of the Bible and the Fathers, the most profound and basic sources for the Church's life and teaching. In this respect the modern renewal is at one with monastic spirituality, for these are precisely the sources from which monasticism has always drawn its life: the staple diet of the *lectio divina.*

On the other hand, there are other aspects of the contemporary renewal which seem to be proceeding in the opposite direction from the traditional monastic outlook. It is not, in fact, monastic spirituality which has given the principal dynamic impetus to the movement of renewal, but rather an approach to spirituality which can be called incarnational. It stems from the realization that nature is essentially good, that the Church's mission is not to rescue men from an evil world, but to sanctify and transform material creation so that men may achieve their salvation in and through it.

Contrary to the forebodings of the "prophets of doom," there is every reason for optimism about the Church's fulfillment of this mission. She must not fear the world, or withdraw into the safety of a fortress to withstand a siege from without, but must bravely gird herself for the tasks which need to be accomplished, and go on the offensive. She must transform herself to meet the exigencies of life in a world which has itself profoundly changed. She must adapt her structure, her theology, her worship, her methods of evangelization to enter into dialogue with the world and become meaningful to men who live within the context of twentieth-century civilization.

The essence of monastic spirituality, on the other hand, is flight from the world. The monk takes refuge in the desert to seek an existence which transcends created good. He does not play a direct role in the construction of a Christian civilization in this world, but looks forward with intense desire to the kingdom of God which is to come. His answer to temporal reality is not incarnation in the world, not missionary zeal for direct action to effect its transformation, but eschatology. He does not seek the values of the city of man; he burns with desire for the city that is above, the heavenly Jerusalem.

These two divergent outlooks may appear to be contradictory. In fact they are not so. Both are fully Christian attitudes, provided that each is tempered by an awareness of the other. Not only are they both legitimate, but both are necessary to realize the fullness of the Church's life. This ambivalent attitude toward the world stands at the very center of the Christian commitment, simply because the Church is what she is: in the world, but not of it; the immaculate Bride of Christ, without spot or wrinkle, and at the same time a community of wretched and imperfect sinners.

Ambivalence toward the world is of the very essence of the Church, for she exists in a state of tension. Tension between this world and the next, between immanence and transcendence, between realized eschatology and future eschatology, between sign and reality, between hierarchical structure and charismatic inspiration, between tranquil contemplation of her Lord and feverish activity to extend his kingdom, between worship and service, between the fruitful use of human values and renunciation of them, between holy prudence and divine folly, between the city of redeemed man and the city of the redeeming God. There are two poles in the Church's existence which draw her in different, though not entirely opposite, directions: her life and development in this world and her destiny in the world to come. She must be incarnate in the world of created reality, and yet keep her gaze fixed upon the transcendent reality of her consummation in the eschatological kingdom.

These two aspects of the Church's being must be present in the life of every Christian. He must live out the paradox, find a balance in the tension between the two poles. In this life the tension is never perfectly resolved: the saints are those who come closest to a solution. Only in the next life can the tension be entirely transcended. Here below every Christian must reckon with the duality of his existence, and seek to establish the best synthesis possible for himself. Because the two elements can be combined in varying proportions, there is no limit to the possibilities of accidental differences in Christian spirituality.

The Church herself, in the multiplicity of her organs, must also find a temporary equilibrium until her pilgrimage is ended. Hence each of the two aspects of her life, incarnation and eschatology, must be realized in stable form in one or the other of her organs. Each member and each institution in the Church must choose a synthesis which is dominated by one of the two poles, without entirely excluding the other. The hierarchy represents the Church as incarnate in the world, structured to meet the missionary task of converting and sanctifying men. The monk is a witness to the eschatological aspect of the Church's being.

This is his role in the Church: to be a witness, to testify, in his own way, to what the Church is in the mystery of her own inner life. What is productive in the monk's life is not what he does, but what he is. He does not exist *for* anything else: like the martyr, he seeks to live by and for God alone, to bury himself in the mystery of Christ's death and exaltation, and thus to bear witness to the transcendence of the demands of God.

So long as the Church exists, there will be need for this kind of witness. Without it the Church would not be fully herself, for she would cease to be a reminder to men of the transitoriness of this life and the transcendence of the kingdom of heaven. Monasticism is not the whole of the Church's life, any more than is her government or her missionary effort: it is all of her organs together which give completeness of life and activity to the Body of Christ.

It is for this reason that the Church, through her *Magisterium*, has never ceased to insist upon the necessity and value of the monastic and contemplative life. In our own time, when the validity of ancient institutions is being questioned, there is perhaps more need for Christians to be reminded of this than in other periods of history. This is why recent popes, while wholeheartedly encouraging the movement of incarnationalism which has given so much vitality to the Church in the twentieth century, have at the same time recalled the value and superiority of the contemplative life, superior precisely because it transcends the merely transitory to attain what is definitive.

Pius XII, speaking to a congress organized for the study of oriental monasticism, said:

> What has been called the spirituality of the desert, that form of contemplative outlook which seeks God in silence and renunciation, is a profound movement of the Spirit, which will never cease so long as there are hearts to hear its voice. It is not fear, nor regret, nor mere prudence, which peoples the solitudes of monasteries. It is the love of God. That there should be in the midst of great modern cities, in the richest countries, as well as in the plains of the Ganges or the forests of Africa, souls capable of satisfying themselves all their life long with praise and adoration, who freely devote themselves to thanksgiving and intercession, who voluntarily become the advocates of humanity before the Creator, the protectors and intercessors on behalf of their brothers before the Father of heaven, what a victory of the omnipotent God, what glory for the Savior! Essentially, monasticism is nothing other than this (Allocution *Nous sommes heureux*, April 11, 1958: AAS 50 (1958) 285).

Pope John XXIII expressed himself in similar terms to the General Chapter of the Cistercians:

> The Church, while such pressure is put upon her by the external apostolate, so necessary in our time, nevertheless attributes the greatest importance to contemplation, and especially in our time when there is so much insistence upon exterior action. In reality, the authentic apostolate consists precisely in a participation in the salvific work of Christ. Now such participation is impossible without an interior spirit of prayer and sacrifice. Christ redeemed the world, enslaved to sin, principally by his prayer and by sacrificing himself: likewise those souls who try to relive this intimate aspect of Christ's mission, even if they do not devote themselves to any external activity, promote the apostolate in an eminent manner (Allocution *C'est à Rome*, Sept. 1, 1962: AAS 54 (1962) 664).

More recently, in his discourse at the consecration of the basilica of Monte Cassino, Pope Paul VI has eloquently testified to the continuing value of the monastic life:

> It is for us to bear testimony to something other than the nature of monastic life; and we can express it in a simple statement: the Church still has need today of this form of religious life; the world still has need of it today . . . yes, the Church and the world, for different but convergent reasons, need for St. Benedict to go forth from the ecclesiastical and social community and surround himself with a barrier of solitude and silence. From there may he let us hear the enchanting tones of his tranquil and recollected prayer, from there may he allure and summon us to the threshold of his monastery, to offer us the blueprint for a workshop 'of the Lord's service,' of a small ideal society, dominated by love, obedience, innocence, freedom from material things and the art of rightly using them, predominance of the spirit, peace—in a word, the Gospel (Allocution *Quale saluto*, Oct. 24, 1964: AAS 56 (1964) 986–987).

The Fathers of the Second Vatican Council have given expression not only to the Church's esteem for the monastic life, but also to the hope that in the future a renewed monasticism may make a fruitful contribution to the prosecution of the Church's mission:

> The venerable institute of monastic life, which in its long history through the centuries has achieved conspicuous merits in the Church and in human society, should be faithfully preserved and, with the passage of time, should shine forth more brightly in its authentic spirit both in the East and in the West. The principal duty of monks is to offer the divine Majesty a service which is humble but at the same time noble within the enclosure of the monastery, whether by devoting themselves wholly to divine worship in the hidden life, or by legitimately taking on certain works of the apostolate or of Christian charity. Preserving therefore the particular character of the institute, they should renew their ancient serviceable traditions and adapt them to the needs of souls today in such a way that monasteries may be, as it were, nurseries for

the building up of the Christian people (*Decree on the Renewal and Adaptation of Religious Life* 9).

Monastic spirituality continues to be relevant to the Church and to the world, in our time as in the past, because it reflects something which is essential to Christianity. In a period which is dominated by incarnationalism and the resurgence of renewed vitality, the message of monasticism has an increasingly important role to play. It is its task to remind Christians that no amount of natural evolution and human activity can bring about the ultimate human good: this is an unmerited gift of God, and can only be sought from the Lord by prayer and penance. It must remind men today that their joy and satisfaction in the value of created goods and their optimism over human achievement must be tempered by the realization that this value and achievement, however noble it may be, is transitory. The ultimate values belong to the world to come.

On the other hand, monks must be aware of the limitations of their own spirituality. It is, in fact, the possession of a minority, and it needs to be complemented by other aspects of the Church's mission. Monks have much to learn from other organs of the Church, much reason to be grateful to them. They must be attuned to the value of the incarnational aspect of the Church's life. Their solitude and separation, far from cutting them off from the life of the Church, should make them all the more concerned about the welfare of their brothers. The knowledge that others are giving generously of themselves to build the kingdom of God in the world should inspire in them a sense of humility, an awareness of their social responsibility and the will to make their own hidden life an apostolically productive force in the Mystical Body.

In these times of renewal, monastic spirituality cannot remain aloof from the vital currents which are stirring the Church to new life. Monasticism, too, has sometimes strayed from its original ideal and sought to exercise influence in the Church and the world through institutional power and activity rather than through the silent witness of withdrawal and renunciation. Monks must also return to the sources of their spirituality and study the problem of how the purity of their witness can best be expressed in the modern world. The monasteries which will have the most fruitful and permanent influence in the Church of the future will be those which have recovered the simplicity of the primitive monastic ideal of living for God alone in solitude, obscurity and poverty, and waiting with humble patience for the manifestation of his glory.

Bibliography

LIST OF ABBREVIATIONS

AAS	*Acta Apostolicae Sedis*
ABR	*The American Benedictine Review*
Anal Mon	*Analecta Monastica*
Aux sources...	J. Leclercq, *Aux sources de la spiritualité occidentale. Etapes et constantes*, Paris 1964
Benedictus...	*Benedictus, der Vater des Abendlandes, 547–1947. Weihegabe der Erzabtei St. Ottilien zum vierzehnhundertsten Todesjahr dargebracht und herausgegeben von H. S. Brechter*, Munich 1947
BGAMB	*Beiträge zur Geschichte des alten Mönchtums und des Benediktinerordens*
BM	*Benediktinische Monatschrift*
BVC	*Bible et vie chrétienne*
C Cis	*Collectanea Cisterciensia* (continuation of *COCR*, 1965–)
CJC	*Codex Juris Canonici*
COCR	*Collectanea Ordinis Cisterciensium Reformatorum*
Denz	H. Denzinger and others, *Enchiridion Symbolorum, Definitionum et Declarationum de Rebus Fidei et Morum*

DR	*Downside Review*
D Sp	*Dictionnaire de spiritualité*
EA	*Erbe und Auftrag* (continuation of *BM*, 1959–)
GL	*Geist und Leben*
Irén	*Irénikon*
LJ	*Liturgisches Jahrbuch*
LM	*Liturgie und Mönchtum*
LMD	*La Maison-Dieu*
LO	*Lex Orandi*
Mél Bén	*Mélanges bénédictins publiés à l'occasion du XIVe centenaire de la mort de saint Benoît par les moines de l'abbaye de saint Jérôme de Rome*, Fontenelle 1947.
Message . . .	*Le message des moines à notre temps (Mélanges Alexis Presse)*, Paris 1958.
MS	*Monastic Studies*
MTZ	*Münchener Theologische Zeitschrift*
NRSM	*Nouvelle revue de science missionaire*
OCA	*Orientalia Christiana Analecta*
OCP	*Orientalia Christiana Periodica*
PL	J. P. Migne, *Patrologia Latina*
RAM	*Revue d'ascétique et de mystique*
R Bén	*Revue bénédictine*
Riv Lit	*Rivista liturgica*
RLM	*Revue liturgique et monastique*
R Mab	*Revue Mabillon*
RR	*Review for Religious*
RTAM	*Recherches de théologie ancienne et médiévale*
SA	*Studia Anselmiana*
SM	*Studia Monastica*
SMGBO	*Studien und Mitteilungen zur Geschichte des Benediktiner-Ordens und seiner Zweige*
Stud Pat	*Studia Patristica*
TG	*Theologie und Glaube*
Théologie . . .	*Théologie de la vie monastique*, Paris 1961
TWNT	*Theologisches Wörterbuch zum Neuen Testament*
VM	*Vita monastica*
VS	*La vie spirituelle*
VSS	*La vie spirituelle (Supplément)*

BIBLIOGRAPHY ON MONASTIC SPIRITUALITY

The best source for current bibliography is the *Bulletin de Spiritualité Monastique*, which has appeared regularly in *COCR* since 1959. The 1962 bulletin, with some entries from 1960 and 1961, is available in English: A. Louf and others, *The Message of Monastic Spirituality*, New York 1964. Sections 1-3 of the 1963 bulletin appeared in English in periodical form: *The Message of Monastic Spirituality*, New Melleray Abbey, Dubuque, Iowa 1963.

The following also contain useful bibliographical information:

The *Bulletin d'Histoire Bénédictine*, appearing regularly in *R Bén* since 1907.

The *Bulletin d'Histoire Monastique*, appearing regularly in *R Mab* since 1926.

R. Bauerreis, *Bibliographia Benedictina 1939-1952*, in *SMGBO* 57 (1939) (1)–(28); 64 (1952) (29)–(127).

R. Bauerreis, *Bibliographie der Benediktinerregel*, in *SMGBO* 58 (1940) 3–20.

O. Kapsner, *A Benedictine Bibliography* (2 vols), Collegeville 1962.

O. Rousseau, "Chronique des publications monastiques," in *Irén* 36 (1963) 110–129.

For papal documents:

A Piel, *Les moines dans l'Eglise. Textes des Souverains Pontifes recueillis et présentés*, Paris 1964.

On Byzantine monasticism:

H.-G. Beck, *Kirche und theologische Literatur im byzantinischen Reich*, Munich 1959, 120–140.

I. WHAT IS RELIGIOUS LIFE?

1. Christian Perfection

E. Mersch, *Morality and the Mystical Body*, New York 1939.

C. Truhlar, *Problemata Theologica de Vita Spirituali Laicorum et Religiosorum*, Rome 1960.

G. Thils, *Christian Holiness*, Tielt 1961.

L. Bouyer, *Introduction to Spirituality*, New York 1961.
R. Schutz, *Living Today for God*, Baltimore 1962.
Collective work: *Laïcs et vie chrétienne parfaite*, Rome 1963.
Collective work: *Sainteté et vie dans le siècle*, Rome 1965.
F. Vandenbroucke, "Retours à l'Evangile," in *VS* 112 (1965) 141–153.

2. *Christian Perfection in Religious Life*

A. Gasquet, *Religio Religiosi. The Object and Scope of the Religious Life*, London 1923².
C. Butler, *Ways of Christian Life*, London 1932.
O. Lottin, *Considérations sur l'état religieux et la vie bénédictine*, Louvain 1946.
Jac. Leclercq, *La vocation religieuse*, Tournai 1951.
E. Heufelder, *Die evangelischen Räte: die biblisch-theologischen Grundlagen des Ordenslebens im Blick auf seine Erneuerung in unserer Zeit*, Vienna 1953.
E. von Severus, "Die christliche Stände in der Ordnung der Heilsökonomie," in *GL* 27 (1954) 406–418.
R. Voillaume, *Seeds of the Desert. The Legacy of Charles de Foucauld*, Chicago 1955.
B. Lavaud, *The Meaning of the Religious Life*, Westminster 1955.
I. Hausherr "I fondamenti teologici della vita religiosa," in *VM* 13 (1957) 51–63.
R. Carpentier, *Life in the City of God. An Introduction to the Religious Life*, New York 1959.
J. Winandy, "Le sens originel des conseils évangéliques," in *COCR* 22 (1960) 105–119.
J. Leclercq, *The Life of Perfection. Points of View on the Essence of the Religious State*, Collegeville 1961.
H. Holstein, "The Mystery of Religious Life," in *RR* 20 (1961) 317–329.
Soeur Jeanne d'Arc, "Fonction de la vie religieuse dans l'Eglise et dans le monde," in *VSS* 66 (1963) 353–382.
J. Tillard, "Religious Life in the Mystery of the Church," in *RR* 22 (1963) 613–633.
J. Tillard, "Religious Life, Sacrament of God's Presence," *ibid* 23 (1964) 6–14.

J. Tillard, "Religious Life, Sign of the Eschatological Church," *ibid* 197–206.

J. Tillard, "Religious Life, Sacrament of God's Power," *ibid* 420–432.

Collective work: *Les religieux aujourd'hui et demain*, Paris 1964.

Collective work: *La vie religieuse dans l'Eglise du Christ*, Paris 1964.

3. *Different Forms of Religious Life*

C. Vagaggini, "La spiritualità e le spiritualità," in *Il senso teologico della liturgia*, Rome 1958 [2], 505–515.

B. Besret, "Le problème des fins de la vie religieuse," in *Les religieux aujourd'hui et demain*, Paris 1964, 27–50.

II. WHAT IS MONASTIC LIFE?

1. *The Origins of Monasticism*

On the origins and early history of monasticism:

I.G. Smith, *The Rise of Christian Monasticism*, London 1892.

J.-M. Besse, *Les moines d'Orient, antérieurs au concile de Chalcédoine*, Paris 1900.

J. Hannay, *The Spirit and Origin of Christian Monasticism*, London 1903.

St. Schiwietz, *Das morgenländische Mönchtum* (3 vols), Mainz and Mödling 1904, 1913, 1938.

H. Workman, *The Evolution of the Monastic Ideal*, London 1913; reprinted Boston 1962.

P. Van Cauwenbergh, *Etude sur les moines d'Egypte depuis le Concile de Chalcédoine (451) jusqu'à l'invasion arabe (640)*, Paris-Louvain 1914.

W. Mackean, *Christian Monasticism in Egypt to the Close of the Fourth Century*, London 1920.

U. Berlière, *L'Ordre monastique des origines au XIIe siècle*, Maredsous 1924[3].

J. Hannah, *Christian Monasticism, A Great Force in History*, London 1924.

H. White, *The Monasteries of the Wâdi 'n Natrûn. Part II: The History of the Monasteries of Nitria and of Scetis*, New York 1932.

K. Heussi, *Der Ursprung des Mönchtums*, Tübingen 1936.

A. Vööbus, *History of Asceticism in the Syrian Orient* (2 vols so far), Louvain 1958, 1960.

A. Vööbus, "Sur le développement de la phase cénobitique et la réaction dans l'ancien monachisme syriaque," in *Recherches de Science Religieuse* 47 (1959) 401–407.

G. Turbessi, *Ascetismo e monachesimo prebenedettino*, Rome 1961.

On the Qumran Sect and monastic origins:

S. Luff, "The Monks of Qumran and St. Benedict's Rule. The Continuity of Monastic Tradition," in *Dublin Review* 474 (1957) 313–321.

E. Hardy, "The Dead Sea Discipline and the Rule of St. Benedict," in *Journal of Bible and Religion* 25 (1957) 183–186.

J. Van der Ploeg, "Les Esséniens et les origines du monachisme chrétien," in *Il Monachesimo Orientale* (*OCA* 153), Rome 1958, 321–339.

A. Penna, "Il reclutamento nell' essenismo e nell' antico monachesimo cristiano," in *Revue de Qumran* 1 (1958–1959) 345–364.

G. Brisebois, "De momento regulae Communitatis seu Unionis Qumrân ad originem vitae religiosae," in *Antonianum* 34 (1959) 3–31.

B. Rigaux, "L'idéal d'un moine de Qumran à la lumière des écrits de la Mer Morte," in *Revue Générale Belge* 98 (1962) 1–19.

On St. John the Baptist and monasticism:

J. Steinmann, *St. John the Baptist and the Desert Tradition*, New York 1958.

G. Penco, "S. Giovanni Battista nel ricordo del monachesimo medievale," in *SM* 3 (1961) 7–32.

On the literature of ancient monasticism:

Th. Camelot, "Les Pères du désert, un guide de lecture," in *VS* 101 (1959) 316–324.

G. Penco, "Osservazioni preliminari sui caratteri dell' antica letteratura monastica," in *Aevum* 35 (1961) 220–246.

J. Quasten, "The Founders of Egyptian Monasticism," in *Patrology*. Vol III: *The Golden Age of Greek Patristic Literature*, Utrecht 1960, 146–189 (with excellent bibliography).

Some translations of monastic texts which have appeared subsequent to the bibliography in Quasten:

A.-J. Festugière, *Les moines d'Orient.* Vol. II: *Les moines de la région de Constantinople,* Paris 1961; Vol III: *Les moines de Palestine* (3 fascicles), Paris 1962, 1964; Vol IV, 1: *Enquête sur les moines d'Egypte (Historia Monachorum in Aegypto),* Paris 1964.

T. Merton, *The Wisdom of the Desert,* New York 1961.

P. Deseille, *L'Evangile au désert, des premiers moines à saint Bernard. Présentation, choix de textes et traduction,* Paris 1965.

R. Meyer, *Palladius: The Lausiac History* (*Ancient Christian Writers* 34), Westminster, Md. 1965.

On the spirituality of ancient monasticism:

K. Holl, *Enthusiasmus und Bussgewalt im griechischen Mönchtum,* Leipzig 1898.

P. Resch, *La doctrine ascétique des premiers maîtres égyptiens du quatrième siècle,* Paris 1931.

W. Seston, "Remarques sur le rôle de la pensée d'Origène dans les origines du monachisme," in *Revue de l'Histoire des Religions* 108 (1933) 197–213.

M. Viller and K. Rahner, *Aszese und Mystik in der Väterzeit. Ein Abriss,* Freiburg im B. 1939.

A. Stolz, *L'ascèse chrétienne,* Chevtogne 1948.

V. Warnach, "Der pneumatische Charakter des Mönchtums," in *SMGBO* 62 (1950) 1–7.

H. Bacht, "Heimweh nach der Urkirche. Zur Wesendeutung des frühchristlichen Mönchtums," in *LM* 7 (1950) 64–78.

L. Bouyer, *The Meaning of the Monastic Life,* New York 1955.

U. Ranke-Heinemann, "Die Gottesliebe als ein Motiv für die Entstehung des Mönchtums," in *MTZ* 8 (1957) 289–294.

O. Rousseau, *Monachisme et vie religieuse d'après l'ancienne tradition de l'Eglise,* Chevtogne 1957.

G. Colombás, "El concepto de monje y vida monástica hasta fines del siglo V," in *SM* 1 (1959) 257–342; condensed English version "The Ancient Concept of the Monastic Life," in *MS* 2 (1964) 65–117.

U. Ranke-Heinemann, "Zum Volkommenheitsideal im frühen Mönchtum," in *EA* 35 (1959) 109–121.

U. Ranke-Heinemann, "Todessehnsucht und Parusieerwartung im frühen Mönchtum," *ibid* 351–356.

P. Deseille, "La spiritualité de l'ancien monachisme," in *Christus* 8 (1961) 412–424.

L. Bouyer, *The Spirituality of the New Testament and the Fathers*, New York 1963.

U. Ranke-Heinemann, *Das frühe Mönchtum: seine Motive nach den selbstzeugnissen*, Essen 1964.

On St. Anthony:

L. Bouyer, *La vie de saint Antoine. Essai sur la spiritualité du monachisme primitif*, Saint-Wandrille 1950.

Collective work: *Antonius Magnus Eremita* (*SA* 38), Rome 1956.

For further bibliography see J. Quasten, *Patrology*. Vol. III: *The Golden Age of Greek Patristic Literature*, Utrecht 1960, 39–45; 148–153.

On St. Pachomius:

P. Ladeuze, *Etude sur le cénobitisme pakhômien pendant le IVᵉ siècle et la première moitié du Vᵉ*, Louvain 1898, reprinted 1961.

H. Bacht, "Pakhôme–der grosse 'Adler'," in *GL* 22 (1949) 375–379.

H. Bacht, "L'importance de l'idéal monastique de S. Pachôme pour l'histoire du monachisme," in *RAM* 26 (1950) 308–326.

H. Bacht, "Vom gemeinsamen Leben. Die Bedeutung des pachomianischen Mönchsideals für die Geschichte des christlichen Mönchtums," in *LM* 11 (1952) 91–110.

H. Bacht, "Antonius und Pachomius. Von der Anachorese zum Cönobitentum," in *Antonius Magnus Eremita* (*SA* 38), Rome 1956, 66–107.

H. M. Biedermann, "Die Regel des hl. Pachomius und die evangelischen Räte," in *Ostkirchliche Studien* 9 (1960) 241–253.

H. Bacht, "La loi du 'retour aux sources'. (De quelques aspects de l'idéal monastique pachômien)," in *R Mab* 51 (1961) 6–25.

H. Bacht, "Mönchtum und Kirche. Eine Studie zur Spiritualität des Pachomius," in *Sentire Ecclesiam (Festschrift H. Rahner)*, Freiburg im B. 1961, 113–133.

H. Bacht, "Pakhôme et ses disciples," in *Théologie . . .*, 39–71.

On St. Basil:

E. Morison, *St. Basil and His Rule: A Study in Primitive Monasticism*, Oxford 1912.

W. Clarke, *St. Basil the Great: A Study in Monasticism*, Cambridge 1913.

M. Murphy, *St. Basil and Monasticism*, Washington 1930.

P. Humbertclaude, *La doctrine ascétique de saint Basile de Césarée*, Paris 1932.

D. Amand, *L'ascèse monastique de saint Basile. Essai historique*, Maredsous 1948.

J. Gribomont, "Obéissance et Evangile selon saint Basile," in *VSS* 21 (1952) 192–215.

J. Gribomont, "L'exhortation au renoncement attribuée à saint Basile," in *OCP* 21 (1955) 375–398.

J. Gribomont, "Le monachisme au IVe siècle en Asie Mineure, de Gangres au Messalianisme," in *Stud Pat* II, Berlin 1957, 400–415.

J. Gribomont, "Les Règles Morales de saint Basile et le Nouveau Testament," *ibid* 416–426.

E. Amand de Mendieta, "Le système cénobitique basilien comparé au système pachômien," in *Revue de l'Histoire des Religions* 132 (1957) 31–80.

J. Gribomont, "Le renoncement au monde dans l'idéal ascétique de saint Basile," in *Irén* 31 (1958) 282–307; 460–475.

B. Drack, "Beschauliches und tätiges Leben im Mönchtum nach der Lehre Basilius des Grossen," in *Freiburger Zeitschrift für Philosophie und Theologie* 7 (1960) 297–309; 391–414; 8 (1961) 93–108.

J. Gribomont, "Saint Basile," in *Théologie . . .*, 99–113.

2. *The Benedictine Tradition*

On the origins of monasticism in the West:

L. Gougaud, "Les critiques formulées contre les premiers moines d'Occident," in *R Mab* 24 (1934) 145–163.

G. Gordini, *Forme di vita ascetica a Roma nel IV secolo*, Rome 1952.

G. Gordini, "Origine e sviluppo del monachesimo a Roma," in *Gregorianum* 37 (1956) 220–260.

G. Ferrari, *Early Roman Monasteries. Notes for the History of the Monasteries and Convents at Rome from the Vth through the Xth Century*, Vatican City 1957.

G. Penco, "Il concetto di monaco e di vita monastica in Occidente nel secolo vi," in *SM* 1 (1959) 7-50; an English version is scheduled to appear in *MS*.

G. Penco, *Storia del monachesimo in Italia dalle origini alla fine del Medio Evo*, Rome 1961.

J. O'Sullivan, "Early Monasticism in Gaul," in *ABR* 16 (1965) 32-46.

On St. Jerome:

P. Antin, "Le monachisme selon saint Jérôme," in *Mél Bén*, 71–105; plus appendix 107–113.

P. Antin, "Saint Jérôme," in *Théologie* . . . ,191–199.

On St. Martin of Tours:

Collective work: *Saint Martin et son temps. Mémorial du XVI*ᵉ *centenaire des débuts du monachisme en Gaule (361–1961)* (*SA* 46), Rome 1961.

On St. Augustine:

C. Lambot, "L'influence de saint Augustine sur la règle de saint Benoît," in *RLM* 14 (1929) 320–330.

M. Mellet, *L'itinéraire et l'idéal monastiques de saint Augustin*, Paris 1934.

A. Zumkeller, *Das Mönchtum des hl. Augustinus*, Würzburg 1950.

A. Manrique, *La vida monástica en San Agustín. Enchiridion histórico-doctrinal y Regla*, El Escorial-Salamanca 1959.

A. Sage, *La Règle de saint Augustin commentée par ses écrits*, Paris 1961.

M. Verheijen, "Saint Augustin," in *Théologie* . . . , 201–212.

On John Cassian:

B. Capelle, "Les oeuvres de Jean Cassien et la Règle bénédictine," in *RLM* 14 (1929) 309–319.

S. Marsili, *Giovanni Cassiano ed Evagrio Pontico. Dottrina sulla carità e contemplazione* (*SA* 5), Rome 1936.

L. Cristiani, *Jean Cassien. La spiritualité du désert* (2 vols), Saint-Wandrille 1946.

M. Rothenhäusler, "Das innere Leben des Zönobiten nach Joh. Cassian und die Regel des hl. Benedikt," in *Vir Dei Benedictus. Eine Festgabe zum 1400. Todestag des heiligen Benedikt dargeboten von Mönchen der Beuroner Kongregation, herausgegeben von Abtpräses Dr. R. Molitor*, Münster 1947, 276–292.

O. Chadwick, *John Cassian: A Study in Primitive Monasticism*, Cambridge 1950.

M. Olphe-Galliard, "Cassien (Jean)," in *D Sp* II, Paris 1953, 214–276.

P. Munz, "John Cassian," in *The Journal of Ecclesiastical History* 11 (1960) 1–22.

J.-C. Guy, *Jean Cassien. Vie et doctrine spirituelle*, Paris 1961.

H. Weber, *Die Stellung des Johannes Cassianus zur ausserpachomianischen Mönchstradition. Eine Quellenuntersuchung*, Münster 1961.

On St. Benedict:

I. Herwegen, *St. Benedict, A Character Study*, St. Louis 1924.

J. Chapman, *St. Benedict and the Sixth Century*, London 1929.

F. Cabrol, *Saint Benedict*, London 1934.

J. McCann, *Saint Benedict*, London 1937.

O. Casel, "Benedikt von Nursia als Pneumatiker," in *Heilige Überlieferung (Festgabe Herwegen) (BGAMB*, Supplementband), Münster 1938, 96–123.

T. Lindsay, *Saint Benedict: His Life and Work*, London 1949.

I. Schuster, *St. Benedict and His Times*, St. Louis 1951.

D. Knowles, "St. Benedict," in *The Month* 23 (1960) 69–83.

L. von Matt and S. Hilpisch, *Saint Benedict*, London 1961.

J. Leclercq, "Monasticism and St. Benedict," in *MS* 1 (1963) 9–23.

On the authenticity and transmission of the *Rule*:

A. Mundó, "L'authenticité de la 'Regula sancti Benedicti'," in *Commentationes in Regulam s. Benedicti* (*SA* 42), Rome 1957, 105–158.

G. Penco, "La prima diffusione della Regola di S. Benedetto," *ibid* 321–345.

G. Penco, "La Regola e le regole," in *VM* 14 (1960) 81–90.

P. Meyvaert, "Towards a History of the Textual Transmission of the 'Regula S. Benedicti'," in *Scriptorium* 17 (1963) 83–110.

On the *Regula Magistri:*

G. Penco, *S. Benedicti Regula. Introduzione, testo, apparati, traduzione e commento*, Florence 1958; contains a full discussion of the problems and a bibliography complete through 1957.

A. de Vogüé, *La Règle du Maître. Introduction, texte, traduction et notes* (3 vols; *Sources Chrétiennes* 105–106–107), Paris 1964, 1965; contains further bibliography, extensive introduction, critical text and valuable indices; the third volume contains a verbal concordance by J.-M. Clément, J. Neufville and D. Demeslay.

Recent bibliography can also be found in M. J. Cappuyns, *Lexique de la Regula Magistri* (Instrumenta Patristica 6), Steenbrugge 1964.

D. Knowles, "The Regula Magistri and the Rule of St. Benedict," in *Great Historical Enterprises; Problems in Monastic History*, Edinburgh 1963, 139–195 (a good introduction to the question).

Editions of the *Holy Rule*:

C. Butler, *Sancti Benedicti Regula Monachorum. Editio Critico-Practica*, Freiburg im B. 1912.

B. Linderbauer, *S. Benedicti Regula, herausgegeben und philologisch erklärt*, Metten 1922; text and apparatus reprinted in *S. Benedicti Regula Monasteriorum* (*Florilegium Patristicum* 17), Bonn 1928.

A. Lentini, *S. Benedetto, La Regola. Testo, versione e commento*, Montecassino 1947.

G. Colombás, L. Sansegundo and O. Cunill, *San Benito, su vida y su regla* (*Biblioteca de Autores Cristianos* 115), Madrid 1954.

P. Schmitz, *Sancti Benedicti Regula Monachorum*, Maredsous 1955[2].

G. Penco, *S. Benedicti Regula. Introduzione, testo, apparati, traduzione e commento*, Florence 1958.

R. Hanslik, *Benedicti Regula* (*Corpus Scriptorum Ecclesiasticorum Latinorum* 75), Vienna 1960.

Translations of the *Holy Rule*:

L. Doyle, *St. Benedict's Rule for Monasteries*, Collegeville 1948.

J. McCann, *The Rule of St. Benedict in Latin and English*, Westminster, Md. 1952.

A. Savaton, *La Règle de saint Benoît*, Lille 1950.

A. Dumas, *La Règle de saint Benoît*, Paris 1963.

B. Steidle, *Die Benediktusregel, lateinisch-deutsch*, Beuron 1964.

Modern translations are also contained in the editions of Lentini, Sansegundo, Schmitz and Penco listed in the preceding section.

Commentaries on the *Holy Rule*:

Smaragdus, *Commentaria in regulam sancti Benedicti*, in *PL* 102, 689–932.

Pseudo Paul the Deacon: *Pauli Warnefridi . . . in sanctam regulam commentarium archi-coenobii Casinensis monachi nunc primum ediderunt*, Monte Cassino 1880.

Hildemar: *Expositio regulae ab Hildemaro tradita et nunc primum typis mandata*, Regensburg 1880.

Bernard of Monte Cassino, *Expositio in Regulam*, Monte Cassino 1894.

P. Boherius: *Petri Boherii in Regulam sancti Benedicti commentarium nunc primum editum cura et studio L. Allodi*, Subiaco 1908.

B. Haeften, *Disquisitionum Monasticarum Libri XII*, Antwerp 1644.

J. Mège, *Commentaire sur la Règle de S. Benoît*, Paris 1687.

E. Martène, *Commentarius in Regulam S. P. Benedicti*, Paris 1690; reprinted in *PL* 66, 205–932.

A. Calmet, *Commentaire litteral, historique et moral sur la Règle de saint Benoît* (2 vols), Paris 1734; Latin translation, Paris 1750.

P. Delatte, *The Rule of St. Benedict*, reprint Latrobe, Penn. 1950.

I. Herwegen, *Sinn und Geist der Benediktinerregel*, Einsiedeln 1944.

I. Schuster, *S. Benedetto: La Regula Monasteriorum. Testo, introduzione, commento e note*, Alba 1945.

I. Schuster, *Historical Notes on St. Benedict's "Rule for Monks,"* Hamden, Conn. 1962.

A. Lentini, *S. Benedetto, La Regola. Testo, versione e commento*, Montecassino 1947.

B. Steidle, *Die Regel St. Benedikts. Eingeleitet, übersetzt und aus dem alten Mönchtum erklärt*, Beuron 1952.

G. Colombás, L. Sansegundo, O. Cunill, *San Benito, su vida y su regla* (*Biblioteca de Autores Cristianos* 115), Madrid 1954.

Collective work: *Commentationes in Regulam s. Benedicti, cura B. Steidle* (*SA* 42), Rome 1957.

H. Van Zeller, *The Holy Rule. Notes on St. Benedict's Legislation for Monks*, New York 1958.

M.-D. Philippe, *Analyse théologique de la Règle de saint Benoît*, Paris 1961.

Works on Benedictine spirituality:

M. Wolter, *The Principles of Monasticism*, St. Louis 1962.

P. Gueranger, *Religious and Monastic Life Explained*, St. Louis 1908.

C. Butler, *Benedictine Monachism. Studies in Benedictine Life and Rule*, London 1919.

J.-M. Besse, *Le moine bénédictin*, Paris 1920.

C. Marmion, *Christ the Ideal of the Monk. Spiritual Conferences on the Monastic and Religious Life*, St. Louis 1926[6].

D. Gorce, "La part des 'Vitae Patrum' dans l'élaboration de la Règle Bénédictine," in *RLM* 14 (1929) 338–399.

D. Knowles, *The Benedictines*, New York 1930; condensed version, *The Benedictines. A Digest for Moderns*, St. Leo, Florida 1962.

P. de Puniet, *La spiritualité bénédictine*, Praglia 1931.

J. Leclercq, "La vie évangélique selon la Règle de saint Benoît,' in *VS* 76 (1947) 848–855.

V. Warnach, "Gesetz und Geist in der Regel des heiligen Benedikt," in *LM* 4 (1948) 63–65.

G. Morin, *The Ideal of the Monastic Life Found in the Apostolic Age*, Westminster, Md. 1950.

I. Van Houtryve, *Benedictine Peace*, Westminster, Md. 1950.

M. Thiel, "Benediktinische Heiligkeit. Zur zönobitischen Vollkommenheitsideal des heiligen Benedikt," in *LM* 11 (1952) 63–72.

M.-A. Denis, *Théologie bénédictine*, Paris 1952.

I. Schuster, *La vie monastique dans la pensée de saint Benoît*, Paris 1953.

T. Merton, *Basic Principles of Monastic Spirituality*, Gethsemani 1957.

T. Merton, *The Silent Life*, New York 1957.

T. Merton, *Monastic Peace*, Gethsemani 1958.

B. Calati, "Historia Salutis. Saggio di metodologia della spiritualità monastica," in *VM* 13 (1959) 3–48; reprinted separately, Rome 1959; partial English translation, "Monastic Spirituality: An Essay on Rule or Methodology," in *ABR* 15 (1964) 437–457.

J. Winandy, "Benedictine Spirituality," in J. Gautier (ed), *Some Schools of Catholic Spirituality*, New York 1959, 17–48.

R. Tschudi, *Die Benediktiner*, Fribourg 1960.
H. Van Zeller, *Approach to Monasticism*, New York 1960.
J. Leclercq, *The Love of Learning and the Desire for God*, New York 1961.
A. Savaton, *Valeurs fondamentales du monachisme*, Paris 1962.
W. Tunink, *Vision of Peace*, New York 1963.
S. Hilpisch, "The Benedictine Ideal Through the Centuries," in *ABR* 15 (1964) 381–394.
A. Kemmer, "Christ in the Rule of St. Benedict," in *MS* 3 (1965) 87–98.
A. de Vogüé, "La Paternité du Christ dans la Règle de saint Benoît et la Règle du Maître," in *VS* 110 (1964) 55–67.
G. Turbessi, *Ascetismo e monachesimo in S. Benedetto*, Rome 1965.

On Benedictine history:
J.-M. Besse, *Les mystiques bénédictins des origines au XIIIe siècle*, Maredsous 1922.
U. Berlière, *L'ascèse bénédictine des origines à la fin du XIIe siècle. Essai historique*, Maredsous 1927.
S. Hilpisch, *Geschicht des benediktinischen Mönchtums in ihren Grundzügen dargestelt*, Freiburg im B. 1929.
H. Leclercq, *L'ordre bénédictin*, Paris 1930.
J. Perez de Urbel, *Historia de la orden benedictina*, Madrid 1941.
P. Schmitz, *Histoire de l'Ordre de saint-Benoît* (7 vols), Maredsous 1942–1956.
D. Knowles, *The Monastic Order in England*, Cambridge 1940.
D. Knowles, *The Religious Orders in England* (3 vols), Cambridge 1948, 1955, 1959.
P. Cousin, *Précis d'histoire monastique*, Paris 1956; contains extensive but often inaccurate bibliography.
S. Hilpisch, *Benedictinism Through Changing Centuries*, Collegeville 1958.
S. Hilpisch, *History of Benedictine Nuns*, Collegeville 1958.
H. Van Zeller, *The Benedictine Idea*, Springfield, Ill. 1959.
L. Daly, *Benedictine Monasticism: Its Formation and Development Through the 12th Century*, New York 1965.

On St. Benedict of Aniane:
J. Narberhaus, *Benedikt von Aniane: Werk und Persönlichkeit (BGAMB 16)*, Münster 1930.

J. Winandy, "L'oeuvre monastique de saint Benoît d'Aniane" in *Mél Bén*, 237–258.

P. Schmitz, "L'influence de saint Benoît d'Aniane, dans l'histoire de l'ordre de saint Benoît," in *Il monachesimo nell' alto Medioevo e la formazione della civiltà occidentale*, Spoleto 1957.

On early medieval monasticism:

M. A. Schroll, *Benedictine Monasticism as Reflected in the Warnefrid-Hildemar Commentaries*, New York 1941.

Collective work: *Il monachesimo nell' alto Medioevo e la formazione della civiltà occidentale (IV settimane di studio del centro Italiano di studi sull' alto Medioevo)*, Spoleto 1957.

J. Leclercq, F. Vandenbroucke and L. Bouyer, *La spiritualité du moyen âge*, Paris 1961.

J. Leclercq, *The Love of Learning and the Desire for God*, New York 1961; contains complete bibliography of Dom Leclercq to 1960.

J. Semmler, "Karl der Grosse und das Frankische Mönchtum," in *Karl der Grosse. Lebenswerk und Nachleben. II. Das geistige Leben*, Düsseldorf 1965, 255–289; cf summary by J. Leclercq, "Charlemagne et les moines," in *C Cis* 27 (1965) 242–245.

J. Leclercq, *Témoins de la spiritualité occidentale*, Paris 1965.

On the medieval monastic crisis:

J. Leclercq, "La crise du monachisme aux XIe et XIIe siècles," in *Bulletino dell' Istituto Storico Italiano per il Medio Evo* 70 (1958) 19–41; reprinted in *Aux sources . . .*, 175–199.

N. Cantor, "The Crisis of Western Monasticism, 1050–1130," in *American Historical Review* 66 (1960–61) 47–67.

On Cluny:

G. de Valous, *Le monachisme clunisien des origines au XVe siècle* (2 vols), Ligugé 1935.

Collective work: *A Cluny. Congrès scientifique*, Dijon 1950.

K. Hallinger, *Gorze-Kluny. Studien zu den monastichen Lebensformen und Gegensätzen im Hochmittelalter (SA 22–23–24–25)*, Rome 1950, 1951.

Collective work: *Spiritualità cluniacense (Convegni del centro di studi sulla spiritualità 2)*, Todi 1960.

J. Leclercq, "Pour une histoire de la vie à Cluny. Qu'est-ce que Cluny?", in *Revue d'Histoire Ecclésiastique* 57 (1962) 385–408; 783–812.

J. Leclercq, "Un sommet: Cluny," in *Aux sources . . .*, 91–173.

J. Leclercq, "Culte et pauvreté à Cluny," in *LMD* 81 (1965) 33–50.

On Citeaux:

T. Merton, *The Waters of Siloe*, New York 1949.

L. Lekai, *The White Monks. A History of the Cistercian Order*, Okauchee, Wis. 1953.

A. King, *Citeaux and Her Elder Daughters*, London 1954.

L. Bouyer, *The Cistercian Heritage*, Westminster, Md. 1958.

M.-A. Dimier, "Les concepts de moine et de vie monastique chez les premiers Cisterciens," in *SM* 1 (1959) 399–418.

H. Daniel-Rops, *Bernard of Clairvaux. The Story of the Last of the Great Church Fathers*, New York 1964.

P. Salmon, "Monastic Asceticism and the Origins of Citeaux," in *MS* 3 (1965) 119–138.

3. Monastic Spirituality in the Church

On the meaning of the term "monk":

A. Adam, "Grundbegriffe des Mönchtums in sprachlicher Sicht," in *Zeitschrift für Kirchengeschichte* 63 (1953–1954) 209–239.

J. Leclercq, *Etudes sur le vocabulaire monastique du moyen âge (SA 48)*, Rome 1961.

On the role of monasticism in the life of the Church:

F. Vandenbroucke, *Le moine dans l'Eglise du Christ*, Louvain 1947.

E. von Severus, "Das Monasterium als Kirche," in *Enkainia*, Maria Laach 1956, 230–248.

O. Rousseau, "Communauté ecclésiale et communauté monastique," in *LMD* 51 (1957) 10–30.

U. Ranke-Heinemann, "Das Verhältnis des frühen Mönchtums zur Kirche," in *GL* 30 (1957) 272–280.

F. Wulf, "Mönchsspiritualität?," in *GL* 31 (1958) 460–463.

D. Rutledge, "The Monk and the Holy People of God," in *Clergy Review* 43 (1958) 333–342.

A. de Vogüé, "Le monastère, Eglise du Christ," in *Commentationes in Regulam s. Benedicti (SA 42)*, Rome 1958, 25–46.

G. Ladner, *The Idea of Reform. Its Impact on Christian Thought and Action in the Age of the Fathers*, Cambridge, Mass. 1959.

F. Vandenbroucke, "Jalons pour une théologie du monachisme," in *SM* 2 (1960) 159–192.

H. Bacht, "Mönchtum und Kirche. Eine Studie zur Spiritualität des Pachomius," in *Sentire Ecclesiam (Festschrift H. Rahner)*, Freiburg im B. 1961, 113–133.

E. Heufelder, "St. Benedikt von Nursia und die Kirche," *ibid* 176–184; also in *EA* 36 (1960) 440–447.

Collective work: *Théologie de la vie monastique*, Paris 1961.

Collective work: *Théologie de la vie monastique d'après quelques grands moines des époques moderne et contemporaine*, Ligugé 1961; *R. Mab* 51 (1961) 91–299 *(Archives de la France monastique* 50*)*.

A. Kassing, "Die Mönchsgemeinde in der Kirche. Eine Skizze," in *GL* 34 (1961) 190–196.

G. Penco, "L'ideale monastico nella vita della Chiesa," in *VM* 18 (1964) 6–18; 63–70.

A. Robles Sierra, "Cuestiones de teología de la vida monástica," in *Yermo* 2 (1964) 75–88.

A. de Vogüé, "Monasticism and the Church in the Writings of Cassian," in *MS* 3 (1965) 19–51.

J. Leclercq, "The Role of Monastic Spirituality Critically Discussed," in *Worship* 39 (1965) 583–596.

III. THE COORDINATES OF MONASTIC SPIRITUALITY: THE BIBLE AND THE LITURGY

1. The Biblical Inspiration of Monasticism

F. Bauer, "Die heilige Schrift bei den Mönchen des christlichen Altertums," in *TG* 17 (1925) 512–532.

P. Volk, *Die Schriftzitate der Regula S. Benedicti*, appendix to E. Munding and A. Dold, *Palimpsesttexte des Codex Latin. Monacensis* 6333 (*Texte und Arbeiten* 15–18) Beuron 1930, (1)–(34).

P. Volk, "Das Psalterium des hl. Benedikt," in *SMGBO* 48 (1930) 83–97.

H. Dörries, "Die Bibel im ältesten Mönchtum," in *Theologische Literaturzeitung* 72 (1947) 215–222.
A. Vaccari, "La Bibbia nell' ambiente di S. Benedetto," in *Biblica* 29 (1948) 321–344.
B. Fischer, "Die Psalmenfrömmigkeit der Regula Benedicti," in *LM* 4 (1949) 22–35; 5 (1950) 64–79.
A. Mundó, "Bibliotheca: Bible et lecture de carême d'après S. Benoît," in *R. Bén* 60 (1950) 65–92.
E. von Severus, "Zu den biblischen Grundlagen des benediktinischen Mönchtums," in *GL* 26 (1953) 113–122.
Collective work: Ecriture sainte et spiritualité," in *D Sp* IV, Paris 1960, 128–278.
C. Augrain, "Les sources bibliques du prologue de la Règle," in *COCR* 22 (1960) 3–10.
J. Bonjorn, "Biblia y monacato en San Jerónimo," *ibid* 249–261.
P. Gordan, "Paulus als Lehrer der Mönche," in *EA* 36 (1960) 163–168.
B. Egli, *Der vierzehnte Psalm im Prolog der Regel des heiligen Benedikt,* Sarnen 1962.
Collective work: *La Bibbia nell' alto Medioevo*, Spoleto 1963.
G. Colombás, "La Biblia en la espiritualidad del monacato primitivo," in *Yermo* 1 (1963) 3–20; 149–170; 271–286; 2 (1964) 3–14; 113–129; an English version is scheduled to appear in *MS.*
P. M. Galopin, "La Bible et saint Benoît," in *BVC* 55 (1964) 65–77.
C. Gindele, "Die Schriftlesung im Pachomiuskloster," in *EA* 41 (1965) 114–122.
S. Pawlowsky, *Die biblischen Grundlagen der Regula Benedicti (Wiener Beiträge zur Theologie IX),* Vienna 1965.

2. *The Liturgical Inspiration of Monasticism*

P. Deseille, "La liturgie monastique selon les premiers cisterciens," in *LMD* 51 (1957) 82–87.
C. Vagaggini, "Liturgia e spiritualità" in *Il senso teologico della liturgia,* Rome 1958^{2}, 505–577.
C. Vagaggini, "Liturgia e questione monastica," in *VM* 12 (1958) 165–173.
B. Besret, "La liturgie monastique," in *Message . . .*, 221–250.

E. von Severus, "Liturgie und Mönchtum," in *LM* 22 (1958) 7–15.

G. Brasó, *Liturgy and Spirituality*, Collegeville 1960.

W. Dürig, "Liturgische Frömmigkeit, in *LM* 27 (1960) 31–40.

E. Dekkers, "Were the Early Monks Liturgical?", in *COCR* 22 (1960) 120–137.

E. Dekkers, "Moines et liturgie," *ibid*, 329–340; also in German in *EA* 39 (1963) 204–213.

E. Dekkers, "Liturgie et vie spirituelle aux premiers siècles," in *LMD* 69 (1962) 29–38.

A.-M. Roguet, "La réforme liturgique et les contemplatives," in *VS* 47 (1965) 78–86.

L. Leloir, "Towards a More Prayerful Liturgy," in *MS* 3 (1965) 99–118.

C. Vagaggini, *Bibbia e spiritualità liturgica*, Rome 1965.

3. *The Eucharist in Ancient Monasticism*

B. Steidle, "Die Eucharistie im frühen Mönchtum," in *Die Regel St. Benedikts*, Beuron 1952, 189–198.

C. Donahue, "The Agape of the Hermits of Scete," in *SM* 1 (1959) 97–114.

G. Penco, "La partecipazione alla vita eucaristica presso il monachesimo antico," in *Riv Lit* 48 (1961) 183–192.

4. *The Eucharist in the Church*

For bibliography on the Eucharist, see A. Piolanti (ed), *Eucaristia: Il mistero dell' altare nel pensiero e nella vita della Chiesa,* Rome 1957, and J. de Baciocchi, *L'Eucharistie*, Tournai 1964.

See also the collective work: *The Eucharist in the New Testament*, Baltimore 1964.

5. *The Eucharist and the Monk*

On the place of the Eucharist in Christian spirituality, see the bibliographies in the volume edited by Piolanti, listed in the preceding section.

See also the articles in *LMD* 24 (1950): *La messe, engagement de charité.*

IV. THE ENTRANCE TO MONASTIC LIFE

1. The Biblical Doctrine of Conversion

J. Behm and E. Würthwein, "metanoeo, metanoia," in *TWNT* IV, Stuttgart 1942, 972–1004.

R. Schnackenburg, "Metanoia," in *Lexikon für Theologie und Kirche* 7, Freiburg im B. 1962, 356–359 (with bibliography).

2. Conversion in the Church

See the articles in *LMD* 55 and 56 (1958): *La pénitence dans la liturgie.*

Also the articles in *Lumière et Vie* 47 (1960): *La conversion.*

Collective work: *Pénitence et pénitences: l'insertion de notre ascèse dans le plan redempteur*, Brussels 1953.

3. Conversion and the Monk

See the entries under Chapter IV, section 5: On monastic profession as a second baptism.

4. The Monk and the Sacrament of Penance

On the penal code in the *Holy Rule:*

M. Frank, "Der Strafkodex in der Regula St. Benedikts," in *BM* 17 (1935) 310–318; 380–388; 465–473.

R. Spilker, "Die Busspraxis in der Regel des hl. Benedikt. Untersuchung über die altmonastiche Busspraxis und ihr Verhältnis zur altkirchlichen Bussdisziplin," in *SMGBO* 56 (1938) 281–339; 57 (1939) 12–38.

G. Oesterle, "De codice poenali in Regula S. Benedicti," in *Studia Benedictina in memoriam gloriosi ante saecula xiv transitus S. P. Benedicti (SA* 18–19*)*, Rome 1947, 173–193.

E. Heufelder, "Strenge und Milde. Die Strafkapitel der Benediktinerregel," in *BM* 28 (1952) 6–18.

On the chapter of faults:

Ph. Schmitz, "Chapitre des coulpes," in *D Sp* II, Paris 1953, 483–488.

G. Penco, "Significato spirituale del capitolo delle colpe," in *VM* 17 (1963) 60–70.

G. Ghislain, "Le chapitre des coulpes, signe de communion," in *C Cis* 27 (1965) 178–193.

L. Van Boxsom, "Coulpes et proclamations, hier et aujourd'hui," *ibid* 202–210.

On spiritual direction:

E. Wellens, "S. Benoît et la direction spirituelle," in *COCR* 9 (1947) 164–176.

On examination of conscience:

J.-C. Guy, "Examen de conscience: III. Chez les Pères de l'Eglise," in *D Sp* IV, Paris 1961, 1801–1807.

A. Liuima and A. Derville, "Examen particulier," *ibid* 1838–1849.

T. Merton, "Examination of Conscience and Conversatio Morum," in *COCR* 25 (1963) 355–369.

J. Bonduelle, "Deux dossiers sur la révision de vie," in *VSS* 66 (1963) 407–452.

J. Bonduelle, *La révision de vie. Situation actuelle*, Paris 1964.

On confession:

H. Dörries, "The Place of Confession in Ancient Monasticism," in *Stud Pat* V, Berlin 1962, 284–311.

The Community of Saint-Severin, *Confession: Meaning and Practice*, Chicago 1959.

A. O'Hagan, "Confession: End-Time Phenomenon," in *RR* 23 (1964) 404–410.

P. Bernadicou, "Penance and Freedom," *ibid* 411–419.

J. Galot, "Confession and the Religious Life," *ibid* 390–402.

5. *Monastic Profession*

On the monastic habit:

D. de Bruyne, "Le costume bénédictin primitif," in *R Bén* 33 (1921) 55–60.

P. Oppenheim, *Das Mönchskleid im christlichen Altertum*, Freiburg im B. 1931.

P. Oppenheim, *Symbolik und religiöse Wertung des Mönchskleides im christlichen Altertum*, Münster 1932.

P. de Meester, "Autour de quelques publications sur les habits des moines," in *Ephemerides Liturgicae* 47 (1933) 446–458.

E. Peterson, *Pour une théologie du vêtement*, Lyons 1943.

On the rite of monastic profession:

M. Rothenhäusler, *Zur Aufnahmeordnung der Regula S. Benedicti* (= Part I of *Studien zur benediktinischen Profess, BGAMB* 3), Münster 1912.

M. Rothenhäusler, "Die Anfänge der klösterlichen Profess," in *BM* 4 (1922) 21–28.

M. Rothenhäusler, "Der heilige Basilius und die klösterliche Profess," in *BM* 4 (1922) 280–289.

R. Molitor, "Symbolische Grablegung bei der Ordensprofess," in *BM* 6 (1924) 54–57.

H. Frank, "Untersuchungen zur Geschichte der benediktinischen Professliturgie im frühen Mittelalter," in *SMGBO* 63 (1951) 93–139.

B. Sause, "The Rite of Monastic Profession," in *Benedictine Review* 18 (1963) 20–29; 40–52.

P. Hofmeister, "Benediktinische Professriten," in *SMGBO* 74 (1963) 241–285.

On the "Benedictine vows":

B. Steidle, "Das Versprechen der 'Beständigkeit,' des 'Tugendwandels' und des 'Gehorsams' in der Regel St. Benedikts," in *EA* 36 (1960) 105–122.

On the profession formula:

I. Herwegen, *Geschichte der benediktinischen Professformel* (= Part II of *Studien zur benediktinischen Profess, BGAMB* 3), Münster 1912.

On the consecration of monks:

R. Molitor, "Von der Mönchsweihe in der lateinischen Kirche," in *TG* 16 (1924) 584–612.

O. Casel, "Die Mönchsweihe," in *Jahrbuch für Liturgiewissenschaft* 5 (1925) 1–47.

P. Oppenheim, "Mönchsweihe und Taufritus. Ein Kommentar zur Auslegung bei Dionysius dem Areopagiten," in *Miscellanea Mohlberg* I, Rome 1948, 259–282.

On monastic life as military service:

A. Harnack, *Militia Christi*, Tübingen 1905.

H. Emonds, "Geistlicher Kriegsdienst. Der Topos der militia spiritualis in der antiken Philosophie," in *Heilige Überleiferung (Festgabe Herwegen) (BGAMB*, Supplementband*)*, Münster 1938, 21–50.

L. Hofmann, "Militia Christi. Ein Beitrag zur Lehre von den kirchlichen Ständen," in *Trierer Theologische Zeitschrift* 63 (1954) 76–92.

J. Auer, "Militia Christi. Zur Geschichte eines christlichen Grundbildes," in *GL* 32 (1959) 340–351.

E. Manning, "La signification de *militare-militia-miles* dans la Règle de saint Benoît," in *R Bén* 72 (1962) 135–138.

On monastic life as imitation of Christ:

U. Ranke-Heinemann, "Zum Motiv der Nachfolge im frühen Mönchtum," in *EA* 36 (1960) 335–347.

On monastic life as martyrdom:

M. Viller, "Le martyre et l'ascèse," in *RAM* 6 (1925) 105–142.

H. von Campenhausen, *Die Idee des Martyriums in der alten Kirche*, Göttingen 1936.

E. Malone, *The Monk and the Martyr*, Washington 1950.

E. Malone, "The Monk and the Martyr," in *Antonius Magnus Eremita* (*SA* 38), Rome 1956, 201–228.

On monastic profession as a second baptism:

F. Vandenbroucke, "La profession, second baptême," in *VS* 76 (1947) 250–263.

B. Capelle, "De quelques témoignages relatifs à l'équivalence: profession monastique-second baptême," in *Sanctae Ecclesiae* 29 (1948) 196–208.

E. Malone, "Martyrdom and Monastic Profession as a Second Baptism," in *Vom christlichen Mysterium (Festschrift O. Casel)*, Düsseldorf 1951, 115–134.

J. Leclercq, "Profession monastique, baptême et pénitence d'après Odon de Cantorbéry," in *Analecta Monastica II (SA* 31), Rome 1953, 124–140.

E. Dekkers, "Profession monastique-second baptême. Qu'a voulu dire saint Jérôme?," in *Historisches Jahrbuch* 77 (1958) 91–97.

J. Leclercq, "Une doctrine de la vie monastique dans l'école de Bec," in *Spicilegium Beccense I*, Le Bec-Hellouin-Paris 1959, 477–488.

G. Penco, "Sulla professione monastica come secondo Battesimo," in *Riv Lit* 47 (1960) 34–39.

H. Hantsch, "Die 'Abrenuntiato' im Taufritus und die Mönchsprofess, ihre Beziehungen zu einander und zu zeitgenossischen Rechtsanschauungen," in *Österreich. Archiv für Kirchenrecht* 11 (1960) 161–189.

B. Neunheuser, "Mönchsgelübde als Zweite Taufe und unser theologisches Gewissen," in *LM* 33/34 (1963–64) 63–69.

V. THE ACTIVE LIFE – THE SPIRITUAL COMBAT

1. Beata Solitudo

On monastic solitude:

G. Turbessi, "La solitudine dell' asceta come expressione ideale della vocazione cristiana," in *Benedictina* 8 (1954) 43–55.

U. Ranke-Heinemann, "Das Verhältnis des frühen Mönchtums zur Welt," in *MTZ* 7 (1956) 289–296.

J. Winandy, "L'idée de fuite du monde," in *Message. . .*, 95–104.

J. Bonjorn, "El concepto de 'aislamiento del mundo' en su verdadera dimensión teológica," in *Cistercium* 10 (1958) 154–160.

T. Merton, "Notes for a Philosophy of Solitude," in *Disputed Questions*, New York 1960, 177–207.

Collective work: *La séparation du monde (Problèmes de la religieuse d'aujourd'hui)*, Paris 1961.

J. Leclercq, " 'Umbratilis'. Pour l'histoire du thème de la vie cachée," in *RAM* 39 (1963) 491–504.

J. Herrera, "Temas neotestamentarios de huída del mundo en la Vida de Antonio, de San Atanasio," in *Yermo* 1 (1963) 287–303.

Z. Alszeghy, "Fuite du monde," in *D Sp* V, Paris 1964, 1575–1605.

K. Truhlar, *Fuite du monde et conscience chrétienne d'aujourd'hui*, Rome 1965.

On monastic silence:

P. Salmon, "Le silence religieux. Pratique et théorie," in *Mél Bén*, 13–57.

H. Duesberg, "Silence, culture et civilisation," in *Revue d'Histoire de l'Eglise de France* 47 (1961) 223–234.

2. *Discretion*

D. Feuling, "Discretio," in *BM* 7 (1925) 339–366.

I. Widnmann, "Discretio. Zur Bedeutungsgeschichte," in *SMGBO* 58 (1940) 21–28.

H. Walter, "Die benediktinische Discretio," in *Benedictus...*, 195–212.

J. Leclercq, "La discrétion bénédictine," in *Prudence Chrétienne*, Paris 1948, 100–107.

I. Hausherr, *Direction spirituelle en Orient autrefois* (*OCA* 144), Rome 1955.

A. Cabassut, "Discrétion," in *D Sp* III, Paris 1957, 1311–1330.

G. Bardy, "Discernement des ésprits: II. Chez les Pères," in *D Sp* III, Paris 1957, 1247–1254.

F. Dingjan, "La discrétion dans les apophtegmes des Pères," in *Angelicum* 39 (1962) 403–415.

3. *Compunction*

B. Steidle, "Die Tränen ein mystisches Problem im alten Mönchtum," in *BM* 20 (1938) 181–187.

I. Hausherr, *Penthos. La doctrine de la compunction dans l'Orient chrétien* (*OCA* 132), Rome 1944.

A. Gomez, "Compunctio lacrymarum. Doctrina de la compunción en el monacato latino de los siglos IV–VI," in *COCR* 23 (1961) 232–253.

4. *Humility*

B. Ullathorne, *The Little Book of Humility and Patience*, Westminster, Md. 1945.

L. Bopp, "Die Demutsstufen der Benediktinerregel," in *Benedictus...*, 241–262.

G. Haverbeque, "L'humilité d'après S. Benoît," in *COCR* 9 (1947)

39–48, 225–230, 317–327; 10 (1948) 173–183, 273–277; 11 (1949) 18–23; 12 (1950) 17–25; 13 (1951) 98–107.
G. Bélorgey, *L'humilité bénédictine*, Paris 1948.

5. *Asceticism*

P. Salmon, "L'ascèse monastique et la spiritualité," in *VSS* 29 (1954) 195–240.
Collective work: *Christian Asceticism and Modern Man*, New York 1955.
Collective work: *Redécouverte du Jeûne*, Paris 1959.
G. Penco, "La vita ascetica come 'Filosofia' nell' antica tradizione monastica," in *SM* 2 (1960) 79–93.
G. Bardy, "Apatheia," in *D Sp* I, Paris 1937, 727–746.

6. *Poverty*

Collective work: *Poverty*, Westminster, Md. 1954.
E. Dupriez, "La pauvreté monastique," in *Message. . .*, 195–206.
A. Louf, "Une théologie de la pauvreté monastique chez le Bienheureux Guerric d'Igny," in *COCR* 20 (1958) 207–222; 362–373.
K. Rahner, "The Problem of Poverty," in *Sponsa Regis* 33 (1961–62) 311–317; "The Motives of Poverty," *ibid* 348–357; "Poverty in the Modern World," *ibid* 34 (1962–63) 15–24; "The Challenge of Poverty," *ibid* 49–57; condensation of these articles, "Religious Poverty in a Changing World," in *Theology Digest* 11 (1963) 51–56.
D. Sanchis, "Pauvreté monastique et charité fraternelle chez saint Augustin," in *SM* 4 (1962) 7–33.
P.-R. Régamey, *La pauvreté et l'homme d'aujourd'hui*, Paris 1963.
A. Gelin, *The Poor of Yahweh*, Collegeville 1964.
A. Lassus, "Il senso della povertà monastica," in *VM* 18 (1964) 155–164.

7. *Virginity*

Collective work: *Chastity*, Westminster, Md. 1955.
A. Lassus, "Le mystère de la virginité dans la pensée cistercienne," in *COCR* 20 (1958) 3–15.

M. Thurian, *Marriage and Celibacy*, London 1959.
A. Motte, "La chasteté consacrée et ses connexions," in *VSS* 54 (1960) 291–306.
L. Legrand, *The Biblical Doctrine of Virginity*, New York 1963.
J. Klimisch, *The One Bride*, New York 1965.

8. Obedience

On the role of the abbot:

B. Steidle, "Heilige Vaterschaft," in *BM* 14 (1932) 215–226.
B. Steidle, "Abba Vater," *ibid* 16 (1934) 89–101.
I. Herwegen, *Väterspruch und Mönchsregel*, Münster 1937.
L. Dürr, "Heilige Vaterschaft im antiken Orient," in *Heilige Überlieferung (Festgabe Herwegen) (BGAMB*, Supplementband), Münster 1938, 1–20.
S. Brechter, "Die Stellung des Abtes nach der Regel des hl. Benedikt," in *SMGBO* 58 (1940) 44–58.
J. Dupont, "Le nom d'abbé chez les solitaires d'Egypte," in *VS* 77 (1947) 216–230.
L. Thiry, "Individu et société dans la Règle de saint Benoît," in *Mél Bén*, 117–141.
B. Steidle, "Abbas Tyrannus. Zur Abtsidee der Regel St. Benedikts," in *BM* 24 (1948) 335–348.
B. Hegglin, *Der benediktinische Abt in Rechtsgeschichtlicher Entwicklung und geltendem Kirchenrecht*, St. Ottilien 1961.
P. Salmon, *L'abbé dans la tradition monastique: contribution à l'histoire du charactère perpétuel des supérieurs religieux en Occident*, Paris 1962.
A de Vogüé, *La communauté et l'abbé dans la Règle de saint Benoît*, Paris 1961.
O. Rousseau, "Chronique monastique," in *VSS* 62 (1962) 471–479; a discussion of the preceding work.
J. Bonduelle, "Autour du pouvoir dominatif," *ibid* 59 (1961) 569–570.
J. Bonduelle, "Le pouvoir dominatif des Abbés," *ibid* 69 (1964) 201–223.
A. de Vogüé, "L'origine du pouvoir des abbés selon la Règle du Maître," *ibid* 70 (1964) 321–324; with a note by J. Bonduelle, 325–326.

H. Bacht, "Der Abt als Stellvertreter Christi. Die Stellung des Abtes im christlichen Altertum im Lichte neuerer Forschung," in *Scholastik* 39 (1964) 402–407.

B. Steidle, " 'Wer euch hört, hört mich' (Lk 10,16). Die Einsetzung des Abts im alten Mönchtum," in *EA* 40 (1964) 179–196.

On obedience and authority:

Collective work: *Obedience*, Westminster, Md. 1953.

A.-M. Henry, "Obéissance commune et obéissance religieuse," in *VSS* 26 (1953) 249–282.

O. Rousseau, "Obéissance et hiérarchie d'après l'ancienne tradition monastique," *ibid* 283–339.

B. Leeming, "The Mysticism of Obedience," in *RR* 15 (1956) 69–90.

C. Capelle, *Le voeu d'obéissance des origines au XIIe siècle*, Paris 1959.

K. Rahner, "Reflections on Obedience. A Basic Ignatian Concept," in *Cross Currents* 10 (1960) 363–374.

A. de Vogüé, "L'obéissance (RB 5 et 7)," in *La communauté et l'abbé dans la Règle de saint Benoît*, Paris 1961, 207–288.

P. Galimard, "De quelques difficultés de l'obéissance religieuse vues par un clinicien," in *VSS* 58 (1961) 337–351.

J. Todd (ed), *Problems of Authority*, Baltimore 1962.

P. Galimard, "Les tentations de l'autorité," in *VSS* 64 (1963) 5–19.

A. Plé, "L'exercice de l'autorité, école de perfection," in *VSS* 64 (1963) 58–71.

A. Brunner, "Religiöser Gehorsam heute," in *GL* 37 (1964) 177–184.

J. Tillard, "Religious Obedience, Mystery of Communion," in *RR* 24 (1965) 66–86.

J. Leclercq, "Religious Obedience According to the Rule of St. Benedict," in *ABR* 16 (1965) 183–193.

J. Leclercq, "L'obéissance, éducatrice de la liberté dans la tradition monastique," in *La liberté évangélique (Problèmes de vie religieuse* 21), Paris 1965.

9. Stability

On pilgrimage:

H. von Campenhausen, *Die asketische Heimatlosigkeit in altkirchlichen und frühmitteraltlichen Mönchtum (Sammlung gemeinverständlicher Vorträge und Schriften* 139), Tübingen 1930.

B. Kötting, *Peregrinatio religiosa. Wallfahrt und Pilgerwesen in Antike und alter Kirche*, Münster 1950.

E. Duckett, *The Wandering Saints of the Early Middle Ages*, New York 1959.

J. Leclercq, "Monachisme et pérégrination," in *Aux sources...*, 35–90; combines articles which originally appeared in *VM* 4 (1961) 99–106; *Römische Quartalschrift* 55 (1960) 212–223; and *SM* 3 (1961) 36–52.

G. Penco, "La vocazione di Abramo nella spiritualità monastica," in *Rivista di ascetica e mistica* 8 (1963) 148–160.

On stability:

M. Rothenhäusler, "Ältestes Mönchtum und klösterliche Beständigkeit," in *BM* 3 (1921) 87–95; 223–237.

M. Rothenhäusler, "Die Beständigkeit des Benediktiners," *ibid* 345–357.

M. Rothenhäusler, "Die rechtlichen Wirkungen der benediktinischen Beständigkeit," *ibid* 440–454.

J. Lahache, "Stabilité monastique," in *Dict de Droit Canonique* 7, Paris 1962, 1078–1086.

On acedia:

G. Bardy, "Acedia," in *D Sp* I, Paris 1937, 166–169.

M. Matthei, "Aflicción y consuelo en los padres del desierto," in *SM* 5 (1963) 7–25.

Note on the meaning of CONVERSATIO MORUM

M. Rothenhäusler, *Zur Aufnahmeordnung der Regula S. Benedicti* (= Part I of *Studien zur benediktinischen Profess*, *BGAMB* 3), Münster 1912.

M. Rothenhäusler, "Conversatio Morum," in *BM* 12 (1930) 145–146.

N. Würmseer, "Conversatio Morum Suorum," in *SMGBO* 57 (1939) 99–112.

F. Friedrich, "Conversatio Morum. Das zweite Gelübde des Benediktinermönches," in *SMGBO* 59 (1941–42) 200–326.

P. Horger, "Initium conversationis. Die Professgelübde der Regula Benedicti," in *Benedictus...*, 213–232.

P. Schmitz, "Conversatio (Conversio) Morum," in *D Sp* II, Paris 1952, 2206–2212.

C. Mohrmann, "La langue de saint Benoît," in P. Schmitz, *Sancti Benedicti Regula Monachorum,* Maredsous 1955², 9–39.

B. Steidle, " 'De conversatione morum suorum.' Zum philologischen Verständnis von Regula S. Benedicti, cap. 58,17," in *Regula Magistri. Regula S. Benedicti. Studia Monastica (SA* 44), Rome 1959, 136–144.

O. Lottin, "Le voeu de 'conversatio morum' dans la Règle de saint Benoît," in *RTAM* 26 (1959) 5–16; reprinted in *Etudes de morale, histoire et doctrine,* Gembloux 1960, 309–321, with reply to objections, 321–328.

J. Winandy, "Conversatio morum," in *COCR* 22 (1960) 378–386.

O. Lottin, "A propos du voeu de 'conversatio morum' chez saint Benoît," in *RTAM* 28 (1961) 154–160.

J. Campos, "Una formula de la 'Regula sancti Benedicti'," in *Salmanticensis* 8 (1961) 183–194.

H. Hoppenbrouwers, *Conversatio: une étude semasiologique (Graecitas et Latinitas Christianorum Primaeva. Supplementa I),* Nijmegen 1964, 45–95.

10. Work

D. Redonet, *El trabajo manual en las reglas monásticas,* Madrid 1919.

H. Dörries, "Mönchtum und Arbeit," in *Forschungen zur Kirchengeschichte und christlichen Kunst (Festschrift J. Ficker),* Leipzig 1931, 17–39.

H. B. de Warren, "Le travail manuel chez les moines à travers les âges," in *VS* 52 (1937) (80)–(123).

A. Geoghegan, *The Attitude Towards Labor in Early Christianity and Ancient Culture,* Washington 1945.

H. Dedler, "Vom Sinn der Arbeit nach der Regel des heiligen Benedikt," in *Benedictus. . .,* 103–118.

A. Morganti, "L'ascetica del lavoro nella Regola di San Benedetto," in *Vita Cristiana* 17 (1948) 131–147.

A. Tabera Araoz, "De labore monastico," in *Commentarium pro Religiosis* 31 (1952) 37–48.

R. Sorg, *Holy Work. Towards a Benedictine Theology of Manual Labor,* St. Louis 1953.

P. Riley, *Manual Labor in Ancient Monastic Literature. The Semi-eremitical Phase,* Ottawa 1953.

M. Ducey, "The Benedictines and Manual Labor," in *ABR* 1 (1950) 467–489.

E. von Severus, " 'Ora et labora.' Gedanken zu einer 'benediktinischen Devise'," in *LM* 28 (1961) 38–43.

I. Herwegen, "Weltarbeit und klösterliches Ideal. Die Gedanken Abt I. Herwegen zu Gebet und Arbeit," *ibid* 44–60.

M. Menapace, "Notas sobre el trabajo manual en la espiritualidad del monacato primitivo," in *Yermo* 3 (1965) 113–126.

M. Pérez de Laborda, "Trabajo y caridad: un aspecto poco conocido del monacato antiguo," *ibid* 127–152.

VI. THE ACTIVE LIFE – THE APOSTOLATE

1. The Apostolate of Monks

J. H. Newman, "The Mission of St. Benedict," in *Historical Sketches*, Vol II, London 1896.

J. Chautard, *The Soul of the Apostolate*, Trappist, Kentucky 1946.

H. Ibach, "Die Welt braucht Mönche," in *LM* 11 (1952) 21–25.

Jac. Leclercq, *Nous avons besoin de l'ordre monastique*, Clervaux 1953.

Y. Congar, *Lay People in the Church: A Study for a Theology of the Laity*, Westminster, Md. 1957.

R. Paissac, "Action et vie contemplative," in *Message . . .*, 279–298.

P. Dupont, "Absolu monastique et engagement pastoral," *ibid*, 341–356.

Y. Congar, "The Theology of Religious Women," in *RR* 19 (1960) 15–39.

J. Leclercq, "Benedictine Rule and Active Presence in the World," in *MS* 2 (1964) 51–63.

M.-H. Vicaire, *L'imitation des apôtres. Moines, chanoines et mendiants (IVe–XIIIe siècles)*, Paris 1963.

2. The Monk and the Priesthood

On monastic priesthood:

J. Winandy, "Les moines et le sacerdoce," in *VS* 80 (1949) 23–36.

I. Dalmais, "Sacerdoce et monachisme dans l'Orient chrétien," *ibid*, 37–49.

R. Foreville and J. Leclercq, "Un débat sur le sacerdoce des moines au XIIe siècle," in *Analecta Monastica IV* (*SA* 41), Rome 1957, 8–118.

O. Rousseau, "Priesthood and Monasticism," in *The Sacrament of Holy Orders*, Collegeville 1962, 168–181.

G. Lafont, "Sacerdoce claustral," in *Commentationes in Regulam s. Benedicti (SA* 42), Rome 1958, 47–72.

A.-M. Henry, "Le sens du sacerdoce monastique," in *Message. . .* , 173–194.

O. Porcel, "San Gregorio Magno y el monacato," in *Monastica I (Scripta et Documenta* 12), Montserrat 1960, 1–95; monasticism and priesthood are treated on pages 79–89.

F. Wulf, "Priestertum und Rätestand," in *GL* 33 (1960) 109–118; 247–261.

A. Real, "Mönchtum und Priestertum," in *LM* 29 (1961) 11–36.

J. Leclercq, "On Monastic Priesthood According to the Ancient Medieval Tradition," in *SM* 3 (1961) 137–155.

O. Nussbaum, *Priestermönch und Privatmesse. Ihr Verhältnis im Westen von den Anfängen bis zum hohen Mittelalter*, Bonn 1961.

J. Leclercq, "The Priesthood for Monks," in *MS* 3 (1965) 53–85.

C. Halflants, "Réflexions à propos d'un article sur 'Le sacerdoce des moines'," in *COCR* 26 (1964) 207–214.

On the lay brotherhood:

J. Bonduelle, "La crise actuelle des convers. Ses causes, ses remèdes," in *VSS* 11 (1949) 243–278.

A.-M. Henry, "Les convers autrefois et aujourd'hui," *ibid* 279–302.

J. Bonduelle, "Convers," in *Dict. de Droit Canonique* 4, Paris 1949, 562–588.

T. Bogler, "Gespräch über die Brüder. Ein Bericht," in *LM* 11 (1952) 34–62.

B. Reetz, "Vom Laienmönchtum," in *BM* 28 (1952) 183–192.

K. Hallinger, "Woher kommen die Laienbrüder?", in *Analecta Sacri Ordinis Cisterciensis* 12 (1956) 1–104.

K. Hallinger, "Ausdrucksformen des Umkehr-Gedankens zu den geistigen Grundlagen und den Entwicklungsphasen der Instituta conversorum," in *SMGBO* 70 (1959) 169–181.

E. Heufelder, *Das Laie im Mönchtum*, Niederaltaich 1963.

V. Hermans, "Le problème des frères convers," in *COCR* 26 (1964) 86–99.
M. Driot, "Réflexions sur l'institution des frères convers," in *VSS* 69 (1964) 183–200.
V. Hermans, "Autour du statut sur l'unification des communautés," *C Cis* 27 (1965) 211–223.

3. *The Corporal Works of Mercy*

On the care of guests, the sick, and the aged:

M. Baccetti, "Vecchi e giovani nella Regola di San Benedetto," in *Rivista di ascetica e mistica* 7 (1962) 458–482.
A. de Vogüé, " 'Honorer tous les hommes.' Le sens de l'hospitalité bénédictine," in *RAM* 40 (1964) 129–138.
B. Steidle, " 'Ich war krank, und ihr habt mich besucht' (Mt 25,36)," in *EA* 40 (1964) 443–458; 41 (1965) 36–46; 99–113; 189–206.

On monks and ecumenism:

J. Leclercq, "Médiévisme," *in Irén* 19 (1946) 6–23.
I. Hausherr, "Spiritualité monachale et unité chrétienne," in *Il Monachesimo Orientale* (*OCA* 153), Rome 1958, 15–32.
O. Rousseau, "I benedettini e l'unità cristiana," in *Il problema ecumenico oggi*, Brescia 1960, 523–544.
E. Lanne, "Reunion with the East. The Role of the Monk," in *COCR* 23 (1961) 217–221.
C. Dumont, "Mönchtum und Einheit," in *EA* 37 (1961) 211–213.
T. Sartory, "Die Benediktiner und die Wiedervereinigung der getrennten Christen," *ibid* 195–210.
L. Klein, "The Role of a Benedictine Monastery in the Ecumenical Movement," in *ABR* 13 (1962) 346–354.
C. Lialine, "Eastern and Western Monasticism," in *MS* 1 (1963) 59–83.
M. Standaert, "Oecuménisme et monastères," in *C Cis* 27 (1965) 224–235.

On Protestant monasticism:

L. Präger (ed), *Frei für Gott und die Menschen*, Stuttgart 1959.
"Two Interviews with Protestant Monastic Founders," in *ABR* 14 (1963) 531–561.
F. Biot, *The Rise of Protestant Monasticism*, Baltimore 1963.

B. Lohse, *Mönchtum und Reformation. Luthers Auseinandersetzung mit dem Mönchsideal des Mittelalters*, Göttingen 1963.

R. Esnault, *Luther et la vie monastique aujourd'hui: lecture actuelle du "De votis monasticis judicium,"* Geneva 1964.

See the articles in *Reformatio*, 1964, Heft 5–6.

4. *Monastic Culture*

On monasticism and cultural pursuits:

J. Mabillon, *Traité des études monastiques*, Paris 1691.

J. O'Connor, *Monasticism and Civilization*, New York 1921.

J. Leclercq, "L'humanisme bénédictin du viiie au xiie siècle," in *Analecta Monastica I* (*SA* 20), Rome 1948, 1–20.

J. Leclercq, "Y a-t-il une culture monastique?", in *Il monachesimo nell' alto Medioevo e la formazione della civiltà occidentale*, Spoleto 1957, 339–356; reprinted in *Aux sources . . .*, 269–283.

J. Leclercq, "Cluny fut-il ennemi de la culture?", in *R Mab* 47 (1957) 172–182

J. Leclercq, "Pour une histoire humaine du monachisme au moyen âge," in *Analecta Monastica IV* (SA 41), Rome 1957, 1–7.

A. Pantoni, "Cultura e studi monastici nel loro spirito e nelle loro tendenze," in *VM* 12 (1958) 110–117.

R. Hesbert, *Science et sainteté. L'étude dans la vie monastique, par Dom Jean Mabillon. Textes recueillis et présentés*, Paris 1958.

D. Schlegel, "Culture and the Contemplative Life," in *Blackfriars* 40 (1959) 336–341.

J. Leclercq, "The Monastic Tradition of Culture and Studies," in *ABR* 11 (1960) 99–131.

V. Cilento, *Medio Evo monastico e scolastico*, Milan-Naples 1961.

J. Leclercq, *The Love of Learning and the Desire for God*, New York 1961.

A. Festugière, *Les moines d'Orient*. Vol I: *Culture ou sainteté. Introduction au monachisme oriental*, Paris 1961.

A. Dimier, "Les premiers Cisterciens étaient-ils ennemis des études?", in *SM* 4 (1962) 69–91.

F. Vandenbroucke, "L'ésprit des études monastiques d'après l'Abbé de Rancé," in *COCR* 25 (1963) 224–249.

Collective work: *Los monjes y los estudios*, Poblet 1963.
J. Decarreaux, *Monks and Civilization*, New York 1964.
A. de Vogüé, "Le procès des moines d'autrefois," in *Christus* 12 (1965) 113–128.
B. Morison, "Studies for Monks," in *C Cis* 27 (1965) 57–66.
P. Deseille, "Les études des jeunes moines," *ibid* 67–70.

On "monastic theology":
J. Leclercq, *Theology and Prayer* (lecture separately published), St. Meinrad 1962.
J. Leclercq, "Théologie traditionelle et théologie monastique," in *Irén* 37 (1964) 50–74.
A. Robles Sierra, "A propósito de 'teología monástica'," in *Yermo* 2 (1964) 193–203.

5. *Monastic Schools*

J. H. Newman, "Benedictine Schools," in *Historical Sketches*, Vol II, London 1896.
G. Bardy, "Les origines des écoles monastiques en Orient," in *Mélanges Jos. de Ghellinck*, Gembloux 1951, 293–309.
G. Bardy, "Les origines des écoles monastiques en Occident," in *Sacris Erudiri* 5 (1953) 86–104.

6. *The Care of Souls*

U. Berlière, "L'exercice du ministère paroissial par les moines dans le haut moyen-âge," in *R Bén* 39 (1927) 227–250.
U. Berlière, "L'exercice du ministère paroissial par les moines du XIIe au XVIIIe siècle," in *R Bén* 39 (1927) 340–364.
P. Hofmeister, "Mönchtum und Seelsorge bis zum 13. Jahrhundert," in *SMGBO* 65 (1953–1954) 209–302.

7. *The Missionary Role of Monasticism*

On the role of monks in the missions:
S. Healy, "Benedictines in the Missions," in *ABR* 1 (1952) 123–134.

L. Deguise, "Aux missions: l'heure des moines," in *Message . . .*, 357–372.

A.-M. Henry, "Les moines et la mission," in *Parole et Mission* 9 (1960) 183–210; also in German in *EA* 38 (1962) 372–383.

See the articles in *Rythmes du Monde* 10 (1962) fascicles 3–4: *Vie monastique et missions.*

I. Auf der Maur, "Das alte Mönchtum im Dienste der Glaubensverbreitung," in *NRSM* 18 (1962) 275–288.

J. Hall, "Benedictines and the Mission Vocation," in *ABR* 15 (1964) 14–45.

On monastic missionary work today:

J. Monchanin and H. Le Saux, *Ermites de Saccidananda. Un essai d'integration chrétienne de la tradition monastique de l'Inde*, Paris 1956.

B. Griffiths, "Experiment in Monastic Life," in *Commonweal* 68 (1958) 634–636.

P. Gordan, "Aufgaben und Probleme des benediktinischen Mönchtums in Afrika," in *NRSM* 16 (1960) 186–192.

J. Winandy, "Le monachisme antillais," in *Parole et Mission* 14 (1961) 410–415.

P. Beach and W. Dunphy, *Benedictine and Moor*, New York 1960.

E. des Allues, *Toumliline. A la recherche de Dieu, au service de l'Afrique*, Paris 1961.

A.-M. Henry, "Toumliline. Le monachisme et l'Afrique," in *Parole et Mission* 14 (1961) 416–421.

J.B. Simon-Vermot, "Attentes monastiques en Inde du nord," *ibid* 16 (1962) 64–71.

J.-M. Déchanet, "En marge du monachisme africain: la Jamaa," *ibid* 18 (1962) 429–436.

B. Besret, "Chronique du monachisme missionaire," *ibid* 23 (1963) 640–643; see also the correspondence in 20 (1963) 145–150; 21 (1963) 320–321 (D. Martin); 23 (1963) 644–648; 23 (1963) 648–651 (J.-M. Déchanet).

J. Hall, "Benedictines and the Planting of the Church," in *ABR* 14 (1963) 90–114.

D. Mbonyimmaana, "Témoignage de pauvreté dans un monachisme missionaire," *in Parole et Mission* 26 (1964) 426–434.

S. Frank, "Kontemplatives Mönchtum in den Missionsländern," in S. Richter, *Das Wagnis der Nachfolge*, Paderborn 1964, 95–117.

J. Leclercq, "Le monachisme africain d'aujourd'hui et le monachisme antique," in *Irén* 38 (1965) 33–56.

On the pan-African monastic conference of Bouaké:

Two brief reports in *Informations Catholiques Internationales* 219 (July 1, 1964) 11–12; and in *Herder Correspondence* 1 (1964) 260–263.

J. Leclercq, "Présent et avenir du monachisme en Afrique," in *Christus* 11 (1964) 567–574.

R. De Salvo, "The Bouaké Conference," in *ABR* 15 (1964) 420–425.

A. Louf, "La réunion de Bouaké," in *COCR* 26 (1964) 305–311.

The acts of the conference have been published in *Rythmes du Monde* 13 (1965) fascicles 1–2: *Bouaké: Rencontre monastique en Afrique.*

Tradition et modernisme en Afrique noire. Recontres internationales de Bouaké, Paris 1965.

8. The Apostolate of the Liturgy

G. Tissot, *Le role liturgique d'un monastère*, Solesmes 1936.

O. Rousseau, *The Progress of the Liturgy. An Historical Sketch from the Beginning of the 19th Century to the Pontificate of Pius X*, Westminster, Md. 1951.

O. Heiming, "Heilige Regel und benediktinische Liturgiereform," in *LM* 14 (1954) 79–102.

See the articles in *LM* 22 (1958): *Mönchisches Leben und liturgischer Dienst;* and 24 (1959): *Liturgische Bewegung nach 50 Jahren.*

J. Jungmann, "Der Beitrag der Benediktiner zur Liturgiewissenschaft," *ibid* 28 (1961) 9–15.

VII. THE CONTEMPLATIVE LIFE

1. The Monk as a Man of Prayer

A. Saudreau, "La prière chez les moines de l'antiquité," in *VS* 8 (1923) 288–293.

M. Marx, *Incessant Prayer in Ancient Monastic Literature*, Rome 1946.

E. Drinkwelder, "St. Benedikt als Erbe urchristlichen Betens," in *Benedictus* . . . , 281–310.

R. Banquet, "Preghiera liturgica e preghiera privata nella Regola di S. Benedetto," in *Vita Cristiana* 17 (1948) 124–130.

I. Hausherr, "Comment priaient les Pères," in *RAM* 32 (1956) 33–58; 284–296.

A. van der Mensbrugghe, "Prayer-time in Egyptian Monasticism," in *Stud Pat* II, Berlin 1957, 435–454.

O. Casel, "Der Mönch–ein Beter," in *LM* 22 (1958) 30–36.

J. Leclercq, "The Unity of Prayer," in *Worship* 33 (1958–59) 408–417.

B. Calati, "Il metodo monastico della preghiera," in *VM* 13 (1959) 147–157; 14 (1960) 147–166.

A. Schönen, "Das immerwährende Gebet," in *LM* 27 (1960) 72–86.

P. Rouillard, "Temps et rythmes de la prière dans le monachisme ancien," in *LMD* 64 (1960) 32–52.

I. Hausherr, *Noms du Christ et voies d'oraison* (*OCA* 157), Rome 1960.

J. Leclercq, "Une parenthèse dans l'histoire de la prière continuelle: la 'laus perennis' du haut moyen âge," in *LMD* 64 (1960) 90–101.

J. Leclercq, "Culte liturgique et prière intime dans le monachisme au moyen âge," *ibid* 69 (1962) 39–55; also in *Aux sources* . . . , 285–303.

Collective work: *La preghiera nella Bibbia e nella tradizione patristica e monastica*, Rome 1964.

A. de Vogüé, " 'Orationi frequenter incumbere.' Une invitation à la prière continuelle," in *RAM* 41 (1965).

2. *Lectio Divina*

On *lectio*:

D. Gorce, *La Lectio Divina des origines du cénobitisme à saint Benoît et Cassiodore*. Vol. I: *Saint Jérôme et la lecture sacrée dans le milieu ascétique romain*, Paris 1925.

J. Leclercq, "La 'lecture divine'," in *LMD* 5 (1946) 21–33.

M. van Assche, " 'Divinae vacare lectioni.' De 'ratio studiorum' van Sint Benedictus," in *Sacris Erudiri* 1 (1948) 13–34; in Dutch with Latin summary.

A. Olivar, " 'Codices per ordinem ex integro legant' (San Benito,

Regula Monasteriorum, c. 48)," in *Revista de Archivos, Bibliotecas y Museos*, 4th series, 3 (1949) 513–521.

C. Dumont, "La lecture de la parole de Dieu," in *BVC* 22 (1958) 23–33.

A. Louf, "Exégèse scientifique ou lectio monastique," in *COCR* 22 (1960) 225–247.

A. Pantoni, "La 'lectio divina' nei suoi rapporti con la Bibbia e la liturgia," in *VM* 14 (1960) 167–174.

On *meditatio*:

E. von Severus, "Das Wort 'Meditari' im Sprachgebrauch der Heiligen Schrift," in *GL* 26 (1953) 365–375.

H. Bacht, " 'Meditatio' in den ältesten Mönchsquellen," in *GL* 28 (1955) 360–373.

E. von Severus, "Das Wesen der Meditation und der Mensch der Gegenwart," in *GL* 29 (1956) 108–116.

J. Leclercq, "Meditation as a Biblical Reading," in *Worship* 33 (1958–59) 562–569.

E. Heufelder, "Christliche Meditation im Geiste der Benediktinerregel," in *EA* 37 (1961) 449–457.

3. *Opus Dei*

On the divine office:

V. Warnach, "Mens concordet voci. Zur Lehre des hl. Benedikt über die geistliche Haltung beim Chorgebet," in *Liturgisches Leben* 5 (1938) 169–190.

J. Froger, *Les origines de Prime*, Rome 1946; see also "Note pour rectifier l'interprétation de Cassien, Inst. 3, 4, 6, proposée dans *Les origines de Prime*," in *Archiv für Liturgiewissenschaft* 2 (1952) 96–102.

I. Hausherr, "Opus Dei," in *Miscellanea Guillaume de Jerphanion* (*OCP* 13), Rome 1947, 195–218.

G. Penco, " 'Bibliotheca' e 'Opus Dei' nella Regula Monasteriorum," in *Riv Lit* 38 (1951) 210–217.

E. Heufelder, "Gotteslob und Frömmigkeit nach der Regel des hl. Benedikt," in *LJ* 5 (1955) 135–144.

B. Luykx, "L'influence des moines sur l'office paroissial," in *LMD* 51 (1957) 55–81.

C. Gindele, "Die römische und monastische Überlieferung im Ordo officii der Regel St. Benedikts," in *Commentationes in Regulam s. Benedicti* (*SA* 42), Rome 1958, 171–222.

C. Gindele, "Zum Offiziumsordnung in der Regula," in *EA* 37 (1961) 60–61; 151–153; 241–243; 321–324; 411–412; 497–499.

O. Heiming, "Zum monastischen Offizium von Kassianus bis Kolumbanus," in *Archiv für Liturgiewissenschaft* 7 (1961) 89–156.

P. Salmon, *The Breviary Through the Centuries*, Collegeville 1962.

Collective work: *La prière des heures* (*LO* 35), Paris 1963.

D. Hadidian, "The Background and Origin of the Christian Hours of Prayer," in *Theological Studies* 25 (1964) 59–69.

P. Salmon, "L'ufficio divino e la sua riforma: prospettive monastiche," in *VM* 18 (1964) 103–112.

On the Christian use of the psalms:

H. Duesberg, *Jésus, le chantre idéal des Psaumes*, Louvain 1931.

S. Hilpisch, "Der Psalmenvortrag nach der Regula Benedicti," in *SMGBO* 59 (1941–42) 105–115.

B. Fischer, *Die Psalmenfrömmigkeit der Märtyrerkirche*, Freiburg im B. 1949; also in French in *LMD* 27 (1951) 86–109.

P. Salmon, "De l'interprétation des psaumes dans la liturgie aux origines de l'office divin," in *LMD* 33 (1953) 21–55.

T. Merton, *Bread in the Wilderness*, New York 1953.

F. Vandenbroucke, "Sur la lecture chrétienne du psautier au Ve siècle," in *Sacris Erudiri* 5 (1953) 5–26.

F. Vandenbroucke, *Les psaumes et le Christ*, Louvain 1955.

T. Merton, *Praying the Psalms*, Collegeville 1956.

L. Bouyer, *The Meaning of Sacred Scripture*, Notre Dame 1958.

C.S. Lewis, *Reflections on the Psalms*, New York 1958.

C. Vagaggini, "Nota sui temi centrali dei singoli salmi e il loro riferimento al mistero di Cristo nella liturgia," in *Il senso teologico della liturgia*, Rome 1958^{2}, 372–385.

T. Worden, *The Psalms are Christian Prayer*, New York 1961.

A. Gelin, *The Psalms are Our Prayers*, Collegeville 1964.

A. George, *Praying the Psalms: A Guide for Using the Psalms as Christian Prayer*, Notre Dame 1964.

P. Drijvers, *The Psalms: Their Structure and Meaning*, New York 1965.

A. Rose, *Psaumes et prière chrétienne*, Bruges 1965.

4. Contemplation

On contemplative prayer:

C. Butler, *Western Mysticism*, New York 1924.

A. Stolz, *The Doctrine of Spiritual Perfection*, St. Louis 1938.

V. Stebler, *Der benediktinische Weg zur Beschauung*, Olten 1947.

J. Winandy, "Vie contemplative et vie monastique," in *Acta et Documenta Congressus Generalis de Statibus Perfectionis II*, Rome 1950, 132–140.

O. Lottin, "Vita contemplativa, vita activa, vita mixta quoad doctrinam et praxim in hodiernis statibus perfectionis," *ibid* 118–126; reprinted in *Etudes de morale, histoire et doctrine*, Gembloux 1961, 297–307.

E. von Severus, "Das kontemplative Mönchtum und unsere Gegenwart," in *LM* 11 (1952) 11–20.

A. Presse, "Le métier de contemplation," in *Message . . .*, 121–138.

P. Ernetti, "Vita monastica attiva o contemplativa," in *VM* 12 (1958) 63–88; with a note by A. Giabbani, 89–91.

P. Ernetti, "A quali condizioni il monaco è contemplativo," *ibid* 13 (1959) 64–71; 107–125.

J. Leclercq, "La vie contemplative dans saint Thomas et dans la tradition," in *RTAM* 28 (1961) 251–268.

M.E. Mason, *Active Life and Contemplative Life. A Study of the Concepts from Plato to the Present*, Milwaukee 1961.

J. Leclercq, *Otia monastica. Etudes sur le vocabulaire de la contemplation au moyen âge* (*SA* 51), Rome 1963.

A. de Vogüé, "La Règle de saint Benoît et la vie contemplative," in *C Cis* 27 (1965) 89–107.

J. Leclercq, "La vie monastique est-elle une vie contemplative?", *ibid* 108–120.

M. Ohligslager, "What is Monastic Contemplation?" in *ABR* 16 (1965) 386–395.

On liturgy and contemplation:

C. Vagaggini, "Liturgy and Contemplation," in *Worship* 34 (1960) 507–523.

B. Haering, "Liturgische Frömmigkeit und christliche Vollendung," in *LJ* 11 (1961) 93–103.

5. The Monastery as Paradise

On the paradise theme:

F. Wulf, "Rückkehr in das Paradies," in *GL* 26 (1953) 101–112.

J. Daniélou, "Terre et paradis chez les Pères de l'Eglise," in *Eranos Jahrbuch* 22 (1954) 433–472.

J. Daniélou, "Catéchèse pascale et retour au Paradis," in *LMD* 45 (1956) 99–119.

J. Leclercq, "Le cloître est-il un paradis?", in *Message . . .*, 141–160.

G. Colombás, *Paraíso y vida angélica: Sentido escatológico de la vocación cristiana*, Montserrat 1958.

On the monk and the animals:

G. Penco, "L'amicizia con gli animali," in *VM* 17 (1963) 3–10.

G. Penco, "Il simbolismo animalesco nella letteratura monastica," in *SM* 6 (1964) 7–38.

6. The Monk and the Angels

On the theme of angelic life:

J. Didier, " 'Angélisme' ou perspectives eschatologiques?", in *Mélanges de Science Religieuse* 11 (1954) 31–48.

U. Ranke-Heinemann, "Zum Ideal der vita angelica im frühen Mönchtum," in *GL* 29 (1956) 347–357.

E. von Severus, "Bios angelikos. Zum Verständnis des Mönchslebens als 'Engeleben' in der christlichen Uberlieferung," in *LM* 21 (1957) 56–70.

G. Colombás, *Paraíso y vida angélica: Sentido escatológico de la vocación cristiana*, Montserrat 1958.

A. Lamy, "Monks and the Angelic Life," in *MS* 1 (1963) 39–57.

E. Peterson, *The Angels and the Liturgy*, New York 1964.

S. Frank, *Angelikos Bios. Begriffsanalytische und begriffsgeschichtliche Untersuchung zum "Engelgleichen Leben" im frühen Mönchtum* (*BGAMB* 26), Münster 1964.

On the monk and the demons:

U. Ranke-Heinemann, "Die ersten Mönche und die Dämonen," in *GL* 29 (1956) 165–170.

A. and C. Guillamont, "Démon. III. Dans la littérature monastique," in *D Sp* III, Paris 1957, 189–212.
B. Steidle, "Der 'schwarze kleine Knabe' in der alten Mönchserzählung. Beitrag zu St. Gregor, Dial. 2, 4," in *BM* 34 (1958) 339–350.

7. *Freedom and Simplicity*

On *parresia:*

E. Peterson, "Zur Bedeutungsgeschichte von parresia," in *Festschrift für R. Seeberg* I, 1929, 283–297.
H. Schlier, "parresia, parresiazomai," in *TWNT* V, Stuttgart 1954, 869–884.
B. Steidle, "Parresia-Praesumptio in der Klosterregel St. Benedicts," in *Zeugnis des Geistes*, Beuron 1947, 44–61.
G. Scarpat, *Parrhesia, storia del termine e delle sue traduzioni in latino*, Brescia 1964.
L. Engels, *Fiducia dans la Vulgate. Le problème de traduction parresia-fiducia (Graecitas et Latinitas Christianorum Primaeva. Supplementa I)*, Nijmegen 1964, 97–141.

On freedom:

E. Heufelder, "Gemeinschaft und Persönlichkeit, Autorität und Freiheit nach der Regel des hl. Benedikt," in *BM* 26 (1950) 181–192; 265–274; 354–363; 451–461.
L. Merton, "Christian Freedom and Monastic Formation," in *ABR* 13 (1962) 289–313.

On simplicity:

J. Leclercq, "The Monastic Tradition of Culture and Studies," in *ABR* 11 (1960) 99–131.
J. Leclercq, "Sancta Simplicitas," in *COCR* 22 (1960) 138–148.
P. Antin, " 'Simple' et 'simplicité' chez saint Jérôme," in *R Bén* 71 (1961) 371–381.

EPILOGUE:
THE RELEVANCE OF MONASTIC SPIRITUALITY

Some studies on monastic renewal:

Un moine bénédictin, "Une fondation monastique en milieu populaire déchristianisé," in *VSS* 11 (1949) 322–331.

H. Romero V. Iturbide, "Monachisme cénobitique au Mexique," *ibid* 308–321.

See the articles in *LM* 11 (1952): *Mönchtum in der Entscheidung.*

A.-M. Henry, "Un monastère simple," in *VSS* 41 (1957) 172–198.

W. Tunink, "Purity of Heart and the Modern Monk," in *ABR* 10 (1959) 205–218; with discussion *ibid* 12 (1961) 505–522 (D. Hassel, H. Carey, W. Tunink); 13 (1962) 123–134 (R. Roloff), 134–150 (W. Tunink), 359–389 (R. Roloff and W. Tunink); 14 (1963) 263–286 (C. Peifer), 286–291 (R. Roloff).

A. Nocent, "Vieillesse ou jeunesse du monachisme?", in *Revue Monastique* 157 (1959) 128–137.

O. Rousseau, "Reviviscence du monachisme oriental," in *Irén* 33 (1960) 385–390.

M. Melot, "Enquête sur le monachisme," in *Lumière du Christ* 161 (1960) 145–156; 162 (1961) 37–48.

R. Sorg, *Religion at King of Martyrs,* Fifield, Wisconsin, n.d.

Collective work: *Problemi e orientamenti di spiritualità monastica, biblica e liturgica,* Rome 1961; see the discussions of this volume in *EA* 39 (1963) 149–154 (H. Nitz); and in *MS* 2 (1964) 137–165 (C. Peifer).

Fr. Gregoire, "Une nouvelle forme de vie monastique: La Fraternité de la Vierge des Pauvres," in *Rythmes du Monde* 36 (1962) 207–215.

P. Minard, "Monastische Erneuerung," in *EA* 38 (1962) 384–398.

T. Merton, "The Monk in the Diaspora," in *Commonweal* 79 (1963–64) 741–745; also in *Blackfriars* 45 (1964) 290–302; reprinted in *Seeds of Destruction,* New York 1964, 184–213.

P. Blumberg, "Gedanken zur monastischen Erneuerung," in *EA* 39 (1963) 246–248.

E. Talley, "Benedictine Authenticity," in *Cross Currents* 13 (1963) 511–512.

J. Leclercq, "Problèmes et orientations du monachisme," in *Etudes* 320 (May 1964) 667–684.

C. Stockford, "Monastic Renewal and the Work of God," in *DR* 82 (1964) 312–324; with an editorial note, 324–326.

P. Higham, "New Movements in the Monastic Order," in *Pax* 54 (1964) 76–83.

Soeur M. Pia, "Pour une meillure organisation du travail monastigue," in *VSS* 68 (1964) 89–100.

J. Leclercq, "Problems Facing Monachism Today," in *ABR* 16 (1955) 47–56.

J. Mareck, "New Methodology in Defining the Monastic Ideal," in *ABR* 16 (1965) 56–60.

T. Doyle, "Signs of the Times: A Call for Monastic Scholars," in *ABR* 16 (1965) 173–180.

P. Deseille, "Vers un renouveau du monachisme," in *VS* 47 (1965) 444–456.

V. Stebler, "Monastische Erneuerung aus dem Geist der heiligen Regel," in *EA* 41 (1965) 175–179.

"Monastic Renewal: Three Documents," in *MS* 3 (1965) 313–322.

E. de Miscault, "'Aggiornamento' dans la vie monastique," in *C Cis* 27 (1965) 37–56.

A. Tkacik, "The Twentieth-Century Monk in the Kingdom of God," in *ABR* 16 (1965) 242–262.

B. Sause, "Current Monastic Renewal," *ibid* 219–241 and 290.

R. Weakland, "Monastic Renewal," in *New Blackfriars* 46 (1965) 511–516.

J. Raasch, "El monacato en los Estados Unidos: esfuerzos para definirse y renovarse," in *Yermo* 3 (1965) 85–100.

J. Loew, "Le monastère: Signe et témoignage," in *C Cis* 27 (1965) 165–168.

M. Pontifex, "The Purpose of Monasticism," in *DR* 83 (1965) 145–158; 237–248; 340–349; with editorial note, 349–350.

See the articles in *Pax,* no. 314, autumn 1965: *Monastic Renewal.*

T. Merton, "The Place of Obedience in Monastic Renewal," in *ABR* 16 (1965) 359–368.

T. Merton, "The Council and Religious Life," in *New Blackfriars* 47 (1965–66) 5–17.

I. Index of References

Numbers in parentheses indicate a multiple occurrence of a reference on the same page.

A. BIBLICAL AND APOCRYPHAL BOOKS

B. CONCILIAR, PAPAL, AND LITURGICAL TEXTS

C. ECCLESIASTICAL WRITERS

I. Index of References

II. Index of Proper Names

Names of places are in italics. Numbers in parentheses, following references to authors listed in the bibliography, indicate a multiple occurrence on the same page. The more important page references are in italics.

II. Index of Proper Names

III. Index of Subjects

The more important page references are in italics.

III. Index of Subjects